The Story of The Great War

History of the European War from Official Sources

COMPLETE HISTORICAL RECORDS OF EVENTS TO DATE. ILLUSTRATED WITH DRAWINGS, MAPS, *and* PHOTOGRAPHS

Prefaced by

WHAT THE WAR MEANS TO AMERICA
MAJOR GENERAL LEONARD WOOD, U. S. A.

NAVAL LESSONS OF THE WAR
REAR ADMIRAL AUSTIN M. KNIGHT, U. S. N.

THE WORLD'S WAR
FREDERICK PALMER

THEATRES OF THE WAR'S CAMPAIGNS
FRANK H. SIMONDS

THE WAR CORRESPONDENT
ARTHUR RUHL

Edited by

FRANCIS J. REYNOLDS
Former Reference Librarian of Congress

ALLEN L. CHURCHILL
Associate Editor, The New International Encyclopedia

FRANCIS TREVELYAN MILLER
Editor in Chief, Photographic History of the Civil War

P · F · COLLIER & SON
NEW YORK

A great war Zeppelin on a bomb-dropping expedition is sailing over an enemy city. High above it are the city's defending aircraft—a biplane and a monoplane—ready to attack the raider with their machine guns

The STORY OF THE GREAT WAR

NEUVE CHAPELLE · BATTLE OF YPRES · PRZEMYSL MAZURIAN LAKES · ITALY ENTERS WAR · GORIZIA THE DARDANELLES

VOLUME III

P · F · COLLIER & SON · NEW YORK

CONTENTS

PART I.—RUSSIAN AND TURKISH CAMPAIGN

CHAPTER PAGE

I. Campaign in the Caucasus 9
II. Turkish Advance Against Egypt 15
III. Failure of "Holy War" Propaganda 21
IV. Results of First Six Months of Turkish Campaign . 25
V. The Dardanelles—Strategy of the Campaign 27
VI. Fortifications and Strength—First Movements . . . 34

PART II.—JAPAN AND THE FAR EAST

VII. Why Japan Joined the Allies 40
VIII. Military and Naval Situation in the Far East . . . 46
IX. Beginning of Hostilities—Attacks on Tsing-tau Forts . 52
X. Capture of Tsing-tau 60

PART III.—THE WAR IN AFRICA

XI. Campaign in Togoland and the Cameroons 62
XII. German Southwest Africa—Rebellion in Union of South Africa 68

PART IV.—THE WESTERN FRONT

XIII. Preparations for an Offensive 79
XIV. Battle of Neuve Chapelle Begins 83
XV. Operations Following Neuve Chapelle 92
XVI. Beginning of Second Battle of Ypres 99
XVII. The Struggle Renewed 106
XVIII. Other Actions on the Western Front 115
XIX. Campaign in Artois Region 121
XX. British Forward Movement—Battle of Festubert . . 128
XXI. Sir John French Attempts a Surprise 134
XXII. Attacks at La Bassée 140
XXIII. Operations Around Hooge 146
XXIV. Franco-German Operations Along the Front 151
XXV. Campaign in Argonne and Around Arras 158
XXVI. Belgo-German Operations 166

PART V.—NAVAL OPERATIONS

CHAPTER		PAGE
XXVII.	THE WAR ZONE	170
XXVIII.	ATTACK ON THE DARDANELLES	174
XXIX.	GERMAN RAIDERS AND SUBMARINES	179
XXX.	ITALIAN PARTICIPATION—OPERATIONS IN MANY WATERS	186
XXXI.	STORY OF THE EMDEN	193
XXXII.	SUMMARY OF THE FIRST YEAR OF NAVAL WARFARE	206
XXXIII.	FIGHTS OF THE SUBMARINES	209
XXXIV.	SINKING OF THE LUSITANIA	222

PART VI.—THE EASTERN FRONT—AUSTRO-RUSSIAN CAMPAIGN

XXXV.	THE CARPATHIAN CAMPAIGN—REVIEW OF THE SITUATION	235
XXXVI.	BATTLE OF THE PASSES	241
XXXVII.	BATTLE OF KOZIOWA—OPERATIONS IN THE BUKOWINA	244
XXXVIII.	FALL OF PRZEMYSL	249
XXXIX.	NEW RUSSIAN OFFENSIVE — AUSTRO-GERMAN COUNTER-OFFENSIVE	258
XL.	CAMPAIGN IN GALICIA AND BUKOWINA—BATTLE OF THE DUNAJEC	264
XLI.	RUSSIAN RETREAT	276
XLII.	AUSTRO-GERMAN RECONQUEST OF WESTERN GALICIA	281
XLIII.	CAMPAIGN IN EASTERN GALICIA AND THE BUKOWINA	289
XLIV.	RUSSIAN CHANGE OF FRONT—RETREAT TO THE SAN	293
XLV.	BATTLE OF THE SAN	297
XLVI.	RECAPTURE OF PRZEMYSL	301
XLVII.	CAPTURE OF LEMBERG	306

PART VII.—RUSSO-GERMAN CAMPAIGN

XLVIII.	WINTER BATTLES OF THE MAZURIAN LAKES	313
XLIX.	THE RUSSIANS OUT OF GERMANY	317
L.	TIGHTENING OF THE NET—REPORT OF THE BOOTY	319
LI.	BATTLES OF PRZASNYSZ—BEFORE MLAWA	324
LII.	FIGHTING BEFORE THE NIEMEN AND BOBR—BOMBARDMENT OF OSSOWETZ	329
LIII.	RUSSIAN RAID ON MEMEL	334
LIV.	GERMAN INVASION OF COURLAND—CAPTURE OF LIBAU	337
LV.	RUSSIAN OFFENSIVE FROM KOVNO — FOREST BATTLES IN MAY AND JUNE	342

PART VII.—RUSSO-GERMAN CAMPAIGN—*Continued*

CHAPTER		PAGE
LVI.	Campaign in Southern Poland—Movement upon Warsaw	345
LVII.	Battle of Krasnik—Capture of Przasnysz	348
LVIII.	Grand Offensive on the Warsaw Salient	356
LIX.	Beginning of the End	361
LX.	Warsaw Falls	366

PART VIII.—THE BALKANS

LXI.	Diplomacy in the Balkans	369

PART IX.—ITALY ENTERS THE WAR

LXII.	Spirit of the Italian People—Crisis of the Government	379
LXIII.	The Decision Made—Italian Strategy	382
LXIV.	Strength of Italian Army and Navy	388
LXV.	First Engagements	392
LXVI.	Fighting in the Mountains	402
LXVII.	Attacks in Gorizia	408
LXVIII.	Fighting in the Alps—Italian Successes	416
LXIX.	More Mountain Fighting—Results of First Campaign	419

PART X.—THE DARDANELLES AND TURKEY

LXX.	Beginning of Operations	423
LXXI.	Preparations for Landing—Composition of Forces	429
LXXII.	Plans of Sir Ian Hamilton—First Landing Made	437
LXXIII.	The British in Danger—Bitter Fighting	446
LXXIV.	Further Efforts at Landing—Failure to Take Krithia	454
LXXV.	Krithia Again Attacked—Heroic Work of "Anzacs"	459
LXXVI.	Russo-Turkish Operations	469

PART XI.—THE WAR IN AFRICA

LXXVII.	The Cameroons	481
LXXVIII.	British Conquest of Southwest Africa	484
LXXIX.	Other African Operations	493

PART XII.—WAR IN ARABIA, MESOPOTAMIA, AND EGYPT

LXXX.	Mesopotamia and Arabia	497
LXXXI.	Syria and Egypt	503

LIST OF ILLUSTRATIONS

ZEPPELIN ATTACKED BY AEROPLANES . . . . *Frontispiece*

OPPOSITE PAGE

BELGIANS RE-FORMING FOR A FRESH ATTACK 78

PRAYER IN A FRENCH CHURCH USED FOR A HOSPITAL 158

GREAT LINER LUSITANIA 222

GRAND DUKE NICHOLAS 270

TRIUMPHAL ENTRY OF AUSTRIANS INTO PRZEMYSL 302

PRINCE LEOPOLD OF BAVARIA IN WARSAW 366

CLOUD OF POISONOUS GAS RELEASED BY ITALIAN TROOPS 414

STORES AT SUVLA BAY, GALLIPOLI 462

LIST OF MAPS

PAGE

Strategic Railway System in Eastern Germany Which Made Quick Concentration Possible (*Colored Map*) . . . *Front Insert*

Gallipoli 29

Kiao-chau (Tsing-tau) 43

German Possessions in Africa 65

Western Battle Line, January 1, 1915 81

Neuve Chapelle, Battle at 88

Ypres, Gas Battle of 113

Fighting in Alsace-Hartmannsweilerkopf 119

Artois, Battles in 126

German Submarine War Zone 172

Emden Landing Party, Cruise of 195

Carpathian Passes and Russian Battle Line 237

Przemysl, Detail Maps of the Forts of 248

Galician Campaign from Tarnow to Przemysl 279

Galician Campaign from Przemysl to Bessarabia 291

Riga, German Advance on 338

Warsaw, German Attempts to Reach, in 1914 358

Warsaw, Advance and Capture of 367

Coasts of Italy and Austria, Showing the Naval Raid in May, 1915 395

Austria, Italian Attack on 410

Dardanelles, Pictorial Map of, Showing Where the Allies Landed 439

German Southwest Africa, Conquest of 491

Mesopotamia—The British Operations from the Persian Gulf . 499

Suez Canal, Turkish Attack on 506

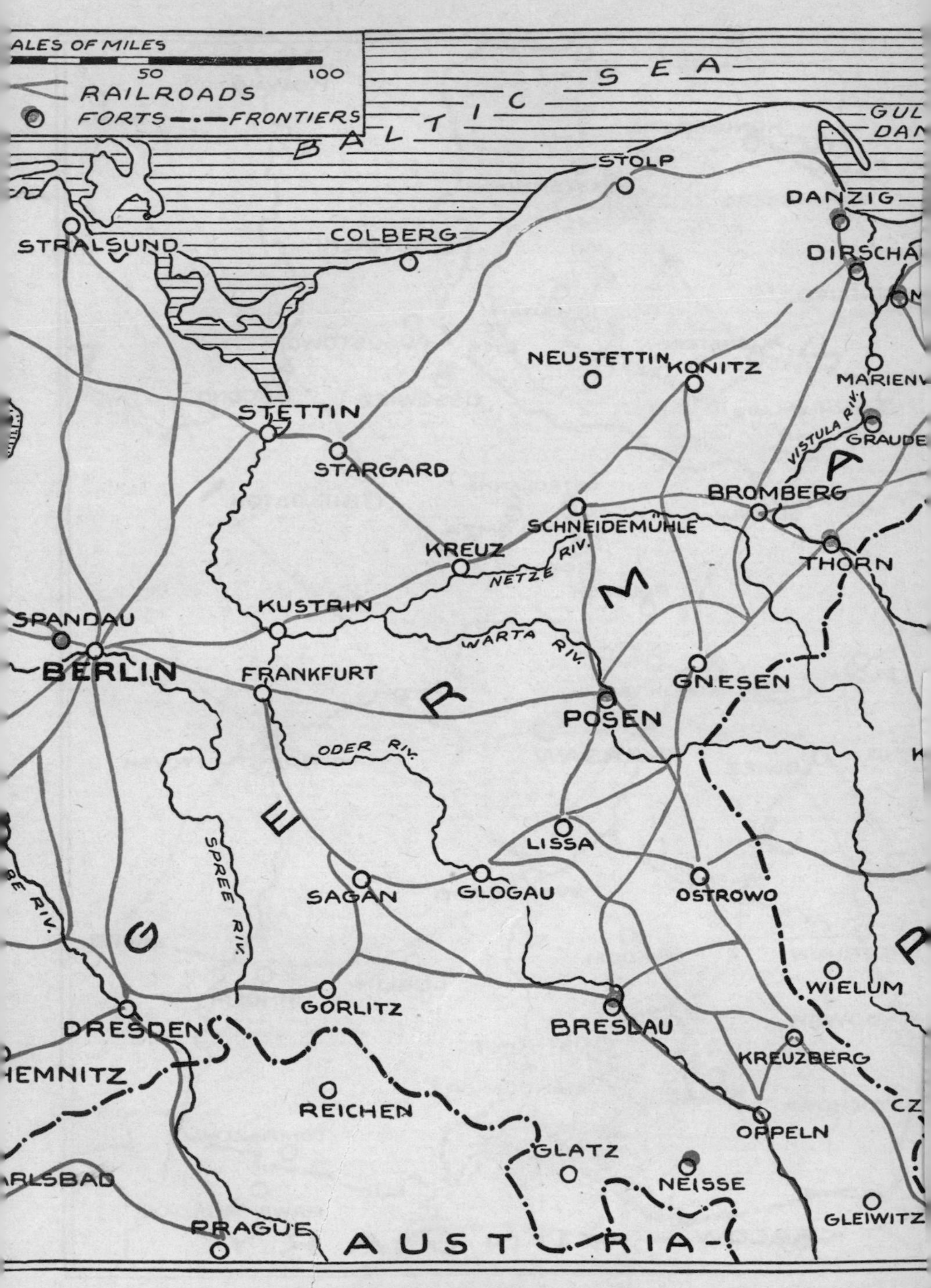

STRATEGIC RAILROAD SYSTEM IN EASTERN GERMANY THAT MADE Q

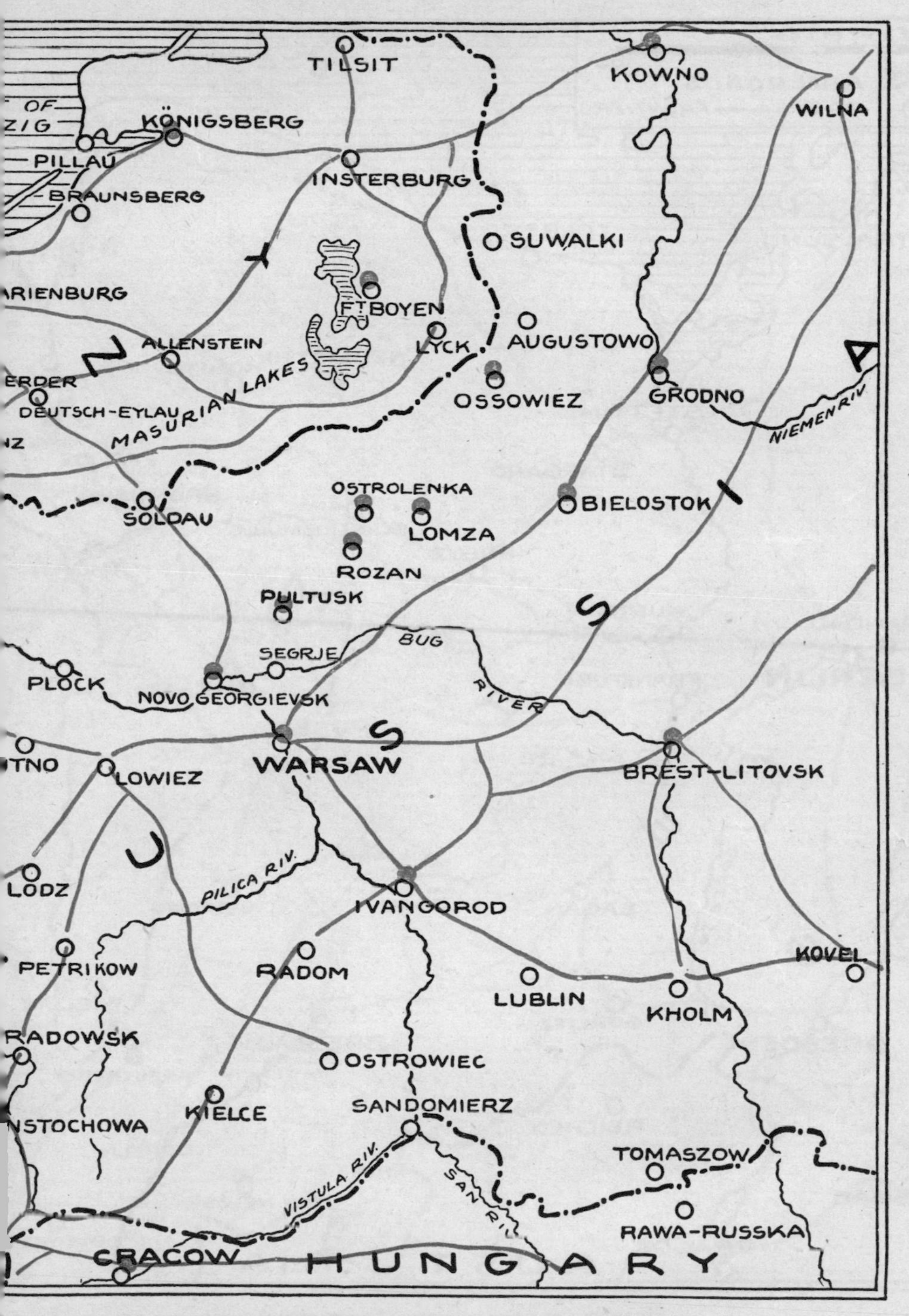

ICK CONCENTRATION AND SHIFTING OF TROOPS POSSIBLE

PART I—RUSSIAN AND TURKISH CAMPAIGN

CHAPTER I

CAMPAIGN IN THE CAUCASUS

DISQUIETING as was the British offensive in Mesopotamia, the Turkish General Staff were not to be drawn by it from considerations of larger strategy. Acting in agreement with the German and Austrian General Staffs, plans were rapidly pushed for an aggressive offensive in the Caucasus, that old-time battling ground of the Russians and the Turks. Germany was being hotly pressed in France by the armies of Belgium, France, and England, and feared an offensive on the part of the Russian army.

Across the great isthmus separating the Caspian and Black Seas run the Caucasus Mountains. Parallel to this range of towering mountains, the highest in Europe, runs the frontier line of Russia and Turkey and Russia and Persia, winding in and out among the Trans-Caucasian Mountains. About two hundred miles from the Russo-Turkish frontier stands Tiflis, the rich and ancient capital of Georgia, and one of the prime objectives of any Turkish offensive. One of the few railroads of this wild country runs from Tiflis through the Russian fortress of Kars, forty-five miles from the Turkish frontier, to Sarikamish, thirty miles nearer. On the Turkish side the fortress of Erzerum stands opposed to Kars, but suffering in comparison by the lack of railroad communication with the interior of Turkey.

Despite all these discouraging circumstances, however, the Turkish General Staff, dominated by the indefatigable and ambitious Enver Pasha, was not to be deterred. A brilliant and daring plan of campaign, aiming at the annihilation or capture of the entire Russian Caucasian army, the seizure of Kars and Tiflis, and the control of the immensely valuable and important Caspian oil fields, was prepared. The unwelcome task of carrying this plan to completion and success was intrusted to Hassan Izzet Pasha, under the general guidance of Enver Pasha and his staff of German advisers.

The heroic efforts of the Turkish troops, their grim but hopeless battle against equally brave troops, appalling weather conditions, and insuperable obstacles, their failure and defeat when on the very verge of complete success, make an intensely interesting story.

Stationed at Erzerum, Turkey had the Ninth, Tenth, and Eleventh Corps. In addition, the Thirty-seventh Arab division had been brought up from Bagdad to strengthen the Eleventh Corps. At Trebizond two divisions of the First Corps had been brought from Constantinople by sea. These forces totaled about 140,000 troops. At and about Kars, General Woronzov, the Russian commander, had between 100,000 and 110,000 troops at his disposal from first to last. But although weaker in numbers he had the inestimable advantage of operating with a line of railroad at his back, whereas the Turkish commander had to depend entirely upon road transit, 500 miles from the nearest railroad.

The conditions absolutely necessary for the success of the Turkish plan were the holding of the Russian force beyond Sarikamish, and the accurate timing of the flanking attacks, otherwise the Russian commander would be able to deal with each force separately and defeat and perhaps destroy them.

The campaign opened on November 20, 1914. The Russians, advancing across the frontier from Sarikamish, took Koprikeui, within thirty miles of Erzerum. There, for some time, they remained while the Turkish command prepared for their great coup.

About the middle of December, 1914, the Eleventh Corps of the Turkish army moved out of Erzerum, engaged the Russians at Koprikeui, defeated them after a short, sharp struggle, and drove them in disorder a dozen miles to Khorasan. While the Eleventh

Corps was thus engaged the Ninth and Tenth Corps, marching forty miles to the north in terrible weather, succeeded in crossing the high mountains that guard the Russian frontier. On Christmas Day they looked down on the town of Sarikamish and the vital railway that stretched away to the eastward. At the same time the two divisions of the First Corps, stationed at Trebizond, making a wider sweep, had, by forced marches through a blinding blizzard that threatened to make necessary the abandonment of the artillery, reached the vicinity of Ardahan.

The Tenth Corps had reached and was threatening the railway east of Sarikamish on the road to Kars. Its defeat was absolutely necessary to the safety of the Russian army. It was therefore the object of General Woronzov's first attack. During four days every available man and gun he could bring up on the railway were thrown against the rapidly dwindling ranks of the Tenth Corps. The Turks fought bravely, but weight of numbers and superiority of communications told in the end, and the Ottoman forces were driven into the mountains to the north.

The defeat and retreat of the Tenth Corps exposed the left flank of the Ninth, commanded by Iskan Pasha. General Woronzov took full advantage of the situation. Iskan and his 40,000 troops were soon fighting a desperate battle against an enveloping movement that threatened to encompass them.

Of the 40,000 troops of the Ninth Corps, a bare 6,000 struggled out of the mountains to the vicinity of Sarikamish, where they were rallied by Iskan Pasha. For six days and nights this heroic band made a determined attempt to capture the town held by a comparatively weak Russian garrison. Finally, when, surrounded by overwhelming Russian forces, it became apparent that no Turkish relief could reach him, Iskan Pasha and the remnant of his once proud corps surrendered.

Sarikamish was defended against Iskan's 6,000 by a mere handful of soldiers. Time and time again urged by their German officers, the Turks hurled themselves against the thin Russian line. It bent but did not break, as step by step, fighting fiercely all the way, it retreated before weight of numbers. And when relief did come to the defenders, and Iskan and his force were compelled to surrender, the brave little Russian band was completely exhausted.

In their pursuit of the remnants of the Tenth Corps the Russians met with some of the difficulties that had been the undoing of the Turks. Furthermore, although the Ninth Corps had been hemmed in so that no relief could reach it, the Turkish command had by no means lost the power of effective counteraction. The Eleventh Corps at Khorasan carried on an energetic campaign against the Russian front, gained a local and tactically important success, and drove the enemy back as far as Kara-Urgan, less than twenty miles from Sarikamish. Indeed, so serious became the threat to the Russian forces that General Woronzov, much against his wishes, was compelled to call off the pursuit of the Tenth Corps and strengthen the Sarikamish front with the troops that had been operating farther to the east.

In the second week of January, 1915, between these forces and the Eleventh Corps of the Turkish army a fierce battle, lasting several days, opened. The struggle was of the utmost intensity, at times developing into a hand-to-hand combat between whole regiments. On January 14 the Fifty-second Turkish Regiment was put to the bayonet by the Russians. At Genikoi a regiment of Cossacks charged, during an engagement with a portion of the Thirty-second Turkish Division, and killed and wounded more than 300.

It must be remembered in judging the terrible nature of the struggle that the armies were fighting in difficult country. The battle of Kara-Urgan, furthermore, was waged in a continual snowstorm. Thousands of dead and wounded were buried in the rapidly falling snow and no effort was made to recover them. By the end of this week, January 16, 1915, owing largely to their superior railway communications and the possibility of reenforcements, the Russians had not only checked the Turkish offensive, but had decisively defeated the Eleventh Corps. Pressing their advantage the Russians pursued the beaten Turks toward Erzerum, but the heavy snows prevented them gaining the full fruits of their victory.

If the Eleventh Corps had not won a victory it had, however, accomplished its object in that it had relieved the pressure on the Tenth and enabled it to make good its escape to the north, where it proceeded to effect a junction with the First Corps. The experience of this First Corps had not been a happy one. We left it on Christmas Day, 1914, overlooking Ardahan. A week later it entered the city and prepared to carry out its rôle in the general offensive by advancing upon the Russian right flank at Kars. It met serious opposition, however, when it attempted to move out of Ardahan, was itself compelled to retreat, and finally sought safety beyond the ridges to the west. There, in the valley of the Chorûk, it joined up with the Tenth Corps. Together they continued their retreat upon Trebizond. Subsequently they tried a new offensive in the Chorûk valley which was undecisive, however, and at the end of January, 1914, the situation had developed into a deadlock.

The Turkish troops in their operation in the Caucasus appeared to have suffered from the difficulty of keeping open their sea communications with Constantinople. Lacking railways they relied too much upon supplies arriving at Trebizond. The Russian fleet in the Black Sea was active, however, and upset the Turkish calculations. In the first week of January, 1915, at Sinope a Russian cruiser discovered the Turkish cruiser *Medjidieh* convoying a transport. After a short engagement the *Medjidieh* was put to flight, and the transport sunk.

On January 6, 1915, the Russian Black Sea fleet ran into the *Breslau* and the *Hamidieh* and damaged them both in a running fight. A week later Russian torpedo boats sank several Turkish supply boats near Sinope.

While this fighting was taking place in the north, farther to the south toward the Persian frontier the Russians were attempting a turning movement against the Turkish right flank. At the same time that the Russian force in the north crossed the Turkish frontier the Russian column entered Turkey fifty miles farther southeast. On November 8, 1914, this force entered the Turkish town of Kara Kilissa. A week later, making its way southwest for a distance of twenty miles, it engaged, near the village of Dutukht, a Turkish force composed largely of Arab troops of the Thirteenth Corps. At the outset the Russians met with a measure of success, but on November 22, 1914, the Turks, having been reenforced by troops from Bagdad, began a fierce offensive. After indecisive fighting in the Alashgird valley the Turks, about the middle of December, 1914, almost caught the Russians in a bold enveloping movement north of Dutukht. In order to escape the Russians were compelled to retreat hurriedly and thus ended their offensive operation in this section.

Still farther to the south, in Persia, the Turks and Russians also battled. Not only because of political conditions, but because of the nature of the country, it was easier for Russia and Turkey to attack each other through Persia than directly across other frontiers, just as it was easier for Germany and France to reach each other across Belgium. At the outbreak of war both Turkey and Russia, recognizing these circumstances, were occupants of Persian territory. Early in November two Russian columns marched across the northwest corner of Persia and into Turkey by the Kotur and Khanesur passes, evidently with the important city of Van, on the lake of that name, as an objective. At a point near Dilman, and again at Serai, they drove the Turkish troops back toward Van, but were checked by reenforcements.

Meanwhile the Turks had a more considerable success to the south. Apparently taking the Russian higher command completely by surprise, Turkish troops advanced almost unopposed to Tabriz, the most important of the cities of northern Persia. Alarmed by this, Russia sent a strong force which, on January 30, 1915, succeeded in recapturing the city.

Thus, up to the end of January, 1915, nothing decisive had been accomplished on the Caucasian front by either Turkey or Russia. The Battle of Sarikamish, resulting in a Turkish loss estimated by the Russian authorities at 50,000, while decisive enough locally, seems to have had no appreciable effect upon the situation as a whole. For reasons resting very largely in the difficulty of finding the troops necessary, as well as in the conditions of the country and the weather, the Russians had been unable to follow up their success. Indeed, the offensive appears to have continued in the hands of the Turks.

It is probably the case that Russia was unwilling to detach any considerable number of troops from her Polish and Galician front, where important events were brewing. Her General Staff rightly regarded the Caucasian front as of secondary importance—and like Austria on her Italian frontier, determined to fight a defensive campaign.

However that may be, conditions after the first few months of campaigning settled down into a stalemate. Engagements or a relatively small scale were reported from time to time, but the balance of advantage remained fairly even. Both countries had fronts where victories would bring larger returns and more immediate effect upon the ultimate outcome of the war.

CHAPTER II

TURKISH ADVANCE AGAINST EGYPT

TO the Turk no operation of the war appeared more important than did the campaign against Egypt. That in the early days of the struggle in 1914 he contented himself with what amounted to little more than a demonstration designed to hold as many British troops in Egypt as possible was due primarily to considerations of larger strategy. Undoubtedly, by his incursion into the Sinai Peninsula and his half-hearted attempt with a hopelessly small force to cross the Suez Canal, he learned many lessons invaluable in any future and more ambitious campaign. Considered as a diversion the early advance upon the Suez was a success: as a serious military operation, resting on its own legs, it was a fiasco.

No operation the Turks might have conducted could have been so unwelcome to the British as was that against Egypt. For weeks in advance it was discussed by English writers and, while they all, naturally, agreed that it was foredoomed to failure, there was an undercurrent of apprehension in official circles. It was realized that many untried problems and theories would be put to a severe test by such a campaign, if undertaken in a serious way by a large and well-equipped force. Of a purely Turkish force, commanded and organized by Turkish officers, there was no fear, but such wonderful organizers had the Germans proved themselves to be that the combination of Teuton brains and Turkish fighting qualities and endurance was regarded as formidable.

It was realized in England also that any measure of success that might come to an invading force would have two very serious results. It would not only threaten, and perhaps sever, the shortest route to the east and so seriously embarrass the trade, military and naval efficiency of the Allies, but it would have a grave and perhaps decisive effect upon Mohammedan malcontents in Egypt and India.

The exact truth of the conditions in India and Egypt will possibly never be known, so rigorous were the operations of the censorship set up by the British War Office. One thing is certain, however: in both countries political conditions were serious before the war and they could not, by any stretch of optimism, be conceived as improving with the coming of a great struggle aimed at the only remaining independent Mohammedan power.

For many months previous to August, 1914, the Indian office in London had been apprehensive of rebellion in India. In Egypt the circumstance that at the beginning of the war the British authorities announced that they would make no use of the native Egyptian army speaks for itself. It was believed in Constantinople and in Berlin that both Egypt and India were ripe for a terrible revolt against the rule of the British Raj: the uprisings of millions of fanatical natives that would forever sweep British control from these two key places to the trade of the world and would institute a Turkish suzerainty, backed and controlled by Berlin. This was thought all the more likely as thousands of the British regular troops had been withdrawn from India and Egypt for service in France, being replaced by raw levies from England and the Colonies.

These, then, were the major considerations that prompted the early offensive against Egypt. It was based upon sound political and military strategy. Just how near it came to complete success, just how much additional worry and effort it added to the burden of Great Britain and France, only a complete revelation of the progress of events in all fields will tell.

In the attack upon the canal the Turks operated primarily from their base at Damascus. As preparations progressed the troops that were to take part in the actual advance were concentrated between Jerusalem and Akabah. Under command of Djemel Pasha, Turkish Minister of Marine, there were gathered some 50,000 troops consisting mostly of first line troops of the best quality, reenforced by about 10,000 more or less irregular Arab Bedouins.

During November and early December, 1914, the force was moved forward by slow and methodical stages, until by December 15 it was awaiting orders to advance, encamped on the confines of the great desert that separated it from its objective.

Here it is well that the reader should have a good idea of the difficulties of the task the Turkish higher command had imposed upon Djemel Pasha and his troops.

The two chief difficulties to be met by the invaders of the Sinai were lack of transport facilities and lack of water. Three routes were possible for the Turkish army, all artificial obstacles being for the moment ignored; two by land, across the Sinai desert, and the third by sea, across the Mediterranean. The latter, however, must be ruled out because the seas were controlled by the Anglo-French fleet. For the same reason, the northern land route had many disadvantages, because it could be commanded for a part of its length by warships. However, it is instructive to examine it in detail.

The whole region crossed by the sea road is desert of the most difficult and forbidding character. By this road all the great invasions—the Roman, Egyptian, Assyrian, Greek, and French—have been made. The road enters the desert at El

Arish and from there to El Kantara on the Suez Canal, the probable point of attack of an army moving by this route, is 100 miles. Over this whole distance there are only three places, once an army has left El Arish, where water can be had. The first is a matter of a day's march, at El Maza, thirty miles away; the second is at Bir-El-Abd, another day's march; and the third at Katieh, within striking distance of the canal. Without the construction of a special railway the transport of a force large enough to efficiently control the canal by this route seems to be out of the question.

The southern route, known as the Hadj, or Pilgrim's Road, running from Akaba to Suez, besides being longer is even worse off in the matter of water. This was the traditional path of pilgrims traveling from Egypt to Mecca, and still is much in use for that purpose.

Something like 150 miles separate Akaba and Suez, yet only two watering places are to be found in the whole distance. The first is three days' march from the former place, at a point called Nakhl, where modern cisterns had been built and an adequate supply of water for a large force probably was obtainable. The next watering place is another three days' march, at Ayun Mousa, or Well of Moses, within a short distance of the canal.

But tremendous as were the problems facing a considerable body of men in attempting to cross the Sinai desert and arrive at the Suez Canal in condition to fight a strong, fresh and fully prepared foe, they were not to be compared to the difficulties that would face such an army when the canal had been reached. We have seen how great an obstacle a wide river, such as the Vistula, proved to be to an army when attempting to cross in the face of a prepared enemy. In the case of the Suez Canal, although there were no strong currents, a force attempting to cross it had to contend with two added difficulties: The Suez Canal could not, in the circumstances be turned, as was the Vistula by the Germans. Furthermore its defensive value was immeasurably increased by the circumstance that it could and did carry warships of the largest type which not only had the value of fortresses mounting the heaviest of guns, but were mobile as well. And finally, because of the nature of the shores of the canal, it was possible for an attacking force to cross it at but few points.

The question of crossing the canal or dominating it in any sense was for the Turks largely a question of bringing to bear a superior force of artillery—a task that had only to be stated to reveal its difficulties. No force with smaller or fewer guns would hope to cross the Suez in the face of the concentration of artillery and naval gunfire that the British could bring to bear at any threatened point.

The defenders on the western side of the canal had the additional advantage of railway communication running along the entire canal from Suez to Port Said, and connecting with interior bases.

There were five points from which, once having conquered the desert and reached the canal, the invaders could advantageously launch an attack or attacks upon the canal defenses. The first is just south of El Kantara, where the old sea road crosses the Suez. Just south of Ismailia a group of heights on the east bank provides a second opportunity. The third is found at the point called the Plateau of Hyena. The fourth is just north of the Bitter Lake, and the fifth is to the south of the same body of water.

Late in December, 1914, Djemel Pasha began active preparations for an advance upon the canal. This campaign the Turks later called a reconnaissance in force and as, of their total strength of 50,000 men, only 12,000 at the outside and possibly less were used, the limited term seems justified. Although the southern route was used by the main force, a small force eluded the watchfulness of the Anglo-French naval patrol operating along the shore commanding the first day's march of the northern, or sea road, and ultimately struck at El Kantara. Furthermore, sometime before one of these two forces—the larger, or southern—reached the vicinity of the canal, it split and conducted an independent attack at Suez.

There had been much speculation among military writers all over the world as to the possibility or probability of the construction by the Turks of a light railway running a part of the distance across the Sinai Desert and linking up with the line to Mecca. It was realized that such a railway would be an enormous help to Djemel Pasha and his army, especially in the transport of supplies, ammunitions, and artillery. Indeed, it was held that only by the construction of such a railway, extending almost to the canal, could the absolutely essential artillery be brought into action. There was serious doubt of the ability of the Turks to build such a line. The strength of the German "stiffening" in the army based upon Damascus was believed to be slight. Djemel Pasha is said to have seriously opposed any great number of Teuton officers, especially in the higher commands. Thus the assistance the Turks could expect from the Germans in the organization and construction of such a railway would be small. Whether or not the scheme was feasible at that time it is impossible to say. At any rate the Turks, for reasons best known to themselves, did not put it to a test.

The British force in Egypt was well supplied with aeroplanes and kept the Turkish army under constant observation. With the exception of the use of the first section of the road, covering a couple of days of time, there was probably no element of surprise in the Turkish attack upon the canal. Realizing the limited possibilities of attack from the east shore, the British, taking their lesson from experience in France, had constructed an elaborate system of trenches to the east of the canal at the five points where attacks would possess some likelihood of successful conclusion.

It was the end of January, 1915, before the Turkish army, marching in easy stages across the desert reached the vicinity of the canal. Their German mentors had constructed for them elaborate carriages with the wheels of enormous width to carry the artillery and the heavy supplies across the soft sands. Also, in preparation of a crossing of the canal, the Turks brought a supply of ready-assembled pontoon bridges, running on wheels and similar to those used by the German army in Europe, except that they were much lighter.

In the transport of all this material the Turks were dependent upon camels, suited as are no other animals for work in the desert. In thousands, they had been collected at Hadj, the cooperation of the Arab Bedouins being specially valuable in this work. The consideration of these events in the campaign which begins in February, 1915, will be found in Volume III of this work.

CHAPTER III

FAILURE OF "HOLY WAR" PROPAGANDA

ONE of the most interesting of the various phases of the war, so far as the participation of Turkey was concerned, was the religious development. Countless pages of learned speculation had been written for years before the struggle in an attempt to forecast the outcome of exactly the conditions that had arisen. It must be said at once that in the first six months of the war reality failed to live up to prophecy. The cataclysm that was expected by many to involve the revolt of millions and a vast change in the political color of much of the earth's surface did not appear. Any change that took place operated so quietly and on so comparatively small a scale that it was lost to view beside the greater interest of the struggle on the battle fields of France and Poland.

It is desirable, however, that the situation be examined. Abbas II, Khedive of Egypt, had early in the war openly shown his lack of sympathy with the British in Egypt. By his actions he left no doubt regarding his attitude. He not only vehemently expressed his adherence to Constantinople but left Cairo, and journeyed to Turkey, safe from British official pressure or persuasion. Whereupon the British Government called upon him to return, threatened him with deposition, and finally took that extreme step, setting up another in his place on December 18, 1914.

Furthermore, the day before, Great Britain declared Egypt a British protectorate independent of Constantinople. In this action Great Britain relied not upon any legal right to take such action, but merely upon the right of actual possession. Since

Great Britain had taken over the government of Egypt in 1883, she had acknowledged the sultan's rights of suzerainty and had countenanced the payment to that ruler of certain considerable yearly sums from the Egyptian exchequer.

Indeed, Great Britain was in Egypt merely by virtue of an international understanding and on a definite agreement to release her control of the country when certain conditions of political and financial stability had been restored. The other nations had, willingly, or unwillingly, become resigned to her possession of this strategically important land. Great Britain a decade before the war, at the beginning of that rapprochement with France which led up to the Entente and which had so many fateful consequences for the whole world, sought to legalize her position in Egypt—at least so far as the other great north African power was concerned. A bargain was struck with France by which the English occupation of Egypt for an indefinite period was recognized in exchange for a free hand in Morocco. Great Britain could now urge that the coming of war, and especially the entry of Turkey into the struggle, placed her administration in Egypt in a position impossible to maintain. In theory she was, so long as she acknowledged the suzerainty of the sultan, in the country merely on that ruler's sufferance. She admitted his ultimate authority and especially the loyalty and duty of the Egyptian army and khedive to him. Strictly she could make no move to prevent an armed occupation of the country by the sultan's troops nor could she call upon the khedive and his cabinet to repudiate Constantinople's sway. To put an end to this condition of affairs was the most legitimate reason for England's action.

Although the native Egyptian is in religion allied to the Turk, his religious fervor was not great enough to induce him to rise against British control. Among the better educated of the Egyptians and especially among those who had traveled, there was a strong "Nationalist" movement. At times, even in the period of peace, this movement had threatened to make matters extremely unpleasant for the British rulers. For some years before the war, German and Turkish agents had been working among these ardent Egyptian patriots, encouraging and advising them, and when war with Turkey came England was seriously alarmed. Using the country as a central base for her Turkish, Persian, and Balkan operations, Great Britain imported thousands upon thousands of troops into Egypt. Just how many hundreds of thousands of armed men passed in and out of the country from first to last only the records of the British war office would show, but it can be said that England never had a force of less than 90,000 trained men in Egypt at any one time.

Any chance of effective action that the Egyptian nationalists might have had was neutralized by the indifference and lack of interest in the vast body of their countrymen. There were more than 10,000,000 Mohammedans in Egypt, but only a small minority of them, under the most promising of circumstances, could have been counted upon to pay the least heed to the call of Constantinople. The Egyptian fellah is anything but a fighter. Lazy, unlearned, unambitious, he is content to accept his daily lot, perhaps conscious that the British rule has brought a certain amount of comparative prosperity even to him.

On the other hand, there were in Egypt something like 600,000 nomads, a very large proportion of whom could be depended upon to follow the lead of Constantinople. The males of these wild tribespeople were remarkable fighters, subject to no control, hating the English sway, and so independent of roads and transport that they could keep busy an even larger force of less mobile troops. Their chief weakness was their lack of cohesion and the impossibility of any concerted action on their part.

This, then, was the native situation in Egypt. In other parts of the world, where Great Britain maintained sway over large numbers of Mohammedans, the situation was equally complicated. With the issue of a call for a Holy War by the Sheik-ul-Islam, the religious ruler of the Mohammedan world, many well-informed observers looked for a large measure of trouble in India. So many were the elements of dissatisfaction, and even open revolt, in India that it was believed the Sheik-ul-Islam's call would be the match applied to the powder magazine.

The attitude of the various Indian potentates was uncertain. Some of them were known to be only outwardly loyal to the British authority. The now famous incident at the visit of King George to India, some years before the war, when one of the richest and most important of the native princes refused to bend the knee, was indicative of very widespread dissatisfaction. Innumerable cases of individual and even concerted violence against British rule immediately preceded the war, and several of these were openly encouraged by native princes.

So far as definite action was concerned, the opening of the war with Turkey and the months that immediately followed falsified all these predictions of disaster to British rule in India. Many of the native princes were effusive in their professions of loyalty to the British Empire, and several offered personal service at the front or financial contributions to the huge cost of the struggle.

Notable, and perhaps decisive, was the open adherence to Britain of the Agar Khan, the immensely powerful ruler of millions of Indian Mohammedans. The Agar Khan had spent many of the years previous to the war in England in daily association with English high society and official circles. At the outbreak of the war with Turkey, in October, 1914, at the request of the British Government, he visited Egypt, and it was largely upon his advice that the former khedive was deposed and the new one elevated to the post. Indeed, at one time there were strong rumors, afterward energetically denied by the British Government, that the Agar Khan had advised a Mohammedan repudiation of the authority of the caliph and the elevation of another to his place under a British guarantee. In support of this plan it was pointed out that Great Britain, judged by the number of adherents under her rule, was the world's greatest Mohammedan power. It was intolerable to many English people, especially to those of strong imperialistic tendencies, that the real control, even in theory, of so large and important a section of the people of the British Empire should be in Constantinople, safe from the "influence" and "persuasion" of the British Government. By these people it was held that the sultan's lineal claim was weak, and that an even better claim to the headship of the Moslems could be established for any one of several other men who might have been named. However, the plan was never achieved.

CHAPTER IV

RESULTS OF FIRST SIX MONTHS OF TURKISH CAMPAIGN

WHAT was the situation as a whole, so far as Turkey and her military actions against the Allies were concerned, as to the outcome of these various operations in three fields—the Caucasus, Mesopotamia, and Egypt—during the first six months of the war? The military narrative is recorded in the chapter following. It will be seen that all of them were inconclusive. Indeed, from what we knew of the circumstances surrounding them, all we are justified in saying is that none of them was serious in the sense that they were not intended to have any decisive effect, directly, upon the progress of the war. Of them all it might be urged by a military authority that they were subsidiary operations, dangerous and wasteful in that they withdrew valuable men, munitions, brains, and energy from the decisive fronts. Their only justification is that they imposed similar action on the part of both armies, and so, in just that degree, scattered their forces. For the Turk it can be urged that at least two of the campaigns were forced upon him by his German mentors, while the third was imposed upon him by a British offensive. Furthermore, the Turk was entirely cut off from his Austro-German allies, and there was no possibility of his bringing his weight to bear in one of the main fields. From that point of view it is possible to justify the Turkish offensives as sound strategy.

Aside from a desire to protect the oil supply in Persia, it is hardly as easy to justify the British offensive in Mesopotamia. As events subsequently demonstrated, it was possible for the Turks to throw an overwhelming number of troops into Bagdad and to the south, and, furthermore, they were fighting under vastly more advantageous conditions than were the invaders. Only on the assumption that the Turks were hopelessly demoralized and disorganized, and that as fighting men they would belie all their past history, was it possible to visualize success for the British operations in Mesopotamia.

Turkey had definitely come to grips with England and with Russia. She had in none of these fields measured swords with France, although she was equally at war with that country. The exact apportionment of the actual work to be done by the individual powers of the Entente seems to have led to considerable disagreement, and resulted at times in serious delay. Such arrangements depend, of course, upon each country's idea of its spheres of influence. Obviously, no country, if it can help it, is going to waste its men or its efforts in a field in which it has only a minor political or commercial interest. So far as France was concerned, the Caucasus, Egypt—aside from the possibility of the closing of the canal—and Mesopotamia were not of enough importance to justify her in participating in the struggle with the Turks even were it physically possible. All these remarks, of course, are subject to modifications imposed by considerations of the larger strategy of the Entente Powers; but for many months of the war the agreement of the Entente Powers in the matter of general strategy was conspicuous by its absence.

With her neighbors in the Balkans Turkey had maintained remarkably good relations considering the bitterness engendered, not only by centuries of strife, but by the recent events of the two Balkan wars. Bulgaria, smarting under the loss of territory through the attack upon her by Serbia, Greece, and Rumania in the Second Balkan War, was openly conducting friendly negotiations with Turkey for the acquisition of valuable territory—a compact that could mean only one thing. Greece, frightened by the menace of the German power, had resisted up to the moment all the blandishments of the Entente Powers, who urged her to active participation in the struggle. Rumania, largely isolated from the Entente Powers, menaced on the north by Austro-German forces, on the south by a revengeful Bulgaria, borrowed heavily from Britain, the universal money bag, but straddled the fence.

Thus Turkey, which in different circumstances might have been in a precarious military situation, felt reasonably secure, despite her isolation. In the early part of the war, however, events moved rapidly and not exactly to her liking. For they threatened to sweep the whole Balkans into the whirl of war, and no man could tell exactly how the various petty states, under the stress of sympathy, military and naval considerations and dynastic control, would align themselves. With these events came, too, the first participation of France in the war against Turkey in the campaign in the Dardanelles, now to be described.

CHAPTER V

THE DARDANELLES—STRATEGY OF THE CAMPAIGN

THE beginning of the bombardments in the Dardanelles opens a remarkable chapter in military and naval warfare. The desperate campaign to batter down the fortifications which lead to Constantinople and the disastrous attempt to conquer the most strongly barricaded city in the world, probably excited more world-wide interest or put to the test more theories of warfare than did the Dardanelles campaign undertaken by Great Britain with the assistance of France. It was fiercely attacked by military critics almost from the start. It was, however, a boldly conceived operation, calculated to have a most important effect upon the war as a whole—certainly upon the war in the southeast corner of Europe.

The Dardanelles campaign was largely conceived and controlled by the Rt. Hon. Winston Spencer Churchill, the remarkable and able British Secretary of the Admiralty. He has been widely condemned for his share of the operation, but revelations that have been made would appear to clear him of a great measure of the blame.

What were the considerations that weighed with the British admiralty in deciding to undertake one of the most difficult operations in the whole world? Primarily it seems to have had the idea of relieving the pressure on Russia. The Turkish offensive in the Caucasus had come to grief about the end of December but a resumption was momentarily expected and feared. Hindenburg's victory at Tannenberg in East Prussia had been a terrible blow to Russia and she had no troops to spare for defense in the Caucasus.

Furthermore, Constantinople, besides being one of the objectives of the war, was Russia's only warm sea gate into Europe. It must have been apparent to the Russian military authorities that the existing supplies of munition and guns of the czar's army would not suffice to withstand a hard German-Austrian drive. In other words the condition that resulted in the defeat of the Russian army in Galicia and Poland in the summer of 1915 were foreseen. Russia called upon England and France to force the Dardanelles. One can find it easy to condemn the operation but few can be found who will deny that it was a glorious failure. One that added luster to the glory of the British army, navy, and many unmatched pages to the story of their bravery. And no less credit and glory did it bring to the Turkish armies.

In addition to the question of war supplies there were other reasons for opening the Dardanelles as soon as possible. Russia's ability to finance a war of the magnitude of the one there being fought, especially where large foreign purchases were made, depended very largely upon the maintenance of foreign commerce. Russia was buying from all the neutral world as well as from her Entente partners. England, for instance, was not only making for her millions of dollars' worth of war supplies, but she was, for the moment, financing many of Russia's purchases abroad.

In return for all this it was important that Russia should export as freely as possible. Now one of her most valuable commodities and one in high demand not only in England, but in other countries, was wheat. Millions upon millions of bushels of Russian wheat were stored in her great Black Sea ports waiting to be shipped through Constantinople when the Bosphorus and the Dardanelles were commanded by Entente guns and ships. Greece, under the leadership of Premier Venizelos was hesitating on the brink of a plunge into the struggle as an ally of the En-

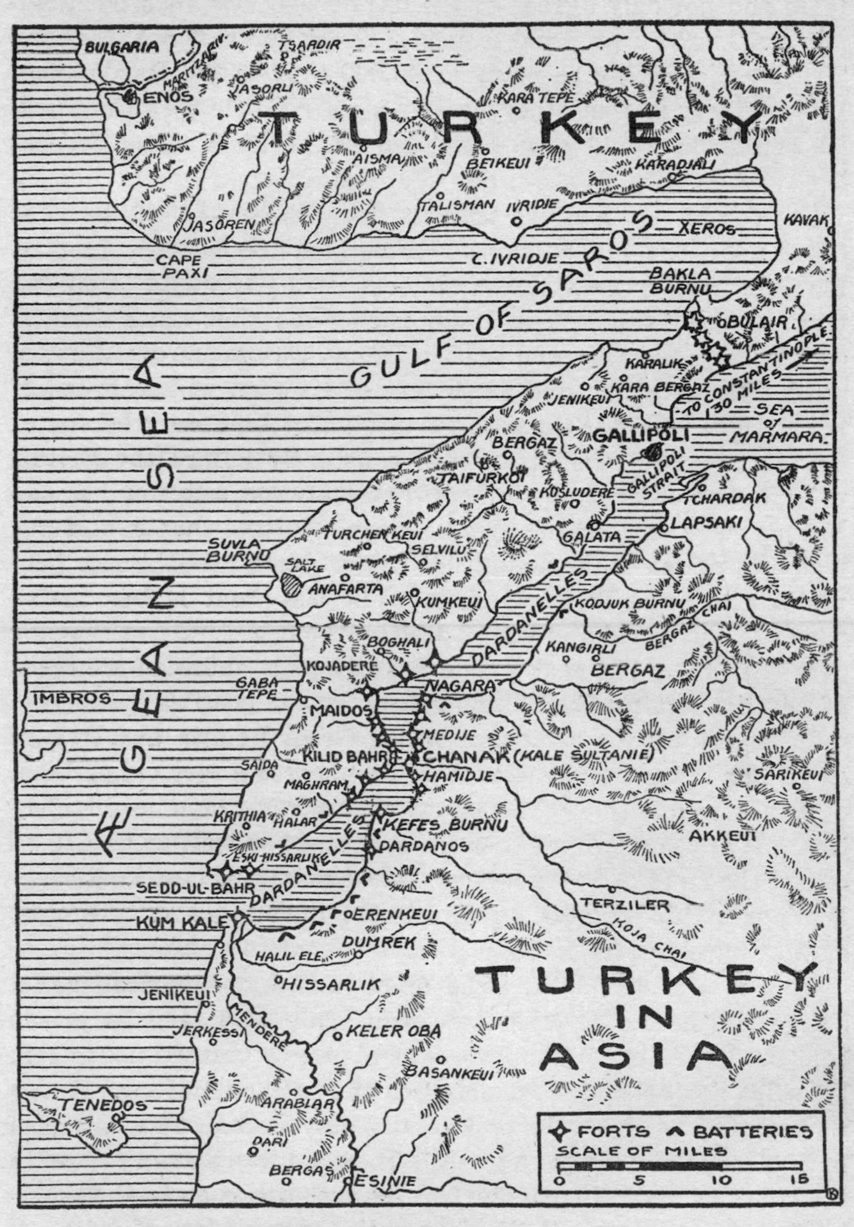
BULGARIA
MARITZA RIV.
TSARDIR
ENOS
JASORLI
KARA TEPE
TURKEY
AISMA
BEIKEUI
KARADJALI
TALISMAN
IVRIDJE
JASÖREN
XEROS
KAVAK
CAPE PAXI
C. IVRIDJE
GULF OF SAROS
BAKLA BURNU
BULAIR
KARALIK
KARA BERGAZ
TO CONSTANTINOPLE 130 MILES
JENIKEUI
SEA of MARMARA
BERGAZ
GALLIPOLI
TAIFURKOI
KUSLUDERE
GALLIPOLI STRAIT
TCHARDAK
LAPSAKI
AEGEAN SEA
SUVLA BURNU
TURCHEN KEUI
SELVILU
GALATA
SALT LAKE
ANAFARTA
KUMKEUI
DARDANELLES
KODJUK BURNU
BERGAZ CHAI
BOGHALI
KANGIRLI
BERGAZ
KOJADERE
GABA TEPE
NAGARA
IMBROS
MAIDOS
MEDIJE
KILID BAHR
CHANAK (KALE SULTANIE)
SAIDA
HAMIDJE
SARIKEUI
MAGHRAM
KRITHIA
HALAR
KEFES BURNU
AKKEUI
ESKI HISSARLIK
DARDANOS
SEDD-UL-BAHR
DARDANELLES
TERZILER
KUM KALE
ERENKEUI
KOJA CHAI
DUMREK
HALIL ELE
HISSARLIK
TURKEY IN ASIA
JENIKEUI
MENDERE
JERKESSI
KELER OBA
BASANKEUI
TENEDOS
ARABLAR
DARI
BERGAS
ESINIE
FORTS
BATTERIES
SCALE OF MILES
0 5 10 15

GALLIPOLI

tente and not only agreed to the use of Greek islands but actually considered a proposal to send a Greek force of not less than 20,000 and possibly as many as 40,000 over to the Dardanelles. Bulgaria was in that state where a striking victory in the Turkish peninsula would have swept her off her feet. Italy was at loggerheads with Austria, her ally, and about to break.

Then from the English point of view there was the possible effect upon the Mohammedan throughout the British Empire. Possibly not for many years, if ever, will the world know the truth of the conditions in India during the war. One thing is certain. In one way and another there was much disaffection, much open rebellion and much fear of an even wider spread of revolt. The need for the maintenance and even strengthening of British prestige must have been constantly before the British ruler and no other campaign could possibly serve this end so efficacious as a successful assault upon Constantinople and the temporal power of the sultan. It would clinch probably for generations to come Britain's claim to be the great Mohammedan power of the world and would destroy the one condition that for years before and at that time especially had contained the seeds of rebellion against the British yoke.

In beginning the campaign which Great Britain and France carried on in the Dardanelles there reappeared a very old problem of war—the question of Warships versus Forts or land fortifications. It appears to have been the consensus of opinion among all except the more extreme exponents of battleships that land fortifications would possess an undoubted advantage in a contest against purely naval forces.

This it seems had been the opinion of the American naval authorities in the Spanish-American War, when the American commander, Admiral Sampson, was expressly warned not to risk his ships against the shore defenses of Santiago Harbor. It also appears to have been the opinion of many British admirals who have placed their views on record. Indeed, there was in existence the views of several competent naval authorities as to the possibilities of a purely naval attack upon this very system of defenses.

It was not by any means the first time that an attempt had

been made to force the Dardanelles. Many such attempts had proved this narrow neck of water running between high banks to be one of the great natural defensive spots of the world. The realization of that obvious and oft-proved fact had made Constantinople through the ages one of the most fought for and schemed for cities of the whole world.

It is necessary to study these attempts in order to understand clearly the difficulties which faced the British and French Allies in 1914. Of the previous attacks that had been made to force a way through the Dardanelles and so up to the city of Constantinople, that of the famous Admiral Hornby in 1877 was one of the most interesting as well as one of the most instructive. Ordered by the British Government to take his fleet past the forts that lined the approaching banks, he proceeded to carry out his orders, but wrote a warning in which he pointed out that, while it might be possible for his fleet to make its way into the Sea of Marmora, once there it would be helpless if the land defenses were controlled by the enemy. Out of coal, ammunition, and food, the ships would be at the mercy of the Turks. "Although the forts might not prevent a strong fleet passing through the Dardanelles, they certainly," wrote Admiral Hornby, "could sink armed and unarmed transports and supply ships." In view of these considerations, Hornby urged the British Government to provide a land force of sufficient strength to carry and hold the land defenses. His superiors, however, did not agree with him, for they told him to go ahead with a purely naval operation. His ideas were never put to a real test because the Turks offered no resistance to his passage of the straits.

The situation in the Great War of 1914 presented Constantinople as the same perplexing military problem. If we go back another three-quarters of a century to 1807, the experience of Admiral Duckworth throws some light on the subject, although conditions had changed radically. Duckworth, with his sailing ships, ran past the forts in the Dardanelles and anchored in front of Constantinople. It was hoped that a threat of bombardment would bring the Turks to their knees, but the latter refused to be intimidated. In the end, the British admiral ran out of food and water and was compelled to leave without accomplishing anything.

The student of the War of 1914 also must consider that during the war between Italy and Turkey, the Italian General Staff is known to have worked out an elaborate plan for an attack upon the Dardanelles. However, at the critical moment, the European powers interfered and forced upon Italy an agreement that the war should not be extended to the mainland of Europe. In the Balkan War, the Bulgarians threatened the lines of Bulair, the narrow neck which connects the Gallipoli peninsula to the mainland, but never launched the attack.

When in 1914 the British and French determined to press a purely naval attack upon the Dardanelles, they appear to have been influenced by two major considerations. At the time there was not ready a sufficient number of troops to make a land campaign successful and, at the last moment, King Constantine of Greece repudiated a personal agreement made by Venizelos, the Greek Premier, with the Allies by which Greece was to provide at least 20,000 troops to assist the France-British fleet. Even after the fall of Venizelos it was still determined to push the naval attack because of the second consideration. In the opinion of the British admiralty the full power of modern naval guns of 11- and 12-inch had never been tested and in their opinion they would suffice to reduce the Dardanelles defenses in a comparatively short time. Furthermore, the British authorities appear to have relied largely upon the new 15-inch guns of the *Queen Elizabeth* and her sister vessels, then nearing completion in British yards. So tremendous was the power of these new guns and so great their range that it was believed the *Queen Elizabeth* and her sister ships could stand miles out of range of the heaviest of the Dardanelles guns and quickly smash them to an unrecognizable mass of ruins.

It was evident that the British naval command held these views even in spite of the experience of British warships off the coast of Belgium earlier in the war. For a while in 1914 British monitors and battleships bombarded almost at will the German troops posted along the coast running from the Dutch frontier line almost to Nieuport. Finally, however, the Germans brought up heavy army and naval guns and, mounting them in concealed spots among the sand dunes, soon drove off the British naval force.

But Turkish guns were not German guns, Turkish gunners were not German gunners, and above all, the munition supply of the Turkish army was not fed by factories able to turn out a quarter of a million shells a day. Some such considerations as these appear to have convinced the British higher command that there was a difference in the two tasks.

The command of the Dardanelles forts at the entrance to Constantinople and the Black Sea is similar, except that it is perhaps more sure as to the command of the entrance to the Baltic by Copenhagen, the Mediterranean by Gibraltar, and, in a lesser degree, of the North Sea by Dover.

The narrow passage of water called the Dardanelles separates the peninsula of Gallipoli and the Asiatic shore of Turkey. It connects the Ægean Sea and the Sea of Marmora, which in turn, through the Bosphorus, connects with the Black Sea. Curiously enough this tremendously important waterway, the only warm sea outlet of Russia, had been closed against that country by the action of the very powers now fighting desperately to smash it open. The Black Sea was a Turkish lake in the seventeenth century but in the century following the growth of Russia in that part of Europe made the question of the control of the Bosphorus and the Dardanelles one of supreme importance to her. Thus we find, in the so-called "will" of Peter the Great, among other injunctions he lays upon his successors, an admonition never to rest until Constantinople had been wrested from the Turk. But whether this "will" is authentic or not, Russian policy has steadily kept that object in view.

The Crimean War was an attempt by France and England to stem the almost resistless tide of Russian expanse toward the southwest. Russian control of Constantinople was regarded as the chief danger that threatened the western powers and, in 1856, by the Treaty of Paris, not only was the strength of the Russian Black Sea fleet expressly limited, but the Dardanelles were closed against the passage of Russia's warships into the Mediterranean. France and England revived what they called "an ancient rule of the Ottoman Empire, in virtue of which it has at all times been prohibited for ships of war of foreign powers to enter the Straits of the Dardanelles and of the Bosphorus."

Turkey was of no mind to leave the enforcement of this "ancient rule" to the powers. She began the construction of more elaborate fortifications commanding both the Bosphorus and the Dardanelles. German advice, especially after the Franco-Prussian War, was asked and obtained and Krupp sent some of his gigantic pieces for the defense of the narrow waters. This German cooperation with the Turks in the strengthening of those positions through all the years that have intervened is significant.

CHAPTER VI

FORTIFICATIONS AND STRENGTH—FIRST MOVEMENTS

LET us inspect the fortifications in the Dardanelles at the beginning of the war in 1914. The Dardanelles, from end to end, have a length of forty-seven miles. From the town of Gallipoli to the Ægean, however, the full distance of the narrow section of the waterway, is a matter of thirty-three miles. At one point the passage is less than 1,400 yards wide and at no point is it more than 7,000. Although there is a good depth in much of the channel, shallows are to be met with in most unexpected places. To make navigation even more difficult, there is a swift and powerful surface current running through the Narrows, on some occasions at a speed of eight knots an hour. In addition there is not only a strong undercurrent, but, as well, many cross currents. At certain seasons of the year the wind and weather make navigation of large vessels almost impossible.

Both sides of the Dardanelles offered natural positions of enormous advantage to a defending force. On the Gallipoli side were a tangled mass of rocks and hills, almost devoid of vegetation except for stubby yellow bushes. In a few of the little valleys, stray clusters of olive trees relieved the monotony of the view. Heights rose upon heights and along the shores of the peninsula nearly perpendicular cliffs made landings almost out of the question.

This whole peninsula was a difficult country to traverse even in times of peace. No large maps existed of its intricate paths, there were few roads, and those that did exist were so commanded by heights and concealed positions for guns and infantry that the progress of an attacking force would inevitably be most difficult and costly.

Water was almost nonexistent. Most of the available supply was so protected that an attacking force would in no case be able to use it until its task of conquest was complete. As such a force advanced inland, these difficulties as well as those of the country would constantly and rapidly increase. From Cape Hellas, at the tip of the peninsula where a sandy beach made a landing possible, if difficult, the ground rapidly rose to a height of 140 feet. Hill country then led to ridges standing 600 feet, while a mile and a half beyond stood 600 feet in the air the commanding peak of Achi Baba, destined to play so large and so tragic a part in the struggle for the peninsula of Gallipoli. At the narrowest part of the Narrows, the real key position to the straits, stood the Kilid Bahr plateau, 700 feet, while to the northwest, almost 300 feet higher, stood the precipitous eminence of Sari Bair, a dense mass of trackless ravines and thickets.

Where the peninsula of Gallipoli joined the mainland is, comparatively speaking, a narrow neck of land. Even this, however, presented tremendous potential difficulties to any force. A hill almost 500 feet in height rose in the center and marshed on either side prevented a turning movement. Furthermore, the difficulties of landing a force in the face of an enemy strongly intrenched on the heights were not lessened by the circumstance that the cliffs rose to a height of 300 feet, almost straight from the water's edge. In short nature seems to have designed the country in every way as a protection against an armed force seeking to force its way either in or out of the Black Sea. To just what extent these natural advantages had been utilized by the Turks it is impossible to say. It is not likely, however, that they, or their German mentors, had been idle, in view of the importance the Allies were known to attach to the straits.

In September, 1914, and probably for some time before, the Turks were known to be busy strengthening the forts. Subsequent events led to the conclusion that they, or their German advisers, were alive to the lessons of the early days of the war in France and Belgium and had made elaborate arrangements for the placing of heavy guns in concealed positions. In addition they perfected the mobility of even the heaviest of pieces, so that it became impossible for observation from the Franco-British ships or from aeroplanes to locate them with any certitude.

The Turks also seem to have secured a plentiful supply of sea mines, with which the waters approaching the Dardanelles and the actual passage of the straits were strewn along the shores. Toward the Narrows were constructed shore batteries for the launching of torpedoes, as well as for the launching of floating mines. The strong current of the straits could be depended upon to carry these latter engines of destruction among the allied ships of war should they venture within the narrow, confined waters of the Dardanelles.

This was the condition of affairs, then, on November 3, 1914, when a joint Anglo-French squadron sailed in close to the tip of the Gallipoli peninsula and opened a bombardment of the outer defenses of the Dardanelles. For this and subsequent naval operations against the Turkish position, England was able to detach from her main theatre of naval activity—the North Sea—a considerable number of old, but still extremely powerful, battleships and battle cruisers. These boats, with the exception of the *Queen Elizabeth,* which later appeared on the scene, were all built previous to the introduction of the dreadnought and were to a considerable extent made obsolete by that vessel. At any rate they could not engage the more modern ships of the German navy and could not be attached to the grand fleet of England because of their lack of high speed and the heaviest of guns. For these reasons, although their loss in any engagement against the Turkish defenses would not be relished by the British authorities, still such a disaster would not be decisive in any war. As Winston Churchill subsequently pointed out, many of them would have, in the ordinary course of events, but a few more years of life in the British navy, so rapidly were modern battleships deteriorating under the rapid advance of naval science.

At the entrance to the straits the Turks had erected two major positions and several minor ones. On the Asiatic shore stood the Kum Kale Fort, known as the "New Castle of Asia." There the main battery consisted of four 10.2-inch guns. A short distance down the coast stood Yeni Shehr, where a main battery of two 9.2-inch guns and a short battery of smaller pieces had been erected. On the European side, opposite Kum Kale, stood Sedd-el-Bahr, with six 10-inch and two 5.9-inch guns. At Cape Hellas, the extreme point of the Gallipoli Peninsula, was the Erteghrul Battery, mounting two 9.2-inch guns and some minor pieces.

Each of the attacking warships fired about a score of shells at these forts and an attempt was made to determine just how much damage had been done. None of the forts were silenced, however, and it was finally decided by the commander of the Anglo-French naval force, Vice Admiral Carden, that conditions were not propitious for pushing home the attack and the vessels retired out to sea, where they maintained a tight blockade of the Dardanelles. Then there followed a long period of naval inactivity, at least so far as the larger vessels were concerned.

About a month later, however, on December 13, 1914, the commander of a British submarine accomplished a feat in the Sea of Marmora that not only aroused his countrymen to enthusiasm but as well won for him the coveted Victoria Cross, the first instance of the winning of that decoration by a naval officer since the beginning of the war.

Lieutenant Holbrook was in command of the *B-11*, a 316-ton submarine launched as far back as 1906. It was in no sense to be compared to the giant underwater crafts that were being launched and used at the outbreak of the war, some of them measuring 800 feet. The *B-11* carried only sixteen men in all—two officers and fourteen men.

Early in the morning of December 13, 1914, she started through the straits. Evidently her commander had knowledge of the disposition of the Turkish mine field, for Lieutenant Holbrook successfully navigated his ship through it, dived under five rows of mines, any one of which would have blown his frail craft into a thousand pieces, and came up under the side of the Turkish battleship *Messudiyeh.* The *Messudiyeh,* in any other navy, would have been retired long before, but Turkey had none two many ships and probably had been saving her to fight against the equally ancient vessels of some other minor power. Launched as far back as 1874, she had been reconstructed and rearmed in 1901. She was lying in the Sea of Marmora, guarding the very mine field under which Holbrook had dived his craft.

Holbrook observed the *Messudiyeh* through the periscope of the *B-11,* maneuvered for position, dived, came up again and launched his torpedo. It struck home and the ancient sides of the *Messudiyeh* gaped wide. Slowly she sank while Holbrook dived to safety. For nine and a half hours the latter felt his way out of the straits and when he returned to the fleet his little vessel and its daring crew received an enthusiastic demonstration from the soldiers of the larger warships. Besides the Victoria Cross, received by Holbrook himself, his second in command, Lieutenant Sydney T. Winn, received the Distinguished Service Order, and each of the fourteen members of the crew received the Distinguished Service Medal.

On the next day, December 14, 1914, the British submarine *B-9* attempted to repeat the feat, but the Turks were prepared. When she came to the surface mines were exploded all around her, and she had all she could do to make good her escape.

On January 15, 1915, not content that the British should have all the danger, or the glory, the French submarine, *Saphir,* entered the straits. Near Nagara Point she struck the bottom in one of those shallow spots that abound in the Dardanelles, was compelled to come to the surface in a disabled condition and was quickly shot to pieces by the Turkish shore batteries.

The movement against the forts in the Dardanelles was now begun. This campaign, which was begun with so much confidence of ultimate success, was destined to become one of the greatest repulses that the Allies had encountered thus far during the war.

PART II—JAPAN AND THE FAR EAST

CHAPTER VII

WHY JAPAN JOINED THE ALLIES

THE battle lines of the Great War on land and sea were now beginning to encircle the earth. While the gigantic armies on the battle grounds of Europe were engaged in the greatest test of "the survival of the fittest" that the world had ever witnessed, while the sharp encounters on the seas were carrying the war around the globe, the outbreaks in the Far East were bringing the Orient and the Occident—the two competitive systems of civilization—into a strange alignment. The Moslem world was dividing against itself as had the Christian world. The followers of Buddha and the Brahmins were in direct conflict.

It is important, therefore, to consider in this chapter the development of events in the Far East, which have been only outlined in the preceding narratives. Of all the powers that joined the coalition against Germany in August, 1914, none could state a clearer cause of action than Japan. From the first outbreak of hostilities there was never any question of whether the "England of the East" would enter the war, and on which side she would be aligned. Japan decided promptly and, having decided, acted with characteristic energy.

For a *casus belli* the Japanese statesmen had only to hold up to the eyes of the world the Anglo-Japanese Alliance, which had been signed on August 12, 1905. The object of this agreement was the maintenance of the general peace in eastern Asia and India, the preservation of the common interests of all powers in China, by insuring the independence and integrity of the Chinese

Empire and the principle of equal opportunities for the commerce and industry of all nations in China, the maintenance of the territorial rights of the high contracting parties in the regions of eastern Asia and of India, and the defense of their special interests in the said regions. If these rights and interests were jeopardized, Japan and Great Britain agreed to discuss fully and frankly what measures should be pursued for defense, and to act in common in case of unprovoked attack or aggressive action wherever arising on the part of any other power or powers.

Thus, in those critical days of August, 1914, one of the first acts of the British Government, when war was declared on Germany, and the empire was reaching out for every possible means of defense and aggression, was to ask Japan for assistance under the terms of this alliance. And Japan did not hesitate—she threw herself vigorously into the Great War. The Japanese Emperor in his declaration of war against Germany did not suggest that Japan acted in response to her ally's direct request for assistance, but the Japanese Foreign Minister, Baron Kato, in his speech explaining the situation to the Diet, laid emphasis upon the treaty as the most important factor in the situation.

"German warships and armed vessels," said the foreign minister, "are prowling around the seas of eastern Asia, menacing our commerce and that of our ally, while Kiao-chau was carrying out operations apparently for the purpose of constituting a base for warlike operations in eastern Asia. Grave anxiety was thus felt for the maintenance of peace in the Far East.

"As all are aware," he continued, "the agreement and alliance between Japan and Great Britain has for its object the consolidation and maintenance of general peace in eastern Asia, and the maintenance of the independence and integrity of China, as well as the principle of equal opportunities for commerce and industry for all nations in that country, and the maintenance and defense respectively of territorial rights and special interests of contracting parties in eastern Asia. Therefore, inasmuch as we are asked by our ally for assistance at a time when commerce in eastern Asia, which Japan and Great Britain regard alike as one of their special interests, is subjected to a constant menace,

Japan, who regards that alliance as a guiding principle of her foreign policy, could not but comply to the respect to do her part."

The Japanese statesman offered this explanation to his people: "Germany's possession of a base for powerful activities in one corner of the Far East was not only a serious obstacle to the maintenance of a permanent peace, but also threatened the immediate interests of the Japanese Empire. The Japanese Government, therefore, resolved to comply with the British request, and, if necessary, to open hostilities against Germany."

Baron Kato's speech was delivered after Japan had declared war. The Western world, when it found time to turn its attention from the absorbing drama already being enacted in Belgium to the minor crisis in the Far East, was not left long in doubt regarding the intentions of Great Britain's ally. War was declared on August 24, 1914, nine days after Japan had dispatched to Germany an ultimatum, which Germany scornfully ignored.

The text of the ultimatum was as follows: "We consider it highly important and necessary in the present situation to take measures to remove the causes of all disturbance of peace in the Far East, and to safeguard general interests as contemplated in the agreement of alliance between Japan and Great Britain.

"In order to secure firm and enduring peace in eastern Asia, the establishment of which is the aim of the agreement, the Japanese Government sincerely believes it to be its duty to give advice to the German Government to carry out the following two propositions:

"(1) To withdraw immediately from Japanese and Chinese waters the German warships and armed vessels of all kinds, and to disarm those which cannot be withdrawn.

"(2) To deliver on a date not later than September 15 to the Japanese authorities, without condition or compensation, the entire leased territory of Kiao-chau, with a view to the eventual restoration of the same to China.

"The Japanese Government announces at the same time that in the event of its not receiving by noon on August 23, 1914, an answer from the German Government signifying unconditional acceptance of the above advice offered by the Japanese Govern-

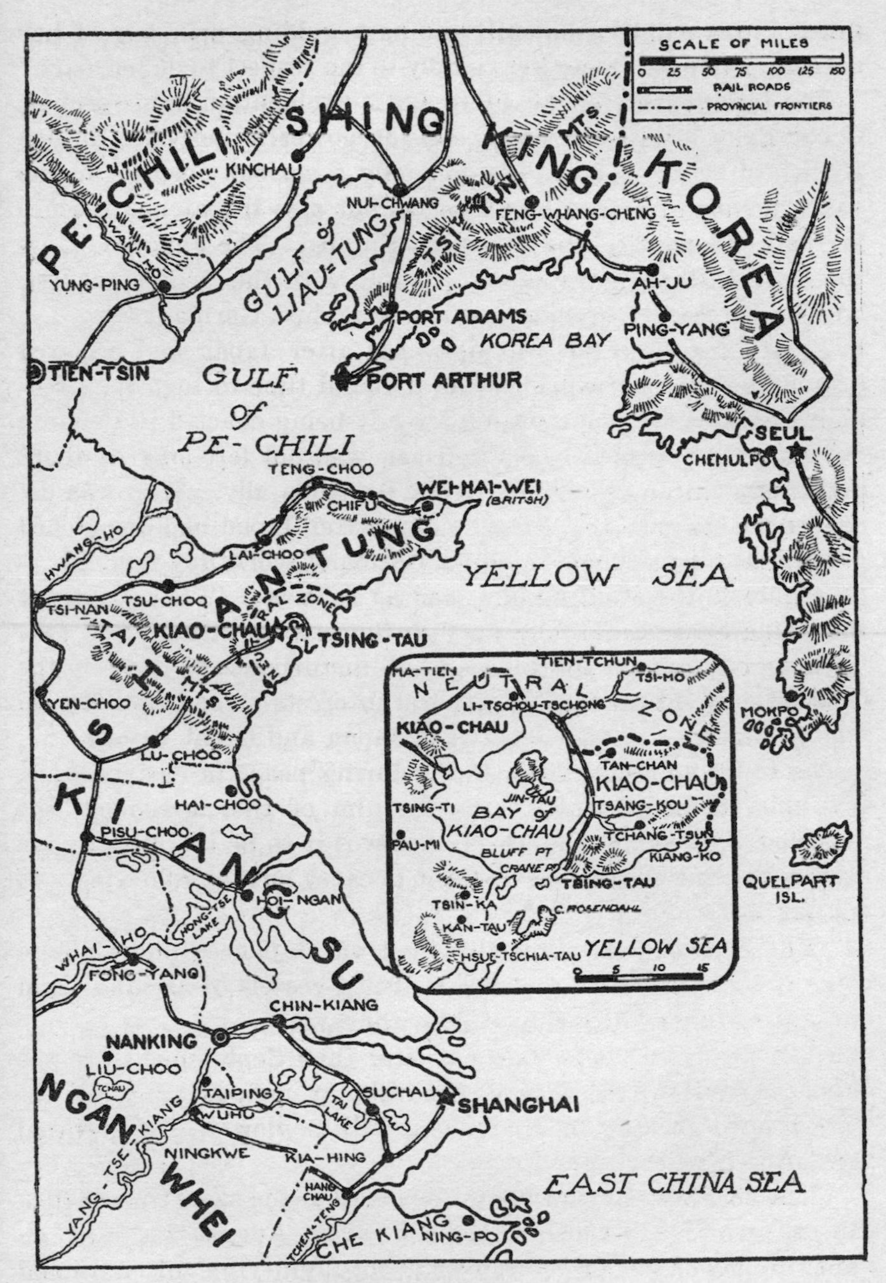

KIAO-CHAU (TSING-TAU)

ment, Japan will be compelled to take such action as it may deem necessary to meet the situation."

The intervention of Japan in the war, welcome as it was to Great Britain, created special problems for that empire. The British in China, and the people of Australia, New Zealand, and western North America had long been uneasy regarding the commercial and political policy of Japan. On the Pacific Coast of the United States and Canada a strong anti-Japanese sentiment had developed. British statesmen were apprehensive lest the entry of Japan into the war might be used to alienate American sympathy from the Allies and diminish the zeal of the Canadian and Australasian colonies for the war.

To meet this situation, the British Government issued a formal statement which said: "It is understood that the action of Japan shall not extend to the Pacific Ocean beyond the China Sea, except in so far as it may be necessary to protect Japanese shipping lines in the Pacific, nor beyond Asiatic waters westward of the China Seas, nor to any foreign territory except territory in German occupation on the continent of eastern Asia." This declaration went far toward allaying uneasiness, especially in the United States.

The Japanese people accepted the situation calmly. There were few noisy demonstrations. Germans living in Japan were not molested, notwithstanding the action of Germany, which immediately after the ultimatum was issued arrested every Japanese subject in Germany and seized funds of the Japanese Government deposited in the Deutsche Bank of Berlin. In Tokyo the chief of police told the people that although the two Governments had entered into hostilities, the people individually were not to cultivate hostility. The German Ambassador remained at the Japanese capital until August 30, 1914. A number of Germans who decided to stay in Japan were allowed to continue their regular occupations.

When no answer came from Germany up to the time of the expiration of Japan's ultimatum, the imperial rescript declaring the existence of a state of war was issued next day.

The emperor said: "We hereby declare war against Germany

and we command our army and navy to carry on hostilities against that empire with all their strength, and we also command all our competent authorities to make every effort in pursuance of their respective duties to attain the national aim within the limit of the law of nations.

"Since the outbreak of the present war in Europe, the calamitous effect of which we view with grave concern, we, on our part, have entertained hopes of preserving the peace of the Far East by the maintenance of strict neutrality, but the action of Germany has at length compelled Great Britain, our ally, to open hostilities against that country, and Germany is at Kiao-chau, its leased territory in China, busy with warlike preparations, while her armed vessels, cruising the seas of eastern Asia, are threatening our commerce and that of our ally. The peace of the Far East is thus in jeopardy.

"Accordingly, our Government and that of his Britannic Majesty, after a full and frank communication with each other, agreed to take such measures as may be necessary for the protection of the general interests contemplated in the agreement of alliance, and we on our part, being desirous to attain that object by peaceful means, commanded our Government to offer, with sincerity, an advice to the Imperial German Government. By the last day appointed for the purpose, however, our Government failed to receive an answer accepting their advice.

"It is with profound regret that we, in spite of our ardent devotion to the cause of peace, are thus compelled to declare war, especially at this early period of our reign, and while we are still in mourning for our lamented mother.

"It is our earnest wish that, by the loyalty and valor of our faithful subjects, peace may soon be restored and the glory of the empire enhanced."

CHAPTER VIII

MILITARY AND NAVAL SITUATION IN THE FAR EAST

WE now pass to the first fighting ground in the Far East. Unlike the campaigns in the west, the war in eastern Asia developed along lines which any observer, possessing the least knowledge of history and international politics and military strategy, could foresee. From both military and commercial standpoints none of Germany's possessions in the Far East could compare in importance with the little tip of the Shantung Peninsula leased for a term of ninety-nine years from China in 1898. This concession, about fifteen miles long and ten miles across, was designated Kiao-chau. In the sixteen years since their tenure began, the Germans had laid out at Tsing-tau, situated at the extreme southern end of the peninsula, a city which was rapidly growing to foremost importance among the ports of the Chinese coast. A large part of the native population was induced to migrate, hills were leveled, roads constructed, trees planted, and waterworks and sewers laid out along the most up-to-date lines.

The Great War found Tsing-tau a modern city, almost European in appearance, with a magnificent harbor, where natural advantages had been enhanced by the construction of immense piers and breakwaters. One line of railway connected the port with Chi-nan, capital of Shantung Province, and Germany held concessions for the construction of two new lines. The census of 1913 showed a total population of 58,000, of which Germans, exclusive of the garrison, numbered 2,500. Non-German Europeans, Americans, and Japanese numbered but 630. The European quarter was distinctly Teutonic.

The attack on Tsing-tau was a foregone conclusion. As a naval base and a seat of menace to the commerce of hostile nations, Tsing-tau occupied an unexcelled situation, almost equidistant from Nagasaki and Shanghai, in virtually the same latitude as

Tokyo, San Francisco, and Gibraltar. Its defenses were second in strength only to those of Port Arthur and Hongkong.

Kiao-chau was under the administration of the German admiralty. The German fleet seized it in 1897 ostensibly to secure reparation for the murder of two German missionaries in Shantung. The ninety-nine-year lease subsequently arranged gave Germany the right to fortify the new concession, and the thoroughness with which this privilege was exercised was proved by the stout resistance the garrison was able to make against far superior forces of besiegers. The whole concession occupied 117 square miles.

Although Kiao-chau was the kaiser's only continental colony in Asia the outbreak of the war found Germany in possession of several islands and groups of islands in the Pacific. These included German New Guinea, the Bismarck Archipelago, the Caroline, Pelew Marrana, Solomon and Marshall Islands and a portion of the Samoan group. But the strongly fortified port on the Shantung Peninsula was the naval base for the protection of all these ocean possessions; and the Japanese statesmen rightly concluded that with Tsing-tau in their grasp the reduction of the other German colonies would be only a formal task of seizure. Therefore the 27th of August, 1914, four days after the declaration of war, saw a Japanese fleet blockading Tsing-tau and Japanese transports carrying troops for landing expeditions in cooperation with the warships.

Germany began the concentration of all available forces inside the Tsing-tau fortifications on August 8, 1914. But she was able to gather there when the siege began only 5,000 men, a handful compared with the great force Japan could muster for the reduction of the fortress. The garrison of peace times was augmented by reservists, who came from treaty ports along the Chinese coast, from Japan, Siberia, and from every part of the Far East near enough to enable German veterans to reach the city before communication was cut off.

The crew of the Austrian cruiser *Kaiserin Elizabeth,* more than 300 men, who had left Tsing-tau by railroad before Austria decided to join her ally in the Far East as well as in Europe.

hurried back in small groups and in civilian clothes to escape detection. Squads of the Landsturm, the last reserve, middle-aged men who had left their families and their business in all parts of China joined the ranks and went to drilling in preparation for the hard fighting expected as soon as the invading fleet passed the outer defenses of the harbor. Altogether the defenders mustered three artillery and infantry regiments and four troops of cavalry. They had three aeroplanes and a few machine guns and in the harbor were four small gunboats in addition to the *Kaiserin Elizabeth.*

Tsing-tau's principal points of defense were Mount Moltke, Mount Bismarck and Mount Iltis. The rugged slopes of these positions commanded the plain. Beyond the plain the important outer line of defense was along the Litsum River, which flows into Kiao-chau Bay and then through the mountains to the sea, a line about eight miles long and about ten miles distant from the city. Preparations to oppose a landing of hostile troops were made at points along the coast of the leased territory for a distance of twenty miles. At the entrance of the bay shore batteries and mines made a bombardment by the Japanese fleet impracticable, except with the support of land forces.

The first line of defense comprised five forts connected by trenches and barbed wire entanglements. The shore defenses consisted of five forts, called respectively: "The Kaiser's," armed with two large guns mounted upon unsheltered platforms and two cannon of medium caliber sheltered; "August Point," a square closed fort with unsheltered gun platforms, and two guns of large medium caliber; "Taisichen," unsheltered with four large cannon; "Kaiser Northeast," unsheltered four cannon; "Yunuisan Point," two cannon of medium caliber. The main line of defense was for both land and sea work; "Fort Moltke" at the base of the German left wing had a shelter trench and guns of medium caliber; "Fort Bismarck" had three heavy gun platforms in addition to a platform for rapid fire guns of large caliber. From this the guns could be turned in any direction. "Fort Iltis" mounted four heavy guns of large and medium caliber besides mitrailleuse of large size. Two heavy guns were mounted in the summit of Mount Iltis.

In command of the German forces was the Governor General of Kiao-chau, Admiral Meyer-Waldeck, a naval officer of experience and reputation. The defenses of both land and sea were under his control.

This entrance of Japan into the war introduced a factor fraught with unknown possibilities. Unlike the other enemies of the Teutonic alliance, Japan had nothing to fear for her home territory or her possessions. Secure from attack, she was able to devote all her energies to the task of driving the Germans out of the Far East. By this accomplishment she not only fulfilled the terms of her alliance with Great Britain, but strengthened her own supremacy in that quarter of the globe.

Tsing-tau, since its occupation by the Germans, had been like a mailed fist brandished in her face. Since Japan's victory over Russia no other European power had occupied a position on the Asiatic coast that offered a threat comparable to this German stronghold. Also, it was only human that the Japanese remembered how Germany compelled them to abandon many of their fruits of victory in their last war with China.

The unknown factor of her participation was just how far Japan would go in aiding her new allies. The military and naval potentialities of the Island Kingdom when the war started were greater than ever before. She was twice as strong as when she went to war with Russia. Her navy was sufficiently formidable to resist, in home waters at least, that of any other power except England. Her army, twice proved during recent years against the soldiers of Russia and China, was steadily increasing its size and equipment. Her predominant position in the Far East was absolutely assured.

The Japanese army, based to a certain extent upon the German model, numbered at the outbreak of the war somewhat over 250,000 men of all ranks. This was its peace strength. Military service was obligatory upon all able-bodied males between the ages of seventeen and forty. This law made available each year 550,000 men, but in practice during times of peace the annual conscription amounted to only 120,000 men taken by ballot from among the number eligible. The total effective military strength of the Empire was estimated at a million and a half trained soldiers.

The army was divided into nineteen divisions, four independent cavalry brigades, three independent field artillery brigades, six regiments of heavy field artillery and a communication brigade. Each divisional unit consisted of two infantry brigades of six battalions each, a cavalry regiment (three squadrons of 120 men each), a field artillery regiment (six batteries of six guns), and a battalion of army service corps. A battalion of mountain guns was attached to certain divisions. Thus the army on a peace footing consisted of seventy-six infantry regiments (228 battalions), twenty-seven regiments of cavalry, 150 field batteries, nine mountain batteries, nineteen battalions of garrison artillery and nineteen battalions of engineers. When the reserves were summoned to the colors the Japanese system provided for an indefinite increase in the number of battalions for each regiment.

The Japanese navy had weathered a storm which at one time threatened to interfere seriously with its steady growth, and the year 1914 found it at a formidable climax of strength and efficiency. The war with Russia had left the nation on the verge of bankruptcy and the annual budgets from 1907 to 1910 contained no appropriations for naval increases. The lull in naval construction, however, was of short duration. The wisest statesmen realized, from the time when Japan first emerged from her Oriental seclusion and eagerly set out to learn the lessons of western civilization, that their country's insular situation made a strong navy the first requisite of national independence. It was the warships of the western world that forced the Japanese to open their door to the foreigner. Fifteen years after the Japanese had seen the foreign men-of-war riding dominant in their harbors, their antiquated collection of war junks had been replaced by an up-to-date navy, manned and officered by sea fighters trained upon the best western models. In 1910 the Japanese began to compare their naval equipment with that of Germany, and from that time their shipbuilding program was designed to make them secure against the chance of German aggression, ever present since the leasing of Kiao-chau.

At the outbreak of the Great War the Japanese navy had nearly doubled its strength since the close of the war with Russia. It included two battleships of the dreadnought class, the *Kawachi* and the *Settsu,* both over 21,000 tons, with a speed of twenty knots, two dreadnought battle crusiers of 27,500 tons each and a speed of twenty-seven knots, the *Kongo* and the *Hiyei;* two semi-dreadnought battleships, the *Aki* and *Satsuma,* between 19,000 and 20,000 tons each and a speed of twenty and eighteen and a quarter knots, respectively; four first-class battle cruisers with speeds ranging from twenty to twenty-three knots and averaging 14,000 tons; six battleships of slightly heavier displacement and slightly less speed; six first-class coast defense ships, averaging 13,000 tons and seventeen and a half knots; nine first-class cruisers ranging from 7,300 to 9,800 tons and twenty to twenty-one knots; thirteen second-class cruisers, some of which had a speed of twenty-six knots; seven second-class coast defense ships; nine gunboats, two first-class destroyers capable of thirty-five knots an hour; two second-class destroyers with a speed of thirty-three knots; and forty-six other destroyers of varying speeds; thirty-one torpedo boats and thirteen submarines, besides auxiliary craft, hospital ships, dispatch boats, etc.

Although the Japanese air fleet gave a good account of itself during the operations before Tsing-tau it developed no surprises, and accomplished no exploits to confirm rumors prevailing before the war that in Japan naval aviation had reached a special and advanced stage. The Japanese Flying Corps conducted itself upon lines made familiar by the British, German and French aviators in Europe.

CHAPTER IX

BEGINNING OF HOSTILITIES—ATTACKS ON TSING-TAU FORTS

HAVING reviewed the military and naval situation in the Far East at the outbreak of war, we come now to the beginning of actual belligerent operations.

Japan's declaration of war against Germany was dated August 23, 1914. The morning of the preceding day witnessed the departure from Japanese war ports of the greatest fleet of warships and transports the Empire had sent to sea since the Russian War. It comprised the Second Squadron, embracing battleships, cruisers, destroyers and hydro-aeroplanes, a dozen in all. The transports carried land forces numbering 22,980 officers and men and 142 guns to be put ashore as soon as the landing forces had ground for their advantageous location.

The Japanese troops included the Eighteenth Division, under Lieutenant General Mítsuomi Kamio, who was Commander in Chief of the expedition; the Twenty-third Brigade of Infantry (Major General B. Horiuchi); the Twenty-fourth Brigade of Infantry, commanded by Major General Hanzo Yamanashi, Chief of Staff, and other divisional troops. The Twenty-ninth Brigade of Infantry (Major General G. Joholi). Siege Artillery Corps (Major General Y. Watanebe), the Miyama Heavy Artillery Regiment, the Yokosuka Heavy Artillery Regiment, the Shimonosoki Heavy Artillery Battalion, and the Tadanoumi Heavy Artillery Battalion. Detachments of Engineers and Army Service Corps from the Sixth and Twelfth Divisions. Two Railway Battalions. Railway Guard Troops, the Eighth Infantry Regiment. Detachment of the Flying Corps. Marine Artillery Detachment. Being intended for siege work this army carried no cavalry, horse artillery or light field artillery.

In command of the fleet was Vice Admiral Hikonojo Kamimura, whose reputation as one of Japan's war idols was established when his squadron had defeated three Russian warships, the *Rurik, Gromoboi* and *Rossia,* off the east coast of Korea. Later his squadron had taken a commanding part in the great battle in the Japan Sea, which put an end to Russia's naval power in the East. Admiral Kamimura was sixty-five years old, and had spent the greater part of his life in naval service. After the final Russian defeat he was rewarded with the title of Baron and invested with the Grand Cordon of the Rising Sun and the first-class of the Golden Kite.

On September 23, 1914, the Japanese were joined by a British force of 1,369 men under command of Lieutenant Colonel Nathaniel Walter Barnardiston, commander of the British forces in North China, including Wei-hai-wei. Although the British did not arrive until a month after the forces sailed from Japan, the distance that separated Laoshan Bay, where the former made their landing on the original leased territory and thus avoided the breach of neutrality against China committed by the Japanese, was so much shorter and the landing place presented so much less difficulty than the Japanese encountered in their preliminary advance, that the British really arrived on the scene of actual operations just as the Japanese were finishing their first engagements in force, on September 28, 1914.

Colonel Barnardiston's command consisted of 910 noncommissioned officers and men of the Second Battalion South Wales Borderers, and 450 non-commissioned officers and men of the Thirty-sixth Sikhs, besides nine staff officers.

The bombardment of the Tsing-tau forts began on August 26, 1914, and on September 1, 1914, the Japanese bluejackets seized several small islands in Kiao-chau Bay, which the Germans were unable to defend except by long range fire from their shore batteries, and by mines with which the harbor had been thickly sown. Mine sweeping therefore occupied the first activities of the fleet. This operation was signalized by one of the many acts of patriotism and bravery that characterized the siege on both sides. One hundred Japanese women who made their living by diving for pearls in these waters offered to enter the water and release the mines from their moorings so that they would be carried away by the tides. Their courageous offer was declined, not because the Japanese admiral believed it could not be carried out, but because the Japanese law expressly prohibited the employment of women in warlike operations. When one of the small boats that acted as mine sweepers was blown up during the dragging that followed the women renewed their offer, but again it was declined.

The first landing on the Shan-tung Peninsula was made September 2, 1914. Ten thousand troops were put ashore; but it was not until September 25, 1914, that the invaders made their first capture of a German outpost, Weihsien. The check on the Japanese advance, however, was due less to the defenders of Tsing-tau than to the torrential rains, which swelled the streams and for a time effectively barred further movements. The Japanese artillery was compelled to return to Lung-chow, their original base on the mainland.

The Japanese leaders proceeded with deliberation and caution. They had the enemy penned up with no hope of reenforcement, and nothing was to be gained by haste or the unnecessary waste of men and equipment. On September 19, 1914, to facilitate the movement of their troops behind the beleaguered city, they seized the railway connecting Tsing-tau with the Chinese province of Shantung, and China, prompted by Berlin, protested against the act as a violation of neutrality. This was the second Chinese protest, the first having been sent to Tokyo after the Japanese made their first landing on Chinese territory at Lung-chow. To the former objection Japan had no answer except to set forth that the landing was a military necessity and made with no intention of permanent occupancy. To the second protest, however, she replied without hesitation that possession of the railway line was justified since it was owned by Germans. The wide area covered by the Japanese investment campaign is shown by the fact that by September 13, 1914, they had established guards at the railway station of Kiao-chau—a town having the same name as the whole German concession—twenty-two miles distant from Tsing-tau.

While the Japanese infantry and engineers waited for the floods the naval airmen were not idle. The first damage inside the city was inflicted by two seaplanes which dropped bombs upon the railway station and barracks. Although one of the planes was hit several times by the German guns, both made a safe return. This raid was the forerunner of a systematic air campaign, designed as much to strike terror and discouragement into the hearts of the garrison and the civil population as to gain any military end by the actual destruction of defense works. Bombs were dropped also upon ships in the harbor. Occasionally the Japanese flyers scattered circulars calling upon the defenders to surrender and pointing out the uselessness of further resistance.

The first serious losses on either side were naval. On August 28, 1914, two days after the first bombardment a typhoon swept the Japanese fleet, causing havoc among the little destroyers and sending one to the bottom. Five days later another destroyer ran aground in Kiao-chau Bay. A German merchant ship in the harbor was set afire by the Japanese aerial bombs and destroyed. The greatest naval losses suffered during the whole engagement were the destruction of the Austrian cruiser *Kaiserin Elizabeth* and of the Japanese cruiser *Takachiho.* The *Kaiserin Elizabeth* was sunk by the naval bombardment; but the loss of the *Takachiho* was due to the German torpedo boat *S-90.*

It was September 26, 1914, before the floods subsided sufficiently to permit the Japanese to resume their advance. On that day they drove the Germans from the high ground between the rivers Pai-sha and Li-tsun, and next day they pushed forward to a point seven miles northeast of Tsing-tau, between the Li-tsun and the Chang-tsun. The following morning found them established within five miles of the fortress. Their casualties were reported as three killed and twelve wounded.

These two days saw the heaviest fighting thus far during the siege. While the land forces were pushing up to the main German forts the fleet carried on a general bombardment, having by this time moved in close enough to make gun fire effective and having learned the range. The Japanese warships were assisted by the British battleship *Triumph,* which had joined them a short time before with the British destroyer *Usk.* These British boats remained throughout the investment, the *Triumph* was a favorite mark for the German gunners, but escaped with comparatively slight damage.

By September 30, 1914, the Germans were driven in from their outer fortifications and Tsing-tau itself was completely surrounded. On that day the defenders made a desperate attempt to regain some of their lost positions, but they were repulsed, and the Japanese settled back for a few days to await the bringing up of their heavy siege guns.

It is said that the failure of this assault, in which the Germans apparently concentrated all their resources, convinced General Kamio that the capture of the city would not prove the long, arduous task that had been expected, and he abandoned forthwith his plans for a long, slow siege and made preparations to take the place by assault. At the same time the Japanese commander showed no disposition to sacrifice his men unnecessarily, and while waiting for their big guns the Japanese worked like beavers with pick and shovel protecting their positions and digging saps and zigzag trenches up to the very face of the German defenses. They labored under a storm of shells but so little exposed that losses under the bombardment were small compared with the casualties of the actual assault operations.

For eight days the Germans poured projectiles into the enemy's works; but for the most part their shooting was a waste of ammunition. Just why the defenders of Tsing-tau were so prodigal of ammunition at this time never has been satisfactorily explained. Military correspondents estimated that during one period of twenty-four hours the forts on the three hills containing the main defensive positions fired more than 2,000 shells without inflicting any loss whatever.

But by October 8, 1914, the German fire slackened perceptibly. They had found that they were wasting their resources and that several positions were almost out of ammunition. The warfare of that period is described in a letter written by an officer with the British expeditionary force:

"That night," he said, "we were working in trenches along a river bed at the bottom of the slope, where the others had been wounded, and *sans doute* most darnation close to the enemy. A beginning had been made on this trench the night before, so there was a little cover. The two redoubts were about 800 yards on our right and left respectively, the enemy's trenches about 350 yards to our front.

"Well, for the first hour after getting down we were left severely alone. Then they started throwing star rockets and sort of Roman candle things which lit up the place like day, and at the same time they peppered us with Maxims, pompoms, and rifle fire from all three places. We had some men hit further back in the communication trench, but funnily enough none in the forward line. . . . We were entertained by a certain amount of shell fire during the rest of the night. Next night we were due to leave for the forward trenches at dusk to carry on, having had our usual entertainment in the afternoon from the Germans, when suddenly they began throwing shrapnel at our trench. For about half an hour it was all over us, and I'm blest if I know why nobody was hit. It was the overhead cover, I fancy, that saved us this time. We came out like a lot of rabbits when it was over and proceeded to get down below.

"The Japanese artillery was supporting us that night, as we were working on the enemy's side of the river, within 200 yards of their advance trenches. Never have I felt a more comforting sensation then when watching those Japanese shells bursting just over our heads, a little in advance, the shrapnel from them going slap into the Germans every time. I must say it was a magnificent sight when the Japanese guns were going, the German rockets, etc., and their machine guns and rifles joining in when they could get their heads up. One had to shout to make oneself heard, and those who saw it from the top of Heinrich Hill in rear said it was very fine."

During the early days of the siege life in the beleaguered city went on about as usual. A large part of the civil population had withdrawn while there was yet time, but enough shops remained open to supply the needs of those who remained. Cafés continued business and meals were served without interruption at the German Club throughout the siege, although toward the end the number of those who gathered at the club's tables dwindled to a few administrative officers and civilians.

In a proclamation the day before the expiration of the Japanese ultimatum, Governor Meyer-Waldeck had expressed the spirit of the little garrison in the following words:

"Never shall we surrender the smallest bit of ground over which the war flag is flying. From this place, which we with love and success have endeavored during the last seventeen years to shape into a little Germany across the seas, we shall not retreat. If the enemy wants Tsing-tau, he must come and take it."

Few, if any, military men in Tsing-tau doubted the outcome of the siege; but every resource was prepared for a desperate resistance. The city did not lack food; and after the surrender it was found that enough still remained to provision the garrison for more than three months longer. The supply of running water ceased about the middle of October. News from the outside world came in until November 5, and invariably it told of German successes.

"I remember one evening," said the Tsing-tau correspondent of the Associated Press, and the only foreign press representative in the city during the siege, "the roar of laughter that went up in the German Club when the news was read that England had asked Portugal for assistance. For two or three days it looked, according to the news, that the British Empire was going to pieces. We heard of revolutions in India, riots in Alexandria, mutiny and martial law in South Africa and even disaffection in Sarawak and North Borneo."

When it became clear that the end was drawing near preparations were made that as few war munitions as possible should fall into the hands of the enemy. The warships in the harbor that had escaped the bombardment were blown up. When the big guns in the forts had fired their last shots the gunners under orders destroyed them. In many cases this was done because without ammunition the guns were useless.

October 31, 1914, the anniversary of the emperor's birthday, was selected by the Japanese and English for their final bombardment. From 142 guns now occupying commanding positions came a deluge of shells that continued for seven days. The gunners by this time had the exact ranges and wasted no ammunition. The staffs of the two expeditionary forces gathered on Prince Heinrich Hill to watch the final act of the passing of German rule in the Far East. The warships ranged in the harbor joined in, and after an hour or two it became evident that the German defenses would be swept away by mere weight of metal. Under cover of this terrific gunfire the Allies' troops drove their saps and trenches up the very edge of the defense works, where they waited orders to take the place by storm.

The Germans replied bravely. A great cloud of smoke and dust arose over the doomed city visible far out at sea. In the city the noncombatants took refuge in their cellars and helped care for the wounded. Almost every German position, except the bombproof casements where the guns stood, was hammered to pieces. The electric power station was destroyed, so that during the last few nights the city was in darkness.

The last handbills dropped into Tsing-tau by the Japanese aviators contained the following appeal: "To the honored officers and men in the fortress: It is against the will of God, as well as the principles of humanity, to destroy and render useless arms, ships of war, and merchantmen, and other works and constructions, not in obedience to the necessity of war, but merely out of spite, lest they fall into the hands of the enemy. Trusting, as we do, that, as you hold dear the honor of civilization, you will not be betrayed into such base conduct, we beg you, however, to announce to us your own view as mentioned above.

(Signed) "The Besieging Army."

It is needless to say that the Japanese plea was not heeded. By November 6, 1914, only spasmodic fire from widely scattered positions answered the Allies' bombardment. That night the Japanese and English charged across open ground and took the middle fort in the first line of defense with surprising ease, capturing 200 prisoners. The charge was led by General Yoshimi Yamada at the head of companies of infantry and engineers. At one point they surprised a squad of Germans in charge of a searchlight.

To have fired upon them would have betrayed the advance to the defenders of the adjacent fort; so, the story says, the Germans were quietly and quickly dispatched by the engineers with picks and shovels.

CHAPTER X

CAPTURE OF TSING-TAU

TSING-TAU fell early on the morning of the next day, November 7, 1914. Encouraged by the unexpected successes of the night, the Japanese commander gave the order for a final grand assault. Nobody was more surprised than the Japanese themselves. They had expected a last-ditch resistance and feared they would have to sacrifice a thousand men before gaining these positions commanding the city. But the Germans, their ammunition almost gone, stunned by the continuous rain of shells and broken by long fighting, had decided that further resistance was useless.

The Japanese infantry occupied the central positions on the main line of defense soon after midnight. Just before dawn they captured the north battery on Shaotan Hill, then the east battery of Tahtungehin and the Chungchiawa fort on the west. The heaviest loss suffered by any of the Japanese detachments in the final assault fell upon a company that was caught by machine-gun fire in an attack upon Redoubt No. 2. Out of 250 men only 87 escaped. The total Japanese casualties in the final assault were 450 killed and wounded. The British casualties were slight.

Daylight found the Japanese and British in possession of every position commanding the city and nearly 20,000 men were awaiting the signal to charge the last line of defenses when a white flag appeared on the Tsing-tau military observatory. Within the next hour flags of surrender were flying from all the other German forts. So unexpected was the sudden collapse of the defense that at six o'clock, when the Governor sent Major von Kayser, his adjutant, with a white flag to make terms, the signal of surrender was not observed and the Japanese, far from suspecting the German officer's purpose, opened fire, killing Von Kayser's trumpeter and shooting his horse under him.

The formal capitulation of Tsing-tau came at 7.50 o'clock on the evening of November 7, 1914, when both sides signed the Japanese terms. The Germans surrendered unconditionally, but were accorded the honors of war. On November 10, 1914, at 10 a. m., Governor Meyer-Waldeck formally transferred possession to General Kamio, and German's last foothold in Asia passed from her possession.

News of the fall of Tsing-tau, although not unexpected, caused great rejoicing throughout Japan and among her allies, and profoundly stirred the German world.

The German attitude was expressed by an editorial in the Berlin "Lokalanzeiger," which said: "Never shall we forget the bold deed of the yellow robbers, or of England that set them on to do it. We know that we cannot yet settle with Japan for years to come. Perhaps she will rejoice over her cowardly robbery. Here our mills can grind but slowly. Even if the years pass, however, we shall certainly not often speak of it, but as certainly always think of it."

The Japanese and British forces made formal entry into the captured city on November 16, 1914. The Germans had done all in their power to destroy supplies, nevertheless the spoils of victory included 100 machine guns, 2,500 rifles, 30 field guns, a small amount of ammunition, about $6,000 in cash, 15,000 tons of coal, 40 motor cars, and a large quantity of provisions. Prisoners taken numbered 4,043, including the governor general and 201 German officers and 3,841 noncommissioned officers and men.

The casualties on both sides, considering the length of the siege and the intensity of the gunfire in both directions, were remarkably small. The Japanese had 236 killed and 1,282 wounded, the British had 12 killed and 63 wounded, including two officers. The Germans estimated their losses in killed and wounded at about 1,000 men. To the Allies' losses must be added 10 killed and 56 wounded, all Japanese, by the explosion of German land mines several days after the surrender.

PART III—THE WAR IN AFRICA

CHAPTER XI

CAMPAIGN IN TOGOLAND AND THE CAMEROONS

THE first shots of the Great War had hardly detonated across Europe when their echoes were heard in Africa. The war fever began to hover over Germany's colonial possessions in Africa—Togoland, the Cameroons, German Southwest Africa, and, greatest of all, German East Africa. Each of these colonies became in turn the scene of armed invasions and fierce conflicts, as important to the small forces involved as the great campaigns on the continent across the seas.

When Great Britain declared war on Germany on August 4, 1914, and the news flashed across the world to the official representatives of the warring nations in Africa, the British acting governor of the Gold Coast and the French governor of Dahomey planned a concerted campaign by land in cooperation with the warships to be found in African waters.

The first blow was struck on August 8, 1914, in Togoland, a country about the size of Ireland, lying between French Dahomey and the British Gold Coast. It is populated by a million Hausas and about 400 whites. At the beginning of the war the military force of Togoland could not have exceeded 250 whites and 3,000 natives. Hemmed in on three sides by French and British territory, with a coast line easily approached by warships, the colony was not in a position to offer much resistance if attacked.

On August 8, 1914, a British cruiser appeared before Lome, the capital of Togoland, and the town was surrendered without a shot being fired. But before the British force landed, the little German army of about 60 Europeans and 400 natives fell back to Atakpame, 100 miles in the interior.

While this was happening at Lome an expeditionary force composed of the Gold Coast Regiment, with British officers and commanded by Captain F. C. Bryant, R. A., crossed the frontier in motor cars on August 8, or 9, 1914, and a French force entered Togoland from the other side. A few days later the Allies had possession of all the southern part of Togoland, and advanced together toward Atakpame to capture an important German wireless station at Kamina in the same region.

The only real fighting in this campaign took place on August 25, 1914, when Captain Bryant and his forces had crossed the Monu River. The Allies drove the enemy from his intrenchments, seized the wireless station, and occupied Atakpame. Their losses were two officers and 21 men killed and about 50 wounded.

On August 26, 1914, the Germans surrendered unconditionally, and the Allies came into possession of three Maxim guns, 1,000 rifles and 320,000 rounds of ammunition. It was stated at the time that the Germans offered such a feeble resistance because many natives, on whom they had counted, refused to take up arms against the British.

Togoland having fallen to the Allies, it was arranged between the officials of Great Britain and France that the colony should be jointly governed, each to control that part of Togoland nearest her possessions. In a few months' time normal trade was resumed in the Allies' colony, and since private property had been respected during the invasion, there was nothing left to show that the country had recently been the scene of small but decisive conflicts, far-reaching in their effects.

The action in the African war drama now shifts to the Cameroons (German Kamerun Colony), which Germany took possession of in 1884. It has a seacoast of about 200 miles on the Bight of Biafra. To the northeast and south are the British Protectorate of Nigeria and French Equatorial Africa. The country is largely mountainous and is 290,000 square miles in extent. Before the war there were less than 2,000 whites among a population of 2,500,000 negroes, principally of the Bantu race.

The Cameroons, though surrounded by territory of the Allies, was a more difficult country to conquer than Togoland, owing to its natural advantages and the difficulties of communication over great distances. The first moves of the Allies met with disaster. It was in the African rainy season and misadventures multiplied as the invading troops marched through a wild and badly mapped country. It was decided between the Allies that two French columns should move from French Congo, while British columns entered at different points on the frontier of Nigeria.

On August 8, 1914, a detachment of mounted infantry of the West African Frontier Force left Kano and, marching 400 miles in seventeen days through West Africa, got in touch with the Germans at Tepe, a frontier station just inside the Cameroons. In the fierce engagement that followed the Germans were repulsed, losing five officers and suffering other casualties.

On August 29, 1914, the river station of Garua was attacked, and here one of the most disastrous battles of the campaign was fought. On August 31, 1914, Lieutenant Colonel Maclear, commanding the Royal Dublin Fusiliers and native troops, left their intrenchments 400 yards from the German forts and advanced to attack. The German gunners having perfect range, poured a murderous fire from machine guns on the British forces. The native troops wavered and fled, leaving British officers in the trenches, and these in turn were soon forced to fly to escape complete annihilation. Lieutenant Colonel Maclear was killed, and of the 31 other officers only 10 escaped, while 40 per cent of the native troops were lost. The remainder of the British force retreated into Nigeria in such an exhausted condition that had the Germans followed up their victory not a man would have escaped.

The second British expedition which entered the Cameroons from a more westerly point along the Nigerian frontier occupied, after slight resistance, the German station of Nsanakong a few miles from the border, where a week later the Germans attacked in force at two o'clock in the morning. The British resisted stubbornly, but, having exhausted their ammunition, the garrison

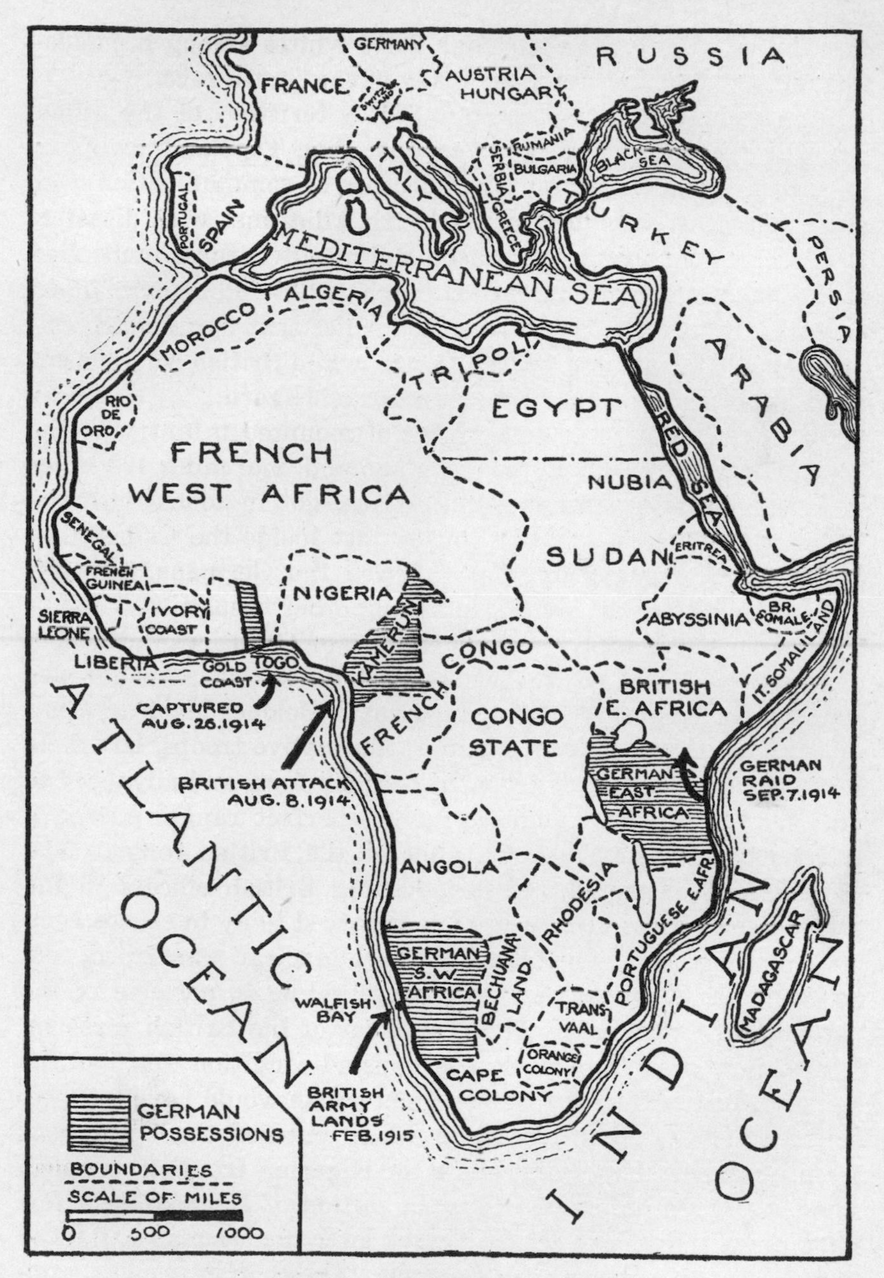

GERMAN POSSESSIONS IN AFRICA

tried to cut their way out with the bayonet. The British lost three officers, while large numbers of native soldiers were killed or made prisoners. The remainder, escaping to the bush, after many hardships found their way back to Nigeria. Another British expedition from Calabar, near the coast, occupied Archibong, August 29, 1914, while about the same time a German force took possession of the Nigerian station of Okuri.

The British had failed by land; they were more successful on the sea, as will be seen in the chapter on Naval Operations. On September 4, 1914, an attempt was made by the Germans to wreck the British gunboat *Dwarf,* which with the cruiser *Cumberland* was watching German ships in the Cameroon estuary. The German merchantman *Nachtigal* tried later to ram the same gunboat and wrecked herself with a loss of 36 men. Further attempts to destroy the *Dwarf* also failed.

The British now taking the offensive cleared the channel for three miles, where the Germans had sown mines and sunk 10 or 12 steamboats to obstruct the waterway to Duala, the capital of the Cameroons. H.M.S. *Challenger* and five troopships joined the *Dwarf* and *Cumberland* on September 26, 1914, and, moving on Duala, bombarded the town.

On September 27, 1914, the Germans offered to surrender Duala unconditionally, and on September 28, 1914, Brigadier General C. M. Dobell came ashore and took it over. About the same time a battalion landing at Bonaberi, across the river from Duala, capitulated after some desultory fighting. The wireless station at Duala was found to have been wrecked, but the British took several hundred prisoners, captured 8 merchantmen with valuable cargoes and the German gunboat *Soden,* which was at once put into commission in the British navy. While the British were successful around Duala, a French force by sea from Libreville, French Congo, escorted by their warship *Surpris,* attacked *Ukoko* on Corisco Bay, south of the Cameroons, during which the armed vessels *Khios* and *Itolo* were sunk.

The Allies had captured the chief port and controlled the coast, but the most difficult work lay before them in the mountainous and almost roadless region still to be conquered. The retreating

Germans occupied a defensive position on a river at Japona, where on October 8, 1914, a French column came up with them, forced a bridge, and compelled them to continue their retreat.

On October 8, 1914, Colonel E. H. Gorges, commanding a British naval and military force and four field guns, sailed up the Wuri in launches and found the enemy intrenched near Jabassi. The British made a spirited attack, but were driven back by the accurate fire of the enemy. After a flank attack failed, the order was given to retreat, and the British returned to Duala.

The Allies reenforced, and with two 6-inch guns resumed the attack on October 14, 1914, when the German batteries were soon silenced. After a brisk engagement the infantry occupied Jabassi, taking ten European prisoners. Minor successes won by the Allies at this time were the defeat of the Germans at Susa, and the occupation of the region around Mora, near Lake Chad by a Nigerian Regiment which had entered the colony from the northeast.

Two columns of Anglo-French troops under Brigadier General Dobell, with Colonel Mayer commanding the French colonial infantry, followed the retreating Germans to Edea on the Sanaga River, some fifty miles from Duala. Part of the road led through a thick forest where snipers were concealed, who harassed the expedition at every step and were dislodged with great difficulty.

On October 26, 1914, Edea was taken without resistance, and the enemy retired to Yaunde, a station far in the interior. Mujuka, a station about fifty miles from Duala, was occupied by the British a few weeks later.

Early in November, 1914, General Dobell planned an attack on the German capital of Buea, and its seaport Victoria. The latter place was bombarded by the French cruiser *Bruix* and the yacht *Ivy;* marines were landed, and after a short and spirited fight it was taken, while the enemy, who had concentrated on the hills leading to Buea, were scattered by the Allies' forces advancing from different directions.

The Germans made a determined effort to regain Edea, but were forced to retire with a loss of 20 Europeans and 54 natives. Meanwhile, in the hinterland, the French General, Aymerich, with a force of men and a steamer loaned by the authorities of the Belgian Congo drove the enemy from the Congo-Ubanghi region, which had been given to Germany in 1911. After two days of strenuous fighting the German posts of Numen and Nola were taken, and some officers, guns, and ammunition.

The greatest campaign in December, 1914, was the capture of the entire northern railway line, with rolling stock, locomotives, two aeroplanes, and about sixty white men. Mendawi, Baré, and Nkongsamba were other posts taken at this period.

At the close of the year the Cameroons were not conquered, but the Germans had been driven into the interior, could not secure supplies, and it was only a question of time when they must surrender or be annihilated. The allied forces were constantly harrying their enemy.

The Allies' next movement was an advance in three columns against Yaunde, where they fought two little battles January 27-28, 1915, and seized the post of Bersona. Near the coast some important operations were successful.

CHAPTER XII

GERMAN SOUTHWEST AFRICA—REBELLION IN UNION OF SOUTH AFRICA

GERMAN Southwest Africa, to which we will now turn, was in a different situation at the outbreak of the war from that of the German colonies of the east and west. Over the frontier was a self-governing dominion, the Union of South Africa, with an independent parliament made up of a strange mixture of different parties. The irreconcilables in the Dutch population who had dreamed of a greater Afrikander Republic, would they not take this opportunity to side with Germany who promised to further their ambitions? Great Britain expected some trouble from this element in the Union, and prepared for the worst, while Germany was equally active, and there was much intriguing to persuade the Dutch to cast in their lot with them. In other parts of Africa, Germany had to fight her battles unaided, but here in the enemy's camp there was every hope of gaining powerful assistance. Until the situation in the Union became clear, it was Germany's part to defend her colony in Southwest Africa, hoping by a brave display of arms to win over the Dutch, who were bitter against England.

German Southwest Africa enjoys many natural advantages. Her capital is far in the interior. Between her railway on the south, which almost reaches the Cape frontier, and her border spreads out the desert of Kalahari and the arid, waterless plains of northwest Cape Colony. The branch railways are separated by about 200 miles from German territory, and on the northern line Kimberley was a little less than 400 miles distant. British forces entering the colony by land must encounter many difficulties, especially in the desert region, which the Germans left undefended because they believed it could not be crossed by troops.

Before the war, according to the official returns, the colony had a force of 3,500 men, mainly whites; but with reserves and volunteers from among the population of German blood it has been variously estimated that an army of from 6,000 to 10,000 men could be gathered together. The Germans were believed to be strong in artillery, and were known to have sixty-six batteries of Maxims. There was also a camel corps 500 strong.

After the declaration of war in August, 1914, Dr. Seitz, the German Governor, began to carry out his plan of defense. In the second week of August, 1914, the Germans abandoned Swakopmund and Lüderitz Bay, their principal stations on the coast, and after destroying the jetty and tugs in harbor, retired with their military stores to Windhoek, the inland capital. In the last weeks in August they made short dashes into British territory, intrenching themselves in some places, and occasionally engaged in a skirmish with farmers on the frontier.

Thus, when the Union Parliament met September 8, 1914, it was informed by General Botha, the Premier, that Germany had begun hostilities against the British colonies. On the following day, as a challenge to the pro-German party, he moved a resolution to convey to King George an address, assuring him of the loyal support of the Union. Upon this General Hertzog moved an amendment to the effect that attacking German territory in South Africa was against the interests of the Union and the empire. But the victory was with General Botha's Government when the questions were voted on. Only 12 of the 104 votes cast were in favor of Hertzog's amendment.

It was evident that many burghers living in districts on the borders of German Southwest Africa shared Hertzog's opinion, and were opposed to taking offensive measures against the German colony as long as the Union was left in peace. From the time that Hertzog had been dropped from Botha's cabinet he had posed as a martyr. His adherents believed that he had been "sacrificed to please the English," and that Botha was merely a tool in the hands of the British Government.

The spirit of rebellion in the Union did not show itself openly for some time, but the leaders—Beyers, De Wet, Maritz, and Kemp—were busy conspiring and stirring up disaffection among the burghers who had never become reconciled to the Union.

De Wet, because of his world-wide fame during the Boer War, has been given undue prominence for the part he played in the rebellion. He was not the head and front of the movement, though his name was one to conjure with among the disaffected Boers, and he proved to be a valuable recruiting agent. His operations during the rebellion, as will be subsequently shown, were generally ineffective in the field, and terminated ingloriously, before he could work any great harm.

General Beyers, the most dangerous foe the Union had in the rebellion, was a direct contrast to the rude and unlettered De Wet. He was young and brave, and had shown himself one of the ablest soldiers the British had to fight against during the Boer War. He looked the dashing officer that he was—tall, straight, black bearded, and with his pleasant manners and easy speech he was just the man to inspire enthusiasm in others.

Colonel Maritz and Colonel Kemp, the other chief leaders in the rebellion, had never been as prominent in South African affairs as Beyers and De Wet. Maritz had shown ability as a leader in the Boer War, had held various military positions since, and at the beginning of the European War was in command of the South African border between the Union and German Southwest Africa, to which he had been appointed by Beyers, who was commandant general of the citizen forces. General Smuts, the Minister of Defense, may have suspected some sinister motives in this appointment, for Maritz had many friends in the German colony, but for the present he had to keep his suspicions to himself and await some overt act of offense.

Colonel Kemp, the remaining chief leader, had never done anything to give him special prominence. He had proved himself an efficient soldier during the Boer War, and appears to have been in command of a training camp in the western Transvaal when the rebellion was started.

Under these four leaders, acting independently, or in conjunction with them, were subleaders, an indefinite number, members of the Government, and men connected with the church and army, whose part in the rebellion was to stir up the people.

An interesting character among the somewhat nebulous subleaders in the rebellion was Van Rensburg, sometimes called "Prophet" Lichtenberg, from the place where he lived. During the Boer War he had predicted a remarkable victory for the Boers, which had resulted in the capture of Lord Methuen, and ever since the burghers of the Union had held him in reverential awe. When the war with Germany broke out he made various prophecies. He discovered that the events foretold in the Book of Revelation would now take place. Germany, he said, had been divinely ordained to conquer the world and purify it. Any attempt to resist this divine ordinance would be punished by the righteous anger of an offended deity. Nor was the "prophet" forgetful of local politics, for he had another "vision" in which he predicted that Generals Delarey, Beyers, and De Wet were divinely appointed leaders, who would restore the old republic. These "prophecies" were spread broadcast throughout the Union, were eagerly believed by the superstitious burghers, and served to hearten up the disaffected who had some grudge against the Government.

A great meeting of the burghers was summoned to meet August 15, 1914, at Treurfontein. This date had been fixed because Van Rensburg in a "vision" had seen "a dark cloud, with blood flowing from it, inscribed with number 15, and General Delarey, the uncrowned king of western Transvaal, returning home without his hat, followed by a carriage full of flowers." Eight hundred burghers attended the meeting, but Delarey, who spoke, had been warned by General Botha, and therefore spoke calmly, urging the burghers to remain cool and await events. Such was Delarey's influence over the assembly, who had come expecting to make a fiery speech, that a resolution expressing confidence in the Government was passed.

On September 15, 1914, General Christian Beyers resigned his position of commandant general of the defense force in a letter which was practically a declaration of war against the British Empire. It developed that for some weeks he had been organizing rebellion. He was secretly arranging a scheme of operations in which the German forces were to take part, while making plans for the Union Government. He hoped to win over General Delarey, leader of the Boers in the western Transvaal, but this officer was accidentally killed by the police near Johannesburg. The patrol out looking for the notorious Jackson gang of bandits, then in the neighborhood, had orders to examine any motor car and fire at once, if when summoned to stop their challenge was ignored. The car bearing Generals Beyers and Delarey had been twice challenged while passing through the town. The third time a policeman fired at the wheel to disable the car, and the bullet ricocheted and killed Delarey.

A thousand armed Boers at this time were encamped at Potchefstroom in Delarey's district. Colonel Kemp, who had sent in his resignation to the Union Government, and was working here for Delarey, had won over their officers, and on parade urged the men to refuse to volunteer for German Southwest Africa. He also collected in his tent such ammunition as he could lay his hands upon.

The death of General Delarey disconcerted General Beyers, and his fellow conspirators, and Colonel Kemp withdrew his resignation from the Union army. Over the grave of Delarey General Beyers, in the presence of General Botha, declared that he had no intention of advising or causing a rebellion, yet the following day, with General De Wet and others, he was urging the Boers who had come to the funeral of their dead leader to revolt against active service should the commandos be called out under the Defense Act.

Botha knew the men who were stirring up rebellion and acted quickly. He called for volunteers, announcing that he would lead in person the Union forces against the Germans, and the immediate response he received was gratifying. The conspirators remained quiet for some weeks, but General Beyers and De Wet were secretly at work against the Government of the Union.

On September 26, 1914, Colonel Grant and a small force of African Rifles and Transvaal Horse Artillery operating at Sandfontein near the German border were trapped by two German battalions while on their way to a water hole. From the heights the German guns swept the circular basin below where the Union force was gathered. The advantage was all in favor of the Germans. High explosive shells from ten guns wrought havoc among the South African soldiers, but not until their ammunition ran out and every man of their gun crews was either killed or wounded would the little band of Boers and Britons surrender. It developed later that Lieutenant Colonel S. G. Maritz, a Boer leader commanding Union forces in the Northwest territory, had turned traitor and arranged the disaster. It was through General Beyers that he had been appointed to an important command on the German border.

Maritz who was now ordered by General Smuts, Minister of Defense, to report to headquarters and give up his command, sent a defiant reply October 8, 1914. He stated that in addition to his own troops he had German guns and men, and had signed an agreement with the Governor of Southwest Africa ceding Walfish Bay (a British possession) and certain portions of Union territory in return for a guarantee of the independence of the South African Republic. All his officers and men who were unwilling to join with him had been sent as prisoners into German territory.

General Botha replied to the rebel by proclaiming martial law throughout the Union. General Brits, with the imperial Light Horse, was sent to capture Maritz, and in an engagement October 15, 1914, at Ratedraai, near Upington, took seventy rebel prisoners.

On October 22, 1914, Maritz with 1,000 rebels and seventy German gunners, attacked at dawn the post of Keimos, where there were only 150 loyalists. The little garrison held out until reenforcements arrived and the battle then turned against Maritz, who offered to surrender for a free pardon. This being refused, the fight went on, and Maritz eventually fled wounded into German territory. Two days later a party of rebels with German gunners were defeated at Kakamas.

General Hertzog, who had represented the pro-German party in the Union Parliament, gathered a commando and broke out in revolt on October 21, 1914. He issued a manifesto complaining of English oppression, and announced that he would tolerate it no longer. Three members of the Union Parliament and a member of the Defense Council, Mr. Wessel-Wessels, came out in arms. In the western Transvaal and the northern Free State the rebel leaders had about 10,000 men in separate groups. Their plan was to join their commandos with a force under Maritz from German Southwest Africa.

The situation from a military point of view seemed to be serious for the Union, but Generals Botha and Smuts were active and resourceful and in a few weeks had 40,000 men in the field. The loyal Boers were in a difficult position, for now they were asked to fight against their own kith and kin for the British Empire. In battle the Dutch generals showed that they were anxious to spare their own kinsmen, and ordered their men to withhold firing to the last moment, hoping that the rebels would surrender. The rebels were not allowed time to join their forces, for General Botha gave them no rest night or day.

On October 27, 1914, General Beyers and his commando

operating near Rustenburg were driven in headlong flight all day long by General Botha and a force of loyalists. Two days later General Beyers was a fugitive. His scattered commandos were defeated by Colonel Alberts at Lichtenburg and again at Zuitpansdrift on November 5, 1914. Meanwhile, Colonel Kemp, who had been acting with General Beyers, now separated from his chief, and with a large force started for German Southwest Africa, pursued by Colonel Alberts. Beyers, trying to get in touch with De Wet, entered the Orange Free State, closely followed by a large loyalist force under Colonel Lemmer.

On November 7, 1914, Beyers's commando was attacked by Lemmer near the Vet River and though Beyers led in person, he was defeated, and, 364 of his men being captured and about 20 killed or wounded, the fugitive remnant returned to Hoopstad. De Wet, whom General Beyers had been prevented from joining by the activity of the loyalist forces, had gathered together in the northern districts of the Orange Free State a poorly organized body of soldiers, but sufficient in numbers to cause the South African Government some anxiety. Negotiations between the Free State leaders and De Wet postponed for a time any military action by the Government, but the old guerrilla captain was not to be pacified. There had been a rivalry between him and Botha in the Boer war, and he seemed anxious to measure strength now with a soldier whom he considered his inferior.

De Wet's name was a power in the land, especially among the "poor whites" and the squatter class, who without much intelligence or education had not prospered under new conditions in the Union. They were without hope for the future and felt that they were being crowded out by the more active spirits in the country. They saw in the rebellion a chance to improve their economic position. There was little to lose and much might be won. A new Afrikander Republic would bring back the old days for which they had never ceased to long for. It was from this class of malcontents that De Wet drew the bulk of his men. The rest were religious fanatics, disgruntled politicians, wastrels and adventurers.

We have said previously that De Wet's recruits were poorly organized. It was a weakness of this brilliant guerrilla fighter that he could not maintain discipline when handling a large body of men, and the sort of troops he was working with in the rebellion called for the sternest kind of authority to make them effective soldiers. He only enjoyed a month of freedom and covered considerable territory, but he accomplished very little from a military point of view. He could not follow the same tactics that he had employed in the Boer war with equal success now. At home on the back of a horse, it was impossible for him to slip through the enemy's lines as of old when there were motor cars to pursue. He began his campaign with an action at Winburg where he defeated a small loyalist commando under Cronje, and where one of his sons was killed.

A battle of considerable importance was fought on November 12, 1914, at Marquard to the east of Winburg. General Botha and his Transvaal commando by a forced night march had reached Winburg the day before and getting in touch with De Wet's forces encircled them on the east and northeast. Colonel Brandt at the same time led his commando from Winburg within easy reach of De Wet, while General Lukin and Colonel Brits moving forward from the west completed the hemming in of the enemy. General Botha's commando attacked De Wet's forces and defeated them with great loss. If General Lukin and Colonel Brits had not been delayed in taking up their positions all the rebels would have been captured. The victory was especially of far-reaching importance because it discouraged De Wet's hopes and strengthened the loyalist cause. All of De Wet's stores of food and ammunition were taken, and a hundred carts, wagons and motor cars, while the prisoners numbered about 250.

De Wet, with a Boer commando in pursuit, now fled up the Vet River, then turning south at Boshof, divided his decreasing force into two divisions. Leading one of these he turned again north, reaching the Vaal River with only 25 men remaining of the 2,000 he had fought with at Marquard.

Beaten back by a loyal outpost he succeeded in crossing the

Vaal on November 21, 1914, closely pursued by Commandant Dutoit and a motor car contingent from Witwatersrand. De Wet's followers had gradually deserted, and he had only four men with him when he succeeded in joining a small commando of fugitives gathered at Schweizer Renek. The heavy rainstorms at this time favored him as he started with this force to follow Colonel Kemp and join Maritz in German Southwest Africa, for the motor cars in pursuit could make small progress over the heavy roads. Crossing Bechuanaland on November 25, 1914, De Wet was pursued by another loyalist force under Colonel Brits who in two days captured half of the fugitives.

On December 1, 1914, at a farm at Waterburg, about a hundred miles from Mafeking, De Wet and his party of 52 men surrendered to Colonel Jordaan without firing a shot, and the onetime Commander in Chief of the Orange Free State forces was imprisoned at Johannesburg to await his trial for high treason.

In the Orange Free State, General Beyers and about seventy men harried by loyal commandos divided his party, and leading one group made a dash for the Vaal River pursued by Captain Uys and Cornet Deneker with a small force. Trapped at daybreak on December 9, 1914, near the Vaal, Beyers and a few men tried to swim the river to the Transvaal under a fierce fire. Beyers was seen to fall from his horse, and was heard to cry for help, but was drowned before anyone could come to the rescue.

General Botha's operations in the northern district of the Orange Free State were made difficult because of the heavy fogs, but early in December, 1914, the rebels were in sore straits, 500 being captured while 200 surrendered to Commandant Kloppers a loyalist, who had been taken a prisoner and was afterwards released.

General Maritz, Colonel Kemp, and the "Prophet" Litchtenburg had fled west, and after some fighting at Kurumun, and two minor successes, surprising two posts at Langklip and Onydas which they were forced to abandon on the arrival of reenforcements, they retired toward the German frontier where they were penned in by the Union forces.

On January 24, 1915, the rebels made their last sally, attacking Colonel Van der Venter at Upington. The rebel force, about 1,200 strong and led by Maritz and Kemp, was easily repulsed. On February 3, 1915, Maritz, having fled to German territory, Colonel Kemp and his commando of 43 officers and 486 men including the "Prophet" Lichtenburg surrendered.

These Belgian soldiers are weary and covered with mud from the trenches, but they are rallying for a fresh resistance to German attacks

PART IV—THE WESTERN FRONT

CHAPTER XIII

PREPARATIONS FOR AN OFFENSIVE

DURING the greater part of the winter of 1914-15, the fighting along the western front had been almost constant, but had resulted in little that either side could justly assert to be a success. The rigors inevitable in such a mode of warfare had become almost beyond human endurance, and commanders on both sides looked forward to a more active campaign.

An immense amount of ammunition had been stored by the French in and around Perthes in anticipation of a forward movement; and, by the second week of February, a quarter of a million men of the French army had been assembled near that place. They were opposite a section of the German trenches which was about twelve miles long, extending from Ville-sur-Tourbe in the Argonne to the village of Souain. Early in the year this section had been held by only two divisions of Rhinelanders. These two divisions had suffered severely from the heavy gun fire which the French had directed against them by means of the successful work of the French aviators. The French infantry also had done effective work in the short rush which they had been making, gaining on an average about twelve yards a day. Following the concentration of French troops, the German commanders brought up reenforcements to the number of 80,000. Some of these were taken from La Bassée, and others from a contingent which had been intended for a northern offensive movement.

Because of the chalk formation of the soil in this section of the front, the excessive moisture of this season of the year drained rapidly, leaving exposed an undulating section on which were small forests of fir trees. The nature of the ground made it an easy matter to move troops even in winter. General Joffre took advantage of this fact, and assembled a quarter of a million men against the German lines in Champagne. This caused the German commanders to mass troops just in front of Perthes. The concentration continued until there were 220,000 German soldiers packed there in close formation. The French attacked, and quickly a rain of more than a hundred thousand shells fell upon the Germans.

The Germans sought to reply by bringing up twenty-two batteries of heavy guns and sixty-four field batteries; but the French gunners kept command of the field. In the twenty days' battle—from February 16 to March 7, 1915—the French won scarcely a mile of ground; but they found and buried 10,000 German dead. The French staff estimated that 60,000 German soldiers had been put out of action. The German staff admitted they had lost more men in this action than in the campaign in East Prussia against the Russians, where fourteen German army corps were engaged. The French lost less than 10,000 men.

In the last week of February, 1915, it had been learned by General Joffre that General von Falkenhayn of the German forces had withdrawn from Neuve Chapelle, and the section north of La Bassée six batteries of field artillery, six battalions of the Prussian Guard, and two heavy batteries of the Prussian Guard. These had been withdrawn for the purpose of checking the supposed French advance at Perthes, as already narrated. Hence it was known that the English, in command of Sir Douglas Haig, at Neuve Chapelle, were opposed by a thin line of German troops who were making a demonstration of force for the purpose of concealing the weakness of their line.

The British officers in the region of Neuve Chapelle received complete instructions on March 8, 1915, in regard to an offensive which they were to start on the 10th. These instructions were supplemental to a communication which had been sent on February 19 by the British commander in chief to Sir Douglas Haig, the commander of the First Army. Neuve Chapelle was to be the

THE WESTERN BATTLE LINE, JANUARY 1, 1915

immediate objective of the prospective engagement. This place is about four miles north of La Bassée at the junction of main roads, one leading southward to La Bassée, and another from Bethune on the west to Armentières on the northeast. It is about eleven miles west of Lille. These roads formed an irregular diamond-shaped figure with the village at the apex of the eastern sides, along which the German troops were stationed. The British held the western sides of this figure.

The land in this part of France is marshy and crossed by dykes; but, to the eastward, the ground rises slowly to a ridge, on the western border of which are two spurs. Aubers is at the apex of one; and Illies at the apex of the other. Both of these villages were held by the Germans. The ridge extends northeast, beyond the junction of the spurs, from Fournes to within two miles southwest of Lille. Along the ridge is the road to Lille, Roubaix, and Tourcoing, all of which are among the chief manufacturing towns of France. The occupation of the ridge was a necessary step to the taking of Lille; and Neuve Chapelle was at the gateway to the ridge. If the Allies could take Lille they would then be in a position to move against their enemy between that point and the sea.

The River Des Layes runs behind Neuve Chapelle to the southeast; and, behind the river, a half mile from the straggling village, is a wood known as the Bois du Biez. Almost at right angles to the river, on the west, the main road from Estaires to La Bassée skirts Neuve Chapelle. There is a triangle of roads north of the village where there were a few large houses with walls, gardens, and orchards. At this point the Germans had fortified themselves to flank the approaches to the village from that section. These trenches were only about a hundred yards from those of the British. The Germans had machine guns at a bridge over the river; and they had another post established a little farther up at the Pietre mill. Farther down the stream, where the road into the village joins the main road to La Bassée, the Germans had fortified a group of ruined buildings which was known as Port Arthur. From there was a great network of trenches which extended northwestward to the Pietre mill. There were also German troops in the Bois du Biez, and in the ruined houses along the border of the wood.

The German trenches were in excellent positions, but were occupied by only a comparatively few soldiers; it was the German plan to keep large bodies of troops in reserve, so that they might be sent to any sector where the need seemed most likely. They have asserted they had only four battalions in the front line here; but that statement is denied by the British.

The British plan of attack embraced a heavy bombardment to demoralize their enemy and prevent reenforcement. This was to be followed by an infantry attack. It was expected that the Germans would be surprised to such an extent it would be impossible for them to make much resistance. Units of the First Army were to make the main attack, supported by the Second Army. The support included a division of cavalry. Among the large force of heavy artillery for the opening bombardment were a number of French guns manned by French artillerymen.

CHAPTER XIV

BATTLE OF NEUVE CHAPELLE BEGINS

THREE hundred and fifty guns at short range began a most terrific bombardment March 10, 1915, at 7.30 a. m. It is said that the discharges of the artillery was so frequent that it seemed as if some gigantic machine gun was in action. Shortly after this bombardment started, the German trenches were covered by a great cloud of smoke and dust and a pall of green lyddite fumes. The first line of German trenches, against which the fire was directed, became great shapeless furrows and craters filled with the dead and dying.

This was the condition all along the line except on the extreme northern end where the artillery fire was less effective, owing, it was said, to a lack of proper preparation by the British staff. This terrific artillery fire was continued for thirty-five minutes;

and then the range was changed from the first line of German trenches to the village of Neuve Chapelle itself. Thereupon the British infantry advanced and made prisoners of the few Germans left alive in the first line. The men found unwounded were so dazed by the onslaught which the guns had made upon their position that they offered no resistance. The bombardment had swept away the wire entanglements; and the British had only the greasy mud with which to contend, when they made their dash forward.

Where the wire entanglements had been swept away, the Second Lincolnshire and the Berkshire regiments were the first to reach the German trenches. These regiments then turned to the right and left, and thus permitted the Royal Irish Rifles and the Rifle Brigade to go on toward the village.

In order to understand the infantry attack in detail it is necessary to know the manner in which the British troops were distributed before they made their dash at the ruined trenches of the Germans. Two brigades of the Eighth Division, the Twenty-fifth to the right and the Twenty-third to the left, were due west of Neuve Chapelle. On a front a mile and a half long to the south of them was the Meerut Division, supported by the Lahore Division. The Garhwal Brigade was on the left and the Dehra Dun Brigade was on its right. In the first attack the Twenty-third dashed to the northeast corner of the village, the Twenty-fifth against the village itself; and the Garhwal Brigade charged on the southwest corner.

The trenches opposite the Twenty-fifth were taken with practically no fighting. The Germans who had manned them were either killed or too dazed to offer resistance. As has already been told, the Second Royal Berkshires and the Second Lincolns took the first line of trenches in front of them, and opened the middle of their line to permit the Second Rifle Brigade and the First Irish Rifles to dash on to the village. The British artillery range was lengthened, thereby preventing the German supports from interference with the well-defined plan of the British. Into the wrecked streets of Neuve Chapelle swung two battalions of the Twenty-fifth Brigade. The few of their enemy who offered resistance were soon overpowered — being captured or slain.

These men of the Twenty-fifth Brigade found terrible scenes of destruction. The village had been knocked literally into a rubbish heap. Even the dead in the village churchyard had been plowed from their graves by the terrific bombardment.

The Garhwal Brigade captured the first line of trenches on the right, and the Third Gurkhas, on the southern outskirts of the village, met the Rifle Brigade. Then it dashed on to the Bois du Biez, passing another rubbish heap which once had been the hamlet known as Port Arthur.

The attack on the left, however, resulted less successfully for the British forces. As indicated above, the preparation for the bombardment at this part of the line had been inadequate for the purpose which the general in command had sought to achieve. Thus on the northeast corner of Neuve Chapelle the German trenches and the wire entanglements in front of them had been damaged but little. The British forces on this part of the line included the Second Devons, the Second West Yorks, the Second Scottish Rifles, and the Second Middlesex, known as the Twenty-third Brigade. The Scottish Rifles charged against intact wire entanglements which halted them in the range of a murderous rifle and machine-gun fire. With daring bravery the Scots sought to tear down the wire with their hands; but were forced to fall back and lie in the fire-swept zone until one company forced its way through an opening and destroyed the barrier. The regiment, as a result of this mishap to the plans of the commanding general, lost its commander, Colonel Bliss, and fourteen other officers.

The Middlesex, on the right, met with the same obstruction and lost many of its men and officers while waiting for the British artillery to smash a way through for them. This the artillery did when word had been carried back telling of the plight of the infantry.

The Twenty-fifth Brigade, to the south, had the good fortune to turn the flank of the Germans north of Neuve Chapelle. Then the entire Twenty-third Brigade forced its way to the orchard northeast of the village, where it met the Twenty-fourth Brigade, which included the First Worcesters, Second East Lancashires, First Sherwood Foresters, and the Second Northamptons. The Twenty-fourth Brigade had fought its way through from the Neuve Chapelle-Armentières road. As soon as this had been accomplished by the British, their artillery proceeded to send such a rain of shrapnel fire between the village and the Germans that a counterattack was quite impossible. This gave the victors an opportunity to intrench themselves practically at their leisure. The plans of the British commander had embraced a forward movement when the troops had reached this point, but they had not included a means of keeping communication with the various units intact. The telegraph and telephone wires had been cut by the shot and shell of both sides; and there was no opportunity to repair them until it was too late to take advantage of the demoralization of the Germans. Moreover, the delay of the Twenty-third Brigade had so disarranged the plans of the British that it is doubtful if they would not have failed in part even if the means of communication had not been destroyed. Nevertheless, Sir John French wrote: "I am of the opinion that this delay would not have occurred had the clearly expressed orders of the general officer commanding the First Army been more carefully observed."

There was also an additional delay in bringing up the reserves of the Fourth Corps. Thus it was not until 3.30 p. m. that three brigades of the Seventh Division, the Twentieth, Twenty-first, and Twenty-second Brigades were in their places on the left of the Twenty-fourth Brigade. Then the left moved southward toward Aubers. At the same time the Indian Corps, composed of the Garhwal Brigade and the Dehra Dun Brigade, forced its way through the Bois du Biez toward the ridge. Strong opposition was met with to such an extent, however, that the Thirty-ninth Garhwals and the Second Leicesters suffered severe losses on reaching a German position which had practically escaped the heavy artillery fire. A German outpost at the bridge held the Dehra Dun Brigade, which was supported by the Jullundur Brigade of the Lahore Division, in its attack farther to the south on the line of the River Des Layes. The First Brigade of the First Corps was rushed forward by Sir Douglas Haig; but it was dark before these troops arrived. Another fortified bridge, farther to the left, checked the Twenty-fifth Brigade; and machine-gun fire stopped the Twenty-fourth Brigade, this fire being from the German troops at the crossroads northwest of Pietre village. The Seventh Division was held by the line of the Des Layes, and the defense of the Pietre mill.

By evening the British had gone forward as far as their artillery fire had been effective; and it was found necessary for them to stop to strengthen the new line which they had established. They had won Neuve Chapelle. They had advanced a mile. They had straightened their line, but they could go no farther.

On the following day, March 11, 1915, the British artillery was directed against the Bois du Biez and the trenches in the neighborhood of Pietre. The Germans, however, had recovered from the surprise of the great bombardment, and they made several counterattacks. Little progress was made on that day by either side. On that night, March 11, the Bavarian and Saxon reserves arrived from Tourcoing, and on the morning of March 12 the counterattack extended along the British front. Because of the heavy mist, and the lack of proper communications, it was impossible for the British artillery to do much damage. The defense of the bridges across the Des Layes kept the British forces from the ridges and the capture of Aubers. The best that the British seemed to be able to do was to prevent the German counterattack from being successful.

An attempt to use the British cavalry was unsuccessful on March 12. The Second Cavalry Division, in command of General Hubert Gough, with a brigade of the North Midland Division, was ordered to support the infantry offensive, it being believed that the cavalry might penetrate the German lines. When the Fifth Cavalry Brigade, under command of Sir Philip Chetwode, arrived in the Rue Bacquerot at 4 p. m., Sir Henry Rawlinson reported the German positions intact, and the cavalry retired to Estaires.

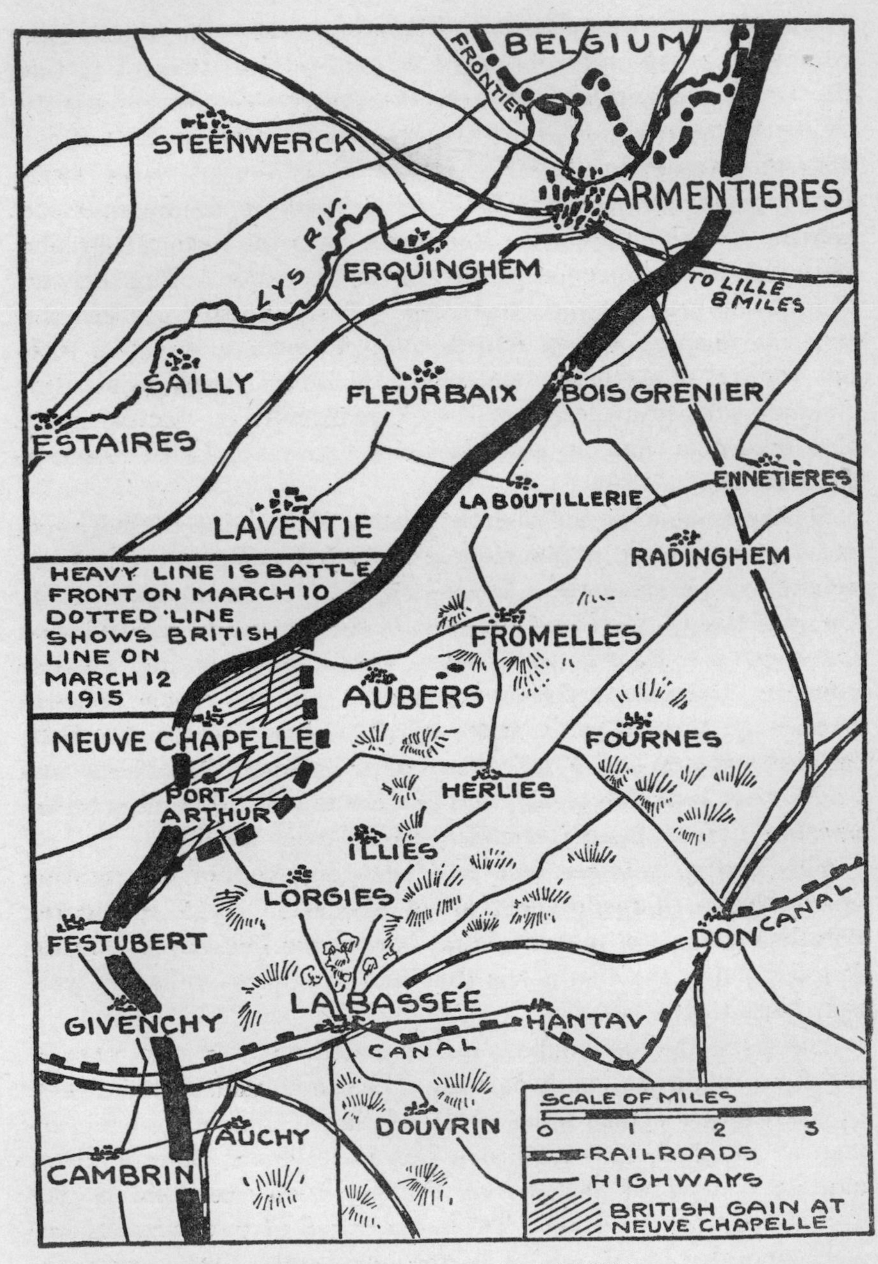

THE BATTLE AT NEUVE CHAPELLE

The attack of the Seventh Division against the Pietre Fort continued all the day of March 12, as did the attempt to take the Des Layes bridges from the Germans, who were valiantly defending their second line of trenches in the Bois du Biez. Probably the fiercest fighting of that day fell to the lot of the Twentieth Brigade, composed of the First Grenadiers, the Second Scots Guards, the Second Border Regiment, and the Second Gordons, with the Sixth Gordons, a Territorial battalion. This brigade fought valiantly around Pietre Mill. Position after position was taken by them, but their efforts could not remain effective without the aid of artillery, which was lacking. The Second Rifle Brigade carried a section of the German trenches farther south that afternoon, but an enfilading fire drove the British back to their former position.

It was evident by the night of March 12 that the British could not gain command of the ridge and that the Germans could not retake Neuve Chapelle. Hence Sir John French ordered Sir Douglas Haig to hold and consolidate the ground which had been taken by the Fourth and Indian Corps, and suspend further offensive operations for the present. In his report General French set forth that the three days' fighting had cost the British 190 officers and 2,337 other ranks killed; 359 officers and 8,174 other ranks wounded, and 23 officers and 1,728 other ranks missing. He claimed German losses of over 12,000.

The British soldiers who had been engaged in the fighting about Neuve Chapelle spent all of March 13, 1915, in digging trenches in the wet meadows that border the Des Layes. On the following day the two corps that had fought so valiantly were sent back to the reserve.

The German commanders, in the meantime, had been preparing for a vigorous counterattack. They planned to make their greatest effort fifteen miles north of Neuve Chapelle, at the village of St. Eloi, and trained a large section of their artillery against a part of the British front, which was held by the Twenty-seventh Division. The preparation of the Germans was well concealed on March 14 by the heavy mist that covered the low country. The bombardment started at 5 p. m., the beginning of which was immediately followed by the explosion of two mines which were under a hillock that was a part of the British front at the southeast of St. Eloi. The artillery attack was followed by such an avalanche of German infantry that the British were driven from their trenches. This German success was followed up by the enfilading of the British lines to the right and left, with the result that that entire section of the British front was forced back.

That night a counterattack was prepared. It was made at 2 a. m., on March 15, by the Eighty-second Brigade, which had the Eightieth Brigade as its support. The Eighty-second Brigade drove the Germans from the village and the trenches on the east. The Eightieth Brigade finished the task of regaining all of the ground that had been lost except the crater caused by the explosion of the mines. Among the regiments that made a most enviable record for themselves in this action were Princess Patricia's Canadian Light Infantry, the Fourth Rifle Brigade, the First Leinsters, the Second Cornwalls, and the Second Royal Irish Fusiliers. The "Princess Pat's," as the Canadian troops were known in the home land, were the first colonial soldiers to take part in a battle of such magnitude in this war. Their valor and their ability as fighting men were causes of great pride to the British.

Before leaving the Neuve Chapelle engagement and what immediately followed it, it is well to give a brief survey of the actions along the line that supported it. To prevent the Germans from taking troops from various points and massing them against the main British attack, the British soldiers all along that part of the front found plenty of work to do in their immediate vicinity. Thus, on March 10, 1915, the First Corps attacked the Germans from Givenchy, but there had been but little artillery fire on the part of the British there, and the wire entanglements stopped them from more than keeping the German troops in the position which they had held. The Second Corps, on March 12, was to have advanced at 10 a. m. southwest of Wytschaete. The fog that prevailed on that day, however, prevented a movement until 4 p. m. Then the First Wiltshires and the

Third Worcesters of the Seventh Brigade began a movement which had to be abandoned when the weather thickened and night fell.

The attack on L'Epinette, a hamlet southeast of Armentières, was much more successful on the same day. The Seventeenth Brigade of the Fourth Division of the Third Corps advanced at noon, with the Eighteenth Brigade as its support. It advanced 300 yards on a front a half mile in length, carrying the village, which it retained in spite of all the counterattacks.

The work of the artillery was not confined to the main attack, for it was very effective in shelling the Quesnoy railway station east of Armentières, where German reenforcements were boarding a train for the front. The British artillery fire was effective as far as Aubers, where it demolished a tall church spire.

The work of the aviators, from March 10 to 12 inclusive, deserves special mention. Owing to the adverse weather conditions, it was necessary for them to fly as low as from 100 to 150 feet above the object of their attack in order to be sure of their aim. Nevertheless they destroyed one of the piers of the bridge over the Lys at Menin. This bridge carried the railroad over the river. They also wrecked the railway stations at Douai, Don, and Courtrai. The daring of the British aviators even took them over Lille, where they dropped bombs on one of the German headquarters.

To summarize the fighting about Neuve Chapelle, it may be said that the British had advanced something more than a mile on a three-mile front, replacing the sag which had existed in their line by a sag in that of the Germans. The British had not won the ridges which were the key to Lille, but they had advanced their trenches close to those ridges. The entire moral effect was a gain for the British; but even that and the gain in advancing the front had been obtained at a too great sacrifice of the life of their men. The words of the Germans in characterizing the tremendous bombardment of the British were: "That is not war; it is murder."

The belief in the supposed superiority of the German artillery was so shaken in the minds of the General Staff as a result of the fighting on the Neuve Chapelle front that they shortly after issued an order to try a series of experiments on animals with asphyxiating gases.

CHAPTER XV

OPERATIONS FOLLOWING NEUVE CHAPELLE

THERE was very little activity on the western front after the fighting at Neuve Chapelle and St. Eloi until the beginning of a renewal of the campaign between La Bassée and the sea. The importance of success in this region was appreciated by both sides. The Germans north of the Lys planned to cross the Comines-Ypres, Yperlee, and Yser Canals, capture Ypres, take all of the ridge of the Mont-des-Cats, and then continue west and take Dunkirk, Calais, and Boulogne. The Allies in their plan included an advance south of the Lys on two sides of Lille, the taking of the Aubers Ridge, and the turning from the north the German salient at La Bassée. This much of the Allies' plan was to be executed by the British. The work of the French was to drive the Germans from the vicinity of Lens and threaten La Bassée from the south and west. The reasons for making these plans are obvious. The German salient was a source of much danger to the joining of the British and French armies, and the possibility of the Germans forcing their way through to Boulogne meant a possibility of a cutting off of the entire British army and the French and Belgian forces between Ypres and the sea near Nieuport. However, if La Bassée was isolated and the Aubers Ridge taken by the British, the chances that the Germans could retain Lille were materially lessened; and if the British got Lille they might start to drive their enemy from Belgium.

During the lull in the fighting on land, to which reference has been made, there was much activity in the air. Reconnaissances and raids were of almost daily occurrence. A Zeppelin dropped twenty bombs on Calais, slaying seven workmen at the railroad station on March 18, 1915. Three days later another, or possibly the same Zeppelin, flew over the town, but this time it was driven away before it could do any harm. "Taubes" bombarded the railroad junction of St. Omer and made a similar attack on Estaires on March 23. Four days after another attack was made on Estaires, and on the same day, March 27, the German airmen did some damage to Sailly, Calais, and Dunkirk. The next day a "Taube" made an attack on Calais, Estaires, and Hazebrouck. A Zeppelin closed the month's warfare in the air for the Germans by making a dash over Bailleul.

Aviators of the Allies, too, were busy. One of their aerial squadrons proceeded along the coast on March 16 and attacked the military posts at Ostend and Knocke. These aviators had as one of their main objective points the German coast batteries at the latter place. But the squadron was seen from a German observation balloon at Zeebrugge, and a flock of "Taubes" made a dash for their enemy's craft. The Germans were not as skillful airmen, however, and they found it necessary to retire. Five British aviators made an attack on the German submarine base at Hoboken, southwest of Antwerp, and destroyed a submarine and wrecked two others. This raid was made without injury to the aviators, the only accident being the necessity of one of the aircraft to descend, which it did, only to find it had landed on Dutch territory and must be interned. The excellence of the Allies' flying was not confined to the English. Belgian and French airmen, as well as British, flew almost constantly over Ostend, Zeebrugge, Roulers, Aubers, and such other places as German soldiers and their supplies were in evidence. The Belgian airmen dropped bombs on the aviation field at Ghistelles on March 27, and on the following day a Zeppelin hangar was destroyed at Berchem-Sainte-Agathe, near Brussels. On March 30, 1915, ten British and some French aviators flew along the coast from Nieuport to Zeebrugge and dropped bombs on magazines and submarine bases. The last day of the month saw the destruction of the German captive balloon at Zeebrugge and the death of its two observers. The Belgian aviators on the same day threw bombs on the aviation field at Handzaeme and the railroad junction at Cortemarck, and, south of Dixmude, the famous birdman, Garros, fought a successful duel in the air with a German aviator.

An aviator of the Allies flew over the aerodrome at Lille on April 1, 1915, and dropped a football. The Germans hastened to cover. When the ball bounced prodigiously as a result of being dropped from such a height, the Teutons thought it was some new kind of death dealer, and remained in their places of safety. In fact, they remained there quite a few minutes after the football had ceased to bounce. When they finally emerged most cautiously and approached the object of their terror, they read this inscription on it: "April Fool — Gott strafe England."

Though the antiaircraft guns, or "Archibalds," as the soldiers called them, were not especially effective except in keeping the flyers at such a height that it was not easy for them to make effective observations, a "Taube" was brought down at Pervyse, and near Ypres another was damaged on April 8. But on April 12 a German flyer inflicted some loss on the Allies' lines and escaped without being even hit. On the following day, presumably emboldened by that success, German aeroplanes threw flares and smoke balls over the British trenches east of Ypres, with the result that the soldiers of King George were subjected to a severe bombardment. All things considered, however, the Allies had ground for their belief that they more than held their own in the air.

Afloat the Allies continued to maintain the supremacy which had been theirs. The French and British battleships held the left of the Allies' line. Their great guns proved their effectiveness on the Germans who were advancing from Ostend on Nieuport. They repeatedly bombarded the position of the kaiser's men at Westende, east of Nieuport. The Germans had trained one of their mammoth pieces of artillery against that town presumably because it held the sluices and locks which regulated the overflowing of the Yser territory. If the means of flooding the land could not be seized, the next best thing to do was to wreck them.

The Belgians, in the meantime, assumed the offensive, their left being protected by the Allied fleet and the French forces in the neighborhood of Nieuport. These troops captured one of the smaller forts east of Lombartzyde on March 11, 1915. There was also fighting at Schoorbakke, north of the Yser loop, where the German trenches were shelled by French artillery. This was on the eastern border of the inundated section. After destroying the German front in the graveyard at Dixmude, the French artillerists battered a German convoy on its way between Dixmude and Essen on March 17, 1915. By March 23 the east bank of the Yser held a Belgian division. In fact, from Dixmude to the sea the Allied troops were advancing.

The Germans, however, advanced south of Dixmude. On April 1, 1915, they shelled the farms and villages west of the Yser and the Yperlee Canals, and took the Driegrachten farm. Thereupon the Germans crossed the canal with three machine guns. Their plan was to proceed along the border of the inundated district to Furnes. But the French balked the plan by shelling the farm, and the Belgians finished the work by driving the Germans back to Mercken on April 6, 1915.

In the meantime, from March 15 to April 17, 1915, the bombardment of Ypres was continued, destroying most of the remaining buildings there. Engagements of importance had not as yet started on the British front. The British had a supply of shrapnel, and the British and French cannon, as well as the rifle- and machine-gun fire, held the Germans in check until they had time to perfect their plans for a vigorous offensive. Nevertheless the British needed a much larger supply of ammunition before they could start on a determined campaign, which was so much desired by the troops. One of the German headquarters, however, was shelled effectively by the British on April 1, 1915, and on the following day mortars in the trenches did considerable damage in the Wood of Ploegsteert. A mine blew up a hundred yards of the trenches that were opposite Quinchy, a village to the south of Givenchy, on April 3, 1915. To offset this the Germans bombarded the British line at that point. They also shelled Fleurbaix, which is three miles southwest of Armentières, on April 5, 1915. The British on the same day wrecked a new trench mortar south of there. On April 6, 1915, the German artillery began to be more active both north and south of the Lys, and the British retaliated by shelling the railway triangle that was near Quinchy. German soldiers were slain and others wounded when a mine was exploded at Le Touquet, on the north bank of the Lys. One of the kaiser's ammunition depots was blown up near Quinchy on April 9, 1915, and his men were driven from their trenches in front of Givenchy by mortar fire.

The comparative quiet along the front was broken by the fight for the possession of Hill 60, which became famous because of the rival claims as to victory. The mound, for it was little more, getting its name on account of its height—sixty meters—was of importance only because it screened the German artillery which was shelling Ypres from the bridge to the west of Zandvoord. British trenches had been driven close to this hill by the Bedfords, whose sappers tunneled under the mound and there prepared three mines. At the same time the Germans were tunneling to plant mines under the Bedfords' trench. In this underground race the Bedfords won on the night of April 17, 1915, when they blew three big craters in the hill, killing almost to a man all of the 150 Germans who were on the little rise of ground. The Bedfords then dashed forward to the three craters they had opened up and took a quarter of a mile of the German trenches.

The Germans were apparently unprepared for the attack which followed the explosion of the British mines, with the result that the British had to overcome little resistance, and had ample opportunity to prepare a defense from the bombardment that followed. The next morning, April 18, 1915, the German infantry in close formation advanced on the hill. This infantry was composed of Saxons, who continued on for a bayonet charge in spite of the downpour of lead that the British rained upon them. But the Bedfords had been reenforced by the West Kents and about thirty motor machine guns. The machine guns raked the charging Saxons in front, and shrapnel tore their flank. Only their dead and dying remained on the hill; but the German commanders continued to send their men against the British there, who were subjected to a murderous cross-fire, the hill forming a salient. As a result of their persistence the German troops managed to get a foothold on the southern part of the hill by 6 p. m. In the meantime a battalion of Highlanders and the Duke of Wellington's regiment had been sent to reenforce the Bedfords and the West Kents. The Highlanders made a desperate charge, using bayonets and hand grenades on the Germans who had gained the southern edge of the hill. The Germans were driven back.

The Duke of Württemberg, the German commander, presumably believing his troops had not only held what they had taken, but had advanced, announced that another German victory had been gained in the capture of Hill 60. Sir John French also sent out a message, but in his report he set forth that Hill 60 was held by the British. Because there had been similar conflict in official reports all too frequently, it seemed as if a tacit agreement was made among the neutrals to determine who was telling the truth. This resulted in making what was a comparatively unimportant engagement one of the most celebrated battles of the war. As soon as Duke Albrecht of Württemberg discovered his mistake he did what he could to make good his statement by attempting to take Hill 60 without regard to sacrificing his men. Sir John French was just as determined to hold the hill. So he moved large numbers of troops toward the shattered mound, the British artillery was reenforced, and the hastily constructed sandbag breastworks were improved with all possible speed.

The Germans then attacked with gas bombs. Projectiles filled with gas were hurled upon the British from three sides. The East Surrey Regiment, which defended the hill in the latter part of the battle for it, suffered severely. Faces and arms became shiny and gray-black. Membranes in the throats thickened, and lungs seemed to be eaten by the chlorine poison. Yet the men fought on until exhausted, and then fell to suffer through a death struggle which continued from twenty-four hours to three days of suffocating agony.

The German artillery kept up its almost incessant pounding of the British. In short lulls of the big gun's work the German infantry hurled itself against the trenches on the hill, using hand grenades and bombs. The fight continued until the morning of May 5, 1915, when the wind blew at about four miles an hour from the German trenches. Then a greenish-yellow fog of poisonous gas was released, and soon encompassed the hill. The East Surreys, who were holding the hill, were driven back by the gas, but as soon as the gas passed they charged the Germans who had followed the gas and had taken possession of the hill. Notwithstanding the machine-gun fire which the Germans poured upon them, many of the trenches were retaken by the Surrey soldiers in their first frenzied rush to regain what they had lost because of the gas. The battle ended when there was no hill left. The bombardment and the mines had leveled the mound by distributing it over the surrounding territory. The British, however, were accorded the victory, as they had trenches near where the hill was and made them a part of the base of the salient about Ypres.

That town has been likened to the hub of a wheel whose spokes are the roads which lead eastward. It is true that one important road went over the canal at Steenstraate, but practically all of the highways of consequence went through Ypres. Thus the spokes of the wheel, whose rim was the outline of the salient, were the roads to Menin, Gheluvelt, Zonnebeke, Poelcapelle, Langemarck, and Pilkem. And the railroad to Roulers was also a spoke. Hence all of the supplies for the troops on the salient must pass through Ypres, which made it most desirable for the Germans to take the town. It will be remembered that they had won a place for their artillery early in November, 1914, which gave them an opportunity to bombard Ypres through the winter. On February 1, 1915, a portion of the French troops which had held the salient were withdrawn and their places taken by General Bulfin's Twenty-eighth Division. Thus, by April 20, 1915, that part of the Allies' front was held as follows: From the canal to east of Langemarck was the Forty-fifth Division of the French army, consisting of colonial infantry. One the French right, to the northeast of Zonnebeke, was the Canadian division, under the command of General Alderson, consisting of the Third Brigade, under General Turner, on the left, and the Second Brigade, under General Currie, on the right. The Twenty-eighth Division extended from the Canadian right to the southeast corner of the Polygon Wood. This division comprised the Eighty-third, Eighty-fourth, and Eighty-fifth Brigades in order from right to left. The next section of the salient was held by Princess Patricia's Regiment of the Twenty-seventh Division, which division, under the command of General Snow, guarded the front to the east of Veldhoek along the ridge to within a short distance of Hill 60, where the Fifth Division, under the command of General Morland, held the line. The greater part of the German troops opposite the salient were from Württemberg and Saxony.

CHAPTER XVI

BEGINNING OF SECOND BATTLE OF YPRES

WHAT is called the second battle of Ypres began with a bombardment of the little city on April 20, 1915. The rain of shells continued on through April 22, 1915, on the evening of which the British artillery observers reported a strange green vapor moving over the French trenches. The wind was blowing steadily from the northeast. Soon the French troops were staggering back from the front, blinded and choking from the deadly German gas. Many of their comrades had been unable to leave the spot where they were overtaken by the fumes. Those who fled in terror rushed madly across the canal, choking the road to Vlamertinghe. A part of the Zouaves and Turcos ran south toward the Langemarck road, finally reaching the reserve battalions of the Canadians. Ere long the Canadians caught the deadly odor also.

But the work of the gas did a much more valuable thing for the German troops than causing the agonizing death of many hundreds and sending thousands in headlong flight. It made a four-mile-wide opening in the front of the Allies. And the Germans were quick to take advantage of that opening. They followed the gas, and were aided in their advance by artillery fire. The French were forced back on the canal from Steenstraate to Boesinghe. The Canadians had not suffered so much from the gas as the French soldiers, but their flank was too exposed for them to do much effective work against the onrushing Teutons. The attempt to rally the Turcos failed. The Third Brigade could not withstand the attack of four divisions, and was forced inward from a point south of Poelcappelle until its left rested on the wood east of St. Julien. There was a gap beyond it, and the Germans were forcing their way around its flank. Because the entire First Brigade of Canadians had been held in reserve it could not be brought up in time to save the situation. Two of the battalions, the Sixteenth and Tenth, were in the gap by midnight. They charged and recovered the northern edge, and the guns of the Second London Division, which had been supporting the French in the wood east of St. Julien. But the British could not hold all they retook, and were forced to abandon the guns because the artillery horses were miles away. So parts of the guns were made useless before the Germans had them again.

Then another counterattack was made by the First and Fourth Ontarios of General Mercer's First Brigade. The Fourth Ontario captured the German shelter trenches and held them for two days, when they were relieved. The Third Canadian Brigade held its position in spite of being opposed by many times their numbers and almost overcome by the gas fumes. The Forty-eighth Highlanders, who had had to withstand the gas, rallied after their retreat and regained their former place in the front. The Royal Highlanders kept their original position. Yet there was every indication of a rout. The roads were clogged by the night supply trains going forward and the rush of men trying to escape from the deadly gas. The staff officers found it impossible to straighten out the tangle, and the various regiments had to act almost as independent bodies. It was not until early the following morning, April 23, 1915, that the first reenforcements of British soldiers appeared to fill the breach. These men, for the most part, were from the Twenty-eighth Division, and had been east of Zonnebeke to the southeast corner of Polygon Wood. So great was the pressure at the section where the break had been made in the line that troops were taken from wherever available, so that the units in the gap varied from day to day. For the men had to be returned to their original positions, such as remained available, as soon as possible. This composite body of troops has been called Geddes's Detachment.

The Germans had captured Lizerne and Het Sas, and Steenstraate was threatened by them. They bombarded with heavy artillery, located on the Passchendaele ridge, the front held by the Canadians, the Twenty-eighth Division, and Geddes's Detachment, on April 23, 1915. The severest fighting was on that part of the front held by the Third Brigade of Canadians. Many men had been killed or wounded in this brigade, and those who survived were ill from the effects of the gas. Furthermore, no food could be taken to them for twenty-four hours. Moreover, they were subjected to a fire from three sides, with the result that they were forced to a new position on a line running through St. Julien. Finally the Germans forced their way around to the left of the Third Brigade, establishing their machine guns behind it.

A terrific artillery attack was started by the Germans on the morning of April 24, 1915, and this was followed by a second rush of gas from their trenches. It rose in a cloud seven feet high and was making its attack on the British in two minutes after it started. It was thickest near the ground, being pumped from cylinders. And it worked with the same deadly effect. The Third Brigade, receiving its second attack of this sort before it had recovered from the first, retreated to the southwest of St. Julien, but soon after regained most of their lost position. The

Second Brigade had to bend its left south. Colonel Lipsett's Eighth Battalion, however, held fast on the Grafenstafel ridge, remaining in their position two days in spite of the gas of which they got a plentiful supply.

By noon of April 24, 1915, the Germans made an attack on the village of St. Julien and that part of the allied front to the east of the village. Thereupon the Third Brigade retreated about 700 yards to a new front south of the village and north of the hamlet of Fortuin. But what remained of the Thirteenth and Fourteenth Battalions was forced by circumstances to remain in the St. Julien line until late that night. Colonel Lipsett's Eighth Battalion at Grafenstafel, in spite of its left being unsupported, held its position which was of great importance to the British front. For, had that part of the front been lost, the Germans in an hour could have worked their way back of the Twenty-eighth Division and the entire eastern sector.

In the meantime the French on the western section of the front made a counterattack from the canal with partial success; but were unable to drive the German troops from the sector entirely. The Teutons took Steenstraate; but their victory there was marred by the fact that the Belgian artillery smashed the bridge behind them. By this time the British reenforcements began to arrive in fairly large numbers. The Thirteenth Brigade of the Fifth Division was placed to the west of Geddes's Detachment, between the Pilkem road and the canal. Territorials who had arrived from England only three days before, the Durham and York Brigades of the Northumbrian Division, supported the Thirteenth Brigade. The Tenth Brigade of the Fourth Division were rushed to support the Third Brigade of Canadians who were south of St. Julien. Other British troops were sent to relieve the tense situation at Grafenstafel.

An attempt to retake St. Julien was made early on Sunday morning, April 25, 1915, by General Hull's Tenth Brigade and two battalions of the Durham and York Brigade. The British worked their way to the few Canadians who had continued on the former front when the main British force had been driven back. There they were checked by the German machine gun fire. The

British lost many men here and the efforts to save the day resulted in such a mixture of fighting units that there were fifteen battalions under General Hull, as well as the Canadian artillery.

At Grafenstafel the Eighth Battalion of the Durham Brigade were bombarded with asphyxiating shells before the German infantry attack. The fighting on this section of the front was fierce throughout the afternoon, but finally the British were forced to retire. At Broodseinde, the extreme eastern point of the allied front, the Germans made a desperate attempt to take the salient, using asphyxiating and other bombs again and again on the men of the Twenty-eighth Division of the British. King George's men, however, repelled the attacks with severe loss to the Teutons, taking many prisoners.

The French on the left, beyond the Yperlee Canal, prevented the advance of the German troops; and, farther to the left, the Belgians checked three attacks in which asphyxiating gas was used, south of Dixmude. Thus it may be seen that the Germans had met with no success worth while, when Sunday, April 25, 1915, closed, so far as the ends of the salient were concerned; but in the center the British situation was so critical that the Second Canadian Brigade, reduced to less than 1,000 men, was once more called into action on the following day. On the same day, April 26, 1915, the Lahore Division of the Indian army was marched north of Ypres. The point of the salient was pushed in on that day at Broodseinde, but the German success there was short-lived. The brigade holding Grafenstafel was attacked fiercely by the Germans. The Durham Light Infantry was forced from Fortuin behind the Haanabeek River. The Teutons made several attacks from the St. Julien district against the section between the Yperlee Canal and the southern part of the village. By this time Geddes's Detachment was almost exhausted, they, with the Canadians, having withstood the heaviest fighting at the beginning of the battle; and most likely saved the Allies a most disastrous defeat. The detachment could stand no more, and the various units of which it was composed were returned to their respective commands.

But the salient was growing smaller as a result of the repeated hammering of the Germans; and that exposed the allied troops to a more deadly fire from three sides. It was evident that the Allies must make a counterattack. General Riddell's Brigade was sent to Fortuin and with the Lahore Division on its left was told to retake St. Julien and the woods to the west of the village. Beyond the Yperlee Canal, on the left, the French made an assault on Lizerne, supported by the Belgian artillery; while the French colonial soldiers poured on Pilkem from the sector about Boesinghe. On the right the allied troops were lined up as follows: the Connaught Rangers, Fifty-seventh Wilde's Rifles, the Ferozepore Brigade, the 129th Baluchis, the Jullundur Brigade, and General Riddell's battalions. The Sirhind Brigade was held in reserve.

The German artillerymen apparently knew the distances and topography of the entire region and poured a leaden hail upon the allied troops. The Indians and the British in their immediate neighborhood charged in short rushes, losing many men in the attempt to reach the German trenches. Before the Germans were in any danger of a hand-to-hand struggle, they sent one of their gas clouds from their trenches and the attack was abandoned, the British and Indians getting back to their trenches as best they could. In this action the British gave great praise to their comrades from India. Riddell's Brigade was stopped in its attack on St. Julien by wire entanglements; and, though the outlaying sections of St. Julien were captured, the brigade was unable to hold them; and the Germans continued to hold the woods west of the village. Nevertheless the British front had been pushed forward from 600 to 700 yards in some places.

By that night, the night of April 26, 1915, the allied front extended from the north of Zonnebeke to the eastern boundary of the Grafenstafel ridge; thence southwest along the southern side of the Haanabeek to a point a half mile east of St. Julien; thence, bending around that village, it ran to Vamhuele—called the "shell trap"—farm on the Ypres-Poelcappelle road. Next it proceeded to Boesinghe and crossed the Yperlee Canal, passing northward of Lizerne after which were the French and the Belgians.

The work of the allied aviators on April 26, 1915, deserves more than passing consideration in the record of that day's fighting. They dropped bombs on the stations of Courtrai, Roubaix, Thielt, and Staden. They discovered near Langemarck an armored train with the result that it was shelled and thus forced to return. And they forced a German aviator to the ground at Roulers.

The Lahore Division with the French on their left attacked the Germans on April 27, 1915, but they met with little success because of the gas which the Teutons sent into the ranks of the attacking party. But the German troops had lost so heavily that they did not seem to be inclined to follow up their apparent advantage. Incidentally the Allies needed a rest as well. Hence there was little fighting the next two days. On April 30, 1915, however, General Putz attacked the Germans with so much force that they were hurled back an appreciable distance near Pilkem. Seven machine guns and 200 prisoners were taken, and the 214th, 215th, and 216th German regiments lost more than 1,000 men. On the same day the London Rifle Brigade, further east, drove back a German forward movement from St. Julien.

West of the Yperlee Canal, however, it soon became known to the commanders of the allied forces that the Germans were in such a strong position that it would be impossible to dislodge their enemy until much greater preparations had been made. In the meantime the communications of the Allies were in danger. Hence Sir John French on May 1, 1915, ordered Sir Herbert Plumer to retreat. The wisdom of this order, the execution of which contracted the southern portion of the salient, was seen when the Germans again attempted to force their way through the allied front by the use of gas. The attempt this time was made between Zonnebeke, on the Ypres-Roulers railroad, and Boesinghe on the Yperlee Canal on Sunday, May 2, 1915. Though the British had been supplied with respirators of a sort, these means of defense were not as effective as they should have been nor as adequate as what was provided later. The Germans, however, suffered large losses in this attack because, as soon as the wall of gas began to approach the British trenches, the men there fired into it, well knowing from past experience that the Germans were following the gas. In this manner many of the Teutons were slain. The Allies adopted other tactics which were quite as effective. On seeing the gas approaching, the soldiers in some parts of the line proceeded to execute a flank movement, thereby getting away from the gas and subjecting the Germans to a deadly fire from a direction least expected.

Between Fortuin and Zonnebeke and south of St. Julien the allied line broke, but the supports with two cavalry regiments were rushed from Potijze, a mile and a half from Ypres on the Zonnebeke Road, and regained the lost ground. By night the Germans decided to discontinue their attempt to advance and left their dead and wounded on the field.

CHAPTER XVII

THE STRUGGLE RENEWED

THE Germans had only stopped the struggle for a breathing spell. On the following morning, Monday, May 3, they made an attempt to force the allied position back again. This attempt was made on the British left, west of the Bois des Cuisenirs, between Pilkem and St. Julien. The Germans cut their wire entanglements and, leaving their trenches and lying down in front of those protecting places, they were ready to advance; but, before they could start forward, the artillery of their enemy did such effective work that the Teutons returned to their trenches, and gave up an attack at that point. But they made an assault against the northern side of the salient which had by this time become very narrow. A German bomb wrecked a section of the British trenches, and the defenders of that part of the line had to go back of a wood that was a little to the northwest of Grafenstafel, where they were able to stop the German onrush.

The Belgians were bombarded with asphyxiating gas bombs beyond the French lines south of Dixmude. The Germans charged the Belgian trenches only to be cut down by machine-gun fire. That night, the night of May 3, 1915, an attack was made on the British front; but it was stopped by the artillery.

Sir Herbert Plumer in the meantime had been executing the order he had received from Sir John French, and shortened his lines so they were three miles less in length than before starting the movement. The new line extended from the French position west of the Ypres-Langemarck Road and proceeded through "shell-trap" farm to the Haanebeek and the eastern part of the Frezenberg ridge where it turned south, covering Bellewaarde Lake and Hooge and bent around Hill 60. This resulted in leaving to the Germans the Veldhoek, Bosche, and Polygon Woods, and Fortuin and Zonnebeke. This new front protected all of the roads to Ypres, and, at the same time, it was not necessary to employ as many soldiers to hold this line. Moreover the defenders of it could not be fired upon from three sides as long as they held it. In some places the British and German trenches had been no more than ten yards apart, but the difficulty of evacuating the British position was completed in safety on the night of May 3, 1915. The work included the taking with them 780 wounded. Sharpshooters were left in the trenches, however, and they maintained such an appearance of activity and alertness that the Germans kept on shelling the trenches all of the following day.

The attempt of General Putz to force the Germans back across the Yperlee Canal on May 4, 1915, was stopped by a combination of machine guns, asphyxiating gas and fog. Then the French spent the next ten days in tunneling to Steenstraate. Their tunnels toward their objective point were through that territory between Boesinghe and Lizerne. On May 5, 1915 the Germans made a careful advance on the British front under the cover of fog and a heavy bombardment, to find only that the British position had been changed. But they intrenched opposite the new alignment, and brought up their big guns. Then they used poisonous gas again with the result that the British retreated and the Teutons followed, in spite of the many men who fell because of the accurate work of the British artillery. The greater part of this action took place around Hill 60, and some of the British trenches to the north of the hill were captured by the Germans. They then penetrated toward Zillebeke to the supporting line. Up to midnight the Germans seemed to be victorious; then, however, the British drove them from the hill only to be driven away in turn by the use of asphyxiating gas. On the following day the Teutons held Hill 60 and some of the trenches north of it.

Asphyxiating gas also had been used in an attempt to break the British front on the left, on both the north and south sides of the Ypres-Roulers railroad. Though this attack failed, the Teutons were ready to make as near superhuman efforts as possible because they knew that the French were getting ready for a decisive action in the Arras territory, which would have the aid of a British attack south of the Lys. Hence it was to the advantage of the Germans to force Sir John French and General Foch to retain most of the British and French soldiers north of the Lys. On May 8, 1915, they turned their artillery on that part of the British front that was near Frezenberg. It destroyed the trenches and killed or wounded hundreds of the defenders. After three hours of this, the Germans commenced an attack on that part of the British front between the Ypres-Menin and the Ypres-Poelcappelle highways, the greatest pressure being brought to bear along both sides of the Ypres-Roulers railroad.

The British fought bravely, but it was impossible for them to hold out against the avalanche of lead. First the right of a brigade went to pieces and then its center and the left of another brigade south of it were forced back. Princess Patricia's Canadian Light Infantry held fast. The Second Essex Regiment also made some little success for their side by annihilating a small detachment of Germans; but that was more than offset by the breaking of the center of another brigade, after which the First Suffolks were surrounded and put out of the fight. Finally the Germans pushed their way on to Frezenberg. Sir Herbert Plumer realized by the middle of the afternoon that a counter-attack was necessary. He had held two battalions in reserve along the Ypres-Menin Road. He also had five battalions with him and reenforcements in the form of a brigade of infantry had arrived at Vlamertinghe Château, back of Ypres. He sent the First Royal Warwickshires, the Second Royal Dublin Fusiliers, the Second Surreys, the Third Middlesex, and the First York and Lancaster Regiments into the break in the line with the result that Frezenberg was retaken. This victory was short-lived, however; for the German machine-gun fire was too fierce for the men to withstand. The British retired to a new front which ran north and south through Verlorenhoek. The Twelfth London Regiment, on the left, though it lost many men, managed to get to the original line of trenches. Next the British were menaced from the north and east. Great bodies of Teutons rushed from the woods south of the Menin highway, when others rushed down the Poelcappelle Road and took Wieltje, which is only about two miles from Ypres.

The fighting continued all night, but shortly after midnight the British charged with the bayonet and retook Wieltje as well as most of that section to the north of it which they had lost. Early on May 9, 1915, the fighting was continued, and, in the afternoon, the Germans charged from the woods in a vain attempt to take Ypres after a severe bombardment of the British trenches. An attacking party of five hundred was slain north of the town. On the eastern side of the salient there were five distinct attacks. An attempt to capture the Château Hooge was made early in the evening, only to result in heaping the ground with German dead. The day closed with 150 yards of British trenches in the hands of the Germans; but they had been taken at a fearful cost to the kaiser's men.

The Germans began the next day, May 10, 1915, by shelling the British north and south of the Ypres-Menin road. They followed the cannonade with a cloud of asphyxiating gas. They then started for the opposing trenches. Many of them, the British allege, wore British uniforms. The British had by now been equipped with proper respirators and could withstand a gas attack with comparative ease. When the Germans were in close range they received a rifle and machine-gun fire that mowed them down almost instantly. Those who had not been shot fell to the ground to escape the leaden hail. But escape was not for them.

Shrapnel was poured upon them, and nearly all of the attacking troops perished.

Another gas attack was made between the Ypres-Menin road and the Ypres-Comines canal. There two batteries of gas cylinders sent forth their deadly fumes for more than a half hour. The cloud that resulted became so dense that it was impossible for the British in the opposite trenches to see anything; so they were withdrawn temporarily; but the troops to the left and right kept the Germans from following up this advantage and the trenches were saved to the British. When the gas had passed away the men returned to their former position. North of the Menin road, however, the Germans were successful in driving the Fourth Rifle Brigade and the Third King's Royal Rifles to a new position, the trenches which the British occupied having been battered by shell fire to such an extent that some of the occupants were buried alive. Hence the British here retreated to a new line of trenches west of the Bellewaarde Wood where the trees had been shelled until they were part of a hopeless entanglement rather than a forest.

The next day, May 11, 1915, was started by the Germans hurling hundreds of incendiary shells into the already ruined town of Ypres. They also fired almost countless high-explosive shells into the British trenches. The British big guns replied with considerable effect. One of the German cannon was rendered useless by the fire of the Thirty-first Heavy Battery, and several howitzers were damaged by the North Midland Heavy Battery. The German cannonade was especially effective near the Ypres-St. Julien road. The Teutons, however, did not confine their work to the artillery, for they made three assaults on the British trenches south of the Menin road. This part of the line was held by Scottish regiments, who, though they were forced out of their trenches, regained them with the aid of other Scots who were supporting them.

By now it was apparent to the British commanding officers that they must still further lessen the projection of their salient. So on May 12, 1915, the Twenty-eighth Division was sent to the reserve. It had experienced continuous fighting since April 22,

1915, and had suffered severe losses. It had only one lieutenant colonel. Captains were in command of most of its battalions. The First and Third Cavalry Divisions took its place. They were under the command of General De Lisle. From left to right the new line was held as follows: The men of the Twelfth Brigade, the Eleventh Brigade, and a battalion of the Tenth Brigade of the Fourth Division guarded the new front to a point northeast of Verlorenhoek. Next came the First Cavalry which held the line to the Roulers railroad. From the railroad to Bellewaarde Lake the Third Division held the line. From the lake to Hill 60 the Twenty-seventh Division had its position. The British admitted that this new position was not strong, because it lacked natural advantages, and the trenches were more or less of hasty construction.

The Germans started a heavy bombardment of the cavalry on May 13, 1915, when the rain was pouring in torrents and a north wind was adding to the discomforts of the British. The fiercest part of this attack was on the Third Division. Some idea of the fierceness of the bombardment can be gained when it is known that in a comparatively short space of time more than eight hundred shells were hurled on a part of the British line which was not more than a mile in length. In places the British were buried alive. In spite of the destructive fire, the North Somerset Yeomanry, commanded by Lieutenant Colonel Glyn, charged the Germans who were advancing on their trenches under cover of the bombardment. The charge was effective, and the Teutons were driven headlong toward their own trenches. But the German artillery had the range of the Seventh Brigade on the right, and poured upon it such a fire that it retreated several hundred yards, leaving the right of the Sixth Brigade exposed. As soon as possible the British made an attempt to remedy the defect in their line, and found it necessary to make a counterattack. In this counterattack very satisfactory results were obtained by the use of the Duke of Westminster's armored motor cars. The British regained the lost ground, but they found it impossible to retain it, for the Teuton's heavy artillery had the range of the position so accurately that no man could live there. The result of the day's fighting was a farther pushing back of the line of the British so that it bent backward from Verlorenhoek and Bellewaarde Lake. In addition to being forced back, the British suffered a large loss of men, especially officers.

The infantry on the left had been fiercely attacked on this same day; but it managed to keep from being driven from its position. One of the defenders of this part of the line was a territorial battalion, the London Rifle Brigade. There were only 278 men in the battalion at the beginning of the day, it having suffered severe losses previously. By night ninety-one more had been lost. Four survivors, under command of Sergeant Douglas Belcher, and two hussars whom the sergeant had added to his squad, held that part of the line in the face of repeated attacks. These plucky men not only made the Germans think the front was strongly defended there by using quick-firing methods, but they undoubtedly saved the right of the Fourth Division. Another especially gallant piece of work on the part of the British was done by the Second Essex, the reserve battalion of the Twelfth Brigade. With a bayonet charge they drove the Germans from Shelltrap Farm, which was between the Langemarck and Poelcappelle highways, and, though it was held by first one side and then the other, the British had it at the close of the day in spite of the bombardment it received.

The French met with better success on the British left. Under the command of General Putz they made an attack on Het Sase and Steenstraate. The sharpshooters of the Zouaves and Algerians took a trench in front of the latter place and entered the village. They fought on to the canal by the end of that day, which was May 15, 1915. More than six hundred Teuton dead were counted after that engagement. At the same time the Zouaves captured Het Sase with great ease, because the artillery had rendered its defenders useless for more fighting. The Germans, however, were not inclined to give up the town so easily. They bombarded Het Sase that night, using asphyxiating shells. Nothing daunted, the Zouaves put on their respirators and drove off with hand grenades and rifle fire the Germans who followed in the wake of the poisonous shells. On the following day it was

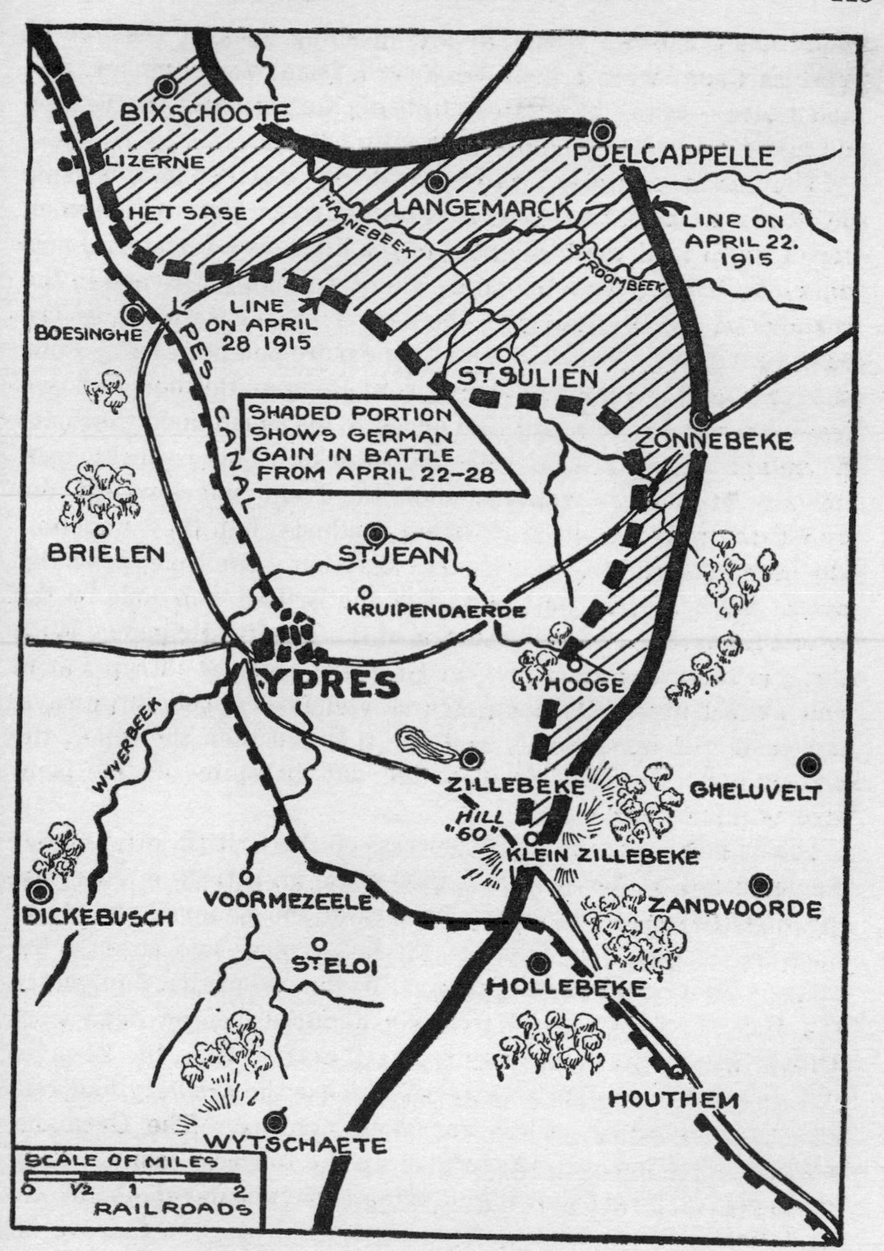

GAS BATTLE OF YPRES

said that the only Germans left alive on the left side of the Yperlee Canal were either wounded or prisoners. The French had destroyed three German regiments, taken three redoubts, and captured four fortified lines and three villages. In this connection it may not be amiss to note that the French reported that, on May 15, 1915, the German Marine Fusiliers who were attempting to hold the Yperlee Canal concluded it was the better part of valor to surrender. Before the Germans could relinquish their places they were shot down by their comrades in the rear.

Fighting along the line of the salient continued with more or less vigor for nearly ten days, but, until May 24, 1915, there were no engagements that had much out of the ordinary. On that date, however, the entire front from Bellewaarde Lake to Shelltrap, a line three miles in length, was bombarded with asphyxiating shells. This was followed by a gas cloud that was sent against the same extent of trenches. The wind sent the cloud in a southwesterly direction, so that the deadly fumes got in their work along nearly five miles of the front. It is asserted that the cloud was 40 feet in height, and that the Germans continued to renew the supply of gas for four and a half hours. It had little effect wherever the British used their respirators, for they managed to stay in their positions without undue inconvenience. Those who suffered the most from the gas cloud were the infantry of the Fourth Division on the left. The cloud which had followed the asphyxiating shells was in turn followed by a severe bombardment from three sides—the east, northeast, and north. The principal attacks were made in the neighborhood of Shelltrap, the British front along the Roulers railroad, and along the Menin road in the vicinity of Bellewaarde Lake. In those places the British were pushed back at least temporarily; but counterattacks were delivered before nightfall, and the greater part of the lost ground regained. Thus, to the disappointment of the Germans, their extra effort, with all the means of warfare at their disposal, had resulted only in reducing the salient at an enormous cost in lives on both sides, but the gain had been for the most part temporary.

Before leaving the consideration of the second battle of Ypres it may be well to estimate what has been gained and lost by both sides. In the attempt to wear down their opponents one side had inflicted as much of a blow as the other, to all intents and purposes, for there had been an almost prodigal waste of human life and ammunition. The distinct advantage that Germany had gained was in pushing back and almost flattening out the prow of the British salient, and they had demonstrated the superiority of their artillery. Britain, on the other hand, had lost no strategical advantage by the change of her line. The knowledge that Germany had a superior artillery acted as a stimulant in making the British provide a better equipment of big guns. But the British had demonstrated the great superiority of their infantry over that of Germany. In fact there was comfort to be derived by the friends of each side as a result of the second battle of Ypres. The fighting had to stop, as far as being a general engagement was concerned. There were other parts of the front in western Europe which were becoming by far too active for either the Germans or the British to neglect them. Hence it is necessary to leave Ypres and the brave men who fell there, and consider what was being done elsewhere.

CHAPTER XVIII

OTHER ACTIONS ON THE WESTERN FRONT

DURING the time in which the foregoing actions had been taking place, there was activity on the part of the Allies and the Germans in other sections of the great western front. It is true that not much was accomplished in Alsace in either April or May; for the fighting in the plains had been for the most part what may be termed trench warfare. The most important engagement had been the effort to take and hold Hartmannsweilerkopf, the spur of the Molkenrain massif, which controls the union of the Thur and the Ill. The top of this rise of ground, it will be remembered, had been won by the Germans on January 21, 1915; but the heights west of it and their slopes were in the possession of the French, who desired to add the spur to their possessions. For this purpose the French artillery bombarded it on March 25, 1915, and continued their work on the following day, March 26, 1915, when the Chasseurs stormed the height, and, after fighting for six hours, gained the top and captured 400 prisoners. But the Germans had no intention of giving their opponents such a hold on the control of the valley of the Ill, so there were many counterattacks.

While the Germans were attempting to retake the summit, the French were making desperate efforts to drive the Teutons from the eastern slopes. The Germans were temporarily successful, but their success was short-lived, for the French retook the top on April 28, 1915. During the next month, May, both sides made claims of success; but what each actually possessed was as follows: The French had the top and all of the western portion; the Germans possessed the summit ridge, and the east and northeast portions. But, until the French held the entire mountain, they could make little use of it in controlling the Ill Valley.

The fighting in the other part of the Vosges had to do principally with the valley of the Fecht. The stream runs from Schlucht and Bramont east, and proceeds past Münster and Metzeral. On its right bank is the railroad from Colmar to Metzeral. The heights in the upper part of the valley were held by the Chasseurs Alpins; and they desired to take both towns. Throughout the month of April the French were fairly successful on both banks of the river. The spur above Metzeral to the northwest was taken by them. The ridge between the two valleys was captured by the French on April 17, 1915. The fighting here was continued throughout May, 1915.

The next scene of activity was north, where there was a wooded plateau between the Moselle and the Meuse. Here the Germans had a salient which was long and quite narrow. The point of this salient was at St. Mihiel, the other side of the Meuse. This point was well protected by the artillery at Camp des Romains, which controlled the section for ten miles in any direction. To the north of the salient there was a railroad from Etain to Metz. There was another line twenty miles to the south. This ran from Metz to Thiaucourt by the Rupt de Mad. The village of Vigneulles was about in the center of the narrow part of the salient, and on the road to St. Mihiel. There was a better road to the south through Apremont. A strategic railroad had been built from Thiaucourt by Vigneulles to St. Mihiel, down the Gap of Spada, which is an opening between the hills of the Meuse Valley. The plateau of Les Eparges is north of Vigneulles. The plateau is approximately 1,000 feet above the sea level, and forms the eastern border of the heights of the Meuse. There was high land on the southern side of the salient, along which ran the main road from Commercy to Pont-a-Mousson. Within the salient the land was rough and, to a considerable extent, covered with wood.

The French did not plan to make an attack on the salient at its apex. The artillery at Camp des Romains would be too effective. The French plan was to press in the sides of the salient and finally control the St. Mihiel communications. The southeastern side of the salient, at the beginning of April, 1915, extended from St. Mihiel to Camp des Romains, thence to Bois d'Ailly, Apremont, Boudonville, Regnieville, and finally to the Moselle, three miles north of Pont-a-Mousson. The northwestern side was marked by an imaginary line drawn from Etain in the north past Fresnes, over the Les Eparges Heights, and thence by Lamorville and Spada to St. Mihiel. The place of most importance, from a military point of view, was the Les Eparges plateau, which controlled the greater part of the northern section of the salient. The taking of this plateau would naturally be the first step in capturing Vigneulles. But the Germans had converted Les Eparges into what had the appearance of being an impregnable fort, when they took it on September 21, 1914. Their trenches lined the slopes, and everything had been made secure for a possible siege. The French in February and March, 1915, however, had taken the village of Les Eparges and a portion of the steep side on the northwest. But of necessity they made progress slowly, because they were in such an exposed position whenever they sought the top. They had planned an assault for April 5, 1915, and, in a heavy rain, with the slope a great mass of deep mud, the French gained some territory. This they were unable to hold when the Germans made a counterattack on the following morning, April 6, 1915. That night the soldiers of the republic forced their way up with the bayonet, taking 1,500 yards of trenches, by the morning of April 7, 1915. Thereupon the Germans brought up reenforcements, which were rendered useless by the French artillery, which prevented them from going forward to the battle line. The German artillery used the same tactics, with the result that the French reenforcements were kept out of the fight. After the cannons had completed their work, both sides were apparently willing to rest for the remainder of the day. But on the morning of April 8, 1915, two regiments of infantry and a battalion of Chasseurs forced their way to the top, which they took after an hour's hard fighting. That pushed the Germans back to the eastern slope. Then the battle was fought on during the remainder of the day, which found the French, at its close, in possession of all except a little triangle in the eastern section.

Some idea of the conditions confronting those who attempted the ascent may be gained when it is learned that fourteen hours were required by the hardy French troops to go up to relieve their comrades who gained the top. This relief was not sent until the following day, April 9, 1915. On that day the Germans in the little triangle were driven off or slain. One of the sudden and dense fogs of the region appeared later and made a cover for a German counterattack. The French were at a disadvantage, but they quickly rallied, and, the fog suddenly lifting, they employed a bayonet charge with such good effect that the Germans were driven off with large losses. The importance of this achievement to the Allies is not likely to be overestimated. The height of Les Eparges dominated the Woevre district, and its capture by the French was one of the most heroic feats of the war. The Germans placed as high a value on the height for military purposes as the French. They had spent the winter in

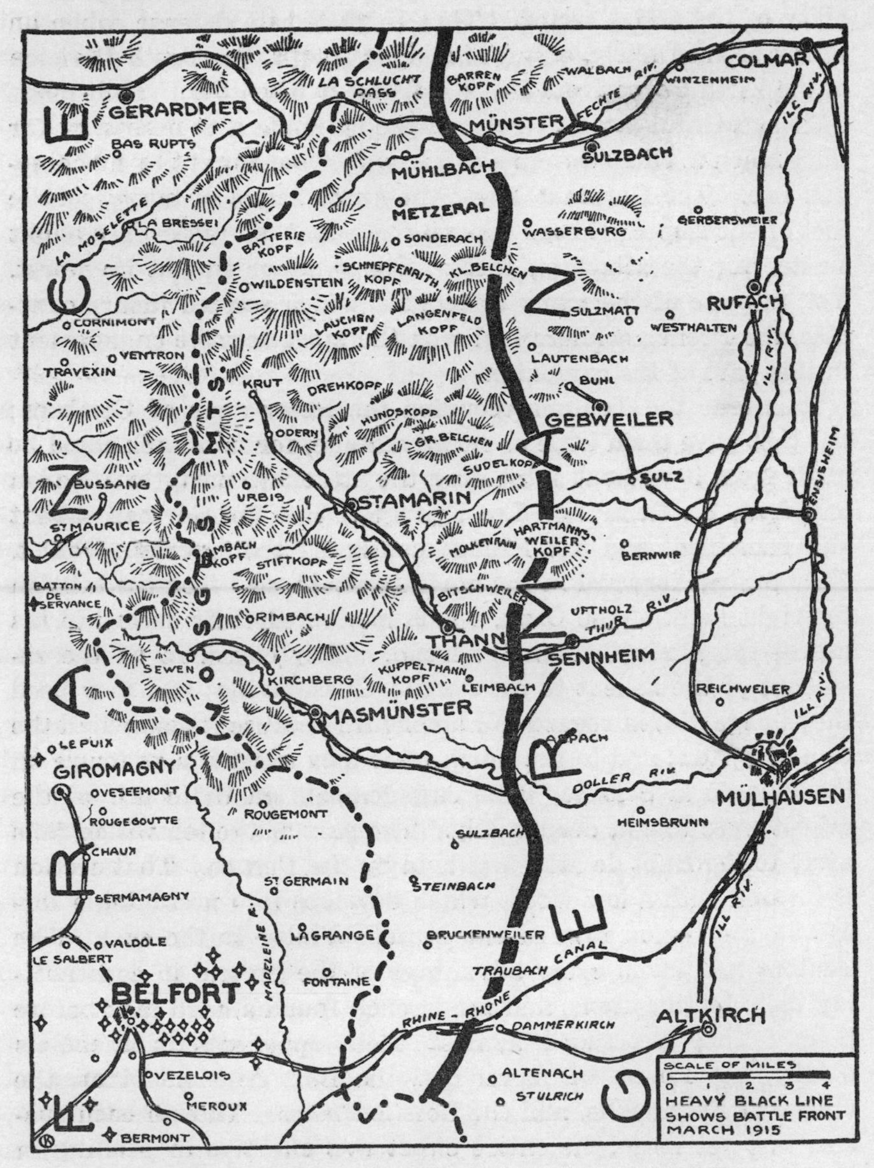

THE FIGHTING IN ALSACE—HARTMANNSWEILERKOPF

adding to what nature had made nearly perfect—the impregnability of the entire sector. They intrusted its defense, when an attack seemed likely, only to first-line troops, the Tenth Division of the Fifth Corps from Posen holding it when the French made their successful attack. To gain the height it was necessary for the French to climb the slimy sides, which were swept by machine-gun fire. The Germans knew the exact range of every square foot of the slopes. There was no place that offered even a slight shelter for the attacking force. The weather was at its worst. Yet, in spite of the many difficulties which seemed insurmountable, the French soldiers had won the most decisive engagement in this part of the campaign.

It is true the Teutons occupied the lesser spur of Combres; but that gave them little or no advantage, for no attack could be made from it without subjecting the attacking party to a leaden hail from St. Remy and Les Eparges. But the German salient still remained, and the French continued their pressure on it. They pushed forward in the north to Etain, and took the hills on the right bank of the Orne, which hampered their enemy in his use of the Etain-Conflans railroad. They closed in on the reentrant of the salient to the north—Gussainville; and they used the same tactics in regard to Lamorville, because it dominated the Gap of Spada; and to the north of it they exerted a pressure on the Bois de la Selouse. The engagements on the south of the salient were fought desperately. The part of the top which falls away to the Rupt de Mad was held by the French. That section is covered with a low wood, which develops into presentable forests in the region toward the Moselle Valley to the east. The Teutons had taken every advantage of the ground in constructing their fortifications, and the French found a hard task before them. They proceeded against their opponents in the Bois d'Ailly, the Forest of Apremont, the Bois de Mont-Mare, the village of Regnieville, and the Bois le Pretre. Though each success was not large, the entire effort was effective in pushing in the southern side of the salient. This brought the soldiers of the republic to within about four miles of Thiaucourt, which, with the control of Les Eparges, threatened St. Mihiel.

The French heavy artillery shelled the southern front of the trenches at Metz on May 1, 1915. The great desire to take Alsace and Lorraine, however, was set aside early in the month. The plight of Russia at this time made it imperative for the Allies to make a great movement on the western front to prevent as much as possible the pressure on the czar's line. Hence the campaign which seemed to be planned by the French was abandoned for a larger opportunity. This was the advance of the Tenth Army in the Artois over the plain of the Scheldt in the direction of Douai and Valenciennes, thereby threatening the communications of the entire Teuton line from Soissons to Lille. Hence the French started a vigorous movement against Lens, while the British sought to take Lille.

CHAPTER XIX

CAMPAIGN IN ARTOIS REGION

TO understand properly the campaign in the Artois, it is necessary to have at least a fair knowledge of the geography and the topography of the territory between La Bassée and Arras.

The valley of the Scarpe is held in on the south by low hills, and on the north by a low plateau, which descends in long ridges to the valley of the Lys and the plains about Lens. The greatest altitude in this section is the ridge known as Notre-Dame de Lorette, running east and west, and containing numerous ravines. To the south of it, in a little valley, is the town of Albain St. Nazaire. Carency is opposite on the next ridge. Next is the Bois de Berthonval in the middle of a wide depression. Beyond, the land ascends to Mont St. Eloi. The valley of the Lys is to the north of the Lorette ridge. To the east the land descends to the long, narrow valley in which is the highway between Arras and Bethune. La Targette and Souchez are along the way. Again the land rolls upward to the hills of Vimy with the Lens-Arras highway beyond them.

The Teutons held a salient in this region at the beginning of May, 1915. The line which bounded this salient ran east of Loos over the Bethune-Lens road, east of Aix-Noulette, and appeared on the Lorette plateau considerably to the west of its tallest spur, where was situated the Chapel of Our Lady; running out to the prow of the salient, it took in Albain; and then proceeded to Carency; bending closely, it ran east of the Bois de Berthonval, taking in La Targette and the Arras-Bethune highway. That part of the German line was called by the French the "White Works," on account of the chalk with which the breastworks were constructed. To the southeast of it was a section known as the Labyrinth. Ecurie was inside the line which finally ran back east of Arras. The salient was constructed for the guarding of Lens, which was considered the entrance to the upper valley of the Scheldt and the lowlands in the direction of Douai and Valenciennes. Of more importance than Lens itself was the railroad back of this front, the capture of which would naturally be a source of great danger to the Germans.

The French had won some ground in the region of the Lorette plateau early in 1915. The Tenth Army in the Artois received enough additional men to give it seven corps. More than 1,100 pieces of artillery, of varying caliber, were taken to this region by the French. The entire preparation for the campaign was under the personal direction of General Foch. In the meantime the Germans, becoming aware that their enemy was becoming more and more active, proceeded to strengthen the front by the addition of three divisions which were known as "divisions of assault." The men composing these additions were from Bavaria, Saxony, and Baden. Even this reenforcement left the Teutons outnumbered, and with less artillery than their opponents; but they held a position which was considered more impregnable than any other on either front. The Germans here had a chain of forts linked together by an elaborate series of trenches, these latter so arranged that the taking of one of the series placed its captors within the zone of fire of several others. Moreover there was an elaborate series of underground works, including mines and wolf pits, the latter being covered over with a thin layer of turf and thickly studded with stakes whose points awaited the charging French.

General Foch was ready on Sunday morning, May 9, 1915, and his artillery began one of the heaviest bombardments in history. The 1,100 French cannon hurled 300,000 shells on the German fortifications that day. The reverberations were deafening and terrifying. They startled the British engaged at the Aubers Ridge. The deluge of projectiles crashed their way through the supposedly impregnable work of engineering that the Germans had erected, and buried their mangled defenders in chaotic ruins. The preliminary work of the artillery was continued for three hours, accompanied by the plaudits of the French infantrymen. Then the infantry were sent to take the wrecks of what had been the pride of the German engineers. They took what was still in existence at La Targette, and the important crossroads there. They waged a fierce fight in and around the village of Neuville St. Vaast, which was stoutly defended by German machine guns. Here there was house-to-house fighting. The French center, farther north, charged over the remnants of the White Works, and went on beyond the Arras-Bethune road. This section of the advance took more than two and a half miles of trenches in an hour and a half. On the left the French were unable to maintain such speed, because of the many ravines. They took the outlying sections of Carency, and worked their way eastward, cutting the road to Souchez. At the end of the first day the French had to their credit three lines of German trenches on a five-mile front, 3,000 prisoners, 10 field guns, and 50 machine guns.

The bombardment was continued all night by the French gunners, while the men who had taken the trenches did their best to make such repairs as were necessary for the protection of the victors. On the morning of the following day, May 10, 1915, the soldiers of the republic had forced their way into the center of the German position. North of the plateau of Notre Dame de Lorette a feint attack was made to hold the German reserves. When the first French line was about to dash forward to complete their work of the day before, they suddenly received an order to remain where they were and seek all cover possible. One of the French aviators had seen a German counterattack getting under way near the sugar factory at Souchez. Preparatory to the Teuton advance the German artillery hurled hundreds of high-explosive shells on the section where the French would have been had they not received the order to keep under cover. To be exposed under such conditions would have meant annihilation. Believing their plans for the counterattack were working favorably, the Germans advanced, only to be mowed down by the French guns. Then the French infantry charged and gained another trench line. So eager were the younger French soldiers that some of those who charged from the south were not content with taking the trench which was their objective point, but dashed on into a ravine that extended in the direction of Ablain. There they killed or made prisoners of the Germans they found. This dash was extremely hazardous in the face of a possible German counterattack, which luckily for the French did not occur as the Teutons retired to Souchez in confusion and were unable to rally for any counterattack. A summary of the day's fighting includes the taking of all of the German trenches across the Bethune-Loos road; the attack on the fortified chapel of Notre Dame de Lorette, and the gaining of the trenches to the south of it, these connecting with Ablain and Souchez; the capture of the cemetery of Neuville St. Vaast; and the defeat of the German reserves who were rushed in motor cars from Lens and Douai. The trenches and approaches being too narrow and deep to allow freedom of action in using rifle and bayonet, the rifle is generally slung on the man's back in bandolier, and the fighting within the trenches is done with short weapons, especially with hand grenades, hence the new military expressions "bombing" and "bombing parties," as the squads are called that are especially detailed for bomb work during the charges.

The fighting continued fiercely throughout May 11, 1915. Late in the day the French took the lower part of the Arabs' Spur. An unsuccessful counterattack was made that night from the Spur of the White Way. But the French were harried by the artillery in Angres and the machine guns in Ablain, and their discomforts were added to by the work of the bursting shells which opened the graves of soldiers who had been slain in previous months.

Carency, surrounded on the east, south and west, and wrecked by the 20,000 shells which had been fired upon it, surrendered on the afternoon of May 12, 1915. The Germans captured there made a total of more than 5,000 prisoners taken by the French. Notre Dame de Lorette with its chapel and fort was also taken this same day, as was Ablain which was in flames when it was surrendered. Thus all of the highland to the west of Souchez was held by the French except a few fortins on eastern ridges.

A north wind and a heavy rain added to the discomforts of the soldiers on May 13, 1915. But physical discomforts were not all that made for more or less unhappiness. The Germans had little reason to be happy; but the French had the edge taken from their elation, because of their victory, by the fact that it seemed as if it must be won again before it would be of use to them. According to the rules of the war game the German line had been broken and the French had made for themselves a right of way; but there were many instances in this war where the rules were not followed; and this was one of the exceptions. It is true the German line had been smashed, but it had not fallen back. Instead the remnants of the line had collected themselves in the series of independent redoubts which had seemingly been prepared for just such an emergency. They were so situated that it was well-nigh impossible to destroy them at long range; but it was impossible to make any forward movement which would not be enfiladed by them. Hence it became necessary for the French, if they were to be really victorious, to reduce each separate redoubt. The most prominent of these were the sugar factory at Souchez, the cemetery at Ablain, the White Road on a spur of the Lorette, the eastern portion of Neuville St. Vaast, and the Labyrinth. The last named was so called because it was an elaborate system of trenches and redoubts in an angle between two roads. The White Road surrendered on May 21, 1915. Ablain was taken on May 29, 1915. The Souchez sugar

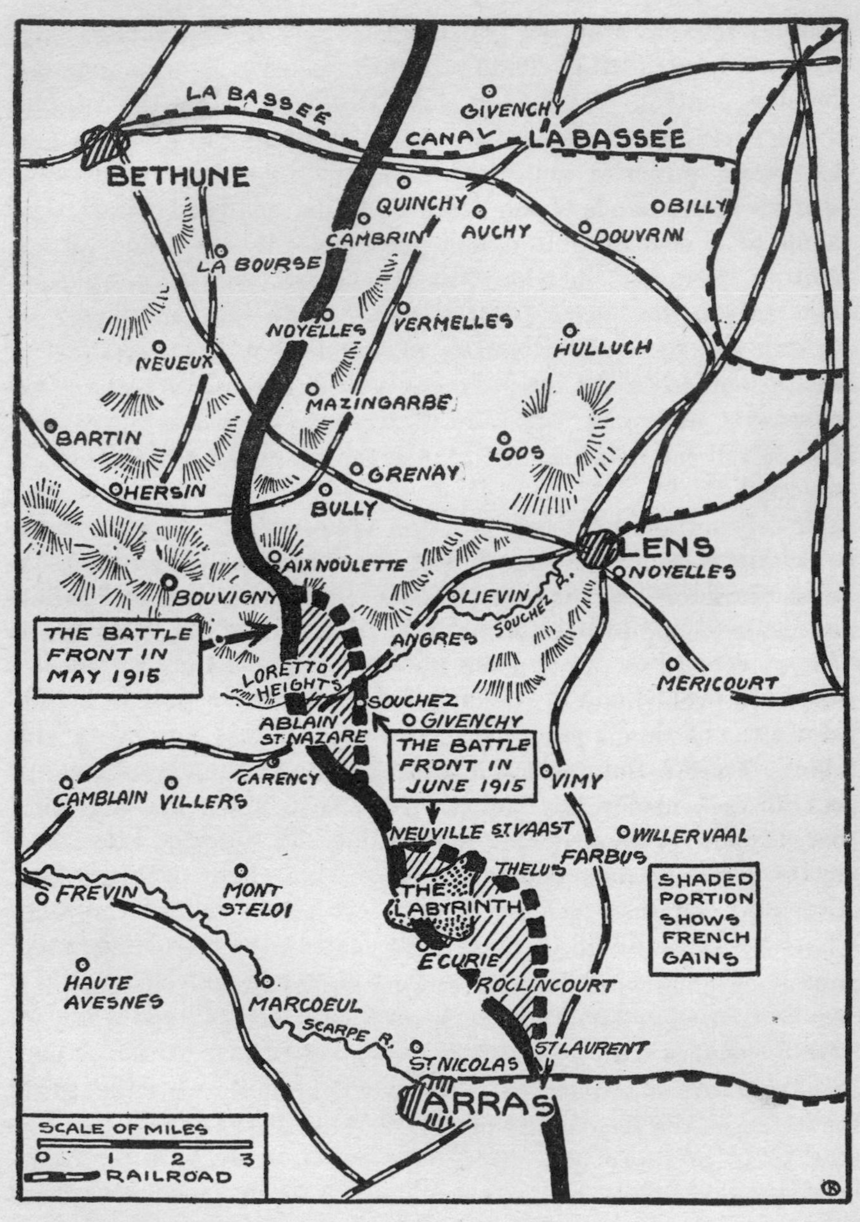

THE BATTLES IN ARTOIS

factory fell on May 31, 1915. Neuville St. Vaast was captured on June 8, 1915. The Labyrinth, however, remained under German control. Part of it was fifty feet below the surface of the earth, much of the fighting there being carried on in underground galleries and by means of mines. It finally was entirely in the hands of the French on June 19, 1915, after being taken to a considerable extent foot by foot. The last of the fighting there was in what was known as the Eulenburg Passage, where the entire 161st German Regiment, consisting of 4,000 men, were slain and a Bavarian regiment suffered a heavy loss in killed and wounded. The French took 1,000 prisoners; and only 2,000 of their own men were unable to answer roll call after the fight, of whom many were only slightly wounded.

In concluding the account of the battle of the Artois it may be admitted that the French had won what has been called a brilliant victory, but it had not been a complete success. They had made an end of the German salient; and only the last defense of Lens remained. How much they had reduced the pressure on Russia is problematical; but there is little doubt they had prevented the Germans from continuing the offensive on the Ypres front. They estimated the German loss at 60,000; and, by a peculiar coincidence, the Crown Prince of Bavaria, whose armies they fought, estimated the French loss at the same figure—60,000. It is known they lost many men in the hand-to-hand struggles; but their great forward movement was so well protected by their artillery that the French loss there was comparatively slight. Some idea can be gained from the fact that one French division killed 2,600 of their enemy and captured 3,000 prisoners with a loss of only 250 slain and 1,250 wounded. But the greatest gain to the French was probably the fact that the battle of the Artois had proved to the soldiers of the republic that their artillery was the equal of the German, which had been the arm in which the Teutons excelled. It also proved that the Germans could not intrench themselves in any manner that was impregnable to the French; for they had taken the Labyrinth, a most complicated series of military engineering feats which were supposed to be able to withstand any assault. And lastly, and perhaps of most importance to the French, the belief in the superiority of the German soldier, as a result of 1870 was shattered in the mind of the Frenchman.

CHAPTER XX

BRITISH FORWARD MOVEMENT—BATTLE OF FESTUBERT

TO aid the French in the Artois, the British made a forward movement in the Festubert region in May, 1915. Its purpose was to prevent the Seventh German Corps from sending troops and artillery to reenforce Lens. Moreover the British, if they succeeded, would take the Aubers ridge, which they had tried to gain in the battle of Neuve Chapelle. If they could capture the Aubers ridge, the way would be opened to Lille and La Bassée. The action began on Sunday morning, May 9, 1915, in the region between Bois Grenier and Festubert, and was a part of the forward movement of the British from Armentières to La Bassée. Part of the First Corps and the Indian Corps marched forward on the right from the Rue du Bois toward the southern part of the Bois du Biez, where there had been much fighting before. The principal attack was made by the Eighth Division on Rouges Bancs, not far from Fromelles and the Aubers ridge, near where the British had been stopped in the battle of Neuve Chapelle. At approximately the same time that General Sir Douglas Haig with the British First Army reached the slightly elevated plateau in front of Lille, General Foch with a large body of French troops made a desperate attack on the Germans on their front from La Bassée to Arras. The French and British had joined their efforts here, not only to relieve the pressure which was being exerted on Ypres and to take Lille, which dominated a region rich in coal, but also for the purpose of keeping the Germans so busy on the western front that none could be sent to the eastern front and further embarrass Russia. The artillery of both the British and French attempted to wreck the German trenches before their infantry should be sent against their foe. In this effort the British, using principally shrapnel, made little headway; but their ally, using high-explosive shells, such as they had been hurling at the Germans for weeks at the rate of a hundred thousand a day, was successful. Soon the Teutons' front was screened by clouds of yellow, green, black and white smoke. But this was not to be a one-sided artillery engagement, and the Germans soon had their artillery in action. They trained it on their enemies' trenches, believing from the size of the bombardment that an assault was soon to be made and that the trenches would be filled with troops. Their surmise was correct, but the Allies had suspected their opponents would reason thus, so the French and British infantry were in covered positions. Of course the Germans did not know how well their opponents were protected, so they sent thousands of shells against the allied positions. And again the allied artillerists replied in kind. This time they caught the German reenforcements, with the result that many of them were slain before they could reach their own front. In this work the British shrapnel was more effective than the French high-explosive shells.

The bombardment was continued vigorously for three-quarters of an hour. That the allied range finders had been doing accurate work was evidenced by the appearance of the German trenches when the British and French fire was turned against the supporting German trenches; but the Teutons' wire entanglements remained intact. Heretofore the big guns had been able to sweep such obstructions away. When the infantry reached the barbed wire, it found the Germans had improved this particular method of defense by using specially manufactured wire cable, well barbed, which was from one and one-half to two inches in diameter. And, to protect their cable entanglements, the Germans had built parapets in front of the entanglements. Their enemy's charging infantry coming upon such an obstruction could not cut it, and the only means of circumventing this new device was for the attacking force to throw their overcoats on the entanglements and crawl across the wire in the face of rifle and machine-gun fire.

For a considerable distance along this part of the front the distance between the German and British trenches was not more than two hundred yards. At not a few sections the opposing trenches were near enough to permit the soldiers to converse with their opponents. The trenches for the most part were built on the marshland with sandbags, those of the British being khaki-colored, and the German being black and white. When the inevitable order to charge was given, the British artillery shifted its range to the German rear and the Eighth Division dashed over the black and white sandbags behind which the Germans were crouching. Beyond them was a ridge, in horseshoe formation, which was the last barrier that lay between the Allies and the plains that led to Lille. This ridge trails off in a northeasterly direction at Rouges Bancs. Near the hamlet there was a small wood which had been taken by the Pathans and Gurkhas before the cannonade started. Among the regiments that led the attack of the Eighth Division were the Kensington Battalion of the London Regiment, the First Gloucesters, the Second Sussex, and the Northamptons. They were supported by the Liverpool Territorials, the First North Lancashires, the Second King's Royal Rifles, and the Sussex Territorials. The Germans had large bodies of reenforcements held at Lille, but they were unavailing; and the British took the first line of trenches though it required fifteen and a half hours to do it. Then they went on until they were on the slope of the ridge. Beyond that, however, it seemed impossible to proceed, for the Germans had such an array of machine guns trained on the approach to their second line of trenches that no human being could live in the face of their deadly fire. The British needed an equipment with which to bombard their enemy with high-explosive shells. Such an equipment they did not possess.

The German commander played a clever trick on the British when their First Army Corps and their Indian Division attempted to make progress in the triangle to the west of La Bassée. He evacuated his first two lines of trenches while the artillery was doing what it could to demolish his parapets; but his men were drawn up in the third line of trenches waiting for the inevitable advance of the British. This third line of trenches was protected with armor plate and concrete. Moreover he had planted a large number of machine guns in the brickfield near La Bassée. The British dashed forward until they were in range of the machine guns. Then they suffered such severe losses that they were forced to retreat, even though they had almost taken the inviting German trenches. The Highlanders and the Bedfords had made a gallant charge and felt especially humiliated to have to withdraw when victory was about to perch on their banners. They believed that a lack of reenforcements was responsible for their nonsuccess.

The day's fighting ended with the First Army of the British driven back except in the center. There the Kensington Territorial Battalion made a remarkable record for itself. In the morning when the British artillery ceased firing, the Kensington men dashed from their trenches and captured three lines of the German trenches at the point of the bayonet. A part of the battalion, in its eagerness to win the day, went on up the ridge. At the same time one of its companies turned to the left and another to the right, and with bayonet and bomb drove the Germans from the trenches for a distance of 200 yards. The Kensingtons were doing the work that had been set for them to do; but two regular battalions, one to their left and the other to their right, were not as able to comply with the orders they had received. The regulars were stopped by wire entanglements that the artillery had failed to smash, and, at the same time, they were raked by machine-gun fire. Hence they were unable to keep up with the Territorials. In fact the regulars never got up to the Kensington men; but were forced to retire. This left the Territorials in a most precarious condition. They had gained such an important point on the German line that a heavy fire was directed against them. But the British would not give up what they had taken. Instead of retiring, they sent for reenforcements which were promised to them. In the meantime the Germans gave up trying to blow the Kensingtons out of their position and made a counterattack. The left wing of the plucky Territorial battalion used bombs effectively to hold their enemy at bay. The right wing at the same time was kept busy in its attempt to prevent being enveloped. In spite of all the Germans could do with their artillery and their repeated counterattacks the West London men maintained their small wedge in the Teuton front. Finally trench mortars were brought against them. Then the Kensington battalion, or what was left of it, received the order to retire. To do that necessitated fighting their way back through the thickening line of their enemy. Those British Territorials had held their peculiar position several hours, and had suffered severely in consequence; but their loss was undoubtedly much larger when retiring to their former line. They fought the greater part of the afternoon and well into the evening in endeavoring to get back; and finally a comparatively few of them succeeded. The last dash to the British trenches was made over a barren piece of ground which was so flat that there was no opportunity for concealment. And here the Germans raked what was left of the battalion with rifle and machine-gun fire. Ultimately, however, a portion of the brave band returned to the British trenches. Previous to withdrawing the survivors from the front, General Sir Henry Rawlinson told them that their gaining the position which they took and holding it as long as they did had not only relieved the pressure on Ypres but had aided General Foch's army to advance between Arras and La Bassée. In conclusion he said: "It was a feat of arms surpassed by no battalion in this great war."

The Sussex and Northampton troops made a desperate effort to get into the German trenches on the morning in which this action started, but they never got nearer than forty yards, being stopped by the deluge of shrapnel, rifle, and machine-gun fire to which they were subjected. When they were ordered to return to the British trenches, those who remained able to make the attempt found it quite as dangerous as trying to go forward. That afternoon the Black Watch and the First Cameronians charged where the Sussex and Northamptons had been repulsed, but the Scotchmen had but little more success. It is true some of the men from the land of the heather got into the German trenches; but they did not survive. The determination of the British was shown when men, who had been wounded in the first charge and been unable to return to their own line, joined the Scots in their mad rush to death. Those men had lain under fire twelve hours before making their dying assault on the German trenches. It had been expected the Scotchmen would get into the opposing trenches and bomb and bayonet the Teutons out. Then reenforcements would be sent from the British line. But the artillery of King George was unable to check the devastating work of the kaiser's big guns and give the reenforcements a clear field through which to go to the aid of the attacking force. The result was that the Germans continued such a leaden hail between the lines that it was sending soldiers to certain death to order them to cross the zone of fire. The remnant of the Scottish regiments was recalled, and it lost as many men on its return as it had in its desperate struggle to reach the German trenches.

Both the Kensingtons and the Scots found groups of German machine guns, doing most destructive work, that could have been rendered useless if the British had had a supply of high-explosive shells. Under the circumstances there was nothing for Sir Douglas Haig to do but to order his men all along the line to retire. They obeyed the order sullenly, and many of them were slain in their attempt to get back to their own trenches. But their comrades felt they had not died wholly in vain; for the woeful lack of lyddite shells thus became known in England and the indignation thus aroused resulted in the appointment of a minister of munitions who organized the manufacture of the necessary explosives on a scale heretofore unattempted by the British. A lesson had been learned, but at a fearful cost to life.

The same lesson was being taught the British public at another section of the battle front. Its soldiers not only were unable to maintain a successful artillery fire, but the fact became so impressed on the German mind that the Teutons in the Ypres and Lille regions felt assured that their infantry had the British at their mercy. Sir John French, however, had a clever knowledge of human nature. He began his efforts to remedy the difficulty by telling the war correspondents his troubles. They spread the news. Then he secretly collected all of the available artillery in the Ypres region, together with his limited supply of shells, and was ready to deal such a blow to the Duke of Württemberg's army when it marched on Ypres the latter part of May, 1915, that it was necessary for the Germans to get reenforcements through Belgium. This was a great surprise to the Teutons and cost them dearly.

CHAPTER XXI

SIR JOHN FRENCH ATTEMPTS A SURPRISE

THE operation of this plan of Sir John French had an excellent effect in the Ypres region, but it had the opposite effect on the British who were trying to take Lille. Moreover it was necessary for the British to continue to occupy the attention of the left wing of the German army, under the command of the Crown Prince of Bavaria, in order to keep him from using his men against General Foch, who was attempting to push his way between Arras and Lille. Inasmuch as the British artillery had proved ineffective because of its lack of enough and the proper kind of ammunition, Sir John French planned another surprise for the Germans. This time he selected the weapon which the Teutons seemed most to fear when it was in the hands of the British—the bayonet. The salient on the German front at Festubert, between La Bassée and Neuve Chapelle, was chosen for the proposed military feat. The territory occupied by the Teutons had the appearance, to the casual observer, of being lowlands on which were wrecked homes, farms, and trees. The actual conditions of this section of the country were much more serious for any body of troops which planned to make an attack. The ground was moist and muddy, in many places being crossed by treacherous ditches filled with slimy water. Moreover the exact range of practically every square foot of it was known to the German artillerymen, whose guns were on the high ground to the west of the lowlands. The British were in trenches from seventy to three hundred yards from those of their enemy. If the men there could dash across the intervening space and get into the German trenches before being annihilated by the kaiser's cannon, they would use the bayonet with deadly effect, and, from past experiences, have reasonable hope of gaining a victory. It was decided to make such an attempt first on that part of the line between Richebourg on the left and Festubert on the right.

The British Seventh Division was sent south to support the attack which was to have been made on May 12, 1915. On that day it was too foggy for the aviators to see with any degree of accuracy; so the movement was delayed. This gave time for the Canadian Division to be sent south and add their strength to the support. The German trenches, at this point where the attack was to be made, were occupied by the Seventh Westphalian Army Corps. This corps had lost many of its men at Neuve Chapelle; and their places had been taken by youths who had not reached the development of manhood and whose immaturity and lack of military training greatly lessened the efficiency of this famous body of troops.

Finally, on Saturday night, May 15, 1915, all conditions for the attack seemed favorable to the British. There was no moon and the sky was dark, though there was not that inky blackness that occasionally occurs under similar weather conditions. The Indian Corps stole from their trenches and began to go forward from Richebourg l'Avoué. But the Germans were alert, and they illumined the movement with innumerable flares which made the Indians easy targets for the machine guns and rifles of the Teutons in that part of the line. So quick was the work to repel the attack that many of the Indians were slain as they were climbing out of their own trenches. As a surprise attack at night, the British were not making much of a success of their plan, but as a method of gaining ground and keeping their enemy busy on that particular part of the line the men of their Second Division were effective. They dashed into the first line of German trenches and cleared them out with the bayonet and hand grenade. The furor of the attack took them on into the second line. By dawn the soldiers of the Second Division had driven a wedge into the German line.

This wedge was widened and driven in harder by Sir Douglas Haig's old command—the First Corps. This corps had suffered heavy losses at the first battle of Ypres; but the men who filled the gaps in the line were hardy young men who made excellent soldiers from the start. Added to their enthusiasm was a desire to show their ability as fighters, with the result that the British right wing was so effective that it, in a great measure, made up for the failure of the Indian troops. The center and the right, with bomb and bayonet, drove the Germans from the trenches; and then together they forced their way into the Teutons' position 600 yards along a front 800 yards in length. Early the next morning, before daylight on May 16, 1915, the British Seventh Division forced its way into the German salient at Festubert. In the meantime the Germans were making hasty preparations for a counterattack. Sir John French's plan, however, had proved effective. It would have required a large supply of high-explosive shells to have made much of an impression on the excellent defenses which the German soldiers had constructed on this part of the front. The British had no such supply of ammunition, and, even if they had had it, it is doubtful if they would have been able to demolish the formidable wire entanglements. Yet in this night attack with the bayonet the British troops had accomplished all they could have done if supplied with proper ammunition. In the desperate charge which they made no wire entanglement could stop the British soldiers. They threw their overcoats or blankets over the barbed wire and then climbed across the obstruction. The Seventh Division took three lines of trenches in this manner, until it was 12,000 yards back of the original line of its enemy.

There were now two wedges driven into the German front, and the British desired to join them and make what might be termed a countersalient, or a salient running into the original salient of the Germans. But the space between the two horns of the British force was a network of trenches. The horns might prod and irritate the Teutons, but they needed artillery again to rid the German breastworks of machine guns and demolish the obstructions which would cost too many lives to take in the same manner in which the British success had been won in its night attack. Nevertheless the British started in to bomb their way toward Festubert, and they even gained forty yards in this hazardous undertaking before they were forced to stop. If they had seemed to be an irresistible force, they had met what had every appearance of being an immovable body—and there was a limit to human endurance.

By May 17, 1915, the British concluded that their most advisable offensive was to clear the space between their two wedges by cutting off the Germans who held that part of their line. To do this the British attempted to cut off the German communication to the north from La Quinque Rue; but, by that time, the Teutons had received reenforcements; and they rained such a shower of lead on the attacking force that the attempt had to be abandoned, but not until many heroic efforts had been made by the British to succeed in their purpose.

Many Germans were made prisoners at all stages of the fighting. The British bayonet seemed to strike them with terror, and the bombs were more potent in scattering them than were the orders of their commanders to repel the attacking force. Between Richebourg l'Avoué and Le Quinque Rue is the farm Cour de l'Avoué. In front of this farm the remains of a battalion of Saxons attempted to surrender. They had arrived on the line as reenforcements to the Westphalians, and had been fighting valiantly until their numbers were so decreased that they were unable to hold out against their foes longer. Whether their commanding officer ordered them to surrender or a common impulse dictated their action, they left their position and advanced toward the British. Not understanding their action, the attacking force fired upon the Saxons who were sufficiently numerous to give the impression that they might be leading a counterattack. Thereupon the Saxons dropped their guns and the firing from the British side ceased, only to be taken up on the German side by the Westphalians. This was followed by an attack on the would-be prisoners by the German artillery until every soldier in the surrendering party was slain. This action horrified the British, but the Germans considered it a means of discipline which would have a salutary effect on any who might prefer the comforts of a prison camp to dying for the Fatherland.

The British Seventh Division at Festubert continued to work south along the German trenches. Its bayonets and bombs cleared the way before it. The plan was for them to continue toward Rue d'Ouvert, Chapelle St. Roch, and Canteleux. In the meantime the Second Division, on the left of the Seventh Division, was to fight its way to Rue du Marais and Violaines. The Indian contingent had received orders to keep in touch with the Third Division. The Fifty-first Division was sent to Estaires to act as a support to the First Army. By the night of May 17, 1915, the British held all of the first line of German trenches from the south of Festubert to Richebourg l'Avoue. For a part of that distance the second and third lines of trenches had been taken and held; and still farther forward the British possessed many important points. Moreover the British soldiers were so inspired with their success that they desired to press on in spite of the fact that the nature of the country was such that they were wet through and covered with mud. It was not all enthusiasm, however. Mingled with the desire for victory was a desire for revenge. The British on this part of the line were enraged by the use of gas at Ypres and the sinking of the *Lusitania.*

On the night of May 17, 1915, the Fourth Cameron Highlanders, a Territorial battalion, met with disaster. The men composing this unit were from Inverness-shire, Skye, and the Outer Islands. Many of them had been gamekeepers and hence were accustomed to outdoor life and the handling of guns, all of which aided them in saving the remnant of their command. They had been ordered to take some cottages, occupied by German soldiers as a makeshift fortification. The Cameronians on the way to the attack fell into a ditch which was both deep and wide. It was necessary for them to swim to get across the ditch in some places. In the meantime Highlanders were being slain by German shells and the rifle fire that the men in the cottages rained upon the Scots. One company was annihilated. Another company lost its way. The rear end of a German communicating trench was reached by a third company. Long before midnight this company was almost without ammunition. Two platoons reenforced it at midnight; but the reenforcements had no machine guns, which would have given at least temporary relief. Under the circumstances the only thing for the Territorials to do was to retreat. The Germans made that quite as perilous a venture as the advance had been. Only half of those who started for the cottages returned. Among the slain was the commander, and twelve other officers were also killed.

The British, in spite of a cold rain, pushed on 1,200 yards north of the Festubert-La Quinque Rue road; and took a defense 300 yards to the southeast of the hamlet. Two farms west of the road and south of Richebourg l'Avoué, the farm du Bois and the farm of the Cour de l'Avoué, in front of which latter the surrendering Saxons were slain, had been held by the Germans with numerous machine guns. The British took both farms by nightfall and found, on counting their prisoners, that they then had a total of 608 as well as several machine guns.

The Second and Seventh Divisions were withdrawn by Sir Douglas Haig on the following day, Wednesday, May 19, 1915. The Fifty-first Division and the Canadians took the places of the men who were sadly in need of relief from active duty. Lieutenant General Alderson received the command of both divisions together with the artillery of both the Second and Seventh Divisions. The cold, wet weather hampered operations and there was comparatively little activity, though hostilities by no means altogether ceased. Each side needed a little rest and time to fill in gaps in their respective lines. Hence it was not until Sunday, May 23, that any fighting on a large scale took place. On that day the Seventh Prussian Army Corps made a desperate effort to break through that part of the British line held by the Canadians near Festubert. The Prussians used their old tactics with the result that the British shrapnel, rifle, and machine-gun fire plowed great holes in their ranks. The Teutons in this instance were without adequate artillery support, for many of their batteries had been made useless by the British. From then on to May 25, 1915, there were several small engagements in which the

British made gains. Then Sir John French concluded to end the activity of his men on this part of the front. In that connection he made the following statement: "I had now reasons to consider that the battle which was commenced by the First Army on May 9 and renewed on the 16th, having attained for the moment the immediate object I had in view, should not be further actively proceeded with.

"In the battle of Festubert the enemy was driven from a position which was strongly intrenched and fortified, and ground was won on a front of four miles to an average depth of 600 yards."

CHAPTER XXII

ATTACKS AT LA BASSÊE

THE British had discovered the futility of attempting to smash through the German lines without an adequate supply of high-explosive shells with which to destroy the heavy wire entanglements. Moreover, in maintaining a curtain of fire between the German lines and potential reenforcements, it was necessary to increase the artillery arm of the service. At this time the Germans could fire four shells to one by the British. Another very essential equipment in which the British were lacking was machine guns. The German army had developed machine-gun warfare apparently to its highest power. They not only used it to increase their volume of fire, but also as a means of saving their infantry. When, for any reason, it was found expedient to move infantry, a few machine-gun crews would take the place of the soldiers with the rifle and maintain a fire which would be almost as effective in checking the British advance as the infantry had been. The British had no such number of machine guns. They lacked this necessary part of their equipment just as they lacked shells, cannon, aircraft, and other war material which the Germans had developed and accumulated in large quantities under the supervision of the German General Staff.

The German munition factories had been making and storing enormous supplies for an army of several millions of men. On the other hand the British had believed in the excellence of their comparatively small army to such an extent that it required all of the fighting from the time their troops landed on the Continent up to Festubert to convince them that they must make and maintain a military machine at least equal, if not superior, to the one her foes possessed. It is true the British needed more men in the ranks, but what was needed more was large additions to the supply of machine guns, artillery, and ammunition.

For those reasons the British generals avoided clashes with the Germans after the battle of Festubert, except when it was necessary to hold as many of the Germans as possible to the British part of the western front. This plan was maintained throughout the summer of 1915. In the meantime the Germans were constructing, beyond their trenches, the most elaborate series of field fortifications in the history of warfare. The German staff realized that the time was coming when the British would again take the offensive. When that time arrived the Germans would thus be prepared to make every foot of ground gained as costly as possible to their foes. In fact they had reason for believing that it would be almost impossible for their opponents to gain ground where it was held by such seemingly impregnable works.

An attack at La Bassée in the first weeks in June, 1915, started with the British Second Army making a pretended advance in the Ypres region. The British in the forest of Ploegsteert drove a mine into the German lines and blew it up. The explosion followed by a British charge, which resulted in the taking of a part of the German trenches. This forest extended northwest of Lille and south of Messines. Under the ground in this section the sappers had built a city, whose streets were named for the thoroughfare of London. Thus there was "Regent Street," "Piccadilly Circus," "Leicester Square," and many others. There was also a "Kensington Garden," in which grew wild flowers transplanted from the forest by the soldiers.

The Germans had been driven out of the forest in the fall of 1914 when they made their dash to reach Calais; but their trenches were only about 400 yards beyond the eastern edge. The earth here was especially adaptable for mines, and both sides made many attempts to work destruction by tunneling forward. In this activity it was soon found necessary to have men in advanced positions in the tunnels to listen to the mining operations of their opponents. As soon as such operations were discovered, a countertunnel was driven in that direction and a mine exploded, thereby destroying the enemy's tunnel and burying his sappers. Sometimes, however, the men in the countertunnel cut through to the other excavation and engaged in a hand-to-hand conflict beneath the surface of the earth. Then primitive methods were used. Though mining had taken place on other sections of the western front, as at Hill 60, it was in this forest area that it was probably brought to its highest development.

The British mine here, as noted above, on June 6, 1915, blew up the German trenches, and the British charged into the crater and drove the Germans out with bayonet and bomb. A similar crater was the result of the mining at La Bassée. Five mines at the end of tunnels constructed by the Germans did not go far enough toward the British trenches, and when the explosions occurred the trenches remained intact.

The sappers, however, had other things to contend with; this was the case when a tunnel was driven toward the German trenches between Rue du Bois and Rue d'Ouvert, near the La Bassée Canal. Water was found below the German intrenchments. The British managed to keep the water out of the tunnel by using sandbags. Then they planted enough dynamite to blow up a large part of the German force. The two trench lines were very close together on this part of the front; and, to prevent accidents, the British left their trenches near the mine before it was fired.

On the night of June 6, 1915, the mine tore open the trenches of both sides, and buried one of the British magazines which was filled with hand grenades and killed several British bomb throwers. At about the same moment another supply of British bombs was exploded when it was struck by a shell from a German howitzer. This occurred at a place on the line called Duck's Bill, and resulted in the British being without an adequate supply of hand grenades. The British troops in this action were the soldiers of a British division and a Canadian brigade. The latter included the First Ontario Regiment, the Second and Fourth Canadian Battalions, the Third Toronto Regiment, and the East Yorkshires.

The Ontario regiment was directed against a fortified part of the German line which was called Stony Mountain. To the south of Stony Mountain, about 150 yards, was another fortified position called Dorchester. This also was to be taken by the Ontario men. If they succeeded in their work the right flank of the British division would be protected. But it was Stony Mountain that was of most importance to the British. Its machine guns and its northern defenses menaced the route which the British must take to make an advance. In order to prevent the Germans from giving their undivided attention to the Canadians, the British division on the left made an advance against the Teutons north of Stony Mountain. The British artillery had been shelling this part of the German line day and night many days as a preparation for this advance. Its projectiles crashed into the brick fields near La Bassée, and in front of the wrecked village of Quinchy.

The German machine-gun crews were hidden behind the brick stacks which were square blocks of burned clay upon which the British shells burst without perceptible effect. The shells that went over the stacks, however, did much damage. Beyond the brick field to the north were the ruins of farm buildings which were also hiding places for the Germans and their machine guns. All the buildings back of the German line had been turned into fortresses whose underground works were concreted and connected with their headquarters by telephone. While the British artillery was attempting to destroy these fortresses it was also hurling lyddite shells into the trenches.

The German artillery fire greatly exceeded the British in volume. Neverthcless the British forces were in the more comfortable position. They had comparatively little to do except wait until they were needed, which would be when their artillery had completed the preparation for the inevitable charge. On the other hand the German soldier had a nerve-racking part to play. He knew from the preparation that an attack in force was about to be made; but he did not know when it would occur nor where. Hence it was necessary for him to be constantly on the alert. Many of the Germans were under arms at all hours of the day and night. In fact few of them on that part of their line got any real rest during the week in which the bombardment continued. The section between the two lines of trenches was illuminated at night, and the cannonade kept up so that there was no opportunity for the Germans to repair the havoc made by the British shells.

The suspense was terminated on the evening of June 15, 1915, by an additional flight of projectiles from the British guns. Every piece of British ordnance on that part of the line was worked at top speed. The Germans, knowing that this immediately preceded an infantry charge, used their artillery to stop it. But the British charge formed in their trenches, with the Canadians on their right. In addition to the shrapnel the Germans made breaks in the lines of their foes by the use of machine guns, but the breaks were quickly filled. On some parts of the front the British and Canadians were successful and reached the trenches. In all the captured trenches extended from Rue du Bois to Rue d'Ouvert.

In the meantime those Canadians who had been directed against Stony Mountain and Dorchester were doing heroic work. The First Company of the Ontario Regiment charged through the débris of the mine explosion, only to run into the deadly hail sent at them by the machine guns. But the Canadians were determined to complete their task, and they took Dorchester and the connecting trench. The fire was too heavy for them to reach Stony Mountain. A group of bombers made a dash forward, but were shot down before they could get near enough to use their weapons.

The second and third companies rushed forward, suffering severely from the deluge of lead, but some of their men got into the German second line and then began to bomb their way to right and left. The captured first trench was utilized by the attacking force. From that vantage the advance was led by a machine gun which was followed by a group of bomb throwers. In working forward the machine-gun base became lost when the man who had it was slain. Thereupon a Canadian "lumberjack" named Vincent became the base, the machine gun being fired from his back. But the German bomb throwers drove the attacking force out of the trench. The Germans kept a rain of lead between the Canadians and the British line of trenches with the result that it was almost suicide for a man to attempt to return for bombs. Nevertheless many braved the ordeal. Only one was successful. He, Private Smith of Southampton, Ontario, seemed to bear a charmed life, for he made the trip five times. The Third Canadian Battalion was sent forward to reenforce the Ontario Regiment which had lost most of its officers, but such a pressure of German forces were brought to bear on the Canadians that the reenforcements were unavailing, and the Canadians were forced to relinquish all they had gained, and return to their own trenches that night.

The retreat was a desperate undertaking; the Germans then had the Canadians in the open and added heavily to the Canadian's death roll. On the other side of Stony Mountain the British had met with no better success than the Canadians. Having started their enemies back, the Germans massed for a counterattack and drove them back a mile, but not without a terrific struggle. The battle field was lighted by the peculiar fireworks used for such purposes and bursting of shells. Jets of flame shot forth from machine guns and rifles. In many places the intermittent light disclosed deadly hand-to-hand conflicts. Suddenly the Germans concentrated their fire on a portion of their lost first line of trenches, and the trenches of their enemies who held them were no more. Having the British and Canadians defeated, as they believed, the Germans proceeded to add to their victory by storming the British and Canadian trenches. They met with resistance, however, that drove them back.

At daybreak on June 16, 1915, the artillery on both sides resumed firing on a large scale. Suddenly, in the afternoon, the British fire increased preparatory to another charge. This time the British commander had selected a smaller section for his attack. This was at Rue d'Ouvert, and the men who had been selected to make the charge were the Territorials and the Liverpool Irish. They got into the first line of German trenches which the Teutons shelled to such an extent that the remnant of the attacking force had to retreat. Then the Second Gordon Highlanders and other Scotch soldiers made a gallant charge at the same place, Rue d'Ouvert, on June 18, 1915, but were forced to retire to their own trenches.

These attacks on this part of the German front resulted in repulses for those who made them; but, at the same time, they helped the Allies win victories elsewhere by keeping the German troops on that part of the line from going to reenforce those who were being hard pressed by the French. In this manner the British and Canadians, who fought so valiantly and with so little apparent success at Stony Mountain and Rue d'Ouvert, were in a measure responsible for the French victories at Angres, Souchez, and the Labyrinth. The Crown Prince of Bavaria could not hold out against both the French and British, but he believed it was more important for him to check the British, because a victory for them would threaten Lille to a greater extent.

CHAPTER XXIII

OPERATIONS AROUND HOOGE

THE next action of importance on the British front occurred at the Château of Hooge on the Menin road about three miles east of Ypres. Here had been the headquarters of Sir John French and Sir Douglas Haig at the first battle of Ypres. From the Château Sir John French had seen the British line break at Gheluvelt, thereby opening the road for the Germans to Calais.

That opening, however, had been closed by the Worcesters. After the Germans began to use their deadly gas in the spring of 1915 they again took possession of Hooge, and used the Menin road for a forward movement which threatened what was left of Ypres.

The Duke of Württemberg was in command of that part of the line opposed to the British, and his forces extended from near Pilkem in the north to near Hill 60 in the south, in the form of a crescent. He made use of the asphyxiating gas cloud and gas bombs so frequently on this part of the front that the British soldiers became expert in donning their hoodlike masks and in using respirators. Moreover, the British were constantly on the alert for the appearance of the poison gas. So that this method of attack was much less effective. Before the Germans discovered how well the British had prepared themselves against the gas, they met with disaster twice when using it. On both occasions they had followed their gas cloud expecting to find their foes writhing on the ground in choking agony—an easy prey for an attack.

But the British had put on their curious-appearing headgear, and were waiting for the men whom they knew would be following the cloud at a safe distance. As soon as the Germans were near enough the British turned loose everything that would hurl a projectile large or small. By the time the gas cloud had cleared, or, to be more accurate, passed on to the rear of the British line and spent itself, the only Germans to be seen were in the piles of dead and wounded in front of the British most advanced trenches. The first time this occurred did not teach the Germans its lesson sufficiently well. A second time the Germans did not follow their gas cloud so closely. The gas-filled shells, however, the British found more difficult. They did not give warning of their coming as did the appearance of the comparatively slow-moving gas cloud. Thus in the first week of May, 1915, Hill 60 was taken by the Germans in a bombardment of asphyxiating shells. The bombardment had been immediately followed by a charge of bomb throwers who made an assault on the hill from three sides at once. That forced the British to retreat to a trench line at the foot of the hill, and gave the top of the hill to the Germans who immediately set up a lookout post for their artillery back of the Zandvoord ridge.

This part of the British line was under the command of Sir Herbert Plumer. His troops occupied themselves from the first week in May to the middle of August, 1915, in fighting in the Hooge district. Most of this fighting was important only because it kept the Germans busy on that section of the line, and prevented them from being able to reenforce the Crown Prince of Bavaria or adding men to the force that was driving the Russians eastward.

The men, fresh from the training camps, fought alongside of hardened veterans and learned much from them. From being what amounted to auxiliaries in these actions the new troops became hardened to actual fighting conditions. For this reason the personnel of the British troops on this part of the line was changed frequently. This was especially true at Hooge. Princess Patricia's Canadian Regiment occupied the Château and village of Hooge on May 8, 1915. The "Princess Pats," as they were known at home, turned over their quarters to the Ninth Lancers who were followed by the Fifteenth Hussars and the Second Camerons.

On May 24, 1915, the Germans made a great gas attack. They had placed along the line from St. Julien to Hooge a great number of gas tanks. They then started a bombardment with asphyxiating shells. When the bombardment was well under way the tanks were opened. The ensuing cloud was five miles long and forty feet high; and it floated over the British trenches from 3 a. m. to 7 a. m. The cloud was followed by three columns of infantry, who dashed forward under the protection of the shells of their artillery. But the Germans made gains in only two places—at Hooge and to the north of Wieltje. For the most part the British regained by counterattacks what they lost; but they were unable to retake the Château of Hooge, though the Ninth Lancers and the Fifteenth Hussars made a heroic attempt to regain it. Thereupon the Third Dragoons received orders to attempt to retake the Château of Hooge. They went into the second line of the British trenches to the south of the Menin road on May 29, 1915. The Germans bombarded the trenches with high-explosive shells while from the German trenches a torrent of small arms fire poured. In spite of the continued hail of lead, the Dragoons held to their position though their trenches were wrecked.

Early in the morning of May 31, the British charged and drove their enemy from the ruins of the Château and its stables. The Germans turned all of their artillery on that part of the line against Hooge, and when the bombardment was finished there was only a heap of ruins left. The British withdrew from the Château, but only for a short distance.

The bombardment was renewed on June 1; on that day the German infantry tried to dislodge the Dragoons, but the attempt was unsuccessful. Again, on June 2, the artillery was used, the German shells being hurled a part of the time at the rate of twenty a minute. Under the cover of this terrific bombardment a part of the German infantry charged from the Bellewaarde Lake region. They got to the Château before a British battery opened fire on them. Again they entered the ruins and made a dash out on the opposite side, where they were met by more machine-gun fire. Three times they tried to escape, but practically all of them were slain. Other attempts were made by the Germans that afternoon, but none of them was successful.

The Dragoons were relieved on June 3, 1915, and their places were taken by a much larger force. It included the Third Worcesters, the First Wiltshires, the First Northumberland Fusiliers, the First Lincolnshires, the Royal Fusiliers, the Royal Scots Fusiliers, and the Liverpool Scottish, a territorial organization.

The British artillery was concentrated in the neighborhood of Hooge and started a bombardment on June 16. After a fairly adequate preparation by cannonade, the infantry charged the German line for a thousand yards near the Château, and took a part of the second line of trenches. Again the British bayonet and bomb had won, though in this attack the greater credit must be given to the bomb. The Germans made an attempt to retrieve the day by battering the British out of the trenches they had won. To do this the German artillery used a plentiful supply of high-explosive shells. They continued the attempt for twenty-four hours; but all they succeeded in doing was driving the British back to the first line of German trenches where they waited for the inevitable attack of the infantry which was repulsed. Finally the Germans seemed inclined to give up trying to accomplish much on this part of their front.

In the first week of July, 1915, the British took two hundred yards of German trenches, eighty prisoners and three trench mortars. The German commander now turned once more to Hooge. An additional reason for his renewed interest in that place was the fact that the British engineers, on July 20, blew up a mine west of the Château, thereby making a great crater in which the British infantry made themselves comparatively secure. The crater was one hundred and fifty feet wide and fifty feet deep.

The Germans made an unsuccessful attempt to take the crater on July 21, 1915; and tried again on July 24. The Duke of Württemberg found his men making comparatively little progress. It is true that the British had not made much more. The gas attacks had gained ground before the British had learned how to avoid the more severe effects of the poison. The result of experience brought into existence a new device. It has been called a flame projector, and has been described as a portable tank which is filled with a highly inflammable coal-tar product. The contents of the tank were pumped through a nozzle at the end of which was a lighting arrangement. The flame could be thrown approximately forty yards.

A large supply of these flame projectors arrived in the German trenches on July 30, 1915. The action began with the usual bombardment of high-explosive shells. Other shells filled with the burning liquid were also used. At the height of the bombardment, the British lines were flame swept. No preparation had been made for such an attack; and the only thing that the British could do was to get out of the way of the flame. Thus they lost their trenches in the crater and at the Château and village of Hooge. The method of attack so infuriated the British that they made a desperate counterattack with the result that they regained most of what they lost with the exception of about five hundred yards of trenches.

CHAPTER XXIV

FRANCO-GERMAN OPERATIONS ALONG THE FRONT

WE have thus far dealt chiefly with the British operations in the western front, but it must not be assumed that the French, in the meantime, were idle. On the contrary, their operations, covering the far greater territory, were proportionally more important than those of their allies.

During the winter months artillery duels along the entire Franco-German front were kept up without intercession. These were varied by assaults on exposed points which were in many cases repeatedly taken and lost by the opposing forces.

The French staff applied itself with the utmost vigor to the accumulation of large stacks of munitions and supplies for the production of active movements when weather conditions should permit. For the most part, however, the Franco-German operations were desultory movements occurring in various portions of the long line. Actions of the first importance began with the attacks in the St. Mihiel salient in April, 1915.

On the night of February 6, 1915, Germans exploded three mines at La Boisselle in front of the houses in the village which the French occupied, but the attempt of the Germans to advance was checked after a small amount of ground had been gained. The next day a counterattack carried out by a French company retook this ground, and inflicted a loss of 200 men. The French seized a wood north of Mesnil-les-Hurles on the night of February 7. Here the Germans had strongly established themselves.

During the first part of February, 1915, the Germans made a series of assaults on the Marie Therese works in the Argonne. Their force comprised about a brigade; but the French repulsed all attacks. Both sides suffered severe losses. On the night of February 9, there was an infantry engagement at La Fontenelle in the Ban de Sapt. Two battalions of Germans took part in the action and gained some ground which the French regained by counterattacks on the following day.

Actions in the Vosges continued in spite of heavy snow. The French carried Hill 937, eight hundred meters northwest of the farm of Sudelle, in the region north of Hartmannsweilerkopf.

About February 9, 1915, there was considerable activity on the part of the German artillery in Champagne, especially before Rheims. The city being again bombarded. There was also a lively cannonade in the region of Lens, around Albert, between the Avre and Oise, in the neighborhood of Soissons, and at Verneuil, northeast of Vailly. In Lorraine the Germans, after having pushed back the French main guard, succeeded in occupying the height of the Xon beacon and the hamlet of Norroy. The Germans were repulsed by a counterattack as far as the slopes north of the beacon.

The French on February 18 made some progress in the region of Boureuilles on Hill No. 263. They also gained a wood south of the Vois de Cheppy. At the same time French troops took four hundred meters of trenches north of Malancourt and about as much south of the Bois de Forges. The Germans made five unsuccessful counterattacks, near Bolincourt, to retake the trenches which the French had captured. On the same day, the French recaptured the village of Norroy. In the Vosges, the French repulsed two infantry attacks north of Wisembach, in the region of the Col de Bonhomme, and consolidated their positions, progressing methodically north and south of the farm of Sudelle. The bombardment of Rheims was continued during these days. On the heights of the Meuse, at Les Eparges, three German counterattacks on the trenches which the French had won on February 17 were stopped by the French artillery fire.

In the Vosges, between Lusse and Wisembach, in the Bonhomme region, the Germans, after succeeding in getting a footing on Hill 607, were dislodged on the morning of February 19, 1915. The French held their position on the height notwithstanding the violent efforts to dislodge them. An attack by the Germans on Le Sattel north of the Sudelle farm was also repulsed.

In the evening of February 19, 1915, the Germans delivered their fourth counterattack against the trenches which the French took at Les Eparges, but the French artillery again beat them back. The Germans were also unsuccessful in a counterattack on Hill 607, at Sattel, south of the Fecht. They succeeded in gaining a footing on the eastern spur of Reichsackerkopf.

After having repulsed a sixth counterattack by the Germans at Les Eparges, the French on February 10, 1915, delivered a fresh attack which enabled them to enlarge and complete the progress they made on the day before. They took three machine guns, two trench mortars, and made two hundred prisoners. among whom were several officers.

They also repulsed a counterattack of the Germans and then took all of their trenches to the north and east of the wood which had been captured by the French on the day before. Two other counterattacks were repulsed, and the French made fresh progress, particularly to the north of Mesnil, where they captured two machine guns and one hundred prisoners. The Germans made their seventh unsuccessful counterattack on Les Eparges on February 21. The French advanced posts fell back on the main line in Alsace on both banks of the Fecht; but the main line was strongly held, and the Germans, attacking in serried and deep formations, suffered heavy losses.

On the Belgian front the French batteries demolished one of the German heavy guns near Lombaertzyde on February 22, 1915. On the same day the French artillery dispersed German troops and convoys between the Lys and the Aisne. The French made progress on the Souain-Beausejour front, taking a line of trenches and two woods, and repulsed two particularly violent counterattacks. Many prisoners were taken by the French in this action. In the Argonne the French artillery and infantry had the better of the almost continuous fighting. This was especially true near Fontaine-aux-Charmes and Marie Therese, as well as at the Bois Bolante.

The bombardment of Rheims continued on February 22, lasting for a first period of six hours, and a second period of five hours. One thousand five hundred shells were fired into all quarters of the town. The cathedral was made a special target and suffered severely. The interior of the vaulted roof, which had resisted up to this time, fell. Twenty houses were set on fire and twenty of the civilian population were killed.

The French captured more trenches in the region of Beausejour and held their gains of previous fighting, on February 23, 1915. Their batteries blew up a German ammunition store to the northwest of Verdun at Drillancourt, in the region of the Bois de Forges, on the same day, February 23, 1915, and stopped an attempted German attack in Alsace from the village of Stossweiler.

There was an action of some importance in the Wood of Malancourt, on February 26, 1915, when the Germans sprayed the French advanced trenches with burning liquid. The French troops evacuated them, the soldiers being severely burned before they could escape. A counterattack was immediately made. This checked the German advance. On the same day, in the region of Verdun and on the heights of the Meuse, the French heavy artillery enveloped with its fire the German artillery, wrecked some guns, exploded about twenty wagons or depots, annihilated a detachment, and destroyed an entire encampment.

In Champagne the French on the night of February 26, 1915, captured five hundred meters of German trenches to the north of Mesnil-les-Hurles.

On February 28, 1915, Rheims was again bombarded and still again on March 2, 1915. About fifty shells fell on the town. In the Argonne, on March 2, 1915, in the Bagatelle-Marie Therese sector, there was mine and infantry fighting in an advanced trench which the French reoccupied after they had been forced to abandon it. At the same time in the region of Vauquois, the

French made some progress and held the ground captured in spite of the counterattacks of the Germans. The French also took some prisoners. In the Vosges, at La Chapelotte, they captured trenches and gained three hundred meters of ground.

The bombardment of Rheims was continued on March 4, 1915, and lasted all day, a shell falling about every three minutes. While the bombardment was in progress the Germans captured an advanced trench from the French to the north of Arras, near Notre Dame de Lorette; but in the Argonne the French made fresh progress in the region of Vauquois. On the following day, March 5, however, the French made successful counterattacks in the region of Notre Dame de Lorette. The Germans lost the advanced positions which they had taken from the French and held them for two days. At Hartmannsweilerkopf, in Alsace, the French captured a trench, a small fort, and two machine guns. They also repulsed a counterattack opposite Uffholz, and blew up an ammunition store at Cernay. On the same night, the French drove back the German advanced posts which were trying to establish themselves on the Sillakerkopf, a spur east of Hohneck.

The French continued to gain ground, on March 7, to the north of Arras in the region of Notre Dame de Lorette, where their attacks carried some German trenches. The German losses were considerable. During this first week in March, 1915, the French carried successively, to the west of Münster, the two summits of the Little and the Great Reichaelerkopf. The Germans made two counterattacks starting from Mühlbach and Stossweiler; but they were unsuccessful. On the right bank of the Fecht the French captured Imburg, one kilometer southeast of Sultzern. This success was completed farther to the north by the capture of Hill 856 to the south of the Hutes Hutles. Finally, at Hartmannsweilerkopf the French repelled a counterattack delivered by a German battalion which suffered heavy losses and left numerous prisoners in the hands of the French.

On March 8, 1915, the French gained two hundred meters on the ridge northeast of Mesnil which they added to the gains of the previous day. Here the French carried a German reaoubt, took a revolver gun and three machine guns, and made some prisoners. The Germans had armored shelters supplied with revolver guns and very deep subterranean chambers. In the Argonne, between Four-de-Paris and Bolante, the French delivered an attack which made them masters of the first line of German trenches of more than two hundred meters in length.

To the north of Rheims in front of the Bois de Luxembourg, the Germans attempted, on March 14, to carry one of the French advanced trenches, but were repulsed. On the same day, between Four-de-Paris and Bolante in the Argonne, the French gained three hundred meters of trenches, and took some prisoners. Two counterattacks which the Germans made were unsuccessful.

In the region of Lombaertzyde on March 15, the French artillery very effectively bombarded the German works. When the Germans attempted to recapture the small fort which was taken from them on the night of March 1 they were repulsed and left fifty dead. The French losses were small. To the north of Arras, a brilliant attack by the French infantry enabled them to capture, by a single effort, three lines of trenches on the spur of Notre Dame de Lorette, and to reach the edge of the plateau. The French captured one hundred prisoners including several officers. They also destroyed two machine guns and blew up an ammunition store. Farther to the south, in the region of Eeurie-Roclincourt, near the road from Lille, they blew up several German trenches and prevented their reconstruction. In Champagne the French made fresh progress. They gained ground in the woods to the northeast of Souain and to the northwest of Perthes. They also repulsed two German counterattacks in front of Ridge 196, northeast of Mesnil, and extended their position in that sector. In the region of Bagatelle in the Argonne two German counterattacks were repulsed. The French demolished a blockhouse there, and established themselves on the site of it. Between Four-de-Paris and Bolante the Germans attempted two counterattacks which failed. At Vauquois the French infantry delivered an attack which gave it possession of the western part of the village. Here they made prisoners. At the Bois-le-Prêtre, northeast of Pont-à-Mousson, the Germans blew up with a mine four of the French advanced trenches which were completely destroyed. The Germans gained a footing there, but the French retook the first two trenches and a half of the third. Between the Bois-le-Prêtre and Pont-à-Mousson, in the Haut de Rupt, the Germans made an attack which was repulsed.

In Champagne, before Hill 196, northeast of Mesnil, on March 19, 1915, the Germans, after violently bombarding the French position, made an infantry attack which was repulsed with heavy losses.

In the Woevre, in the Bois Mortmore, on March 20, 1915, the French artillery destroyed a blockhouse and blew up several ammunition wagons and stores. At La Boisselle, northeast of Albert, the Germans, after a violent bombardment, attempted a night attack which was repulsed with large losses.

The Germans bombarded the Cathedral of Soissons again on March 21, 1915, firing twenty-seven shells and causing severe damage to the structure. On the same day Rheims was bombarded, fifty shells falling there.

Near Bagatelle the French, on March 22, blew up three mines; and two companies of their troops stormed a German trench in which they maintained their position in spite of a strong counterattack. Five hundred yards from there, the Germans, after exploding two mines, and bombarding the French trenches, rushed to an attack on a front of about two hundred and fifty yards. After some very hot hand-to-hand fighting the assailants were hurled back in spite of the arrival of their reenforcements. The French artillery caught them under its fire as they were falling back, and inflicted very heavy losses.

The French then retreated some fifteen meters at Vauquois on March 23, 1915, when the Germans sprayed one of their trenches with inflammable liquid.

CHAPTER XXV

CAMPAIGN IN ARGONNE AND AROUND ARRAS

THERE were some weak places in the French line from Switzerland to the North Sea; and one of them was that part in the region between the Forest of the Argonne and Rheims. General Langle de Cary was in command of the army which held this section. It requires no military genius to comprehend that the French center and the right wing from Belfort to Verdun were not safe until the Germans had been forced back across the Aisne at every place. The French general had made an effort to drive the Germans under General von Einem from Champagne Pouilleuse. The preliminary effort had been to stop the Germans from using the railroad which ran from near the Nort to Varennes through the Forest of the Argonne and across the upper Aisne to Bazancourt.

After the battle of the Marne, the crown prince's army, severely handled by the Third French Army under General Sarrail, pushed hastily toward the north and established itself on a line running perpendicularly through the Argonne Forest, at about ten or fifteen kilometers from the road connecting Ste. Ménéhould with Verdun. Almost immediately there developed a series of fights that lasted during a whole year and were really among the bloodiest and most murderous combats of the war. The German army in the Argonne, commanded by the crown prince, whose headquarters had long been established at Stenay, consisted of the finest German troops, including, among others, the famous Sixteenth Corps from Metz, which, with the Fifteenth Corps from Strassburg, is considered the cream of the Germanic forces. This corps was commanded by the former governor of Metz, General von Mudra, an expert in all branches of warfare relating to fortresses and mines. Specially reenforced by battalions of sharpshooters and a division of Württembergers, the Twenty-Seventh, accustomed to forest warfare, this corps made the most

Prayer in a French church which the exigencies of war have converted into a Red Cross hospital

violent efforts from the end of September, 1914, to throw the French troops back to the south and seize the road to Verdun. The crown prince evidently meant to sever this route and the adjoining highway, leading from Verdun to Ste. Ménéhould. The road then turns to the south and joins at Revigny, the main line of Bar-le-Duc to Paris via Chalons, forming, in fact, the only possible line of communication for the fortress of Verdun. The other line, running from Verdun to St. Mihiel, was rendered useless after the Germans had fixed themselves at St. Mihiel in September, 1914.

Up to the first months of 1916 there was only a small local railway that could be used between Revigny and Ste. Ménéhould by Triaucourt. Of the two big lines, one was cut by the Germans, and the other was exposed to the fire of their heavy artillery.

The violence of the German attacks in the Argonne prove that so long ago as September, 1914, they already dreamt of taking Verdun. Their aim was to force the French troops against Ste. Ménéhould and invest the fortress on three sides to bring about its fall.

These Argonne battles were invested with a particular interest and originality. They were in progress for a whole year, in a thick forest of almost impenetrable brushwood, split with numerous deep ravines and abrupt, slippery precipices. The humidity of the forest is excessive, the waters pouring down from high promontories. The soldiers who struggled here practically spent two winters in the water.

One can hardly imagine the courage and heroism necessary to bear the terrible hardships of fighting under such conditions. All the German soldiers made prisoners by the French describe life in the Argonne as a hideous nightmare.

From the end of September, 1914, the Germans delivered day and night attacks, generally lasting ten days. These attacks were made with forces of three or four battalions up to a division or a division and a half. In each attack the Germans aimed at a very limited objective—to capture the first or second line of trenches, to seize some particular fortified point. That object once attained, the Germans held on there, consolidated the occupied terrain, fortified their new positions and prepared for another push forward. It was thus by a process of nibbling the French trenches bit by bit that the Germans hoped to attain the Verdun-Ste. Ménéhould line.

The tactics employed in these combats were those suited to forest fighting; sapping operations methodically and minutely carried out to bring the German trenches as near as possible to the French; laying small mines to be exploded at a certain hour. Two or three hours before an attack the French positions were bombarded by trench mortars and especially heavy mine throwers.

At the short distances the effect would naturally be to cause considerable damage; trenches and their parapets were demolished, shelters, screening reserves, were torn open. At that moment when the attack is to be launched, the German artillery drops the "fire curtain" behind the enemy trenches to prevent reenforcements from arriving. Such are the tactics almost constantly employed by the Germans.

Despite their most furious efforts during the winter of 1914 and the spring and summer of 1915, in at least forty different attacks, the German gains were very insignificant, and if one considers the line they held after the battle of the Marne and compares it with their present position, one may gather some idea of how little progress they have made.

It was in June and July, 1915, that the Germans displayed their main efforts in the Argonne. Their three great attacks were made with greater forces than ever before (two or three divisions), but the results were as profitless as their predecessors. The heroism of the French barred the way.

At Arras in June, there was almost as much activity as at Ypres. During the last part of the campaign in the Artois, General d'Urbal began an advance between Hebuterne and Serre. The former had been held by the French and the latter by the Germans. The two villages were each on a small hill and not quite two miles apart. There were two lines of German trenches in front of the farm of Tout Vent which was halfway between the villages.

The trenches were held by the Seventeenth Baden Regiment which was attacked by the French on June 7, 1915. The French troops consisted of Bretons, Vendeans, and soldiers from Savoy and Dauphiné. The work of the infantry was preceded by a heavy bombardment to which the German artillery replied. Then the French charged with a dash that seemed irresistible.

On the following day, June 8, 1915, the French gained more ground to the north in spite of the activity of the German artillery. June 9, 1915, saw desperate fighting in the German communicating trenches, and on June 10, 1915, several hundred yards of trenches to the south were taken. The Seventeenth Baden Regiment was only a name and a memory when the fighting ceased; and two German battalions had fared but little better. Of the five hundred and eighty prisoners taken ten were officers.

General de Castelnau, on the day before the fighting at Hebuterne, made a break in the German line east of Forest of l'Aigle which is a continuation of the Forest of Compiègne but is separated from it by the Aisne. Within the French lines were the farms of Ecaffaut and Quennevieres. The Germans held Les Loges and Tout Vent. There was a German salient opposite Quennevieres with a small fort at the peak of the salient. Defenses had been built also where the northern and southern sides of the salient rested on the main line of trenches. There were two lines of trenches on the arc of the salient with three lines on a portion of the arc. An indented trench held the chord of the arc. The Germans had placed several guns in a ravine which ran down toward Tout Vent. Four companies of the Eighty-sixth Regiment had held the salient.

On June 5, 1915, the reserve troops were taken from the Tout Vent ravine for reenforcements. Their places were occupied then by other German troops. The French artillery bombarded the fort at the peak of the salient, and all of the trenches and defenses of the Germans in that neighborhood and the French infantry kept up a rifle and machine-gun fire which was an aid in preventing the Germans from repairing the damage done their defenses. The bombardment continued all day and all night and increased in volume and intensity on the morning of June 6, 1915. Then it was continued intermittently. A mine under the fort at the peak of the salient blew up. The Germans who sought refuge in their dugouts found them unavailing. The shells had blown the roofs from those places of supposed safety. In many instances their occupants had been buried in the débris and suffocated. The French artillery lengthened its range and made a curtain of fire between the Germans on the front and the German supports in the rear. Then the French infantry charged. The men had dispensed with knapsack that they might not be hampered with unnecessary weight. All had three rations and two hundred and fifty rounds of ammunition. They were also provided with two hand grenades and a sack. The last was to be filled with earth. The filled sacks were sufficient to form breastworks with which any place taken might be held. With a cheer the French infantry ran across the two hundred yards between the two lines. The German infantry's nerves had been so badly shaken by the bombardment that only a scattering fire, badly directed, greeted the French. It was but the work of minutes to take the first line of German trenches. The two hundred and fifty survivors of two German battalions were made prisoners. The German reserves in the ravine on the Tout Vent farm made a dash to aid their fire line; but the French artillery shells accounted for them before the reserves ever reached those whom they would have relieved. Thus in less than an hour 2,000 Germans were put out of the fight. The French who had been selected for this work included Bretons, Zouaves, and chasseurs.

The Zouaves then made a dash for the ravine on the Tout Vent front. There they came upon a field work equipped with three guns. This work was protected by wire entanglements. The German artillerymen retreated to their dugouts, but the Zouaves captured them and their fortification. At that stage of the fighting the French aviators saw German reenforcements on their way to take part in the battle. The aviators signaled to their troops this information. Two German battalions were being hurried in motor cars from Roye to the east of the Oise; but before they reached the scene of the fighting the Germans managed to mass for a counterattack. It was ill-planned and executed. French shrapnel and machine guns annihilated those making the counterattack. In the meantime the French sappers were fortifying with sacks of earth the ends of the salient, so that by night the French were in a position to hold what they had gained. The precautions which the French had made were shown to be extremely timely, for that night the reenforcements from Roye made eight desperate attacks.

The lack of success throughout the night did not prevent the Germans from making a reckless attack on the French works at both ends of the salient on the morning of June 7. The Germans made their advance along the lines of the communicating trenches. They were greeted with a shower of hand grenades. By nightfall the Germans seemed to have wearied of the attacks. The total German loss in killed in this engagement was three thousand. The French had lost only two hundred and fifty killed and fifteen hundred wounded. They captured a large amount of equipage and ammunition, besides twenty machine guns.

The French front south of Pont-à-Mousson, on the Moselle, through the gap of Nancy to the tops of the Vosges experienced only slight changes during the spring and summer of 1915. The Germans assumed the offensive in the region of La Fontenelle, in the Ban-de-Sapt, in April and June. The French engineers had built a redoubt to the east of La Fontenelle on Hill 627. The Germans found they could not take it by an assault; so their sappers went to work to tunnel under it; but they had to bore through very hard rock and the work was necessarily slow. The French, learning of the mining operations of their foes, started a countereffort with the result that there was a succession of fierce skirmishes under the surface of the earth. Finally the German sappers were lured into a communicating tunnel which had been mined for the purpose and they all perished. The greatest activity of the sappers was between April 6 and April 13, 1915. On the night of the latter date the officers of the Germans tried to rally their men for further operations, but their soldiers had had enough and refused to renew their work.

The Germans, however, did not give up in their attempts to take Hill 627, which they called Ban-de-Sapt, and in an assault they made upon it on June 22 they took the hill. Thereupon the general in command of the Thirtieth Bavarian Division made the following announcement:

"I have confidence that the height of Ban-de-Sapt will be transformed with the least possible delay into an impregnable fortification and that the efforts of the French to retake it will be bloodily repulsed."

On the night of July 8 the French began a bombardment which was followed by an infantry charge which forced its way through five lines of trenches and gained the redoubt on the top of the hill, in spite of its corrugated iron and gun-shield defenses to which had been added logs and tree trunks. At the same time the French made an attack on the German trenches on the left and surrounded the hill from the eastward. The Germans on the right flank of the French were kept busy by another attack. In this battle two battalions of the Fifth Bavarian Ersatz Brigade were taken from the German ranks either by death or as prisoners. The French captured eight hundred and eighty-one, of whom twenty-one were officers, who, for the most part, were men of more than ordinary education.

The principal work of the French troops at this time was in the valley of the Fecht and the neighboring mountains. They planned to go down through the valley to Münster and take the railroad to which the mountain railroads were tributaries. In connection with this campaign in the mountains the achievement of a company of French Chasseurs serves to illustrate the heroic and hardy character of these men. They were surrounded by German troops on June 14, 1915, but refused to surrender. Instead they built a square camp which they prepared to hold as long as one of them remained alive. When their ammunition began to give out, they rolled rocks down on their enemy and hurled large stones at the advancing foe. At the same time the French artillery aided them by raining shells on the Germans, though the artillery was miles from the scene of action. Thus the Chasseurs were able to hold their position until they were relieved on June 17, 1915. In the meantime the French proceeded down the valley of the Fecht and up the mountains overlooking the valley. An assault was made on the top of Braunkopf and an attack was made on Anlass on June 15 and 16, 1915. The French captured Metzeral on June 19, 1915, the Germans having set fire to it before being driven out. The soldiers of the republic then began to bombard Münster with such success that they destroyed a German ammunition depot there. The Sondernach ridge was held by the French about the middle of July, 1915, and they continued to gain ground so that they were near Münster by the end of July, 1915. In these actions the French mountaineers were pitting their skill against the mountaineers from Bavaria.

By midsummer the lines on both sides of the western front were an elaborate series of field fortifications. The shallow trenches of the preceding fall were practically things of the past. And these fortifications extended from the Vosges to the North Sea. They naturally varied with the nature of the region in which they were built. The marshy character of the soil along the Yser and about the Ypres salient made it impossible to go down very deep. Hence it was necessary to build up parapets which were easy marks for the artillery. The Germans had the better places on the higher levels from Ypres to Armentières; but the British line opposing them showed remarkable engineering skill. The advances of the Allies had resulted in making the first line of trenches somewhat temporary in character in the sections about Festubert, La Bassée, and the Artois; but in these regions there were strong fortifications in the rear of both lines. The condition of the ground from Arras to Compiégne was excellent for fortification purposes. The Teutons had the better position in the chalky region along the Aisne, though the chalk formation did not add to the comfort of the men. In the northern part of Champagne trench life was more bearable. The forests in the Argonne, the Woevre, and the Vosges made the trenches the best of all on the western front. The greater part of these so-called trenches, the like of which had never before been constructed, could not be taken without a bombardment by heavy artillery. And. in the rear of each line there was a series of other fortifications quite as impregnable. This condition was a gradual growth which had developed as a result of the increasingly new methods of attack. As new means of taking life were invented, new means of protection came into existence, until, for the present, the inventive genius of man seemed to be at a standstill. But all this activity and preparation at the front meant a greater activity in the rear of the opposing lines. Fighting men were a necessity; but, under existing conditions of warfare, they were useless unless they were kept supplied by an army of artisans and another army of men to transport munitions to the soldiers on the firing line. In fact it was being forced on the minds of the commanding officers that the war could be won in the workshop and laboratory rather than on the battle field.

CHAPTER XXVI

BELGO-GERMAN OPERATIONS

FOR the most part the activity of the Belgian army in February, 1915, consisted of a continuous succession of advanced-post encounters, in which detachments of from thirty to forty soldiers fought with the Germans on the narrow strips of land which remained inundated, while the artillery of the contending forces bombarded the trenches and the machine-gun forts. The intermittent artillery duel continued through the forepart of February, 1915, and on February 14, 1915, the Germans bombarded Nieuport, Bains and the Dune trenches, and continued the bombardment on February 15, 1915, and again on February 20, 1915.

Near Dixmude on February 28, 1915, the Belgian artillery demolished two of the German trenches, and their infantry occupied a farm on the right bank of the Yser. One of their aviators dropped bombs on the harbor station at Ostend.

By the beginning of March, 1915, strips of dry land began to be seen in the flooded region; and, along these, the Belgians advanced at Dixmude and the bend of the Yser. They won additional bridgeheads on the northern bank of the river. By the middle of the month, March, 1915, the Belgians had obtained a strategical point by possessing Oudstuyvenkerke on the Schoorbakke highway. From there they could force the Germans back until they were in a position that would prevent any German action against the Dixmude bridgehead.

On March 18, 1915, the Belgian army continued its progress on the Yser, and on March 23, 1915, the artillery destroyed several German observation points. A division of the Belgian army made some progress on the right bank of the Yser on March 24, 1915; while another was taking a German trench on the left bank. The almost continuous artillery fighting was more active in the Nieuport region on March 26, 1915; and farther south a farm north of St. Georges in advance of the allied lines was taken and held.

But the Belgian army was unable to take any decisive action against the left wing of the German army during the spring and summer of 1915, both on account of the wetness of the land and the activity of the German artillery. Yet it harassed the Germans by so much activity that the Teutons continued to add to their heavy howitzers and large caliber naval guns. Nevertheless the Belgian strategy gained for its little army many advantages of tactical importance. It seemed to be a part of the plan of the Belgian generals to give their new troops, which were filling up the previously thinned ranks, a training under heavy bombardments without risking the lives or liberty of many of their men. They held the old cobbled roads which remained about the waters, using an almost innumerable number of trenches for that purpose.

The Germans sought to obviate this check to their activities by approaching on rafts on which were machine guns, from which attempts were made to pour an enfilading fire on the trenches. Thereupon the Belgian sharpshooters became especially active and exterminated the machine-gun crews before the Germans could take advantage of the position they had gained by using the rafts.

Finally the waters subsided and the mud which remained dried. As soon as the ground became firm enough to support troops the Belgians became so active that the Germans desired more men, but their soldiers were also needed in many other sections of the western front, and for the time being none could be sent against the Belgians. Hence King Albert's troops continued to make progress.

The Germans made an attack between Nieuport and the sea on May 9, 1915, but were repulsed. To the north of Dixmude the Belgians were violently attacked during the night of May 10, 1915, by three German battalions. They were repulsed and suffered large losses.

On the night of May 16, 1915, the Germans threatened with complete envelopment by the successful attacks of preceding days, evacuated the positions which they had occupied to the west of the Yser Canal, and they gained nothing on the eastern bank. The Germans left about two thousand dead and many rifles when they were forced from the western bank. On the following night, May 17, 1915, the positions on the eastern bank were consolidated, and a German counterattack, which was preceded by a bombardment, was repulsed. The Germans gained a footing in the trenches to the east of the Yser Canal in an attack made on the night of May 20, 1915, but they were driven out and lost some of the ground they had held before making the attack.

The Germans made a violent attack on the edge of the Belgian front at Nieuport in order to prevent the Belgians from aiding in the defense of Ypres, but the Belgians defended Nieuport with one army corps and made an advance on Dixmude with another corps, with the result that they assisted the Zouaves in taking the German bridgeheads on the western bank of the canal above Ypres. These bridgeheads were protected by forts manned by machine guns, and the approaches were commanded by heavy artillery fire, but defense was destroyed in the middle of May, 1915.

The Germans concentrated their efforts against the Belgians at one point between Ypres and Dixmude. They bombarded the trenches, using bombs filled with poisonous gas. When they believed the Belgians had been overcome by the gas the German infantry charged. The Belgians, however, had kept their faces close to the ground, thus escaping most of the fumes from the shells. When the Germans arrived within easy range they were greeted with machine-gun fire to such an extent that the companies leading the charge were slain.

A battalion of Belgian troops on June 14, 1915, gained the east bank of the Yser south of the Dixmude railroad bridge, and established themselves there. The Belgians also destroyed a German blockhouse in the vicinity of the Château of Dixmude. The Belgian troops, south of St. Georges, captured a German trench, all the defenders of which were killed or made prisoners on June 22, 1915.

After the canal line was won, and the Belgians were in position to hold it, they could make little headway eastward. Their advance was checked by a series of batteries which were concealed in the Forest of Houthulst. These batteries, containing many guns of large caliber, continued to shell the Belgian trenches to such an extent that it was necessary for their inhabitants to keep close to the bomb-proof chambers with which the trenches were liberally supplied. But the Belgians kept so many of the German troops occupied that, in this way, they gave great aid to their allies, and enabled the French and British to regain much of the territory which was lost in the first attack which the Germans made with poisonous gas. The remainder of the summer was occupied with intermittent artillery duels and minor engagements between the opposing trench lines. In the meantime the Belgian army was adding to the number of its troops and gathering munitions for an aggressive movement.

PART V—NAVAL OPERATIONS

CHAPTER XXVII

THE WAR ZONE

THE war on the seas, with the long-expected battle between the fleets of the great nations, developed during the second six months of the war into a strange series of adventures. The fleets of the British and the Germans stood like huge phantoms—the first enshrouded in mystery somewhere in the Irish and North Seas; the second held in leash behind the Kiel Canal, awaiting the opportune moment to make its escape.

These tense, waiting days were broken by sensational and spectacular incidents—not so much through the sea fights of great modern warships as through the adventures of the raiders on the seven seas, the exploits of the submarines, and the daring attempt of the allied fleets to batter down the mighty forts in the Dardanelles and bombard their way toward Constantinople—the coveted stronghold of the Ottoman Empire. The several phases of these naval operations are described in special chapters in this volume, therefore we will now confine ourselves to the general naval developments.

In the spring of 1915 the threat made by Admiral von Tirpitz that Germany would carry on war against British and allied shipping by sinking their vessels with submarines, was made effective. The submersible craft began to appear on all the coasts of the British Isles. It infested the Irish Sea to such an extent that shipping between England and Ireland was seriously menaced.

A particularly daring raid took place on the night of February 1, 1915, when a number of submarines tried to scuttle ships lying at Dover. The attack failed, but drew fire from the guns of the fort here.*

On the 5th of February, 1915, the German Naval Staff announced that beginning February 18, 1915, the waters around Great Britain would be considered a "war zone." This was in retaliation for the blockade maintained against Germany by the British navy. The proclamation read as follows:

"The waters round Great Britain and Ireland, including the whole of the English Channel, are herewith proclaimed a war region.

"On and after February 18, 1915, every enemy merchant vessel found in this war region will be destroyed without its always being possible to warn the crew or passengers of the dangers threatening.

"Neutral ships will also incur danger in the war region, where, in view of the misuse of the neutral flags ordered by the British Government and incidents inevitable in sea warfare, attacks intended for hostile ships may affect neutral ships also.

"The sea passage to the north of the Shetland Islands and the eastern region of the North Sea in a zone of at least thirty miles along the Netherlands coast is not menaced by any danger.

"(Signed) Berlin, February 4, 1915, Chief of Naval Staff,
VON POHL."

The effect of this proclamation, which was in truth nothing more than official sanction for the work that the submarines had been doing for some weeks, and which they continued to do, was to bring Germany into diplomatic controversy with neutral countries, particularly the United States; such controversy is taken up in a different chapter of this history. In connection with the naval history of the Great War it suffices to say that such a proclamation constituted a precedent in naval history. The submarine had heretofore been an untried form of war craft. The rule had formerly been that a merchantman stopped by an enemy's warship was subject to search and seizure, and, if it offered no resistance, was taken to one of the enemy's ports

* See chapter on "Exploits of the Submarines."

THE GERMAN SUBMARINE WAR ZONE

as a prize. If it offered resistance it might be summarily sunk. But it was impossible for submarines to take ships into port on account of the patrols of allied warships; and the limited quarters of submarines made it impossible to take aboard them the crews of ships which they sank.

Reference made to the use of neutral flags quoted in the German proclamation had been induced by the fact that certain of the British merchant ships, after Germany had begun to send them to the bottom whenever one of its submarines caught up with them had gone through the waters where the submarines operated flying the flag of the United States and other neutral powers in order to deceive the commanders of the submarines. The latter had little time to do more than take a brief observation of merchantmen which they sank, and one of the first things they sought was the nationality of the flag that the intended victims carried; unless they could be sure of the identity of a ship through familiarity with the lines of her hull, they ran the risk, in attacking a ship flying a neutral flag, of sinking a vessel belonging to a neutral power.

Here was another matter that opened up diplomatic exchanges between Germany and the United States, and between the United States and England. It suffices here to give not only the controversy or the points involved, but the record of events. The first use of the flag of a neutral country by a ship belonging to one of the belligerents in the Great War occurred on January 31, 1915, when the Cunard liner *Orduna* carried the American flag at her forepeak in journeying from Liverpool to Queenstown. She again did so on February 1, 1915, when she left the latter port for New York. And another notable instance was on February 11, 1915, when the *Lusitania,* another Cunard liner, arrived at Liverpool flying the American flag in obedience to orders issued by the British admiralty. It was only the prominence of these vessels which gave them notoriety in this regard; the same practice was indulged in by many smaller ships.

"What will happen after the 18th?" was the one important question asked during February, 1915, by the public of the neutral as well as belligerent countries.

February 18, 1915, arrived and saw Von Pohl's proclamation go into effect, and from that date onward the toll of ships sunk, both of neutral and belligerent countries, grew longer daily.

But before the German submarines could begin the new campaign, those of the British navy became active, and it was admitted in Berlin on February 15, 1915, that British submarines had made their way into the Baltic, through the sound between Sweden and Denmark, where they attacked the German cruiser *Gazelle* unsuccessfully.

Nor was the British navy inactive in other ways, though it had been greatly discredited by the fact that the German submarines were playing havoc with British shipping right at England's door. A fleet of two battleships and several cruisers drew up off Westende and bombarded the German trenches on the 4th of February, 1915.

Only one day after the war-zone proclamation went into effect the Allies brought out their trump card for the spring of 1915.

CHAPTER XXVIII

ATTACK ON THE DARDANELLES

BY the middle of February, 1915, the Allies completed the arrangement for the naval attack on the Dardanelles. The military part of the campaign in these regions is treated in the chapter on the "Campaign in the Dardanelles"; hence we must confine ourselves at present to the general naval affairs. The naval operations began with the concentration in the adjacent waters of a powerful fleet consisting of both French and British ships.

The ships engaged were the *Queen Elizabeth,* with her main battery of 15-inch guns, the *Inflexible,* veteran of the fight off the Falkland Islands, the *Agamemnon, Cornwallis, Triumph,* and *Vengeance.* In addition to these British ships there were the French battleships *Suffren, Gaulois,* and *Bouvet,* and a fleet of destroyers. The senior British officer was Vice Admiral Sackville Carden, and the French commander was Admiral Guepratte. A new "mother ship" for a squadron of seaplanes was also part of the naval force; this was the ship *Ark Royal.* At eight in the morning on February 19, 1915, this powerful fleet started "The Great Attempt."

After bombarding the Turkish forts till three in the afternoon without receiving a single reply from the guns of the forts, the warships ceased firing and went in closer to the shore, the allied commanders believing that the forts had not replied because they all had been put out of action. The fallacy of this belief was discovered when, at the shortened range, shells began to fall about the ships. None was hit; when dusk came on they retired.

Stormy weather prevented further action on the part of the warships for almost a week, but on February 25, 1915, they resumed their bombardment. The *Irresistible* and *Albion* had by then joined the other British ships, and the *Charlemagne* had augmented the French force.

At ten o'clock in the morning of February 25, 1915, the *Queen Elizabeth, Gaulois, Irresistible,* and *Agamemnon* began to fire on the forts Sedd-el-Bahr, Orkanieh, Kum Kale, and Cape Hellas —the outer forts—at long range, and drew replies from the Turkish guns. It was out of all compliance with naval tradition for warships to stand and engage land fortifications, for lessons learned by naval authorities from the Spanish-American and Russo-Japanese wars had established precedents which prohibited it. But here the larger warships were carrying heavier guns than those in the forts. Whereas the *Queen Elizabeth* carried 15-inch guns, the largest of the Turkish guns measured only 10.2 inches.

At 11.30 o'clock in the morning of February 25, 1915, the *Agamemnon* was hit with a shell which had traveled six miles, but it did not damage her beyond repair. Meanwhile the *Queen Elizabeth* had silenced Cape Hellas, firing from a distance far beyond the range of the forts' guns. And then, just before noon, and after the larger ship had silenced the main battery at Cape

Hellas, the ships *Vengeance* and *Cornwallis* dashed in at shorter range and destroyed the minor batteries there. The *Suffren* and *Charlemagne* also took part in this phase of the engagement, and later, in the afternoon, the *Triumph* and *Albion* concentrated fire on Sedd-el-Bahr, silencing its last guns by five o'clock in the evening.

The larger ships needed the respite during the night of February 25, 1915, while trawlers, which had been brought down from the North Sea for the purpose, began to sweep the entrance to the forts for mines, and cleared enough of them out by the morning of the 26th to enable the *Majestic*—which had by then joined the fleet—and the *Albion* and *Vengeance* to steam in between the flanking shores and fire at the forts on the Asiatic side. It was known by the allied commanders that they might expect return fire from Fort Dardanos, but this they did not fear, for they knew that its heaviest gun measured but 5.9 inches. But they had a surprise when concealed batteries near by, the presence of which had not been suspected, suddenly began to fire. Believing now that the Turks were abandoning the forts at the entrance, the allied ships covered the landing of parties of marines.

Long-range firing had by the end of February 26, 1915, enabled the allied fleets to silence the outer forts and to clear their way to the straits. They now had to take up the task of destroying the real defenses of the Dardanelles—the forts at the Narrows, and this was a harder task, for long-range firing was no longer possible. The guns of the forts and those of the ships would be meeting on a more equal basis.

But this was not to be essayed at once, for more rough weather kept the fleets from using their guns effectively, their trawlers continued to sweep the waters for mines near the Narrows. By March 3, 1915, however, the commanders were ready to resume operations. The *Lord Nelson* and the *Ocean* had by then also arrived on the scene, and in the subsequent operations were hit a number of times by the Turkish guns; and the *Canopus, Swiftsure, Prince George,* and *Sapphire,* though they did not report being hit, were also known to have been present.

The new "eyes" of the fleets located new and concealed batteries placed in position by the Turks, and at two o'clock in the afternoon of February 3, 1915, they ascended to direct the fire of the ships' guns by signal. The bombardment was kept up till darkness fell, but it was resumed on the next day.

On March 4, 1915, the *Queen Elizabeth,* so great was the range of her guns, was able to reach the forts Hamadieh I, Tabia, and Hamadieh II, firing across the Gallipoli Peninsula. Three times she was hit by shells from field pieces lying between her and her target, but no great damage was done to her. While her guns roared out, the *Suffren, Albion, Prince George, Vengeance,* and *Majestic* went inside the straits and had attacked the forts at Soundere, Mount Dardanos, and Rumili Medjidieh Tabia, and were fired upon by Turkish guns from the forts and from concealed batteries which struck these ships, but not a man was killed or a ship put out of action.

March 7, 1915, the *Agamemnon* and *Lord Nelson* attacked the forts at the Narrows, their bombardment being covered by the four French battleships. All of the ships were struck, but again none of them was put out of action. After heavy shelling forts Rumili Medjidieh Tabia and Hamadieh I were silenced.

While these operations were going on, another British fleet, consisting of battleships and cruisers, on March 5, 1915, began an attack on Smyrna. For two hours, and in fine, clear weather, Fort Yeni Kale was damaged after being subjected to heavy bombardment, but it was not silenced when dusk interrupted the attack.

Little was accomplished for some days afterward. Some of the forts which had been reported silenced were getting ready to resume firing; their silence had been due to the fact that the defenders often had to leave their guns while the gases generated by the firing cleared off, and they had also thought it wiser to conserve ammunition rather than fire ineffective shots. Sedd-el-Bahr and Kum Kale were able to resume firing in a few days, for though the shells of the allied fleets had damaged the structural parts of these defenses, they had not landed troops out to occupy them, with the result that the Turks were enabled to intrench near the ruins and there reset their guns.

On the morning of March 15, 1915, the small British cruiser *Amethyst* made a dash into the Narrows, which when reported led the British and French public to believe that the defense had been forced, but, as a matter of fact, this exploit was a bit of stratagem, being only designed to draw the fire of concealed batteries.

On March 18, 1915, "The Great Effort" was made to force the defenses with naval operations, all previous work having been preliminary. The battleships *Agamemnon, Prince George, Queen Elizabeth, Lord Nelson, Triumph,* and *Inflexible* steamed right up to the Narrows. Four of them bombarded Chanak and a battery which lay opposite it, and the forts at Saghandere, Kephez Point, and Dardanos were kept busy by the *Triumph* and the *Prince George.* After the fleet had been at it for an hour and a half they received the support of the four French ships which steamed in close and attacked the forts at a shorter range. When the forts ceased firing the six battleships *Ocean, Swiftsure, Majestic, Albion, Irresistible,* and *Vengeance* came in and tried to carry the attack further. While the French squadron maneuvered to allow freedom of action for this newer British squadron the Turkish guns resumed fire. Then came the first of a series of disasters. Three shells struck the *Bouvet,* and she soon began to keel over. When the underwater part of her hull came into view it was seen that she had been hit underneath, probably by one of the mines which the Turks had floated toward the crowded ships. She sank almost immediately, carrying the greater part of her crew down with her. Only two hours later another mine did damage to the *Irresistible,* and she left the line, listing heavily. While she floated and while she was under heavy fire from Turkish guns a destroyer took off her crew. She sank just before six o'clock. Not fifteen minutes later the *Ocean* became the third victim of a floating mine, and she also went to the bottom. Destroyers rescued many of her crew from the water. The guns from the forts were also able to do damage; the *Gaulois* had been hit again and again, with the result that she had a hole in her hull and her upper works were damaged badly. Fire had broken out on the *Inflexible,* and a number of her officers and crew had been either killed or wounded. The day ended with the forts still able to return a lively fire to all attacks, and "The Great Attempt" on the part of the allied fleets had failed.

On the other end of the passage there had also been some naval operations, when, on March 28, 1915, the Black Sea Fleet of the Russian navy had bombarded the forts on the Bosphorous. Smyrna was again attacked on April 6, 1915. The operations of allied submarines were the next phases of the attack on the Dardanelles to be reported. The *E-5* grounded near Kephez Point on April 17, 1915, but before she could be captured by the Turks picket boats from the allied fleet rescued her crew and then destroyed her. It was just two months now since the naval operations had begun at the Dardanelles; it was seen then that all attempts to take them by naval operations alone must fail as did the attack of March 18, 1915.

CHAPTER XXIX

GERMAN RAIDERS AND SUBMARINES

THE next important event in the naval history of the war occurred in far-distant waters. On March 10, 1915, there ended the wonderful career of the German auxiliary cruiser *Prinz Eitel Friedrich,* Captain Thierichens, which on that date put in at the American port of Newport News, Va., for repairs, after making the harbor in spite of the watch kept on it by British cruisers. She brought with her more than 500 persons, 200 of them being her own crew, and the remainder being passengers and crews of French, British, Russian, and American ships that had been her victims in her roving over 30,000 miles of the Atlantic and Pacific oceans since leaving Tsing-tau seven months before.

She had sent eight merchant ships to the bottom, one of them being the *William P. Frye,* an American vessel carrying wheat, three British ships, three flying the French flag, and one Russian ship. Their total tonnage came to 18,245. The fact that she had sunk an American ship on the high seas opened up still another diplomatic controversy between Germany and the United States, which cannot be treated here.

When she left Tsing-tau she took as her crew the men from the German gunboats *Tiger* and *Luchs,* and had their four 4.1-inch and some of their one-pounder guns as her armament. Soon afterward she stopped the British ship *Schargost* and expected to refill her coal bunkers from those of the merchantman, but in this she was disappointed, for those of the latter were almost empty. Her next victim was a French sailing vessel, *Jean,* and on board this was found a pleasant surprise for the German raider, for the vessel was laden with coal. Captain Thierichens had her towed 1,500 miles, to Easter Island, where the coal was transferred to the bunkers of the *Eitel Friedrich,* and the crews of her first three victims were put ashore. These marooned men were burdens to the white inhabitants of the island, for there was not too much food for the extra forty-eight mouths. Finally, on February 26, 1915, the Swedish ship *Nordic* saw them signaling from the island and took them off, landing them at Panama on the day after the *Prinz Eitel Friedrich* entered Newport News.

By the beginning of December, 1914, the German raider was in the South Atlantic, and while there heard wireless messages exchanged between the ships of the British fleet that took part in the battle off the Falkland Islands. The bark *Isabella Browne,* flying the Russian flag, was the next ship overtaken by the *Eitel Friedrich,* on January 26, 1915. She was boarded and all of her provisions and stores were removed to the German ship; after her crew and their personal effects were taken aboard the German ship she was dynamited and sank. On that same morning the French ship *Pierre Loti* was sighted, and while the *Prinz Eitel Friedrich* put an end to her, after first taking off her crew, the captive crew of the *Isabella Browne* was sent below, but was allowed to come on deck to watch the sinking of the French ship. The American ship *William P. Frye* was sunk soon afterward, and her crew, also, was made part of the party on board the raider. After sinking the French bark *Jacobsen* the *Prinz Eitel Friedrich* stopped the *Thalasia* on February 8, 1915, and let her go on her way, but on February 18 the British ships *Cindracoe* and *Mary Ada Scott* were sunk. On the 19th the French steamer *Floride* was overtaken off the coast of Brazil; all persons aboard her were transferred to the German ship and most of her provisions were also taken aboard the latter; the *Floride*, the largest steamer destroyed by the German ship, was set afire and left to burn. On February 20, 1915, the British ship *Willerby* was overtaken and nearly sank the *Prinz Eitel Friedrich* before being boarded. As the German ship passed across the stern of the other at a short distance the British captain, knowing that the end of his own ship was near, decided to take his captor down with him. He tried to ram the German ship with the stern of his ship, but failed in the attempt.

On the evening of February 20, 1915, the wireless operator of the *Prinz Eitel Friedrich* heard British cruisers "talking" with each other, one of them being the *Berwick*. The German captain now saw that his long raiding cruise was up, for though he could replenish his stores and bunkers from captured ships he could not make the many repairs which his vessel needed. To put them off at a neutral port or to let them go in one of the ships he captured would mean that his position would be reported to British ships within a week. He therefore decided to end his raiding and put in at Newport News. His vessel was interned in the American port.

We may now return to the story of the blockade against Germany and the retaliation she sought. The Allies were now stopping as much shipping on its way to Germany as they dared without bringing on trouble with neutral powers. The *Dacia*, formerly a German merchantman, was taken over, after the outbreak of the war, by an American citizen and sailed from New Orleans for Rotterdam with a cargo of cotton on February 12, 1915. She was stopped by a French warship and taken to a

French port February 27, 1915, and there held till the matter of the validity of her transfer of registry could be settled.

On the other hand the German submarine exploits continued and found among their victims a British warship, along with the many merchantmen. On March 11, 1915, the British auxiliary cruiser *Bayano,* while on patrol duty became the victim of a German torpedo off the Scotch coast. She went down almost immediately, carrying with her the greater part of her crew.

But not always were the submarines immune. Only the day before the British destroyer *Ariel* rammed the German submarine *U-12* and sent her to the bottom, after rescuing her crew. She was of an older type, built in 1911, of submarine, and had played an active part in the raiding in British waters. On February 21, 1915, she had sunk the Irish coasting steamer *Downshire* in the Irish Sea, and her destruction was particularly welcome in British shipping circles.

Once more an incident in the naval warfare of the Great War was to involve diplomatic exchanges between the belligerents and the United States. The African liner *Falaba,* a British ship on her way from Liverpool to Lisbon, was torpedoed in St. George's Channel on the afternoon of March 28, 1915. She had as one of her passengers an American, L. C. Thrasher, who lost his life when the ship sank.

The naval warfare was proceeding like a game of checkers. When on March 14, 1915, there came the end of still another of the German raiding cruisers, the *Dresden.* She was a cruiser built in 1907 and having a displacement of 3,544 tons. Her speed was good—24.5 knots—and her armament of ten 4.1-inch guns and eight 5-pounder guns made her quite a match for enemy warships of her class and superior as for merchantmen. She was a sister ship to that other famous raider the *Emden.* In 1909 she had taken her place among the other foreign warships in the line in the Hudson River, participating in the Hudson-Fulton Celebration. In the spring of 1914 she was in the neighborhood of Central America and rescued a number of foreign refugees who fled from Mexico, and also took Senor Huerta from Puerto Mexico.

She was still in that neighborhood when the war broke out, and was immediately sought after by British and French warships which were near by. She managed to get away from these pursuers and sank the British steamers *Hyades* and *Holmwood* off the Brazilian coast during the latter part of August, 1914. She then went south, rounded the Horn and joined the other ships under command of Admiral Von Spee, taking part in the battle off Coronel, on November 1, 1914.

She remained with that squadron and took part in a second battle—that off the Falkland Islands—on December 8, 1914. When Admiral von Spee saw that he had little chance of winning the battle he gave orders that the lighter ships should leave the line and seek safety in flight. The *Dresden* was one of the ships which escaped, to the chagrin of the British Admiral. She then turned "raider."

Five days later, on December 13, 1914, she had appeared off Punta Arenas, in the Straits of Magellan, stopped at that port long enough to take on some provisions and put to sea again, with British and Japanese warships on her trail. She was too closely hunted to be able to sink many ships, but during the week of March 12, 1915, she sank the British steamer *Conway Castle,* off the coast of Chile, and took coal and provisions from the two German steamers *Alda* and *Sierra Cordoba.*

On March 14, 1915, she was sighted by the British cruisers *Glasgow, Kent* and *Orama* near Juan Fernandez Island. What then ensued is in doubt, owing to conflicting reports made by the senior British officer and by the captain of the German cruiser. The latter insisted that, seeing his ship was at the end of her career, he ordered his men to leave her and then blew her up. The former declared that shots were exchanged, that she was set afire and was otherwise badly damaged by the British fire. At any rate, she was destroyed, and all of her men were saved. It was estimated that the amount of damage she inflicted on allied trade amounted to $1,250,000.

Thus at the end of March, 1915, only the *Karlsruhe* and *Kronprinz Wilhelm,* of the eleven German warships that were detached from the main German fleet in the North Sea at the outbreak of the war, and of the few ships which slipped out of various ports as converted auxiliary cruisers, were still at large on the high seas.

Naval activity in the northern waters of Europe did not abate. The British admiralty on March 25, 1915, had announced that the German submarine *U-29*, one of the most improved craft of the type in use, had been sunk. This loss was admitted by the German admiralty on April 7, 1915. It was a serious loss to the German navy, for its commander was Otto von Weddigen, he who, in the *U-9*, had sent the *Cressy*, *Aboukir* and *Hogue* to the bottom in September, 1914.

The naval warfare at the Dardanelles proceeded in the same desultory fashion. A Turkish torpedo boat caught up with the British transport *Manitou*, and opened fire on her, killing some twenty of the soldiers on board.

In answer to calls for help from the *Manitou* the British cruiser *Minerva* and some torpedo boats went to the scene and attacked the Turkish craft on April 7, 1915, driving it ashore off Chios and destroyed it as it lay beached. But during April, 1915, it seemed as though there would be another pitched fight between British and German warships in the North Sea. On April 23, 1915, the German admiralty announced that "the German High Sea Fleet has recently cruised repeatedly in the North Sea, advancing into English waters without meeting the sea forces of Great Britain." The British admiralty had undoubtedly been aware of this activity on the part of their enemy, but for reasons of their own did not choose to send British ships to meet the German fleet, and the expected battle did not take place.

France, on April 26, 1915, was to sustain a severe loss to her navy; she had up to this time not lost as many ships as her ally, England, or her enemy, Germany, but her navy was so much smaller than either of them that the sinking of the *Leon Gambetta* on that date was a matter of weight. The *Gambetta* was an armored cruiser, built in 1904, and carrying four 7.6-inch guns, sixteen 6.4-inch guns and a number of smaller caliber. She had a speed of twenty-three knots. While doing patrol duty in the Strait of Otranto she was made the victim of the Austrian submarine *U-5,* and sank, carrying with her 552 men.

On April 28, 1915, there occurred another incident which gave rise to diplomatic exchanges between Germany and the United States. On that date a German seaplane attacked the American merchantman in broad daylight in the North Sea, but fortunately for its crew the ship was not sent to the bottom. The first American ship to be struck by a torpedo in the war zone established by the German admiralty's proclamation of February 5, 1915, was the *Gulflight.* This tank steamer was hit by a torpedo fired by a German submarine off the Scilly Islands, on the 1st of May, 1915.

But of more importance, because of the number of American lives lost, the standing of the matter in international law and the prominence of the vessel, was the sinking of the Cunard liner *Lusitania,* on May 7, 1915. This is fully described in the chapter on submarines, and in the diplomatic developments discussed in the chapter on the United States and the War. The *Lusitania* had left New York for Liverpool on the 1st of May, 1915. She was one of the fastest ships plying between the Eastern and Western Hemispheres. Larger than any warship afloat at the time, she was able to make the trip from Liverpool to New York in a little under five days. On her last crossing she carried 2,160 persons, including passengers and crew, many of the former being Americans, some of them of great prominence. While off Old Head of Kinsale, on the southeastern end of Ireland, at about half past two, on the afternoon of May 7, 1915, with a calm sea and no wind, she was hit by one or more torpedoes from a German submarine without warning.

Those on board immediately went to the life boats, but it was only twenty minutes after she had first been hit that she sank, and not enough of the small craft could be gotten over her side in that time to rescue all those on board. Out of the 2,160 souls aboard at least 1,398 were lost. Of these 107 were American citizens. Small boats in the neighborhood of the disaster hurried to the scene and rescued those whom they could reach in the water and brought them to Queenstown. The sacks of mail which the liner carried and which went down with her were the first American mail sacks ever lost at sea as a result of war. The controversies which this disaster gave rise to between England, Germany and the United States are given elsewhere.

Against British warships the submarine warfare was also effective during the month of May, 1915. On the 1st day of that month the old British destroyer *Recruit* was sent to the bottom of the North Sea by a German submarine, but the two German destroyers which had accompanied the submarine that did this were pursued immediately by British destroyers and were sunk. On the same day that the *Lusitania* went down a German mine ended the career of the British destroyer *Maori*.

CHAPTER XXX

ITALIAN PARTICIPATION—OPERATIONS IN MANY WATERS

THE month of May, 1915, saw new characters enter the theatres of naval warfare. Italy had now entered the war and brought to the naval strength of the Allies a minor naval unit.

At the time Italy entered the war she possessed six dreadnoughts, the *Caio Duilio* and the *Andrea Doria,* completed in 1915, the *Conte di Cavour, Giulio Cesare,* and *Leonardo da Vinci,* completed in 1914, and the *Dante Alighieri,* completed in 1912. Each of these dreadnoughts had a speed of 23 knots. The *Dante Alighieri* displaced 19,400 tons and had a main battery of twelve 12-inch guns, and a complement of 987 men. Each of the other five had thirteen 12-inch guns and a complement of 1,000 men. The displacement of vessels of the 1914 type was 22,340 tons; that of the 1915 type 23,025 tons. There were many lesser craft flying the Italian flag, but these larger ships were the most important additions to the naval forces of the Allies in southern waters.

The chief operations of the Italian navy were directed against Austria. On May 28, 1915, the Italian admiralty announced the damage inflicted on Austrian maritime strength up to that date. On May 24, 1915, the Austrian torpedo boat *S-20* approached the canal at Porto Corsini, but drew a very heavy fire from concealed and unsuspected batteries which forced her to leave immediately. The Austrian torpedo boat destroyer *Scharfschütze,* the scout ship *Novara* and the destroyer *Ozepel,* all of the Austrian navy, came to the assistance of the *S-20* and also received salvos from the Italian land batteries. But on the same day the Italian destroyer *Turbine,* while scouting gave chase to an Austrian destroyer and the Austrian cruiser *Helgoland.* The strength of these Austrian ships was too much for the *Turbine* and she put on speed with the intention of escaping from their fire, but she was severely damaged by Austrian shells, and not having enough ammunition aboard to give a good account of herself, she was scuttled by her own crew.

It is now necessary to take up again the story of the German raiding ships at large on the high seas. As has been told above, after the *Prinz Eitel Friedrich* ended her career by putting in at Newport News the only German ships of the kind remaining at large were the *Karlsruhe* and *Kronprinz Wilhelm.* But on the 1st of April, 1915, the *Macedonia,* a converted liner which since November, 1914, had been interned at Las Palmas, Canary Islands, succeeded in slipping out of the harbor laden with provisions and supplies for use of warships and made her way to South American waters in spite of the fact that she had run through lines patrolled by British cruisers.

The *Kronprinz Wilhelm's* career as a raider ended on April 11, 1915, when, like the *Prinz Eitel Friedrich,* she succeeded in getting past the British cruisers and slipped into Newport News, Virginia. How this former Hamburg-American liner had slipped out of the harbor of New York on the night of August 3, 1914, with her bunkers and even her cabins filled with coal and provisions, with all lights out and with canvas covering her port holes has already been told. From that date until she again put in at an American port she captured numerous merchant ships, taking 960 prisoners and doing damage amounting to more than $7,000,000. She kept herself provisioned from her captives, and it was only the poor condition of her plates and boilers that made her captain give up raiding when he did. Her movements had been mysterious during all the time she was at large. She was known to have reprovisioned the cruiser *Dresden* and to have taken an almost stationary position in the South Atlantic in order to act as a "wireless station" for the squadron of Admiral von Spee. But when the latter was defeated off the Falkland Islands, she resumed operations as a raider of commerce. When she came into Newport News more than 60 per cent of her crew were suffering from what was thought to be beri-beri; she had but twenty-one tons of coal in her bunkers and almost no ammunition.

The total damage inflicted on the commerce of the Allies by the *Emden, Karlsruhe, Kronprinz Wilhelm, Prinz Eitel Friedrich, Königsberg, Dresden* and *Leipzig* amounted, by the end of May, 1915, to $35,000,000. Sixty-seven vessels had been captured and sunk by them.

In the Dardanelles the naval operations were resumed, to some extent, during the month of May, 1915. For a number of weeks after the allied fleet had made the great attempt to force the Dardanelles on March 19, 1915, their commanders attempted no maneuvers with the larger ships, but the submarines were given work to do. On April 27, 1915, the British submarine *E-14,* under command of Lieutenant Commander Boyle, dived and went under the Turkish mine fields, reaching the waters of the Sea of Marmora. In spite of the fact that Turkish destroyers knew of its presence and hourly watched for it in the hope of sinking it, this submarine was able to operate brilliantly for some days, sinking two Turkish gunboats and a laden transport. Similar exploits were performed by Lieutenant Commander Nasmith with the British submarine *E-11,* which even damaged wharves at the Turkish capital.

But when the military operations were getting under way during May, 1915, the larger ships of the fleets were again used.

The Germans realizing that these great ships, moving as they did slowly and deliberately while they fired on the land forts, would be good targets for torpedoes, sent some of their newest submarines from the bases in the North Sea, down along the coasts of France and Spain, through the passage at Gibraltar and to the Dardanelles. Destroyers accompanying the allied fleets kept diligent watch for attacks from them. The *Goeben,* one of the German battle cruisers that had escaped British and French fleets in the Mediterranean during the first weeks of the war, and which was now a part of the Turkish navy, was brought to the scene and aided the Turkish forts in their bombardment of the hostile warships.

On May 12, 1915, the British battleship *Goliath,* of old design and displacing some 12,000 tons, was sunk by a torpedo. This ship had been protecting a part of the French fleet from flank attack inside the straits, and under the cover of darkness had been approached by a Turkish destroyer which fired the fatal torpedo. It sank almost immediately.

The submarines of the German navy which had made the long journey to participate in the action near the Dardanelles got in their first work on May 26, 1915, when a torpedo fired by one of them struck the British battleship *Triumph* and sent her to the bottom. Of interest to naval authorities all over the world was the fact that this ship at the time she was struck had out torpedo nets which were supposed to be torpedo-proof; but the German missile tore through them and reached the hull. A hunt was made for the hostile submarine by the British destroyers, but she was found by the British battleship *Majestic;* but before the British ship could fire a shot at the German submarine, the latter fired a torpedo that caught the battleship near her stern and sank her immediately. Apprehension was now felt for the more formidable ships such as the *Queen Elizabeth* and others of her class which were in those waters; inasmuch as the operations at the Dardanelles assumed more and more a military rather than a naval character, the British admiralty thought it wiser to keep the *Queen Elizabeth* in safer waters; she was consequently called back to England. Only old battleships and cruisers were left to cooperate with the troops operating on the Gallipoli Peninsula.

Naval warfare in southern waters was continued against British warships by the Austrian navy. On June 9, 1915, the Austrian admiralty announced that a cruiser of the type of the *Liverpool* had been struck by a torpedo fired by an Austrian submarine while the former was off San Giovanni di Medua, near the Albanian coast. Reports of the incident issued by the Austrian and British naval authorities differed, the former claiming that the cruiser had sunk, and the latter that it had remained afloat and had been towed to an Adriatic port.

Most unique was an engagement between the Italian submarine *Medusa* and a similar craft flying the Austrian flag on June 17, 1915. This was the first time that two submarines had ever fought with each other. On that day the two submarines, the presence of each unknown to the other, lay submerged, not a great distance apart. The *Medusa,* after some hours, came up, allowing only her periscope to show; seeing no enemy about, her commander brought the rest of her out of the water. She had not emerged many moments before the Austrian vessel also came up for a look around and the commander of the latter espied the Italian submarine through his periscope. He immediately ordered a torpedo fired; it found a mark in the hull of the *Medusa* and she was sent to the bottom. One of her officers and four of her men were rescued by the Austrian submarine and made prisoners.

Italy's navy was not to continue to act as a separate naval unit in the southern naval theatre of war, for on June 18, 1915, the Minister of Marine of France announced that the "Anglo-French forces in the Mediterranean were cooperating with the Italian fleet, whose participation made possible a more effective patrol of the Adriatic. Warships of the Allies were engaged in finding and destroying oil depots from which the enemy's submarines had been replenishing their supplies." This effective patrol did not, however, prevent an Austrian submarine from sinking an Italian torpedo boat on June 27, 1915.

In the Baltic Sea the naval activity had at no time during the first year of the war been great, but during the month of June, 1915, there was a minor naval engagement at the mouth of the Gulf of Riga, during which the Germans lost a transport and the Russians an auxiliary cruiser. In the other northern waters the Germans lost the submarine *U-14*, which was sunk on June 9, 1915. The crew were brought to England as prisoners. Three days later the British admiralty admitted that two torpedo boats, the *No. 10* and the *No. 12* had been lost. The loss of two such small boats did not worry Britain as much as did the loss of many merchant ships in the war zone right through the spring and summer of 1915, and to show that British warships were not immune from submarine attack, in spite of the fact that many of the underwater craft of Germany were meeting with disaster, the British cruiser *Roxburgh* was struck by a torpedo on June 20, 1915, but was able to get away under her own steam. The rest of the month saw small losses to nearly all of the fleets engaged in the war, but none of these were of importance.

The twelfth month of the first year of war was not particularly eventful in so far as naval history was concerned. On July 1, 1915, the Germans maneuvered in the Baltic Sea with a small fleet which accompanied transports bearing men who were to try to land on the northern shores of Russia. The port of Windau was the point at which the German bombardment was directed, but Russian torpedo boats and destroyers fought off the invading German fleet—which must have been small—and succeeded in chasing the German mine-layer *Albatross*, making it necessary for her captain to beach her on the Swedish island of Gothland, where the crew was interned on July 2, 1915. On the same day a German predreadnought battleship, believed to have been the *Pommern*, was sunk at the mouth of Danzig Bay by a torpedo from a British submarine.

In the Adriatic Austria lost a submarine, the *U-11*, through a unique action. The submersible was sighted on July 1, 1915, by a French aeroplane. The aviator dropped two bombs which found their mark on the deck of the submarine and sank her. Austria had, during that month, made an attempt to capture the Austrian island of Pelagosa, which had been occupied by the Italians on July 26, 1915. But July 29, 1915, the fleet of Austrian cruisers and destroyers, which made the attack, was driven off by unnamed units of the Italian navy. But a loss by the latter had been incurred on July 7, 1915, when the armored cruiser *Amalfi,* while scouting in the upper waters of the Adriatic Sea, was sighted and torpedoed by an Austrian submarine. She sank, but most of her men were saved. Another Austrian submarine had the same success on July 17, 1915, when it fired a torpedo at the Italian cruiser *Giuseppe Garibaldi,* and saw her go down fifteen minutes later. Italy endeavored to imitate the actions of Germany when, on July 6, 1915, she proclaimed that the entire Adriatic Sea was a war zone and that the Strait of Otranto was in a state of blockade. All the ports of Dalmatia were closed to every kind of commerce.

Near the coasts of Turkey, toward the end of the first year of war, there was fought the second duel between submarines. This time the vanquished vessel was the French submarine *Mariotte,* which, on July 26, 1915, was sunk by a torpedo from a German submarine in the waters right near the entrance to the Dardanelles. Britain ended the first year of naval warfare by destroying the German cruiser *Königsberg,* which, since the fall of the year before, had been lying up the Rufiji River in German East Africa, after having been chased thence by a British cruiser. It was decided to destroy her in order that she might not get by the sunken hulls that the British had placed at the mouth of the river in order to "bottle her up." Consequently, on the morning of July 4, 1915, after her position had been noted by an aviator, two British river monitors, *Severn* and *Mersey,* aided by a cruiser and minor vessels, began to fire upon the stationary vessel. Their fire was directed by the aviator who had discovered her, but it was at first almost ineffective because she lay so well concealed by the vegetation of the surrounding jungle. She answered their fire and succeeded in damaging the *Mersey,* but after being bombarded for six hours she was set on fire. When the British monitors had finished with her she was a total wreck.

CHAPTER XXXI

STORY OF THE "EMDEN"

WE now return to the exploits of the *Emden*, its mysterious disappearance and the narrative of its heroes—a great epic of the sea.

When in Volume II the story of the sinking of the German cruiser *Emden* was related, mention was made of the escape of the landing party belonging to that ship from Cocos Island. This party consisted of fifty men, headed by Captain Mücke, and from the time their ship went down on November 9, 1914, until they reported for duty again at Damascus, Syria, in May, 1915, they had a series of adventures as thrilling as those encountered by the heroes in any of the Renaissance epics.

Before the *Emden* met the Australian cruiser *Sydney*, and had been sunk by the latter, she had picked up three officers from German steamers which she had met. This proved to be a piece of good fortune, for extra officers were needed to board and command the prize crews of captured vessels. The story of the raiding of the *Emden* has already been given; but here the story of the landing party is given as told by Captain Mücke himself on May 10, 1915, at Damascus:

"On November 9, 1914," he said, "I left the *Emden* in order to destroy the wireless plant on Cocos Island. I had fifty men, four machine guns, about thirty rifles. Just as we were about to destroy the apparatus it reported, 'Careful; *Emden* near.' The work of destruction went smoothly. The wireless operators said: 'Thank God. It's been like being under arrest day and night lately.' Presently the *Emden* signaled us, 'Hurry up.' I packed up, but simultaneously the *Emden's* siren wailed. I hurried to the bridge and saw the flag 'Anna' go up. That meant 'Weigh anchor.' We ran like mad to our boat, but already the *Emden's* pennant was up, the battle flag was raised, and they began to fire from the starboard."

"The enemy," explained Captain Mücke, "was concealed by the island and therefore not to be seen, but I saw the shells strike the water. To follow and catch the *Emden* was out of the question, as she was going at twenty knots, and I only four with my steam pinnace. Therefore I turned back to land, raised the flag, declared German laws of war in force, seized all arms, set up my machine guns on shore in order to guard against a hostile landing. Then I ran out again in order to observe the fight. From the splash of the shells it looked as though the enemy had 15-centimeter guns, bigger, therefore, than the *Emden's*. He fired rapidly but poorly. It was the Australian cruiser *Sydney*."

According to the account of the Englishmen who saw the first part of the engagement from the shore, the *Emden* was cut up rapidly. Her forward smokestack lay across the deck, and was already burning fiercely aft. Behind the mainmast several shells struck home.

"We saw the high flame," continued Captain Mücke, "whether circular fighting or a running fight now followed, I don't know, because I again had to look to my land defenses. Later, I looked on from the roof of a house. Now the *Emden* again stood out to sea about 4,000 to 5,000 yards, still burning. As she again turned toward the enemy, the forward mast was shot away. On the enemy no outward damage was apparent, but columns of smoke showed where shots had struck home. Then the *Emden* took a northerly course, likewise the enemy, and I had to stand there helpless, gritting my teeth and thinking; 'Damn it; the *Emden* is burning and you aren't aboard!' "

Captain Mücke, in relating his thrilling adventure, then explained: "The ships, still fighting, disappeared behind the horizon. I thought that an unlucky outcome for the *Emden* was possible, also a landing by the enemy on the Keeling Island, at least for the purpose of landing the wounded and taking on provisions. As there were other ships in the neighborhood, according to the statements of the Englishmen, I saw myself faced with the certainty of having soon to surrender because of a lack of ammunition. But for no price did I and my men want to get into English

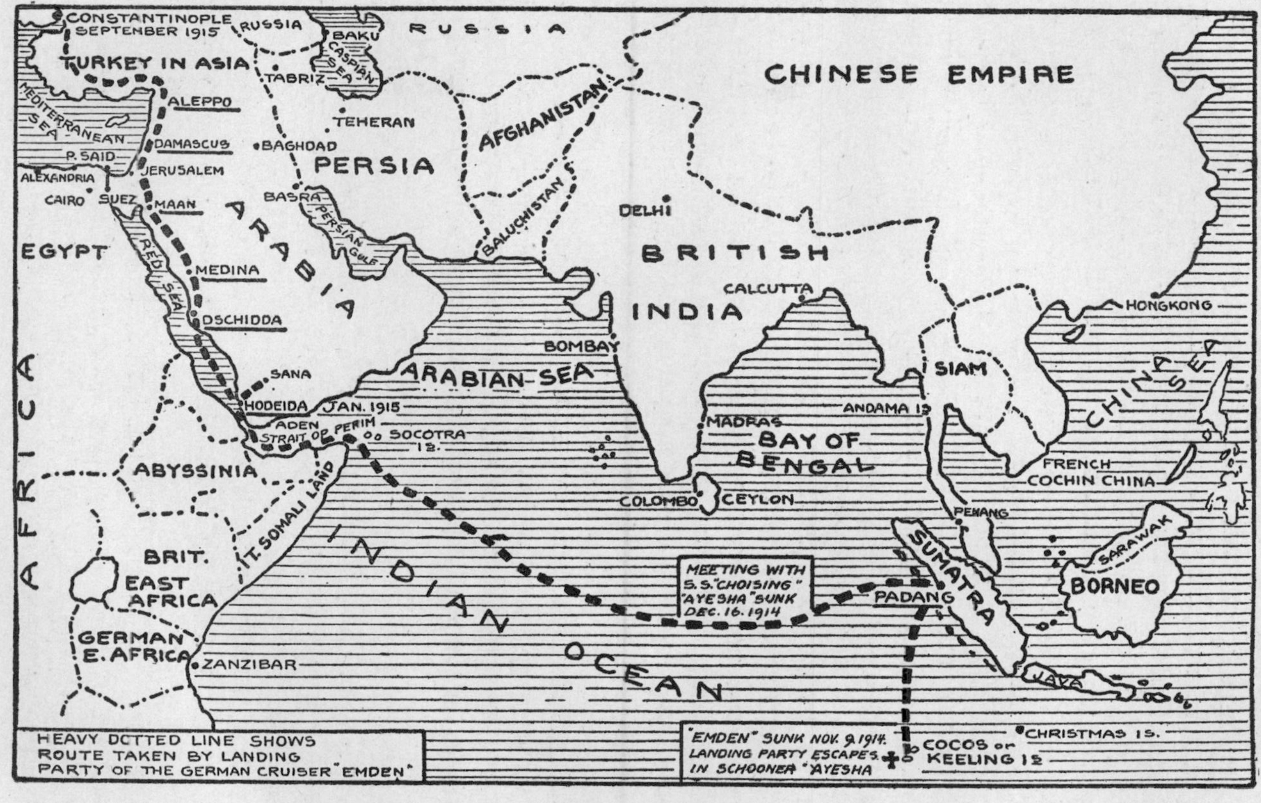

THE CRUISE OF THE "EMDEN" LANDING PARTY

imprisonment. As I was thinking about all this, the masts again appeared on the horizon, the *Emden* steaming easterly, but very much slower. All at once the enemy, at high speed, shot by, apparently quite close to the *Emden*. A high white waterspout showed amidst the black smoke of the enemy. That was a torpedo. I saw how the two opponents withdrew, the distance growing greater and greater between them; how they separated, till they disappeared in the darkness. The fight had lasted ten hours.

"I had made up my mind to leave the island as quickly as possible. The *Emden* was gone; the danger for us growing. In the harbor I had noticed a three-master, the schooner *Ayesha*. Mr. Ross, the owner of the ship and of the island, had warned me that the boat was leaky, but I found it quite a seaworthy tub. Now provisions for eight weeks, and water for four, were quickly taken on board. The Englishmen very kindly showed us the best water and gave us clothing and utensils. They declared this was their thanks for our 'moderation' and 'generosity.' Then they collected the autographs of our men, photographed them and gave three cheers as our last boat put off. It was evening, nearly dark, when we sailed away.

"The *Ayesha* proved to be a really splendid boat. We had only one sextant and two chronometers on board, but a chronometer journal was lacking. Luckily I found an 'Old Indian Ocean Directory' of 1882 on board; its information went back to the year 1780.

"I had said: 'We are going to East Africa.' Therefore I sailed at first westward, then northward. There followed the monsoons, but then also, long periods of dead calm. Only two neutral ports came seriously under consideration; Batavia and Padang. At Keeling I had cautiously asked about Tsing-tau, of which I had naturally thought first, and so quite by chance I learned that it had fallen. Now I decided for Padang, because I knew I would be more apt to meet the *Emden* there, also because there was a German consul there, because my schooner was unknown there and because I hoped to find German ships there, and learn some news. 'It'll take you six to eight days to reach Batavia' a captain had told me at Keeling. Now we needed eighteen days to reach Padang, the weather was so rottenly still."

The suffering of the crew of the *Emden* on their perilous voyage is here told in the captain's words: "We had an excellent cook aboard; he had deserted from the French Foreign Legion. We had to go sparingly with our water; each man received but three glasses daily. When it rained, all possible receptacles were placed on deck and the main sail was spread over the cabin roof to catch the rain.

"At length as we came in the neighborhood of Padang, on the 26th of November, 1915, a ship appeared for the first time and looked for our name. But the name had been painted over, because it was the former English name. As I thought, 'You're rid of the fellow' the ship came up again in the evening, and steamed within a hundred yards of us. I sent all my men below deck, and I promenaded the deck as the solitary skipper. Through Morse signals the stranger gave her identity. She proved to be the Hollandish torpedo boat *Lynx*. I asked by signals, 'Why do you follow me?' No answer. The next morning I found myself in Hollandish waters, so I raised pennant and war flag. Now the *Lynx* came at top speed past us. As it passed I had my men line up on deck, and gave a greeting. The greeting was answered. Then, before the harbor at Padang, I went aboard the *Lynx* in my well and carefully preserved uniform and declared my intentions. The commandant opined that I could run into the harbor, but whether I might come out again was doubtful.

"Three German ships were in the harbor at Padang," continues Captain Mücke. "The harbor authorities demanded the certification for pennant and war flag, also papers to prove that I was the commander of this warship. For that, I answered, I was only responsible to my superior officer. Now they advised me most insistently to allow ourselves to be interned peacefully. They said it wasn't at all pleasant in the neighborhood. We'd fall into the hands of the Japanese or the English. As a matter of fact, we again had great luck. On the day before a Japanese warship had been cruising around here. Naturally, I rejected all the well-meant and kindly advice, and did this in the presence of my lieutenants. I demanded provisions, water, sails, tackle, and clothing. They replied we could take on board everything which we had formerly had on board, but nothing which would mean an increase in our naval strength.

"First thing, I wanted to improve our wardrobe, for I had only one sock, a pair of shoes, and one clean shirt, which had become rather threadbare. My comrades had even less. But the master of the port declined to let us have, not only charts, but also clothing and toothbrushes, on the ground that these would be an increase in armament. Nobody could come aboard, nobody could leave the ship without permission. I requested that the consul be allowed to come aboard. The consul, Herr Schild, as also did the brothers Bäumer, gave us assistance in the friendliest fashion. From the German steamers boats could come alongside and talk with us. Finally, we were allowed to have German papers. They were, to be sure, from August only. From then until March, 1915, we saw no papers.

"Hardly had we been towed out of the harbor again after twenty-four hours, on the evening of the 28th of November, 1914, when a searchlight flashed before us. I thought, 'Better interned than prisoner.' I put out all lights and withdrew to the shelter of the island. But they were Hollanders and didn't do anything to us. Then for two weeks more we drifted around, lying still for days. The weather was alternately still, rainy, and blowy. At length a ship, a freighter, came in sight. It saw us and made a big curve around us. I made everything hastily 'clear for battle.' Then one of our officers recognized her for the *Choising*. She showed the German flag. I sent up light rockets, although it was broad day, and went with all sails set, that were still setable, toward her. The *Choising* was a coaster from Hongkong to Siam. She was at Singapore when the war broke out, then went to Batavia, was chartered, loaded with coal for the enemy, and had put into Padang in need, because the coal in the hold had caught fire. There we had met her.

"Great was our joy now. I had all my men come on deck and line up for review. The fellows hadn't a rag on. Thus, in nature's garb, we gave three cheers for the German flag on the *Choising*.

The men of the *Choising* told us afterward 'We couldn't make out what that meant, those stark-naked fellows all cheering.' The sea was too high, and we had to wait two days before we could board the *Choising* on December 16, 1914. We took very little with us; the schooner was taken in tow. In the afternoon we sank the *Ayesha* and were all very sad. The good old *Ayesha* had served us faithfully for six weeks. The log showed that we had made 1,709 sea miles under sail since leaving Keeling. She wasn't at all rotten and unseaworthy, as they had told me, but nice and white and dry inside. I had grown fond of the boat, on which I could practice my old sailing maneuvers. The only trouble was that the sails would go to pieces every now and then, because they were so old.

"But anyway, she went down quite properly. We had bored a hole in her; she filled slowly and then all of a sudden disappeared. That was the saddest day of the whole month. We gave her three cheers, and my next yacht at Kiel will be named *Ayesha*, that is sure.

"To the captain of the *Choising* I had said, when I hailed him, 'I do not know what will happen to the ship. The war situation may make it necessary for me to strand it.' He did not want to undertake the responsibility. I proposed that we work together, and I would take the responsibility. Then we traveled together for three weeks, from Padang to Hodeida. The *Choising* was some ninety meters long, and had a speed of nine miles, though sometimes only four. If she had not accidentally arrived I had intended to cruise along the west coast of Sumatra to the region of the northern monsoon. I came about six degrees north, then over toward Aden to the Arabian coast. In the Red Sea the north-eastern monsoon, which here blows southeast, could bring us to Djidda. I had heard in Padang that Turkey was still allied with Germany, so we would be able to get safely through Arabia to Germany.

"I next waited for information through ships, but the *Choising* did not know anything definite, either. By way of the *Luchs*, the *Königsberg* and *Kormoran* the reports were uncertain. Besides, according to newspapers at Aden, the Arabs were said to have fought with the English; therein there seemed to be offered an opportunity near at hand to damage the enemy. I therefore sailed with the *Choising* in the direction of Aden. Lieutenant Cordts of the *Choising* had heard that the Arabian railway already went almost to Hodeida, near the Perin Strait. The ship's surgeon there, Docounlang, found confirmation of this in Meyer's Traveling Handbook. This railway could not have been taken over by the Englishmen, who always dreamt of it. By doing this they would have further and completely wrought up the Mohammedans by making more difficult the journey to Mecca. Best of all, we thought, 'We'll simply step into the express train and whizz nicely away to the North Sea.' Certainly there would be safe journeying homeward through Arabia. To be sure, we had maps of the Red Sea; but it was the shortest way to the foe whether in Aden or in Germany.

"On the 7th of January, 1915, between nine and ten o'clock in the evening, we sneaked through the Strait of Perin. It lay swarming full of Englishmen. We steered along the African coast, close past an English cable layer. That was my greatest delight—how the Englishmen will be vexed when they learn that we passed safely by Perin. On the next evening we saw on the coast a few lights near the water. We thought that must be the pier of Hodeida. But when we measured the distance by night, three thousand meters, I began to think that must be something else. At dawn I made out two masts and four smokestacks; that was an enemy ship and, what is more, an armored French cruiser. I therefore ordered the *Choising* to put to sea, and to return at night.

"The next day and night the same; then we put out four boats—these we pulled to shore at sunrise under the eyes of the unsuspecting Frenchmen. The sea reeds were thick. A few Arabs came close to us; then there ensued a difficult negotiation with the Arabian coast guards. For we did not even know whether Hodeida was in English or French hands. We waved to them, laid aside our arms, and made signs to them. The Arabs, gathering together, began to rub two fingers together; that means 'We are friends.' We thought it meant 'We are going to rub against you and are hostile.' I therefore said: 'Boom-boom' and pointed to the warship. At all events, I set up my machine guns and made preparations for a skirmish. But, thank God, one of the Arabs understood the word 'Germans'; that was good.

"Soon a hundred Arabs came and helped us and as we marched into Hodeida the Turkish soldiers who had been called out against us saluted us as Allies and friends. To be sure, there was not a trace of a railway, but we were received very well and they assured us we could get through by land. Therefore, I gave red-star signals at night, telling the *Choising* to sail away, since the enemy was near by. Inquiries and deliberations concerning a safe journey by land proceeded. I also heard that in the interior about six days' journey away, there was healthy highland where our fever invalids could recuperate. I therefore determined to journey next to Sana. On the kaiser's birthday we held a great parade in common with the Turkish troops—all this under the noses of the Frenchmen. On the same day we marched away from Hodeida to the highland.

"Two months later we again put to sea. The time spent in the highland of Sana passed in lengthy inquiries and discussions that finally resulted in our foregoing the journey by land through Arabia, for religious reasons. But the time was not altogether lost. The men who were sick with malaria had, for most part, recuperated in the highland air.

"The Turkish Government placed at our disposal two sambuks (sailing ships), of about twenty-five tons, fifteen meters long and four wide. But, in fear of English spies, we sailed from Jebaua, ten miles north of Hodeida. That was on March 14, 1915. At first we sailed at a considerable distance apart, so that we would not both be captured if an English gunboat caught us. Therefore, we always had to sail in coastal water. That is full of coral reefs, however."

Captain Mücke had charge of the first sambuk. Everything went well for three days. On the third day the order was given for the sambuks to keep near together because the pilot of the first one was sailing less skillfully than the other. Suddenly, in the twilight the men in the second sambuk felt a shock, then another, and a third. The water poured into it rapidly. It had run upon the reef of a small island, where the smaller sambuk had been able to pass on account of its lighter draft. Soon the stranded boat began to list over, and the twenty-eight men aboard had to sit on the gunwale.

"We could scarcely move," narrated Lieutenant Gerdts, who commanded the stranded boat. "The other boat was nowhere in sight. Now it grew dark. At this stage I began to build a raft of spars and old pieces of wood that might keep us afloat. But soon the first boat came into sight again. The commander turned about and sent over his little canoe; in this and in our own canoe, in which two men could sit at each trip, we first transferred the sick. Now the Arabs began to help us. But just then the tropical helmet of our doctor suddenly appeared above the water in which he was standing up to his ears. Thereupon the Arabs withdrew: We were Christians, and they did not know that we were friends. Now the other sambuk was so near that we could have swum to it in half an hour, but the seas were too high. At each trip a good swimmer trailed along, hanging to the painter of the canoe. When it became altogether dark we could not see the boat any more, for over there they were prevented by the wind from keeping any light burning. My men asked: 'In what direction shall we swim?' I answered: 'Swim in the direction of this or that star; that must be about the direction of the boat.' Finally a torch flared up over there—one of the torches that was still left from the *Emden*. But we had suffered considerably through submersion. One sailor cried out: 'Oh, psha! It's all up with us now, that's a searchlight.' About ten o'clock we were all safe aboard, but one of our typhus patients wore himself out completely by exertion and died a week later. On the next morning we went over again to the wreck in order to seek the weapons that had fallen into the water. You see, the Arabs dive so well; they fetched up a considerable lot—both machine guns, all but ten of the rifles, though these were, to be sure, all full of water. Later they frequently failed to go off when they were used in firing.

"Now we numbered, together with the Arabs, seventy men on the little boat. Then we anchored before Konfida and met Sami Bey. He had shown himself useful, even before, in the service of the Turkish Government, and had done good service as a guide in the last months of the adventure. He procured for us a larger boat of fifty-four tons. We sailed from the 20th of March, 1915, to the 24th, unmolested to Lith. There Sami Bey announced that three English ships were cruising about in order to intercept us. I therefore advised traveling a bit overland. I disliked leaving the sea a second time, but it had to be done."

Captain Mücke explained that Lith is nothing but desert, and therefore it was very difficult to get up a caravan at once. They marched away on March 28, 1915, with only a vague suspicion that the English might have agents here also. They could travel only at night, and when they slept or camped around a spring, there was only a tent for the sick men. Two days' march from Jeddah, the Turkish Government having received word about the crew, sent sixteen good camels.

"Suddenly, on the night of April 1, 1915, things became uneasy," said Captain Mücke. "I was riding at the head of the column. All our shooting implements were cleared for action, because there was danger of an attack from Bedouins, whom the English had bribed. When it began to grow a bit light I thought: 'We're through for to-day'; for we were tired—had been riding eighteen hours. Suddenly I saw a line flash up before me, and shots whizzed over our heads. Down from the camels! We formed a fighting line. You know how quickly it becomes daylight there. The whole space around the desert hillock was occupied. Now we had to take up our guns. We rushed at the enemy. They fled, but returned again, this time from all sides. Several of the gendarmes that had been given to us as an escort were wounded; the machine-gun operator fell, killed by a shot through the heart; another was wounded. Lieutenant Schmidt was mortally wounded. He received a bullet in the chest and another in the abdomen.

"Suddenly, they waved white cloths. The sheik, to whom a part of our camels belonged, went over to them to negotiate, then

Sami Bey and his wife. In the interim we quickly built a sort of wagon barricade, a circular camp of camel saddles, of rice and coffee sacks, all of which we filled with sand. We had no shovels, and had to dig with our bayonets, plates, and hands. The whole barricade had a diameter of fifty meters. Behind it were dug trenches, which we deepened even during the skirmish. The camels inside had to lie down, and thus served very well as cover for the rear of the trenches. Then an inner wall was constructed, behind which we carried the sick men. In the very center we buried two jars of water, to guard us against thirst. In addition we had ten petroleum cans full of water; all told, a supply for four days. Late in the evening Sami's wife came back from the futile negotiations, alone. She had unveiled for the first and only time on this day of the skirmish, had distributed cartridges and had acted faultlessly.

"Soon we were able to ascertain the number of the enemy. There were about 300 men; we numbered fifty, with twenty-nine machine guns. In the night Lieutenant Schmidt died. We had to dig his grave with our hands and with our bayonets, and to eliminate every trace above it, in order to protect the body. Rademacher had been buried immediately after the skirmish with all honors.

"The wounded had a hard time of it. We had lost our medicine chest in the wreck; we had only little packages of bandages for skirmishes; but no probing instrument, no scissors, were at hand. On the next day our men came up with thick tongues, feverish, and crying: 'Water, water!' But each one received only a little cupful three times each day. If our water supply became exhausted we would have to sally forth from our camp and fight our way through. At night we always dragged out the dead camels that had served as cover and had been shot.

"This continued about three days. On the third day there were new negotiations. Now the Bedouins demanded arms no longer, but only money. This time the negotiations took place across the camp wall. When I declined the Bedouin said, 'Lots of fight.' I said, 'Please go to it.'

"We had only a little ammunition left, and very little water. Now it really looked as if we would soon be dispatched. The mood of the men was pretty dismal. Suddenly, at about ten o'clock in the morning, there bobbed up in the north two riders on camels, waving white cloths. Soon afterward there appeared, coming from the same direction, far back, a long row of camel troops, about a hundred; they drew rapidly nearer, rode singing toward us, in a picturesque train. They were the messengers and the troops of the Emir of Mecca.

"Sami Bey's wife, it developed, had in the course of the first negotiations, dispatched an Arab boy to Jeddah. From that place the governor had telegraphed to the emir. The latter at once sent camel troops with his two sons and his personal surgeon; the elder, Abdullah, conducted the negotiations, and the surgeon acted as interpreter in French. Now things proceeded in one-two-three order, and the whole Bedouin band speedily disappeared. From what I learned later I know definitely that they had been corrupted with bribes by the English. They knew when and where we would pass, and they had made all preparations. Now our first act was a rush for water; then we cleared up our camp, but had to harness our camels ourselves, for the camel drivers had fled at the very beginning of the skirmish.

"Then, under the safe protection of Turkish troops, we got to Jeddah. There the authorities and the populace received us very well. From there we proceeded in nineteen days by sail boat to Elwesh, and under abundant guard with the Suleiman Pasha, in a five-day caravan journeyed to El Ula."

"Have I received the Iron Cross?" was the first question Captain Mücke asked when he got to that place, and old newspapers which he found there told him that he had. A few days later the party was on train, riding toward Germany.

CHAPTER XXXII

SUMMARY OF THE FIRST YEAR OF NAVAL WARFARE

THE first year of the war came to an end in August, 1915, with the naval situation much the same as it stood at the end of the first six months. The navy of practically every belligerent was intact; the Allies enjoyed the freedom of the seas, but the fact that a German fleet lay intact in the North Sea, and an Austrian fleet lay intact in the Adriatic Sea, indicated only the naval supremacy of the Allies, but not that they had won decisive naval victories.

As there had been no victory there had been no defeat, yet there had been losses to all concerned. The mine and the submarine had changed somewhat the methods of naval warfare—the enemies "nibbled" at their opponents' fleets. Battleships were lost, though the first year of the Great War had seen no pitched battle between ships of that class.

During the second six months of the war England lost the five old battleships *Irresistible, Ocean, Goliath, Triumph,* and *Majestic;* the destroyers *Recruit* and *Maori;* and the submarine *E-15* and another unidentified; and the auxiliary cruisers *Clan McNaughton, Bayano,* and *Princess Irene.* Her ally France had lost, during the same period, the old battleship *Bouvet,* the cruiser *Leon Gambetta,* the destroyer *Dague,* and the submarines *Joule, Mariotte,* and one unidentified.

The losses on the other side were confined to the German navy, with the exception of the Turkish cruiser *Medjidieh.* Germany lost the battleship *Pommern;* the cruisers *Dresden* and *Königsberg;* the submarines *U-12, U-29, U-8,* one of the type of the *U-2,* and another unidentified; two unidentified torpedo boats; and the auxiliary cruisers *Prinz Eitel Friedrich* (interned), *Holger, Kronprinz Wilhelm* (interned), and *Macedonia.* Also the destroyer *G-196,* the mine layer *Albatross,* and the auxiliary cruiser *Meteor.*

In retaliation for having her flag swept from the seas, Germany's submarines, during the second six months of the war, had sunk a total of 153 merchant ships, including those belonging to neutral countries as well as to her enemies. The total tonnage of these was about 500,000 tons; 1,643 persons died in going down with these ships.

Not of the least importance were the precedents that were established, or attempted to be established, by Germany in conducting naval warfare with her submarine craft. In a note delivered to the United States Government, the German Government declared that British merchant vessels were not only armed and instructed to resist or even attack submarines, but often disguised as to nationality. Under such circumstances it was assumed to be impossible for a submarine commander to conform to the established custom of visit and search. Accordingly, vessels of neutral nations were urgently warned not to enter the submarine war zone. The war zone which she proclaimed about Great Britain had no precedent in history, and it immediately brought to her door a number of controversies with neutrals, particularly the United States. The sinking of liners carrying passengers claiming citizenship in neutral countries was another precedent, which had the same effect with regard to diplomatic exchanges.

Predictions that had been made long before the war came were found to be worthless; there were those who had predicted that Germany in the event of war with England would give immediate battle with her largest ships; but twelve months went by without an actual battle between superdreadnoughts. "Der Tag" had not come. There were those who had predicted that the British navy would force the German ships out of their protected harbors. "We shall dig the rats out of their holes," said Mr. Winston Churchill, British Secretary of State for the Navy in the early months of the war. Mr. Churchill was removed from his position, and twelve months passed by with the German ships still in their "holes."

Certain lessons had been taught naval authorities of all nations through the actual use of the modern battleship in war. The first year showed that the largest ships must have very high speed and long gun range. To some extent the fact that the fighting ships of nearly all of the belligerent countries were thus equipped changed battle tactics.

When the allied fleets had started their bombardment of the Turkish forts at the Dardanelles they were breaking certain well-defined rules which had been axiomatic with naval authorities. The greatest of modern battleships were designed to fight with craft of their like, but not to take issue with land fortifications. For weeks, while the fleets succeeded in silencing for a time some of the Turkish forts, it was thought that this rule no longer held good. But when, after March 19, 1915, the fleets ceased attempting to take the passage without military cooperation, the worth of the rule was reestablished. The ease with which the bombarding ships were made victims of hostile submarines was greatly instrumental in making the rule again an axiom.

The naval supremacy of the allied powers brought them certain advantages—advantages which they had without winning a decisive victory. Germany and Austria were cut off from the Western Hemisphere, and were troubled, in consequence, by shortage in food for their civilian populations to a greater or lesser degree. This was perhaps a negative benefit derived by the Allies from their naval supremacy; the affirmative benefit was that their own communications with the Western Hemisphere were maintained, enabling them not only to get food for their civilian populations, but arms and munitions for their armies; and even financial arrangements, which, if their emissaries could not pass back and forth freely could not have been made, depended on their control of the high seas.

They were able to keep the Channel clear of submarines long enough to permit the passage of the troops, which England from time to time during the first year of the war sent to the Continent, and permitted the participation of the troops of the British overseas dominions, the troops from Canada joining those in France, and the troops from New Zealand and Australia taking their places in the trenches along the Suez Canal and on the Gallipoli Peninsula. Thus, to a certain extent, the advantage of continuous railroad communication which was enjoyed by the Teutonic allies "inside" the arena of military operations was offset by the naval communication maintained by the Entente Powers "outside" the arena of military operations.

CHAPTER XXXIII

FIGHTS OF THE SUBMARINES

WHEN, on the 5th of February, 1915, the German admiralty proclaimed a "war zone" around the British Isles and announced that it would fight the sea power of the Allies with submarines, a new era in naval warfare had opened. In all previous wars, and in the earlier months of the Great War, submarines were employed as auxiliaries to the larger naval units. The Germans were the first to use them as separate units. The idea of sending a fleet of submarines out on to the high seas was a new one, and had been impossible in the last war in which they had been used—that between Russia and Japan. But the improvements which had been made in their design and equipment since then had made an actual cruising submarine possible, and made possible the new phase of naval warfare inaugurated by the German admiralty.

While Germany was the last great sea power to adopt the submarine as a weapon, both England and Germany, in the years immediately preceding the war, had spent the same amounts of money on this sort of craft—about $18,000,000—but while the Germans had later given as much attention to them as to any other sort of naval craft, the British authorities did not figure on employing the submarine as a separate offensive tactical unit being sufficiently equipped in large ships carrying large guns. And being weaker in capital ships Germany was compelled to rely upon underwater warfare in her campaign of attrition. Not only were the naval authorities of the rest of the world uninformed about the improvements that German submarines carried, but they were fooled even as to the actual number which Germany had built.

The most modern of the German submarines at the time had a length of 213 feet and a beam of twenty feet, these dimensions giving them sufficient deck space to mount thereon two rapid-fire guns, one of 3.5 inches and another of 1.4 inches. Their displacement was 900 tons, and they could make a speed of 18 knots when traveling "light" (above water), and 12 knots when traveling submerged. These speeds made it possible for them to overtake all but the fastest merchantmen, though not fast enough to run away from destroyers, gunboats, and fast cruisers. Their range of operation was 2,000 miles, and in the early months of 1915, it was possible for Germany to send two or three of them from their base in the North Sea to the Mediterranean. Germany was at the same time experimenting with a larger type, with a displacement of 1,200 tons and an operating distance of 5,000 miles.

The ordinary submarine in service at the beginning of the war could remain below the surface for twenty-four hours at least. Reserve amounts of air for breathing were carried in tanks under pressure, and in the German type there were also chemical improvements for regenerating air. Contrary to the opinion of laymen, submerging was accomplished both by letting water into ballast tanks, and also by properly deflecting a set of rudders; every submarine had two sets of rudders, one of which worked in vertical planes and pointed the prow of the ship either to the left or the right; the other pair worked in horizontal planes and turned the prow either upward or downward. A pair of fins on the sides of the hull assisted action in both rising and diving. The action of water against the fins and rudders when the ship was in motion was exactly the same as that of the air against the planes of a kite; to submerge one of the craft it was necessary to have it in motion and to have its horizontal rudders so placed that the resistance of the water would drive the ship downward; the reverse operation drove it upward. And here lay a danger, for if the engines of a diving submarine stopped she was bound to come to the surface. Her presence, while moving entirely submerged could be detected by a peculiar swell which traveled on the water above; if submerged only so much as to leave the tip of her periscope still showing, the latter left an easily discernible wake.

The periscope was merely a tube in which there were arranged mirrors so that anything reflected in the first mirror, the one above the surface of the water, was again reflected till it showed in a mirror at the bottom of the tube, within the hull of the vessel, where its commander could observe it safely. A crew of about twenty-five men was necessary to operate one of these crafts, and theirs was an unpleasant duty, first because of the danger that accompanied each submergence of their vessel; second because of the discomforts abroad. The explosive engines which drove the craft, whether burning oil or the lighter refinements such as gasoline, gave off gases that caused headaches and throbbing across the forehead; and it was almost impossible to heat the interior of the craft.

Though merchantmen had gone to the bottom as victims of German submarines before the proclamation of a "war zone" was issued they were individual cases; the first instance of a merchant ship being sunk as a result of the new policy of the German admiralty was the sinking of the British steamer *Cambark* on the 20th of February, 1915. This ship was bound for Liverpool, from Huelva, Spain. While off the north coast of Wales, on the morning of the 20th, the periscope of a hostile submarine was sighted only 200 yards ahead. The engines of the steamship were immediately reversed, but she had no time to make off, for a torpedo caught her amidships and she started to sink immediately. Her crew managed to get off in small boats, but all of their personal belongings were lost.

The small Irish coasting steamer *Downshire* was made a victim on the 21st of February, 1915, but instead of sending a torpedo into her hull, the commander of the *U-12*, the submarine which overhauled her, resorted to boarding. After trying to elude the submarine by steering a zigzag course, the *Downshire* was finally overtaken. The crew was ordered to take to the small boats, while nineteen men of the submarine, which had come above water, watched the operations from the deck. A crew from the submarine took one of the small boats of the steamship and rowed toward her. They placed a bomb in a vital spot and set it off, sinking the merchantman. In this way the submarine's commander had saved a torpedo. A conversation which took place between the captains of the two craft revealed the methods by which the submarine commanders were able, not only to steal up on their intended victims, but to elude being sighted by the patrolling British warships. Some fishing smacks had been in the vicinity while the *Downshire* was sunk, and the British captain asked the German captain why they had not been attacked. The latter hinted that his plans worked best if the fishing boats were unmolested. When asked whether he had hidden behind one these little boats he changed the subject, but it was learned later that the commanders of the submarines made a practice of coming to the surface right near fishing boats and bade them act as screens while they lay in wait for victims. By keeping the small boats covered with a deck gun or by putting a boarding crew aboard, it was possible for the commanders of the submarines to keep their persicopes or the hulls of their vessels behind the sails of the fishing boats, unobservable to lookouts on larger ships.

By the 23d of February, 1915, the success of German submarines had been so marked that the insurance rates on merchantmen went up. Lloyd's underwriters announced that the rate on transatlantic passage had gone up nearly one per cent. And on the same day it was announced that the British Government would thereafter regulate steamship traffic in the Irish Sea. Certain areas of the Irish Sea were closed to all kinds of traffic; lines of passage were defined and had to be followed by all merchantmen, and vessels of all descriptions were ordered to keep away from certain parts of the coast from sunset to sunrise.

The comparatively small size of the submarines made it possible for the German admiralty to load them on to trains in sections and transport them where needed, and in this manner some were sent from the German ports on the North Sea to Zeebrugge, there assembled and launched. Others were sent to the Adriatic, arriving at Pola on the 25th of February, 1915. These were intended for use in the Mediterranean as well as in the Adriatic Sea.

Neutral ships, in order to escape attack by German submarines had to resort to unusual methods of self-identification. The use of flags belonging to neutral countries by the merchantmen of belligerent powers made the usual identification by colors almost impossible, the German admiralty claiming that the commanders of submarines were unable to wait long enough, after stopping a vessel, to ascertain whether she had a right to fly one flag or another. Consequently the ships belonging to Dutch and American lines had their names painted with large lettering along their sides. At night, streamers of electric lights were hung over the sides to illuminate these letterings; and on the decks of many of the neutral ships their names and nationalities were painted in large letters so that they might be identified by aircraft. Owing to such precautions the Dutch steamship *Prinzes Juliana* escaped being sunk by a torpedo on the 3d of March, 1915. A submarine ran a parallel course to that followed by the Dutch ship, but after examining the lettering on her sides the commander of the German craft saw that she was not legitimate game and turned off.

Not always did the German submarines themselves succeed in escaping unharmed in their raiding of allied merchantmen. Rewards were offered in Great Britain for the sinking of German submersibles by the commanders of British merchantmen. Instructions were issued in the British shipping periodicals, showing how a submarine might be sunk by being rammed. It was officially announced on the 5th of March, 1915, by the British admiralty, that the *U-8* had been rammed and sunk by a British warship. The crew of twenty-nine was rescued and brought to Dover. For the British this was a stroke of good fortune, for while the *U-8* was of an earlier type it was a dangerous craft, having a total displacement of 300 tons, a radius of operation of 1,200 miles, a speed of 13 knots when traveling "light" and a speed of 8 knots when submerged. On the same day the French minister of marine announced that a French warship had come upon a German submarine of the type of the *U-2* in the North Sea and that after firing at the hull of the vessel and hitting it three times it was seen to sink and did not reappear.

During the last week of February and the first week of March, 1915, bad weather on the waters surrounding the British Isles hampered the operations of German submarines to an extent which led the British public to believe that the submarine warfare on merchantmen had been abandoned, but they were disillusioned when on the 9th of March, 1915, three British ships were sunk by the underwater craft. The steamship *Tangistan* was torpedoed off Scarborough, the *Blackwood* off Hastings and the *Princess Victoria* near Liverpool. Part of this was believed to be the work of the *U-16*.

In the three days beginning March 10, 1915, eight ships were made victims of German submarines in the waters about the British Isles. Most novel was the experience of a crowd gathered on the shore of one of the Scilly Islands on March 12, 1915, when two of these eight ships, the *Indian City* and the *Headlands*, were torpedoed. At about eight in the morning the islanders on St. Mary's Island saw a German submarine overtake the former and sink her. The German vessel then remained in the adjacent waters to watch for the approach of another victim, while two patrol boats near by put out and opened fire on her. The crowd saw the enemies exchange shots at a distance of ten miles off shore. But neither side put in any effective shots, and the combat ended when the submarine dived and retired.

The steamship *Headlands* was then sighted by the commander of the submarine and he immediately started to pursue her. The steamship steered a zigzag course, but the submarine got in a position to launch a torpedo, and at about half past ten in the morning the crowd on the shore saw steam escaping from her in large quantities. Some time after they saw a large volume of black smoke and débris fly upward and they knew that another torpedo had found its mark. She then settled, her crew and the men from the *Indian City* reaching St. Mary's in small boats.

To keep British harbors free from the German submarines the British admiralty had to set their engineers to work to devise some method of trapping the underwater craft automatically, for there seemed to be no sort of patrol which they could not elude. Steel traps, not unlike the gill nets used by fishermen, were finally hit upon as the best thing to use against the submarines, and by March 13, 1915, a number of these were installed at entrances to some of the British harbors. They were made of malleable iron frames, ten feet square, used in sets of threes, so arranged that they might hold a submarine by the sides and have the third of the set buckle against its bottom. They were suspended by buoys about thirty feet below the surface of the water. When a submarine entered one of these it was held fast, for the frame which came up from the bottom caught the propeller and made it impossible for the submarine to work itself loose. The disadavantage to the submarine was that, while traveling under water, it traveled "blind"; the periscopes in use were good only for observation when the top of them were above water; when submerged the commander of a submarine had to steer by chart. By the end of March, 1915, a dozen submarines had been caught in nets of this kind.

By the 18th of March, 1915, three more British ships had been made the victims of German torpedoes. The *Atlanta* was sunk off the west coast of Ireland only a day before the *Fingal* was sunk off Northumberland. And the *Leeuwarden* was sunk by being hit from the deck guns of a German submarine off the coast of Holland. There was no loss of life except during the sinking of the *Fingal*, some of whose men were drowned when she dragged a lifeboat full of men down with her.

By way of variety the Germans attempted to sink a British ship in the "war zone" with bombs dropped from an airship, the news of which was brought to England by the crew and captain of the *Blonde* when they reached shore on March 18, 1915. This ship had been German originally, but being in a British port when the war started was taken over and run by a British crew. Two or three mornings before the men landed they had noticed a Taube aeroplane circling over their ship at about 500 feet altitude. It then swept downward and took a close look at the vessel. Two bombs which fell into the water near the ship, were dropped by the German aviator. The captain of the *Blonde* ordered that the rudder of his ship be fastened so that she might drive in a circle and her engines were set at full speed, with the intention of making a more difficult target for the airship's bombs. The whistle of the ship was set going and continued to blow in the hope of attracting help from other ships. More bombs were near the vessel, but none of them found its mark. After one more attempt, when only 300 feet above the ship's deck, the aviator let go with his last supply, but again being unsuccessful he veered off to the north and allowed the *Blonde* to escape.

The naval attack on the Dardanelles is told in another chapter, but the work of the Allies' submarines there included the use of French submarines, which is not narrated elsewhere. On the 19th of March, 1915, Rear Admiral Gueprattе of the French navy reported that one of his submarines had attempted, without success, to run through the Dardanelles. The object of the attempt was to sink the Turkish battle cruiser *Sultan Selim,* formerly the *Goeben.* The submarine submerged and got as far as Nagara. But she had to travel "blind" and her captain, being unfamiliar with those waters, struck some rocks near the shore and immediately brought her to the surface. She became a target for the land guns of the Turks at once and was sunk, only a few of her men, who were taken prisoners, escaping death.

On the 19th of March, 1915, the British admiralty reported that the three British ships, *Hyndford, Bluejacket,* and *Glenartney* had been torpedoed in the "war zone" without warning, with the loss of only one man. Beachy Head in the British Channel had been the scene of most of the operations of German submarines against British ships, and consequently, when on the 21st of March, 1915, the collier *Cairntorr* was torpedoed in that region, no unusual comment was made by the admiralty. Heretofore the scene of the latest attack had been thought worthy of mention on account of the unusual and unexpected places that submarines chose for action.

A new phase of the submarines' activities was opened on March 21, 1915, when two Dutch ships *Batavier V* and *Zaan-*

stroom were held up and captured. The *U-28* had for some days been hiding near the Maas Lightship, and had been taking shots with torpedoes at every ship which came within range. The *Batavier V* had left the Hook of Holland on March 18, 1915. At about five o'clock that morning she came near the Maas Lightship on her way to England, whence she was carrying provisions and a register of fifty-seven persons, including passengers and crew; among the former there were a number of women and children. Suddenly a submarine appeared off her port bow, and her captain was ordered to stop his ship. This he did readily, for he had been thus stopped before, only to be allowed to proceed. But this time the commander of the submarine, the *U-28,* shouted to him through a megaphone: "I am going to confiscate your ship and take it to Zeebrugge."

While the two commanders were arguing over the illegality of this, the *Zaanstroom* was sighted, and was immediately overtaken by the submarine. An officer and a sailor from the submarine had been placed on the *Batavier V,* and this prevented her escaping while the pursuit of the *Zaanstroom* was on. A similar detail was now placed on the latter, and her captain was ordered to follow the *U-28* which returned to the *Batavier V.* "Follow me to Zeebrugge" was the order which the commander of the submarine gave the two ships, and their captains obeyed. They arrived at Zeebrugge at noon, and were immediately unloaded. Those of the passengers and crews who were citizens of neutral countries were sent to Ghent and there released, while all those aboard, such as Belgians and Frenchmen, were detained.

When possible, the commanders of the German submarines saved their costly torpedoes and used shell fire instead to sink their victims. This was done in the case of the steamship *Vosges,* which was sunk on March 28, 1915. For two hours, while the engines of the steamship were run at full speed in an attempt to get away from the submarine, she was under fire from two deck guns on board the submersible. Though the latter made off at the approach of another vessel, her shells did enough damage to cause the *Vosges* to sink a few hours later.

Up to the middle of March, 1915, all the ships which had become victims of German submarines had been of the slower coasting variety. There had been numerous unconfirmed reports that the faster transatlantic ships had been chased, but no credence had been given to them. On the 27th of March, 1915, however, when the *Arabic* arrived at Liverpool it was reported by those on board that she had given a submarine a lively chase and had gotten away safely. At about nine o'clock the evening before the submarine was sighted off Holyhead. She was only 200 yards ahead, and while her commander jockeyed for a position from which he could successfully launch a torpedo, the commander of the *Arabic* gave the order "Full speed ahead." His passengers lined the rail of the ship to watch the maneuvers. Soon the steamship had up a speed of 18 knots, which was a bit too fast for the submarine, and she fell to the rearward. Her chance for launching a torpedo was gone, but she brought her deck guns into action, firing two shots which went wild. The *Arabic* proceeded to port unmolested.

At times even the cost of shell fire was figured by the commanders of German submarines, and pistol and rifles were used instead. This was done in the case of the *Delmira* on the 26th of March, 1915. This steamship was sunk off Boulogne. Ten minutes were given by the crew of the submarine to the crew of the steamship for them to get off. The submarine had come up off the bow of the *Delmira,* and men standing on the deck of the former had fired shots toward the bridge of the latter to make her captain bring her to a stop. The latter ordered his engines started again at full speed, with the intention of ramming the enemy, but his Chinese stokers refused to obey the order, and his ship did not move. The crew of the steamship got into their small boats, and for an hour and a half these were towed by the submarine so that their row to shore would not be so long. Though torpedoed, the *Delmira* did not sink, and was last seen in a burning condition off the French coast near Cape de la Hogue.

The sinking of the steamship *Falaba,* which is mentioned, though not narrated in full, in another chapter, was the last act of German submarines during the month of March, 1915. This ship on the 29th of March, 1915, was overtaken by a German submarine in St. George's Channel. She was engaged in the African trade, voyaging between the African ports and Liverpool. On her last journey she carried a crew of 90 men and some 160 passengers, many of the latter being women and children. The commander of the submarine brought his craft to the surface off the bow of the *Falaba,* and gave the captain of the steamship five minutes in which to put his crew and passengers into lifeboats. A torpedo was sent against her hull and found the engine room, causing a tremendous explosion. One hundred and eleven persons lost their lives because they had not been able to get off in time, or because they were too near the liner when she went down. This was the most important merchantman which had been sent to the bottom by a submarine since the proclamation of February 15, 1915.

The next two victims of this sort of warfare were the steamships *Flaminian* and the *Crown of Castile,* one of which was sunk by the *U-28,* and the other by an unidentified submarine on April 1, 1915. They went down off the west coast of England with no loss of life, though the *Crown of Castile* was torpedoed before her crew could get off. The *Flaminian* had tried to get away, but had to stop under fire from deck guns on the submarine. The shells did not hit her in vital spots, however, and it was necessary to send a torpedo into her hull to sink her.

The ease with which submarines had been able to bob up in unexpected places and to sink British merchantmen, in spite of the patrols maintained by British warships, caused the captains of merchant vessels to petition the British Government to be allowed to arm their vessels on April 1, 1915. This was not granted, because their being armed would have made the steamship legitimate prey for the submarines, nor was any attention paid to the demand made by the British press that the crews and officers of captured German submarines be treated, not as prisoners of war, but as pirates. Reprisals on the part of the Germans was feared.

Beachy Head on the 1st of April, 1915, was again the scene of two successful attacks on merchantmen by submarines. On that day the French steamship *Emma,* after being torpedoed, went to the bottom with all of the nineteen men in her crew. The same submarine sank the British steamer *Seven Seas,* causing the deaths of eleven of her men.

In order to indicate the amount of harm which the submarine warfare caused British shipping, the admiralty on April 1, 1915, announced that though five merchantmen had been sent to the bottom and one had been only partially damaged by submarines during the week ending March 31, 1915, some 1,559 vessels entered and sailed from British ports during the same period.

Efforts were made to damage the base, from which many of the German submarines had been putting out at Zeebrugge, with aircraft. On the 1st of April, 1915, the British Government's press bureau announced that bombs had been dropped, with unknown success, on two German submarines lying there, and that on the same day a British airman had flown over Hoboken and had seen submarines in building there.

The steamship *Lockwood,* while off Start Point in Devonshire, was hit abaft the engine room by a German torpedo on the morning of April 2, 1915, and though she went down almost immediately, her crew was able to get off in small boats and were picked up by fishing trawlers.

The *U-28,* which had done such effective work for the Germans during the month of March, 1915, was relieved of duty near the British Isles during the first week of April by the *U-31,* which sank the Russian bark *Hermes* and the British steamship *Olivine* off the coast of Wales on April 5, 1915.

The British admiralty decided in April, 1915, to use some other means besides the employment of torpedo boats and destroyers to keep watch for German submarines, and innocent-looking fishing trawlers were used for the purpose. While these could give no fight against a submarine, it was intended that they would carefully make for land to report after sighting one of the hostile craft. The Germans, discovering this strategy, then began to sink trawlers when they found them. On the morning of April 5, 1915, one of these small craft was sighted and chased by the *U-20.* After a pursuit of an hour or more the German ship was near enough for members of her crew to fire on the trawler with rifles. Her crew got into the small boat and were picked up later by a steamer. The trawler was sent to the bottom.

The *U-20* still kept up her raiding. On the 5th of April, 1915, she overtook the steamer *Northland,* a 2,000-ton ship, and torpedoed her off Beachy Head. The crew of the steamer were able to escape, although their ship went down only ten minutes after the submarine caught up with it.

The use of nets to catch submarines was vindicated, when on the 6th of April, 1915, one of these vessels became entangled in a steel net near Dover and was held fast. The loss of the *U-29,* which was commanded by the famous Otto von Weddigen, who commanded the *U-9* when she sank the *Hogue, Cressy,* and *Aboukir* in September, 1914, was confirmed by a report issued by the German admiralty on April 7, 1915, after rumors of her loss had circulated throughout England and France for a number of weeks.

In order to encourage resistance on the part of crews of British vessels attacked by German submarines, the British Government rewarded the crew of the steamship *Vosges.* It was announced on April 9, 1915, that the captain had been given a commission as a lieutenant in the Royal Naval Reserve and the Distinguished Service Cross; the remaining officers were given gold watches, and the crew were given $15 per man.

Rumors had reached the outside world that the German submarines were using hidden spots to store fuel and provisions so that they might go about their raiding without having to return to German ports for reprovisioning. Neutral nations, such as the Netherlands and Norway, found it necessary, to maintain their neutrality, to keep watch for such action. On the 9th of April, 1915, Norwegian airmen reported to their Government that such a cache had been discovered by them behind the cliffs in Bergen Bay. Submarines found there were ordered to intern or to leave immediately, and chose to do the latter.

Certain acts of the commanders of German submarines seemed to make it evident that their intention was to sink ships of every description, no matter where found, in order to make the "war zone" a reality, and to make it shunned by neutral as well as belligerent ships. Thus the Dutch steamship *Katwyk,* which lay at anchor seven miles west of the North Hinder Lightship off the Dutch coast, was sunk. This lightship was maintained by the Netherlands Government and stood at the mouth of the River Scheldt, forty-five miles northwest of Flushing. The *Katwyk* was stationary there on the night of April 14, 1915, when the crew felt a great shock and saw that their ship was rapidly taking water. They managed to reach the lightship in their lifeboats just as their vessel sank. The same submarine sank the British steamer *Ptarmigan* only a few hours later.

Among victims flying the flags of neutral nations the next ship was of American register. This was the tank steamship *Gulflight,* which was torpedoed off the Scilly Islands on the 29th of May, 1915. The hole made in her hull was not large enough to cause her to sink, and she was able to get to port. But during the excitement of the attack her captain died of heart failure and two of her crew jumped into the sea and were drowned. Three days later the French steamship *Europe* and the British ship *Fulgent* were sent to the bottom, probably by the same submarine.

The month of May, 1915, had opened with greater activity on the part of German submarines than had been shown for many weeks previous. Between the 1st and the 3d of that month seven ships were torpedoed, four of them being British, one Swedish, and two Norwegian. By the 5th of May, 1915, ten British trawlers had been sunk; some of these were armed for attack on either German submarines or torpedo boats.

CHAPTER XXXIV

SINKING OF THE "LUSITANIA"

ON the 7th of May, 1915, came the most sensational act committed by German submarines since the war had started—the sinking of the Cunard liner *Lusitania.* The vessel which did this was one of the *U-39* class. In her last hours above water the

The great liner, "Lusitania," which was torpedoed by a German submarine, not far from Old Kinsale Head, Ireland, May 7, 1915

giant liner was nearing Queenstown on a sunny day in a calm sea. When about five miles off shore, near Old Head of Kinsale, on the southeastern coast of Ireland, a few minutes after two o'clock, while many of the passengers were at lunch and a few of them on deck, there came a violent shock.

Five or six persons who had been on deck had noticed, a few moments before, the wake of something that was moving rapidly toward the ship. The moving object was a torpedo, which struck the hull to the forward on the starboard side and passed clean through the ship's engine room. She began to settle by the bows immediately, and the passengers, though cool, made rushes for lifebelts and for the small boats. The list of the boat made the launching of some of these impossible.

The scenes on the decks of the sinking liner were heartrending. Members of families had become separated and ran wildly about seeking their relatives. The women and children were put into the lifeboats—being given preference.

"I was on the deck about two o'clock," narrated one of the survivors, "the weather was fine and bright and the sea calm. Suddenly I heard a terrific explosion, followed by another, and the cry went up that the ship had been torpedoed. She began to list at once, and her angle was so great that many of the boats on the port side could not be launched. A lot of people made a rush for the boats, but I went down to my cabin, took off my coat and vest and donned a lifebelt. On getting up again I found the decks awash and the boat going down fast by the head. I slipped down a rope into the sea and was picked up by one of the lifeboats. Some of the boats, owing to the position of the vessel, got swamped, and I saw one turn over no less than three times, but eventually it was righted."

Not all of the women and children got off the liner into the small boats. "Women and children, under the protection of men, had clustered in lines on the port side of the ship," reported another survivor. "As the ship made her plunge down by the head, she finally took an angle of ninety degrees, and I saw this little army slide down toward the starboard side, dashing themselves against each other as they went, until they were engulfed."

Even under the stress of avoiding death the sight of the sinking hull was one that held the attention of those in the water. One of the sailors said afterward: "Her great hull rose into the air and neared the perpendicular. As the form of the vessel rose she seemed to shorten, and just as a duck dives so she disappeared. She went almost noiselessly. Fortunately her propellers had stopped, for had these been going, the vortex of her four screws would have dragged down many of those whose lives were saved. She seemed to divide the water as smoothly as a knife would do it."

Twenty minutes after the torpedo had struck the ship she had disappeared beneath the surface of the sea. "Above the spot where she had gone down," said one of the men who escaped death, "there was nothing but a nondescript mass of floating wreckage. Everywhere one looked there was a sea of waving hands and arms, belonging to the struggling men and frantic women and children in agonizing efforts to keep afloat. That was the most horrible memory and sight of all."

Fishing boats and coasting steamers picked up many of the survivors some hours after the disaster. The frightened people in the small boats pulled for the shore after picking up as many persons as they dared without swamping their boats. Some floated about in the waters for three and four hours, kept up by their lifebelts. Some, who were good swimmers, managed to keep above water till help came; others became exhausted and sank.

Probably the best story, covering the entire period from the time the ship was hit till the survivors were landed at Queenstown, was told by Dr. Daniel V. Moore, an American physician: "After the explosion," said Dr. Moore, "quiet and order were soon accomplished by assurances from the stewards. I proceeded to the deck promenade for observation, and saw only that the ship was fast leaning to the starboard. I hurried toward my cabin below for a lifebelt, and turned back because of the difficulty in keeping upright. I struggled to D deck and forward to the first-class cabin, where I saw a Catholic priest.

"I could find no belts, and returned again toward E deck and saw a stewardess struggling to dislodge a belt. I helped her with hers and secured one for myself. I then rushed to D deck and noticed one woman perched on the gunwale, watching a lowering lifeboat ten feet away. I pushed her down and into the boat, then I jumped in. The stern of the lifeboat continued to lower, but the bow stuck fast. A stoker cut the bow ropes with a hatchet, and we dropped in a vertical position.

"A girl whom we had heard sing at a concert was struggling, and I caught her by the ankle and pulled her in. A man I grasped by the shoulders and I landed him safe. He was the barber of the first-class cabin, and a more manly man I never met.

"We pushed away hard to avoid the suck, but our boat was fast filling, and we bailed fast with one bucket and the women's hats. The man with the bucket became exhausted, and I relieved him. In a few minutes she was filled level full. Then a keg floated up, and I pitched it about ten feet away and followed it. After reaching the keg I turned to see what had been the fate of our boat. She had capsized. Now a young steward, Freeman, approached me, clinging to a deck chair. I urged him to grab the other side of the keg several times. He grew faint, but harsh speaking roused him. Once he said: 'I am going to go.' But I ridiculed this, and it gave him strength.

"The good boat *Brock* and her splendid officers and men took us aboard.

"At the scene of the catastrophe the surface of the water seemed dotted with bodies. Only a few of the lifeboats seemed to be doing any good. The cries of 'My God!' 'Save us!' and 'Help!' gradually grew weaker from all sides, and finally a low weeping, wailing, inarticulate sound, mingled with coughing and gargling, made me heartsick. I saw many men die. Some appeared to be sleepy and worn out just before they went down."

Officials of the Cunard Line claimed afterward that three submarines had been engaged in the attack on the liner, but, after all evidence had been sifted, the claim made by the Germans that only one had been present was found to be true. The commander of the submarine had evidently been well informed as to just what route the liner would take. Trouble with her engines, which developed after she had left New York, had brought her speed down to 18 knots, a circumstance which was in favor of the attacking vessel, for it could not have done much damage with a torpedo had she been going at her highest speed; it would have given her a chance to cross the path of the torpedo as it approached. No sign of the submarine was noticed by the lookout or by any of the passengers on the *Lusitania* until it was too late to maneuver her to a position of safety. A few moments before the white wake of the approaching torpedo was espied, the periscope had been seen as it came to the surface of the water. From that moment onward the liner was doomed.

The German admiralty report of the actual sinking of the ship, which was issued on the 14th of May, 1915, was brief. It read: "A submarine sighted the steamship *Lusitania,* which showed no flag, May 7, 2.20 Central European time, afternoon, on the southeast coast of Ireland, in fine, clear weather.

"At 3.10 o'clock one torpedo was fired at the *Lusitania,* which hit her starboard side below the captain's bridge. The detonation of the torpedo was followed immediately by a further explosion of extremely strong effect. The ship quickly listed to starboard and began to sink.

"The second explosion must be traced back to the ignition of quantities of ammunition inside the ship."

The sinking of the *Lusitania* was one of the most horrible and unjustifiable deeds of the war. The German people, however, struck a medal to commemorate the event. Attacks by submarines on neutral ships did not abate, however, for on the 15th of May, 1915, the Danish steamer *Martha* was torpedoed in broad daylight and in view of crowds ashore off the coast of Aberdeen Bay.

The sinking of ships in the "war zone" continued in spite of rumors that the German admiralty was expected to discontinue operations of the submarines against merchantmen on account of the unfriendly feeling aroused in neutral nations, particularly the United States. On the 19th of May, 1915, came the news that the British steamship *Dumcree* had been torpedoed off a point in the English Channel. A torpedo fired into her hull failed to sink her immediately, and a Norwegian ship came to her aid, passing her a cable and attempting to tow her to port. But the submarine returned, and fearing attack, the Norwegian ship made off. A second torpedo fired at the *Dumcree* had better effect than the first one, and she began to settle. When the submarine left the scene the Norwegian steamship again returned to the *Dumcree* and managed to take off all of her crew and passengers. Three trawlers, one of them French, were sunk in the same neighborhood during the next forty-eight hours.

As soon as Italy entered the war an attempt was made by the Teutonic Powers to establish the same sort of submarine blockade in the Adriatic which obtained in the waters around Great Britain. This was evinced when the captain of the Italian steamship *Marsala* reported on May 21, 1915, that his ship had been stopped by an Austrian submarine, but the latter not wishing to disclose its location to the Italian navy, allowed his ship to proceed unharmed.

The suspicion that the German admiralty maintained bases for their submarines right on the coasts of Great Britain where the submersible craft could obtain oil for driving their engines, as well as supplies of compressed air and of food for the crew, was confirmed on the 14th of May, 1915, when it was reported that agents of the British admiralty had discovered caches of the kind at various points in the Orkney Islands, in the Bay of Biscay, and on the north and west coasts of Ireland.

In order to damage shipping in the "war zone" by having ships go wrong through having no guiding lights an attack was made by a German submarine on the lighthouse at Fastnet, on the southern coast of Ireland, on the night of May 25, 1915. Shortly after nine in the evening the submarine was sighted in the waters near the lighthouse by persons on shore. She was about ten miles from Fastnet, near Barley Cove. When she came near enough to the lighthouse to use her deck guns, men on shore opened fire on her with rifles, and she submerged, not to reappear in that neighborhood again.

But this same submarine managed to do other damage. The American steamship *Nebraskan* was in the neighborhood on its way to New York. The sea was calm and the ship was traveling at 12 knots, when some time near nine o'clock in the evening a shock was felt aboard. A second later there came a terrific explosion, and a subsequent investigation showed that a large hole, 20 feet square, had been torn in her starboard bow, not far from the water line. When she began to settle the captain ordered all hands into the small boats. They stayed near the damaged ship for an hour and saw that she was not going to sink. When they got aboard again they found that a bulkhead was keeping out the water sufficiently to allow her to proceed under her own steam. In crippled condition she made for port, being convoyed later by two British warships which answered her calls for help.

In spite of the sharp diplomatic representations which were at the time passing back and forth between Germany and the United States over the matter of the German submarine warfare, the craft kept up as active a campaign against merchant ships as they did before the issues became pointed. On May 28, 1915, there came the news that three more ships had been sent to the bottom. The *Spennymoor*, a new ship, was chased and torpedoed off Start Point, near the Orkney Islands. Some of her crew were drowned when the lifeboat in which they were getting away capsized, carrying them down. On the same day the large liner *Argyllshire* was chased and fired upon by the deck guns of a hostile submarine, but she managed to get away. Not so fortunate, however, was the steamship *Cadesby*. While off the Scilly Islands on the afternoon of May 28, 1915, a German submarine hailed her, firing a shot from a deck gun across her bows as a signal to halt. Time was given for the crew and passengers to get into small boats, and when these were at a distance from the ship the deck guns of the submarine were again brought into action, and after firing thirty shots into her hull they sank her. The third victim was the Swedish ship *Roosvall*. She was stopped and boarded off Malmoe by the crew of a German submarine. After examining her papers they permitted her to proceed, but later sent a torpedo into her, sinking her.

A new raider, the *U-24*, made its appearance in the English Channel during the last week in May, 1915. On the twenty-eighth of the month this submarine sank the liner *Ethiope*. The captain of the steamship attempted some clever maneuvering, which did not accomplish its object. He paid no attention to a shot from the deck guns of the submarine which passed across his bow. The hostile craft then began to circle around the liner, while the rudder of the latter was put at a wide angle in an effort to keep either stern or bow of the ship toward the submarine, thus making a poor target for a torpedo. But the commander of the submarine saw through the movement and ordered fire with his deck guns. After shells had taken away the ship's bridge and had punctured her hull near the stern the crew and passengers were ordered into the small boats. They had hardly gotten twenty feet from their ship when she was rent by a violent explosion and went down.

The transatlantic liner *Megantic* had better luck, for she managed to escape a pursuing submarine on May 29, 1915, as she was nearing Queenstown, Ireland, homeward bound. A notable change in the methods adopted by the commanders of submarines as a result of orders issued by the German admiralty in answer to the protests throughout the press of the neutral nations after the sinking of the *Lusitania* was the giving of warning to intended victims. By the end of May, 1915, in almost every instance where a German submarine stopped and sank a merchantman the crew was given time to get off their ship and the submarine did not hesitate to show itself. In fact, warning to stop was generally given when the submarine's deck was above water and the gun mounted there had the victim "covered." This was done in the case of the British steamship *Tullochmoor*, which was torpedoed off Ushant near the most westerly islands of Brittany, France.

On the 1st of June, 1915, there came the news of the sinking of the British ship *Dixiana*, near Ushant, by a German submarine which approached by aid of a clever disguise. The crew managed to get off the ship in time; when they landed on shore they reported that the submarine had been seen and on account of sails which she carried was thought to be an innocent fishing boat. The disguise was penetrated too late for the *Dixiana* to make its escape.

The clear and calm weather which came with June, 1915, made greater activity on the part of German submarines possible. On the 4th of June, 1915, it was reported by the British admiralty that six more ships had been made victims, three of them being those of neutral countries. In the next twenty-four hours the number was increased by eleven, and eight more were added by the 9th of June, 1915.

On that date Mr. Balfour, Secretary of the British admiralty, announced that a German submarine had been sunk, though he did not state what had been the scene of the action. At the same time he announced that Great Britain would henceforth treat the captured crew of submarines in the same manner as were treated other war prisoners, and that the policy of separating these men from the others and of giving them harsher treatment would be abandoned.

On the 20th of June, 1915, the day's reports of losses due to the operations of German submarines, issued by the British Government, contained the news of the sinking of the two British torpedo boats, the *No. 10* and the *No. 20.* No details were made public concerning just how they went down.

On the same day the Italian admiralty announced that a cache maintained to supply submarines belonging to the Teutonic Powers and operating in the Mediterranean, had been discovered on a lonely part of the coast near Kalimno, an island off the southwest coast of Asia Minor. Ninety-six barrels of benzine and fifteen hundred barrels of other fuel were found and destroyed. It was believed that this supply had been shipped as kerosene from Saloniki to Piraeus. How submarines belonging to Germany had reached the southern theatre of naval warfare had been a matter of speculation for the outside world. But on the 6th of June, 1915, Captain Otto Hersing made public the manner in which he took the *U-51* on a 3,000 mile trip from Wilhelmshaven on the North Sea to Constantinople. He was the commander who managed to torpedo the British battleships *Triumph* and *Majestic*.

He received his orders to sail on the 25th of April, 1915, and immediately began to stock his ship with extra amounts of fuel and provisions, allowing only his first officer and chief engineer to know the destination of their craft. He traveled on the surface of the water as soon as he had passed the guard of British warships near the German coast; traveling "light" allowed him to make six or seven knots more in speed. As he passed through the "war zone" he kept watch for merchantmen which might be made victims of his torpedo tubes. His craft was sighted by a British destroyer, however, off the English coast and he had to submerge to escape the fire of the destroyer's guns. He then proceeded cautiously down the coast of France, encountering no hostile ships. When within one hundred miles of Gibraltar he was again discovered by British destroyers, but again managed to escape by submerging his craft.

Passage through the Strait of Gibraltar was made in the early morning hours, while a mist hung near the surface of the water and permitted no one at the fort to see the wake of the *U-51's* periscope. Once inside the Mediterranean he headed for the south of Greece, escaping attack from a French destroyer and proceeding through the Ægean Sea to the Dardanelles. The journey ended on the 25th of May, just one month after leaving Wilhelmshaven.

The British ships *Triumph* and *Majestic* were sighted early in the morning, but attack upon them was difficult on account of the destroyers which circled about them; one of the destroyers passed right over the *U-51* while she was submerged. Captain Hersing brought her to the surface soon afterward and let go the torpedo which sank the *Triumph*. For the next two days the submarine lay submerged, but came up on the following day and found itself right in the midst of the allied fleet. This time the *Majestic* was taken as the target for a torpedo and she went down. Again submerging his vessel Captain Hersing kept it down for another day, and when he again came to the surface he saw that the fleets had moved away. He then returned to Constantinople.

On the 23d of June, 1915, the British cruiser *Roxborough,* an older ship, was hit by a torpedo fired by a German submarine in the North Sea, but the damage inflicted was not enough to prevent her from making port under her own steam.

The deaths of a number of Americans occurred on the 28th of June, 1915, when the Leyland liner *Armenian,* carrying horses for the allied armies, was torpedoed by the *U-38,* twenty miles west by north of Trevose Head in Cornwall. According to the story of the captain of the vessel, the submarine fired two shots to signal him to stop. When he put on all speed in an attempt to get away from the raider her guns opened on his ship with shrapnel, badly riddling it. She had caught fire and was burning in three places before he signaled that he would surrender. Thirteen men had meanwhile been killed by the shrapnel. Some of the lifeboats had also been riddled by the firing from the submarine's deck guns, making it more difficult for the crew to leave the ship. The German commander gave him ample time to get his boats off.

To offset the advantage which the Germans had with their submarines the British admiralty commissioned ten such craft during the week of June 28, 1915. These vessels were of American build and design and were assembled in Canada. During the week mentioned they were manned by men sent for the purpose from England. Each was manned by four officers and eighteen men, to take them across the Atlantic. Never before in history had so many submarines undertaken a voyage as great. They got under way from Quebec on July 2, 1915, and proceeded in column two abreast, a big auxiliary cruiser, which acted as their escort steaming in the center.

The next large liner which had an encounter with the German submarine *U-39* was the *Anglo-Californian.* She came into Queenstown on the morning of July 5, 1915, with nine dead sailors lying on the deck, nine wounded men in their bunks, and holes in her sides made by shot and shell. She had withstood attack from a German submarine for four hours. Her escape from destruction was accomplished through only the spirit of the captain and his crew, combined with the fact that patrol vessels came to her aid forcing the submarine to submerge.

A variety in the methods used by the commanders of German submarines was revealed in the stopping of the Norwegian ship *Vega* which was stopped on the 15th of July, while voyaging from Bergen to Newcastle. The submarine came alongside the steamship at night and the commander of the submarine supervised the jettisoning of her cargo of 200 tons of salmon, 800 cases of butter, and 4,000 cases of sardines, which was done at his command under threat of sinking his victim.

The week of July 15, 1915, was unique in that not one British vessel was made the victim of a German submarine during that period, though two Russian vessels had been sunk. Figures compiled by the British admiralty and issued on the 22d of July, 1915, gave out the following information concerning the attacks on merchantmen by German submarines since the German admiralty's proclamation of a "war zone" around Great Britain went into effect on the 18th of February, 1915.

The official figures were as follows:

Week ending	Vessels lost	Lives lost
Feb. 25, 1915	11	9
March 4, "	1	None
March 11, "	7	38
March 18, "	6	13
March 25, "	7	2
April 1, "	13	165
April 8, "	8	13
April 15, "	4	None
April 22, "	3	10
April 29, "	3	None
May 6, "	24	5
May 13, "	2	1,260
May 20, "	7	13
May 27, "	7	7
June 3, "	36	21

Week ending		Vessels lost	Lives lost
June 10, 1915	....	36	21
June 17, "	....	19	19
June 24, "	....	3	1
July 1, "	....	9	29
July 8, "	....	15	2
July 15, "	....	12	13
July 22, "	....	2	None
		235	1,641

The first year of the Great War came to an end with the German submarines as active in the "war zone" as they had been during any part of it. On the 28th of July, 1915, the anniversary of the commencement of the war, there was reported the sinking of nine vessels. These were the Swedish steamer *Emma*, the three Danish schooners *Maria, Neptunis,* and *Lena,* the British steamer *Mangara,* the trawlers *Iceni* and *Salacia,* the *Westward Ho,* and the Swedish bark *Sagnadalen.* No lives were lost with any of these vessels.

The first year of the war closed with a cloud gathered over the heads of the members of the German admiralty raised by the irritation the submarine attacks in the "war zone" had caused. Germany's enemies protested against the illegality of these attacks; neutral nations protested because they held that their rights had been overridden. But the German press showed the feeling of the German public on the matter—at the end of July, 1915, it was as anxious as ever to have the attacks continued. Conflicting claims were issued in Germany and England. In the former country it was claimed that the attacks had seriously damaged commerce; in the latter it was claimed that the damage was of little account.

PART VI—THE EASTERN FRONT—AUSTRO-RUSSIAN CAMPAIGN

CHAPTER XXXV

THE CARPATHIAN CAMPAIGN—REVIEW OF THE SITUATION

IN the beginning of 1915 comparative calm reigned over the Austro-Russian theatre of war, so far as actual hostilities were concerned. But it was not altogether the variable climatic conditions of alternate frost and thaw—the latter converting road and valley into impassable quagmires—that caused the lull. It was a short winter pause during which the opposing forces—on one side at least—were preparing and gathering the requisite momentum for the coming storm.

During January, 1915, the Russian armies were in a decidedly favorable position. In their own invaded territory of Poland, as we have seen, they held an advanced position in front of the Vistula, which circumstance enabled them to utilize that river as a line of communication, while barring the way to Warsaw against Von Hindenburg. Lemberg, the capital of Galicia, which they had captured in September, 1914, was still in their hands. Sixty miles away to the west there lay the great fortress of Przemysl, invested by the Russians under General Selivanoff, and completely cut off from the outer world since November 12, 1914. At least 150,000 troops and enormous quantities of stores and munitions were locked up in the town and outlying forts, together with a population of 50,000 inhabitants, mostly Polish. In addition to these material advantages, the Russians held all the Carpathian passes leading from Galicia into the vast plains of

Hungary, and a strong advanced position on the Dunajec in the west, which, besides threatening Cracow, the capital of Austrian Poland, served also as a screen to the mountain operations. Finally, to the far east of the range, they had occupied nearly the whole of the Bukowina right up to the Rumanian frontier.

Such, briefly, was the situation on the Austro-Russian front when the second winter campaign opened. For Austria the situation was extremely critical. Her armies, broken and scattered after a series of disastrous reverses, could scarcely hope by their own efforts to stem the threatened invasion of Hungary. General Brussilov, however, made no serious attempt to pour his troops through the passes into the plain below; although what was probably a reconnaissance emerged from the Uzsok Pass and penetrated as far as Munkacs, some thirty miles south, while on several occasions small bands of Cossacks descended from the Dukla and Delatyn (Jablonitza) passes to raid Hungarian villages. General Brussilov evidently regarded it inadvisable to risk an invasion of the plain, especially as he did not hold control of the southern exits from the passes, beyond which he would be exposed to attack from all sides and liable to encounter superior forces. The main Austrian anxiety for the moment was the precarious position of Przemysl, to relieve which it was first essential to dislodge Brussilov or to pierce his line. Again, in the hour of her extremity, Austria's powerful ally came to the rescue.

Under the command of the Archduke Eugene the Austrian troops — all that were available — were formed into three separate armies. For convenience sake we will designate them A, B, and C. Army A, under General Boehm-Ermolli, was ordered to the section from the Dukla Pass to the Uzsog. It was charged with the task of cutting a way through to relieve Przemysl. Army B, under the German General von Linsingen, who also had some German troops with him, was to assail the next section eastward, from the Uzsog to the Wyszkow Pass; and Army C, under the Austrian General von Pflanzer-Baltin, likewise supplied with a good "stiffening" of German soldiers, was accredited to the far-eastern section—the Pruth Valley and the

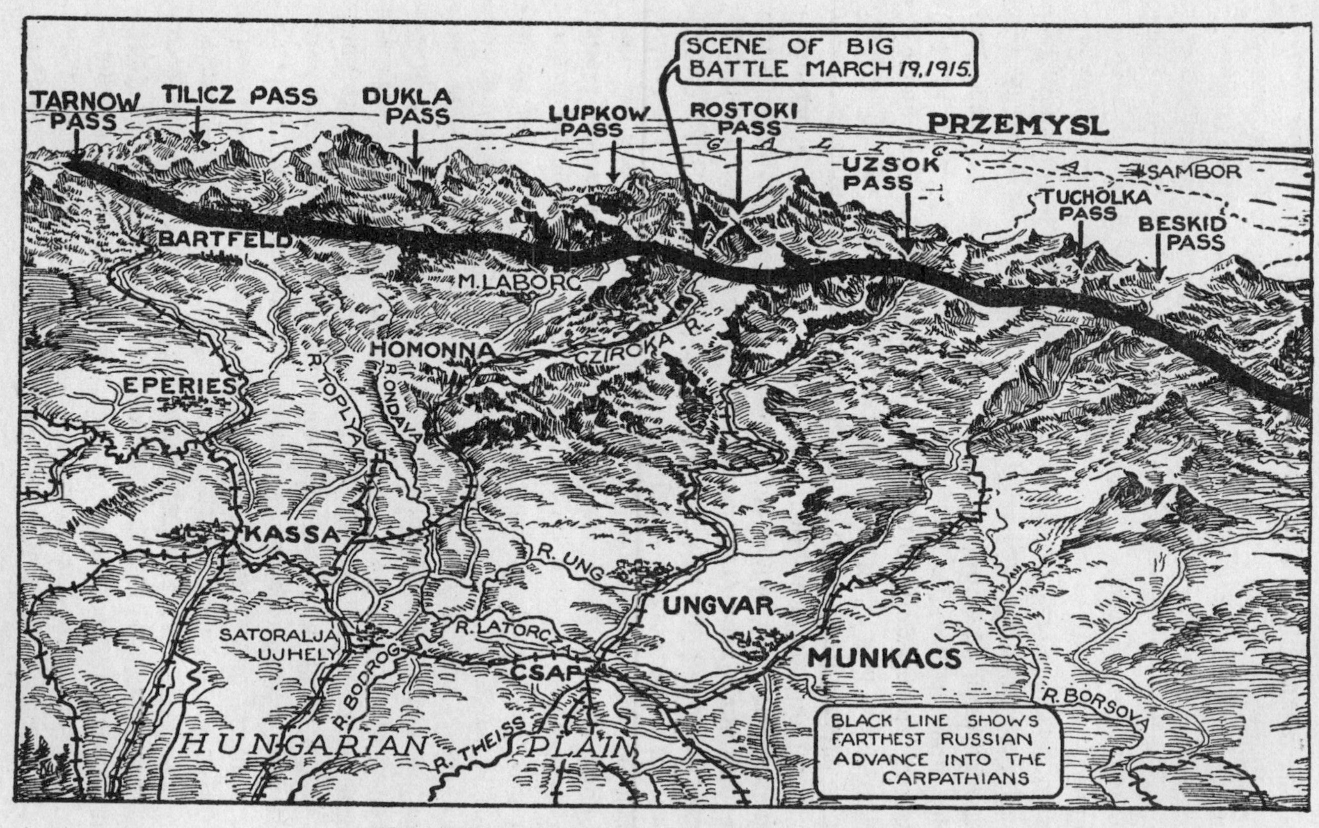

THE CARPATHIAN PASSES AND RUSSIAN BATTLE LINE

Bukowina. These three armies represented the fighting machine with which Austria hoped to retrieve the misfortunes of war and recover at the same time her military prestige and her invaded territories. We have no reliable information to enable us to estimate the exact strength of these armies, but there is every reason to believe that it was considerable, having regard to the urgency of the situation and the bitter experience of the recent past. Hence the figure of 400,000 men is probably approximately correct. Somewhere about January 23, 1914, after a period of thaw and mud the weather settled down to snow and hard frost. Then the machine began to move. A snow-clad mountain rampart lay spread before; over 200 miles of its length embraced the area of the projected operations. Here we may leave this army for a while in order to review some of the political and strategic considerations underlying the campaign, which is the scope of this chapter.

The Russian occupation of the Bukowina, which was undertaken and accomplished by a force far too small to oppose any serious resistance, appears to have been carried out with the definite political object of favorably impressing Rumania, and to guide her into the arms of the Allies. From her geographical position Rumania commands nearly the whole western frontier of the Dual Monarchy. Her fertile soil supplied the Central Powers with grain, dairy produce, and oil. Furthermore, Rumania's foreign policy leaned to the side of Italy, and the general European impression was, after the death of King Carol, October 10, 1914, that if one of the two countries entered the war, the other would follow suit. As subsequent events have shown, however, that expectation was not realized. Rumania, too, had aspirations in the direction of recovering lost territories, but her grievance in this respect was equally divided between Russia and Austria, for, while the one had despoiled her of Bessarabia, the other had annexed Transylvania (Siebenbürgen). Hence the Russian tentative conquest and occupation of the Bukowina paved the way for Rumania, should she decide on intervention. The road was clear for her to step in and occupy the Bukowina (which Russia was prepared to hand over), and probably

Transylvania as well, which latter the proximity of a Russian force might—at the time—have enabled her to do. But the bait failed, no doubt for weighty reasons. Even if Rumania had favored the Triple Entente, which there is strong ground to presume she would, by entering the war, have found herself in as perilous a position as Serbia, with her Black Sea littoral exposed to hostile Turkey and her whole southern boundary flanked by a neighbor—Bulgaria—whose intentions were as yet unknown. However, on January 27, 1915, the Bank of England arranged a $25,000,000 loan to Rumania—an event which further heightened the probability of her entry into the arena.

We may safely take it for granted that these considerations were not overlooked by the German staff, in addition to the patent fact that the Russians were persistently gaining ground against the Austrians. German officers and men were therefore rushed from the eastern and western fronts to the south of the Carpathians to form the three armies we have labeled A, B, and C. The points of attack for which they were intended have already been stated; but the roundabout manner in which they traveled to their respective sections is both interesting and worthy of notice. At this stage a new spirit seemed to dominate Austro-Hungarian military affairs; we suddenly encounter greater precision, sounder strategy, and deeper plans: a master mind appears to have taken matters in hand. It is the cool, calculating, mathematical composite brain of the German General Staff. As the formation and dispatching of three great armies can hardly be kept a secret, especially where hawk-eyed spies abound, a really astute piece of stage management was resorted to. Wild rumors were set afloat to the effect that the Austrian Government had decided to undertake a great offensive—for the third time—against Serbia, and erase her from the map, with the assistance of four German army corps. The concentration one for operations against either Serbia or the Russian front in the Carpathians was naturally in the central plains of Hungary. But to cover the real object of Austro-German concentration active demonstrations were made on the Serb border in the form of bombardments of Belgrade, and occupation of Danube islands.

These demonstrations made plausible the Teutonic assertion that the concentration of troops was being carried out with a view to an invasion of Serbia. So successful was the ruse, and so well had the secret been kept that on February 1, 1914, a Petrograd "official" gravely announced to an eagerly listening world: "The statement is confirmed that the new Austro-German southern army, intended for the third invasion of Serbia, consists of six Austrian and two German corps or 400,000 men, under the command of the Archduke Eugene(!)" At the very time this appeared the new Austro-German "southern" army had been already, for quite a week, making its presence severely felt in the eastern and central sections of the Carpathians, and still the Russian authorities had not recognized the identity of the forces operating there.

A brief description of the battle ground will enable the reader to follow more easily the course of the struggle. Imagine that length of the Carpathian chain which forms the boundary between Galicia and Hungary as a huge, elongated arch of, roughly, 300 miles. (The whole of the range stretches as a continuous rampart for a distance of 900 miles, completely shutting in Hungary from the northwest to the east and south, separating it from Moravia [Mähren], Galicia, the Bukowina, and Rumania.) Through the curve of this arch run a number of passes. Beginning as far west as is here necessary, the names of the chief passes eastward leading from Hungary are: into Galicia—Beskid, Tarnow, Tilicz, Dukla, Lupkow, Rostoki, Uzsok, Vereczke (or Tucholka), Beskid* (or Volocz), Wyszkow, Jablonitza (or Delatyn); into the Bukowina—Strol, Kirlibaba, Rodna; into Rumania—Borgo. In parts the range is 100 miles in width, and from under 2,000 to 8,000 feet high. The western and central Carpathians are much more accessible than the eastern, and therefore comprise the main and easiest routes across. The Hun and Tartar invasions flooded Europe centuries ago by this way, and the Delatyn is still called the "Magyar route." The passes vary in height from under a thousand to over four thousand feet. The Dukla and Uzsok passes were to be the main ob-

* There are two passes named Beskid.

jective, as through them lay the straightest roads to Lemberg and Przemysl. The former is crossed by railway from Tokay to Przemysl, and the latter by rail and road from Ungvar to Sambor. A railroad also runs through the Vereczke from Munkacs to Lemberg, and another through Delatyn from Debreczen to Kolomea. So far as concerned means of communication, matters were nearly equal, but geographical advantage lay with the Russians, as the way from Galicia to Hungary is by far an easier one than vice versa.

CHAPTER XXXVI

BATTLE OF THE PASSES

BEFORE proceeding with the opening of the second winter campaign in the Carpathians, the reader should remember that, as stated in the beginning of this narrative, a Russian army under General Radko Dmitrieff (a Bulgarian), held an advanced position on the Dunajec-Biala line, extending from the Vistula to Zmigrod, northwest of Dukla. This force was consequently beyond the zone of the Austro-German offensive, but, as events proved, it had not been overlooked, for it was here that the heaviest blow was finally to fall. It is also important to bear in mind that the Russian armies occupying Galicia and the northern slopes of the Carpathians were not conducting an isolated campaign on their own account; they formed an integral part of the far-flung battle line that reached from the shores of the Baltic down to the Rumanian frontier, a distance of nearly 800 miles. Dmitrieff's force represented a medial link of the chain—and the weakest.

Over the slushy roads of the valleys and into the snow-laden passes the Germanic armies advanced, each of the widely deployed columns with a definite objective: From Dukla, Lupkow, and Rostoki to relieve Przemysl; from Uzsok through the valley of the Upper San to Sambor; through Beskid and Vereczke northward to Stryj, thence westward also to Sambor; over Wyszkow to Dolina; via Jablonitza to Delatyn; and across Kirlibaba and Dorna Vatra into the Bukowina. Opposed to them were the Russian Generals Brussilov, Ivanoff, and Alexieff, respectively.

Correspondents with the Teutonic troops in these weeks wrote in wonderment of the scenes of the slowly forward toiling advance into the mountains which they had seen. On every road leading into Galicia there was the same picture of a flood rolling steadily on. Everywhere could be seen the German and Austro-Hungarian troops on the move, men going into the firing line to fight for days, day after day, with the shedding of much blood, among the peaks and valleys, under changing skies.

Here is a word picture of the supply columns winding upward into the Carpathians to the support of the Teutonic troops furnished by a German correspondent:

"Truly fantastic is the appearance of one of these modern supply caravans, stretching in zigzag, with numerous sharp corners and turns, upward to the heights of the passes and down on the opposite side. Here we see in stages, one above the other and moving in opposite directions, the queerest mixture of men, vehicles, machines and animals, all subordinated to a common military purpose and organization by military leadership, moving continually and regularly along. The drivers have been drummed up from all parts of the monarchy, Serbs, Ruthenians, Poles, Croats, Rumanians, Hungarians, Slovaks, Austrians, and turbaned Mohammedans from Bosnia. Everyone is shouting to his animals and cursing in his own language. The whole mix-up is a traveling exhibition of most variegated characteristic costumes, for the most part, of course, extremely the worse for wear. Common to all these are the little wagons adapted to mountain travel, elastic and tough, which carry only half loads and are drawn by little ponylike, ambitious horses. In between are great German draft horses, stamping along with their broad high-wheeled baggage and ammunition wagons, as though they belonged to a nation of giants.

"Gravely, with a kind of sullen dignity, slow-stepping steers drag at their yokes heavily laden sledges. They are a powerful white breed, with broad-spreading horns a yard long. These are followed in endless rows by carefully stepping pack animals, small and large horses, mules and donkeys. On the wooden pack-saddles on their backs are the carefully weighed bales of hay or ammunition boxes or other war materials. Walking gingerly by the edges of the mountain ridges they avoid pitfalls and rocks and walk round the stiff, distended bodies of their comrades that have broken down on the way. At times there ambles along a long row of working animals a colt, curious and restlessly sniffing. In the midst of this movement of the legs of animals, of waving arms, of creaking and swaying loaded vehicles of manifold origin, there climbs upward the weighty iron of an Austrian motor battery, with an almost incomprehensible inevitableness, flattening out the broken roads like a steam roller.

"From the first pass the baggage train sinks down into the depths, again to climb upward on the next ridge, to continue striving upward ever toward higher passages, slowly pushing forward toward its objective against the resistance of numberless obstacles.

"The road to the battle field of to-day crosses the battle field of recent weeks and months. Here there once stood a village, but only the stone foundations of the hearths are left as traces of the houses that have been burned down. Sometimes falling shots or the terrors of a brief battle in the streets have reduced to ruins only a part of a village. The roofs of houses have been patched with canvas and boards to some extent, and now serve as quarters for troops or as stables. In the narrow valleys the level places by the sides of streams have been utilized for encampments. Here stand in order wagons of a resting column and the goulash cannons shedding their fragrance far and wide, or the tireless ovens of a field bakery. Frequently barracks, hospital buildings, and shelters for men and animals have been built into the mountain sides. Here and there simple huts have been erected, made of a few poles and fir twigs. Often they are placed in long rows, which, when their inmates are warming themselves by the fire at night turn the dark mountain road into a romantic night encampment, and everywhere fresh crosses, ornamented at times in a manner suggestive of the work of children, remind us of our brothers now forever silenced, who, but a short time before went the same road, withstood just such weather and such hardships, talked perhaps in these same huts of the war, and dreamt of peace.

"The saddest spectacle, however, were the lightly wounded, poor fellows, who might under ordinary conditions have readily walked the distance from the first aid station to the central gathering point, but who here on account of the ice or muddy roads require double and three times the usual time."

CHAPTER XXXVII

BATTLE OF KOZIOWA—OPERATIONS IN THE BUKOWINA

OWING to the topographical conditions under which fighting must be carried on in the central Carpathians, some weeks might be expected to elapse before a general engagement developed along the entire front. Lateral communication or cooperation between the advancing columns was out of the question; the passes were like so many parallel tunnels, each of which must first be negotiated before a reunion can take place at the northern exits.

We will follow the achievements of the three groups in separate order. Army A, under Boehm-Ermolli, crossed Uzsok and Rostoki, and forced part of the Russian line back upon Baligrod, but Brussilov held it fast on Dukla and Lupkow, strongly supported by Dmitrieff on his right. Here the attack failed with severe losses; the Germanic forces were thrown back into Hungary, and the Russians commanded the southern ends of the passes around Dukla. The Uzsok Pass was of small strategical value to the Austrians now that they had it. It is extremely vulnerable at every point; steep, narrow, and winding roads traverse its course nearly 3,000 feet high, with thickly wooded mountains up to 4,500 feet overlooking the scene from a close circle. Regarded merely as a short cut to Przemysl and Lemberg, the Uzsok was a useful possession provided always that the northern debouchment could be cleared and an exit forced. But the Russians held these debouchments with a firm grip, and the pass was consequently of no use to the Austrians. About February 7, 1915, the Russians attempted to outflank the Austrian position in the Lupkow Pass from the eastern branch of the Dukla by pushing forward in the direction of Mezo-Laborc on the Hungarian side. The movement partially succeeded; they took over 10,000 prisoners, but failed to dislodge the Austrians from the heights east of the pass. Severe fighting raged round this district for over a month, the Russians finally capturing Lupkow, as well as Smolnik at the southern exit of Rostoki. Had the Russians succeeded in getting between Uzsok and the Austrian line of communication, as was undoubtedly their aim, the Austrians would have been compelled to relinquish the pass without even a fight. However, General Boehm-Ermolli's mission proved a failure.

Army B, under Von Linsingen, succeeded in traversing all the passes in its appointed section. Crossing by the railway pass of Beskid and the two roads leading through Vereczke and Wyszkow, they pushed forward in the direction of Stryj and Lemberg, but never reached their destination. Barely through the passes, the Germans struck upon Lysa Gora, over 3,300 feet high. This mountain range is barren of all vegetation— no sheltering trees or shrubs adorn its slopes. The route of the Germans crossed Lysa Gora south and in front of the ridge of Koziowa, where the Russian lines, under General Ivanoff, lay in waiting. Passing down the bald slopes of Lysa Gora toward the valley of the Orava River, the advancing German columns presented a conspicuous target for the Russians on the opposite slopes of Koziowa, screened by thick forests. Here one of the most desperate battles of the campaign ensued on February 6, 1915, between Von Linsingen's Austro-German army and Brussilov's center.

In close formation and with well-drilled precision the Germans attempted to storm the position at the point of the bayonet. Again and again they returned to the charge, only to be repulsed with severe losses. As many as twenty-two furious bayonet charges were made in one day, February 7. Wherever a footing was gained in the Russian lines, there a few minutes ferocious hand-to-hand *mêlée* developed—Saxon and Slav at death grips—the intruders were expelled or hacked down. Great masses of Austro-German dead and wounded were strewn over the lower slopes of Koziowa. For five weeks Von Linsingen hammered at the Russian front without being able to break through. So long as the Russians held the heights it was impossible for their enemy to emerge from the passes. These two, Vereczke and Beskid, so close together, may literally be described as twin tunnels. Owing to the highland between them, the two columns moving through could not cooperate; if one side needed reenforcements from the other, they had to be taken back over the range into Hungary to the junction where the roads diverged. It was sound strategy on the Russian side to select Koziowa as the point from which to check the Germanic advance. For the time being, with Dukla and Lupkow in their hands and the exits of Uzsok and Rostoki strongly guarded, the defense of Koziowa held Galicia safe from reconquest. The attacks against Koziowa continued beyond the middle of March, 1915. On the 16th of that month the Russians captured a place called Oravcyk, about four miles westward, from where they could threaten the German left, which had the effect of keeping Von Linsingen still closer to his mountain passages. The fighting in this region represents one of the important phases of the war, for it prevented the relief of Przemysl; temporarily saved Stryj and Lemberg for the Russians; enabled them to send reenforcements into the Bukowina, and, finally, inspired the German General Staff to plan the great and decisive Galician campaign, which was to achieve the task wherein Boehm-Ermolli and Von Linsingen had both failed.

Meanwhile, what had Von Pflanzer-Baltin accomplished with Army C—the third column? His path lay through Jablonitza, Kirlibaba, and Dorna Vatra; his task was to clear the Russians out of the Bukowina, and either to force them back across their own frontiers, or to turn the extreme end of their left flank. We have seen that the Russian occupation of the Bukowina was more in the nature of a political experiment than a serious military undertaking, and that their forces in the province were not strong enough to indulge in great strategical operations. Hence we may expect the Austrian general's progress to be less difficult than that of his colleagues in the western and central Carpathians. To some extent this presumption is correct, for on February 18, 1915, after launching out from the southern corner of the Bukowina at Kimpolung and via the Jablonitza Pass down the Pruth Valley, they captured Czernowitz, and after that Kolomea, whence the railway runs to Lemberg. Within three days they reached Stanislawow, another important railway center, defended by a small Russian force, and a big battle ensued. Altogether, the Germanic troops in the Bukowina were reported at 50,000 in number, though these were split up into two columns, one of which was making but slow progress farther east.

Russian reenforcements were thrown into the town, and the struggle for the railway, which lasted a week, appears to have been of a seesaw nature, for no official reports of the fighting were issued by either side. Still the Austrians pushed westward in the hope of reaching the railways which supplied those Russian armies which were barring the advance through the central passes. The Russians were forced to withdraw from Stanislawow, and their opponents now held possession of the line running to Stryj and Przemysl—a serious menace to the Russian main communications. This meant that Von Pflanzer-Baltin had succeeded in getting to the rear of the Russians. But assistance came unexpectedly from the center, whence Ivanoff was able to send reenforcements to his colleague, General Alexeieff, who was continually falling back before the Austrians. Furious counterattacks were delivered by the Russians at Halicz and Jezupol, the

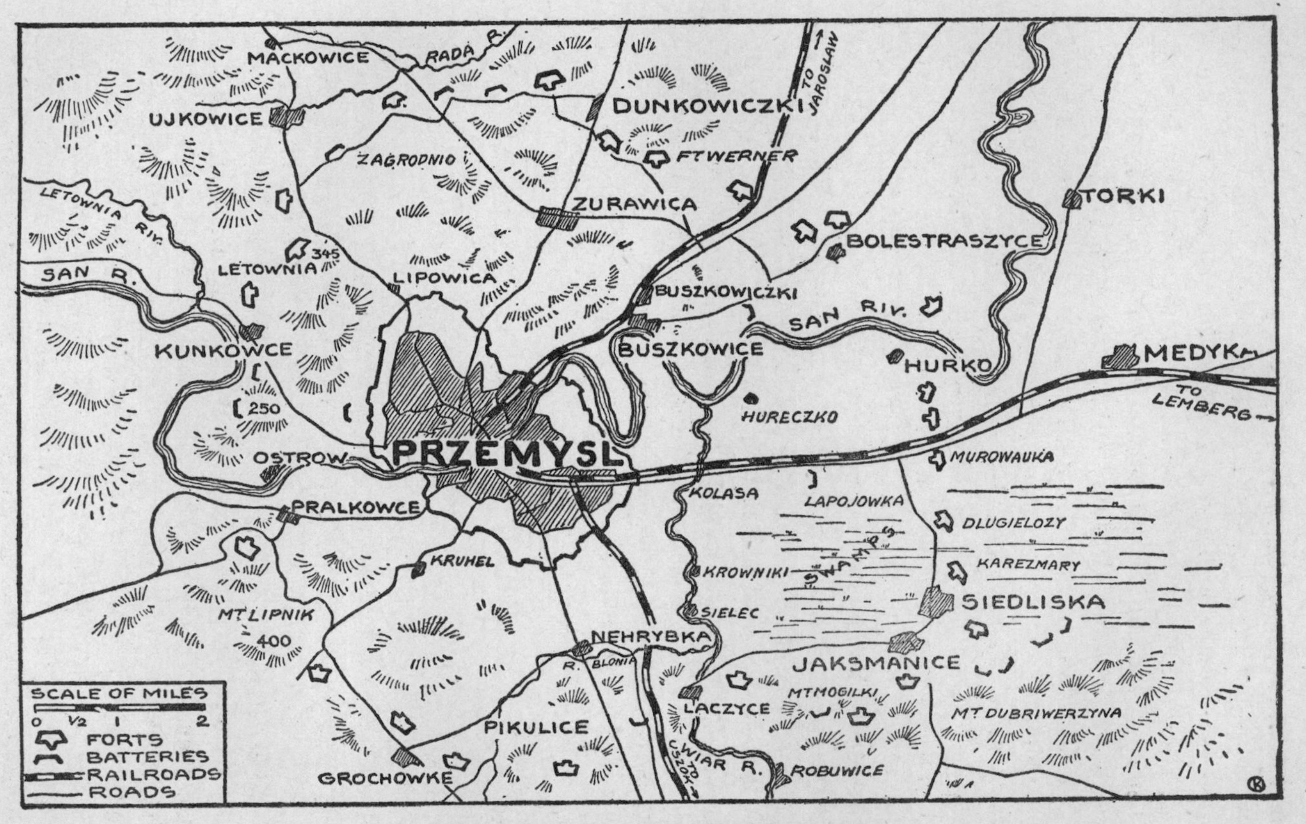

DETAIL MAP OF THE FORTS OF PRZEMYSL

bridgeheads of the southern bank of the Dniester. If the Austrians could not force a victory at these points, their position in Stanislawow would be untenable, since the Russians still had a clear road to pour reenforcements into the fighting area between the Dniester and the Carpathians. On March 1, 1915, the Austrians were defeated at Halicz in a pitched battle, and on the 4th the Russians reentered Stanislawow. According to their official communiqué the Russians captured nearly 19,000 prisoners, 5 guns, 62 machine guns, and a quantity of stores and munitions. About March 16 the opposing forces came again into touch southeast of Stanislawow on the road to Ottynia, but nothing of importance appears to have happened. To sum up the results of the Germanic offensive, we must remember what the objectives were. Of the latter, none was attained. The Russians had not been expelled from Galicia; Przemysl was no nearer to relief than before, and Lemberg had not been retaken. With the exception of Dukla and Lupkow, all the passes were in Austrian hands; but the Russians dominated the northern debouchments of all of them excepting Jablonitza.

CHAPTER XXXVIII

FALL OF PRZEMYSL

THE town and fortress of Przemysl formally surrendered to the Russian General Selivanoff on Monday, March 22, 1915. The first investment began at the early stages of the war in September, 1914. On the 27th of that month the Russian generalissimo announced that all communications had been cut off. By October 15, 1914, the Russian investment had been broken again, and for a matter of three weeks, while the road was open, more troops, provisions, arms, and munitions were rushed to the spot. As we have seen, however, the Russians recovered their lost advantage, for, after the fall of Jaroslav, the fortress to the north of Przemysl, their troops were hurried up from east, north, and west, and within a few days the Austrians were sent back along the whole front. From the region of Przemysl three railroads cross the Carpathians to Budapest, along all of which the Russians had pushed vigorously, besides advancing on the west. As regarded railroad communications, the fate of Przemysl was sealed by the capture of Chyrow, an important junction about twenty miles south of the fortress. Przemysl itself was important as a road junction and as a connecting link with the Uzsok and Lupkow passes. The garrison prepared to make a stubborn resistance with the object of checking the Russian pursuit. A week later the Russians had broken up their heavy artillery and had begun a steady bombardment. By November 12, 1914, Przemysl was once more completely besieged by General Selivanoff with not more than 100,000 troops.

Przemysl is one of the oldest towns of Galicia, said to have been founded in the eighth century. It was once the capital of a large independent principality. In the fourteenth century Casimir the Great and other Polish princes endowed it with special civic privileges, and the town attained a high degree of commercial prosperity. In the seventeenth century its importance was destroyed by inroads of Tatars, Cossacks, and Swedes. Przemysl is situated on the River San, and was considered one of the strongest fortresses of Europe.

The original strategic idea embodied in the purpose of the fortress was purely defensive; in the event of war with Russia only the line of the San and Dniester was intended to be held at all costs, while the whole northeastern portion of Galicia was to be abandoned. With the fortress of Cracow guarding the west, Przemysl was meant to be the first defense between the two rivers and to hold the easiest roads to Hungary through the Dukla, Lupkow, and Uzsok passes. Within the last ten years, however, the Austrian War Staff altered its plans and decided upon a vigorous offensive against Russia should occasion offer, and that Eastern Galicia was not to be sacrificed. Hence a network of strategic railways was constructed with a view to attacking the prospective enemy on a wide front extending from the Vistula near Cracow on the west to the Bug on the east, where the latter flows into Austrian territory and cuts off a corner of eastern Galicia. The plan does not appear to have worked successfully, for, before the war was many days old, the Russians had taken Lemberg, swept across the Dniester at Halicz, across the San at Jaroslav, just north of Przemysl, and had already besieged the fortress, which at no time imposed any serious obstacle in the path of their progress. Perhaps the only useful purpose that Przemysl served was that it restrained the Russians from attempting an invasion of Hungary on a big scale, by holding out for nearly seven months. Not having sufficient siege artillery at their disposal, the Russians made no attempt to storm the place. General Selivanoff surrounded the forts with a wide circle of counterdefenses, which were so strongly fortified that the garrison would have found it an almost hopeless task to attempt a rush through the enemy's lines. The Austrian artillery was naturally well acquainted with the range of every point and position that lay within reach of their guns; and Selivanoff wisely offered them little opportunity for effective practice. Considering it too expensive to attack by the overland route, he worked his way gradually toward the forts by means of underground operations. To sap a position is slow work, but much more economical in the expenditure of lives and munitions. The weakness of Przemysl lay in the fact that its garrison was far too large for its needs, and that provisions were running short. In the early part of the campaign the Germanic armies operating in the San region had drawn freely on Przemysl for supplies, and before these could be adequately replaced the Russians had again forged an iron ring around the place. The Russian commander, moreover, was aware that a coming scarcity threatened the town, and that he had only to bide his time to starve it into submission. Whilst he was simply waiting and ever strengthening his lines, the Austrians found it incumbent on them to assume the offensive. Several desperate sorties were made by the garrison to break through the wall, only to end in complete disaster. General Herman von Kusmanek, the commander in chief of the fortress, organized a special force, composed largely of Hungarians, for "sortie duty," under the command of a Hungarian, General von Tamassy. These sorties had been carried out during November and December, 1914, especially during the latter month, when the Austro-German armies were pouring across the mountains. So critical was the Russian position at the time that the relief of Przemysl was hourly expected. According to an officer of General Selivanoff's staff, "The Austrians in the fortress were already conversing with the Austrians on the Carpathians by means of their searchlights. The guns of Przemysl could be heard by the Austrian field artillery. The situation was serious, and General Selivanoff took prompt measures. He brought up fresh troops to the point of danger and drove the sortie detachments back to the fortress." It is stated from the Austrian side that one of the sortie detachments had succeeded in breaking through the Russian lines and marching to a point fifteen miles beyond the outer lines of the forts. A Russian official announcement states that during two months of the siege the Austrian captures amounted only to 4 machine guns and about 60 prisoners, which occurred in an engagement where two Honved regiments fell on a Russian company which had advanced too far to be reenforced in time. On their part in repulsing sorties by the garrison, frequently made by considerable forces, the Russians made prisoners 27 officers and 1,906 soldiers, and captured 7 machine guns, 1,500,000 cartridges, and a large quantity of arms. In two sorties the garrison in the region of Bircza had more than 2,000 killed and wounded, among them being many officers. No further sorties were undertaken in that particular region. During January and February, 1915, very little fighting took place around Przemysl; sorties were useless as there was no Austro-German force anywhere near the fortress, and the Russians were tightening the pressure around it. The only means of communication with the outer world was by aeroplane, so that, despite the rigid investment, the Austro-German war staff were kept fully informed of the straits in which Przemysl found itself. General Boehm-Ermolli, with Army A, was making desperate efforts to extricate himself from the Russian grip round Uzsok, Lupkow, and Dukla; he did not get beyond Baligrod, as the crow flies, thirty miles south of Przemysl.

On March 13, 1915, the Russians stormed and captured the village of Malkovise, on the northeast, breaking through the outer line of the defense. From this position they began to bombard parts of the inner ring. About the beginning of the third week in March, 1915, a new spirit of activity appeared to seize the beleaguered garrison: they commenced a terrific cannonade which, however, elicited no response. It was but the energy of despair: they were firing to get rid of their ammunition, hoping at the same time to hit something or somebody. The end was at hand.

On March 18, 1915, a Petrograd "official" laconically reports that: "In the Przemysl sector the fortress guns continue to fire more than a thousand heavy projectiles daily, but our troops besieging the fortress lose only about ten men every day." It is also on March 18 that General von Kusmanek issued the following manifesto to the defenders of Przemysl:—"Heroes, I announce to you my last summons. The honor of our country and our army demands it. I shall lead you to pierce with your points of steel the iron circles of the enemy, and then march ever farther onward, sparing no efforts, until we rejoin our army, which, after heavy fighting, is now near us."

Just before the surrender two Austrian officers escaped from the fortress in an aeroplane. These reported concerning the last days of the siege:

"On the 18th of March the last provisions had been dealt out and at the same time the last attempt at breaking through the line of the besiegers had been ordered. This was carried out on the night of the 19th of March. It was shattered, however, against the unbreakable manifold ring of the Russian inclosing lines and against the superior forces which were brought in time to the threatened points. Our men were so weakened by their long fasting that it took them fully seven hours to make the march of seven kilometers, and even in this short stretch many of them had to lie down from exhaustion, yet they fought well and were bravely led by their officers.

"In spite of all this," Captain Lehmann, one of the escaped officers, reported, "the heroic garrison fought on, after their last sortie, for fully forty-eight hours, against assaults of the Russians which now set in with terrific violence. The men of the fortress were fully informed of the situation by an announcement of the commander. They knew that the provisions were at an end and this very knowledge spurred them on to make their last sacrifice. Practically all the nations of the monarchy were represented in the fortress. Tyrolese Landsturm held the south, Hungarians the west, Ruthenians and Poles the north, and lower Austrians the east. To this last battle the troops marched out singing, striving thus to master their weakness. On this occasion the above mentioned notice had fallen into the hands of the Russians and the prospect had thus been opened to them to seize the fortress with little effort. For two days and nights all the works of Przemysl were taken under an uninterrupted terrible artillery fire, including that of modern howitzers of all calibers, up to eighteen centimeters. Then followed an assault at night on the east front, which, however, was again bloodily repelled."

Starvation is conducive neither to good feeling nor heroism, especially when it is superimposed upon an unbroken series of more or less disastrous experiences. Misfortune and the so-called "tradition of defeat" had dogged the steps of Austria's troops from the beginning of the war; unlucky generals—Dankl, Auffenberg, and others—had been relieved of their commands and replaced by "new blood"—Boehm-Ermolli, Boroyevitch von Bojna, and Von Pflanzer-Baltin. Of these three, two had as yet failed in carrying to success the German plans which had taken the place of those of their own strategists. Hence it is not at all improbable that the reports of dissensions among the garrison, which leaked out at the time, were substantially accurate. That jealousies broke out among the numerous races forming the Austrian Army—especially between the Slavonic and Germanic elements—is supported by strong evidence. The sentiments of the Slav subjects of Austria leaned more toward Russia than the empire of which they formed a considerable portion, while there was never any love lost between them and the Magyars. However that may be, the Slav regiments were reported to have refused obedience to the general's order for the last sortie, which was eventually undertaken by a force composed of the Twenty-third Hungarian Honved Division, a regiment of Hussars, and a Landwehr brigade, altogether about 30,000 men. Everything depended upon the venture, for not only were all their food supplies used up, but they had already eaten most of their horses. Instead, therefore, of making southward to where their comrades were fighting hard to tear themselves away from the Carpathian passes, the sortie turned toward the east, in the direction of Mosciska, twenty miles off, which was supposed to be the Russian supply base. This attempted foraging expedition—for it was nothing else—can only be defended on the broad general principle that it is better to do something than nothing as a last resort. Supplies were essential before any more could be undertaken to cut a passage through the strong double set of Russian lines that lay between the Carpathians and Przemysl; but that these supplies were stored at Mosciska was a pure speculation. Further, considering that the whole country was in their opponents' hands, a strength of 30,000 men was insufficient to attempt so hazardous an adventure. Even if they succeeded in breaking through, their return to the fortress was not assured. In that case, if they could not get back, they would have to go forward: eastward lay Lemberg, held by the Russians; northward was the Russian frontier, and southward stood the Russian forces holding the passes. Thus, in any case, however successful the expedition might prove, it meant breaking at least twice through lines which the enemy had spent months in strengthening or fortifying. Undeterred by the almost certain possibility of failure, the expedition of the "forlorn hope" set out across the plain of the San—and speedily came to grief. They had to pass by the strongest Russian artillery position, which was stationed in the low hollow through which the railway runs to Lemberg. Here a terrific hail of shells burst over their heads; rattle of machine guns and rifle fire tore great holes in their ranks; the stoutest courage and bravest hearts were unavailing against an enemy who could not be reached nor even seen. The number of killed and wounded in that fatal sortie has not been made public; that it was an enormous figure is certain. The Russians took 4,000 prisoners of those who survived the ordeal, and captured the forts on the western side directly after the struggling remnants had regained their starting place. General von Kusmanek issued his manifesto in the morning, and by the same night the sortie ended in disaster. Like the misdirected charge of the Light Brigade at Balaclava in 1854, it was "brilliant, but it wasn't war."

One more attempt was made on Saturday, March 20, 1915, toward Oikovice, but it was easily frustrated by the vigilant Russians. On Sunday and Monday, the 21st and 22d of March, a number of explosions were heard in and around Przemysl. The Austrians were destroying everything possible previous to surrendering. Large quantities of explosives were thrown in the river; all kinds of arms were destroyed or rendered useless; three bridges were crippled; the few remaining horses were shot, and a railway bridge over the Wiar, which possessed no strategic value, was also destroyed. These tactics of destroying approaches naturally isolated the town more than ever, and made it exceedingly difficult afterward to convey food supplies to the starving population.

On Monday morning, March 22, 1915, the Austrian chief of staff appeared outside the lines of Przemysl under a flag of truce. He was blindfolded, driven by automobile to Russian headquarters, and ushered into the presence of General Selivanoff. When the bandage had been removed from his eyes, the Austrian officer handed over a letter of capitulation from General von Kusmanek, which ran as follows:

"In consequence of the exhaustion of provisions and stores, and in compliance with instructions received from my supreme chief, I am compelled to surrender the Imperial and Royal Fortress of Przemysl to the Imperial Russian Army."

The Russians took charge without any triumphal display. Some officers were sent to receive the surrender and take stock of the spoils. General von Kusmanek himself supplied the inventory, in which were listed 9 generals, 93 superior officers, 2,500 "Offiziere und Beamten" (subalterns and officials), and 117,000 rank and filc, besides 1,000 pieces of ordnance, mostly useless, and a large quantity of shells and rifle cartridges.

General Artamoff was appointed military governor and to superintend the process of dispatching the prisoners into Russian territory, which was carried out at the rate of 10,000 a day. Extensive arrangements were set on foot to supply the inhabitants with food, drink, and other necessaries of life. As the Russians had not bombarded the town, its natural and artificial beauties had suffered no damage beyond that which the Austrians had themselves inflicted; only the outskirts and the fortifications had been injured by fire and explosion.

Thus fell, on March 22, 1915, Przemysl, "by its own momentum like an overripe fruit," and with a garrison twice as large as would have been adequate to defend it. To Austria the blow was a severe one, for it cost her about four army corps; the immediate advantage it brought to the Russians was the release of Selivanoff's army of 100,000 men, who were urgently required elsewhere. It was only a week earlier that the commander in chief of all the Austro-Hungarian armies, the Archduke Frederick, had granted an interview to an American journalist (Dr. J. T. Roche), in the course of which he stated: "We have only recently reached the point where we are really prepared to carry on a campaign as it should be carried under modern conditions of warfare. Now that our organization has been completed and all branches of the service are working harmoniously, we entertain no doubts as to our ability to hold the enemy at all points and to drive him back from that section of Galicia which is still in his possession."

CHAPTER XXXIX

NEW RUSSIAN OFFENSIVE—AUSTRO-GERMAN COUNTEROFFENSIVE

THREE days before the fall of Przemysl the Russians abandoned the defensive and commenced a vigorous attack on the Carpathian front. Active preparations for the advance had been completed when the capitulation of the fortress was to be expected any hour. Having so far held the Germanic armies in check, it was necessary for the Russians to regain complete control of the Carpathians and the passes before the snow should begin to melt, especially if they decided on an invasion of Hungary. On the other hand, before any offensive could be undertaken against the Germans in Poland, or the Austrians at Cracow, it was imperative to secure the southern flank in Galicia. They had by this time partially grasped one particular feature of German strategy, namely, to parry a blow from one direction by striking in another. A further consideration may have been the absolute certainty that Germany would dispatch more reenforcements to the aid of her ally. Selivanoff's siege army was distributed between Dmitrieff, Brussilov, and Ivanoff, but they could not be employed to full advantage owing to the restricted area presented by the Germanic front. Being largely composed of siege artillery as well as cavalry, a considerable portion of Selivanoff's army was unsuited for mountain warfare. Cavalry were converted into infantry, but could not be supplied with the necessary equipment; they had no bayonets, and most of the fighting was hand-to-hand.

Great masses of Germanic reserves were concentrating in northern Hungary, into which the Russians had driven a thin wedge south of Dukla, where they held an isolated outpost near Bartfeld. To leave this position undeveloped meant compulsory withdrawal or disaster. With the continual influx of reenforcements on both sides, the struggle for the main passes gradually develops into an ever-expanding and unbroken battle front: all the gaps are being filled up. From Dukla westward to the Dunajec-Biala line and the Carpathian foothills a new link is formed by the Fourth Austrian Army, commanded by the Archduke Joseph Ferdinand, with two and a half army corps and one German division. In the Central Carpathians a fifth army, under the command of the Austrian General von Bojna, appears between the forces of Boehm-Ermolli and those of Von Linsingen. Right away eastward the purely Austrian army of Von Pflanzer-Baltin was holding the Pruth Valley. The Germanic chain was complete, with every link welded together.

When the Russian offensive opened on March 19, 1915, the entire battle line still rested on the northern side of the Carpathians, and here the struggle was resumed. The Russian grand attack was directed between the Lupkow and Uzsok passes, where great forces of the enemy, concentrated for the purpose of relieving Przemysl, were stationed. In the western sector, facing Dmitrieff, the Archduke Joseph Ferdinand held the roads leading from Novy-Sacz and Grybow to Tarnow, covering Cracow; and from south of the range the two roads diverging from Zboro to Gorlice and Jaslo were in Russian possession, though the Austrians held their junction at Zboro, eight miles north of Bartfeld. Of the actual fighting that took place in this region very few details were published by the Russian official communiqué. One of these documents, dated April 18, 1915, announced that on March 23, "our troops had already begun their principal attack in the direction of Baligrod, enveloping the enemy positions from the west of the Lupkow Pass and on the east near the sources of the San. The enemy opposed the most desperate resistance to the offensive of our troops. They had brought up every available man on the front from the direction of Bartfeld as far as the Uzsok Pass, including even German troops and numerous cavalrymen fighting on foot. The effectives on this front exceeded 300 battalions. Moreover, our troops had to overcome great natural difficulties at every step. In the course of the day, March 23, 1915, we captured more than 4,000 prisoners, a gun, and several dozen machine guns."

On March 24, 1915, the battle was in full progress: "Especially severe is the fighting for the crest of the mountain south of Jasliska and to the west of the Lupkow Pass. The forests which cover these mountains offer special facilities for the construction of strong fortifications." March 25: "The woods in the Lupkow region are a perfect entanglement of barbed wire . . . surrounded by several layers of trenches, strengthened by deep ditches and palisades. On this day our troops carried by assault a very important Austrian position on the great crest of the Beskid Mountains." The Russian captures for the day amounted to 100 officers, 5,600 men, and a number of machine guns. Advancing from Jasliska the Russians seriously threatened the Austro-German position in the Laborcza Valley, to which strong reenforcements were sent on March 25. With terrific violence the battle raged till far into the night of the 27th, the Russians forcing their way to within seven miles of the Hungarian frontier.

In eight days they had taken nearly 10,000 prisoners. By the night of March 28, 1915, the entire line of sixty miles from Dukla to Uzsok was ablaze—the storm was spreading eastward. Like huge ant hills the mountains swarmed with gray and bluish specks—each a human being—some to the waist in snow, stabbing and hacking at each other ferociously with bayonet, sword, or lance, others pouring deadly fire from rifle, revolver, machine gun, and heavy artillery. Over rocks slippery with blood, through cruel barbed-wire entanglements and into crowded trenches the human masses dash and scramble. Here, with heavy toll, they advanced; there, and with costlier sacrifice, they were driven back. Fiery Magyars, mechanical Teutons and stolid muzhiks mixed together in an indescribable hellbroth of combative fury and destructive passion. Screaming shells and spattered shrapnel rent the rocks and tore men in pieces by the thousand. Round the Lupkow Pass the Russians steadily carved their way forward, and at the close of the day, March 29, 1915, they had taken 76 officers, 5,384 men, 1 trench mortar, and 21 machine guns. Along the Baligrod-Cisna road the fighting proceeded, up to March 30, by day and night.

Gradually the Russians pushed toward Dvernik and Ustrzyki south of Lutoviska, threatening the Austrian position in the Uzsok and lines of communications to the south. German reserves were hurried up from the base at Ungvar, but could not prevent the capture of 80 Austrian officers, over 5,000 men, 14 machine guns, and 4 pieces of cannon. Ivanoff had been careful to hold his portion of Selivanoff's army in reserve; their presence turned the scale.

On the day and night of March 31, 1915, the Russians stormed and carried the Austrian positions 4,000 feet high up on the Poloniny range during a heavy snowstorm. So deep was the snow in places that movement was impossible; the trampling of the charging battalions rushing down over the slopes dislodged avalanches of snow, overwhelming both attackers and defenders. By April 1, 1915, the Russians approached Volosate, only twelve miles from the rear of the Uzsok Pass, from which they were now separated by a low ridge. Holding full possession of the Poloniny range farther west, they commanded the road from Dvernik to Vetlina. From the north other Russian columns captured Michova on the Smolnik-Cisna railroad, crossed the Carpathians, and penetrated into the Virava Valley. Occupying the entire loop of the Sanok-Homona railway north and south of Lupkow, and Mezo-Laborcz toward Dukla, the Russians now threatened the Austrian mountain positions between Lupkow and the Vetlina-Zboj road from the western flank as well. Violent winter storms raged across the Carpathians on April 2 and 3, 1915; nature spread a great white pall over the scenes of carnage. While the elements were battling, the weary human fighting machine rested and bound its wounds. But not for long. Scarcely had the last howls of the blizzard faded away when the machine was again set in motion.

South of Dukla and Lupkow and north of Uzsok fighting was resumed with intense vigor. Painfully digging through the snowdrifts the Austrians retired from the Smolnik-Kalnica line, now no longer tenable. Storm hampered the pursuing enemy, who captured the Cisna railway station on April 4, 1915, with all its rolling stock and large stores of munitions.

On April 6, 1915, a Russian communiqué announced that "during the period from March 20 to April 3, 1915, we took prisoners in the Carpathians, on the front from Baligrod to Uzsok, 378 officers, 11 doctors, and 33,155 men. We captured 17 guns and 101 machine guns. Of these captives 117 officers, 16,928 men, 8 guns, and 59 machine guns were taken on a front of fifteen versts (10 miles)."

The Russians again advanced along their whole front on April 4, 1915; forcing their way along the Rostoki stream, they carried the village of Rostoki Gorne with the bayonet and penetrated the snow-bound Rostoki Pass. Their first line arrived at a Hungarian village called Orosz-Russka, five miles from Nagy Polena, at the foot of the pass. The Austrians attempted to drive them back, but they held their ground.

While fortune was steadily following the efforts of the czar's troops in the Lupkow-Uzsok sector, the German War Staff were preparing their plans for the great decisive blow that was soon to be struck. South of the Carpathians, barely thirty miles away, formidable reenforcements were collecting; they arrived from the East Prussian front, from Poland, and even from the west, where they had faced the French and British. There were also new formations fresh from Germany. General von der Marwitz arrived in the Laborcza Valley with a whole German army corps. These gigantic preparations were not unknown to the Russians; they, also, strained every nerve to throw all available reenforcements behind and into the battle line, strengthening every position *except one*. South of the Lupkow the Germanic forces opened their counteroffensive on April 6, 1915. Official reports on the first day's fighting differ somewhat. The Russians admit a slight German advance, but assert that they were able to withstand all further attacks. The Germans, on the other hand, claim great successes and the capture of 6,000 Russian prisoners.

The Germanic armies in this case, however, certainly did advance, for the Russians withdrew from the Virava Valley, which they had entered four days earlier. The first object of the counteroffensive was to save the Austrians who were holding the frontier south of Lupkow from being enveloped and cut off. But on April 9, 1915, the Russians again moved forward, and recovered part of the Virava Valley. By this day the whole mountain crest from Dukla to Uzsok, a distance of over seventy miles, had been conquered by the Russians. By the same night they had repulsed a counterattack near the Rostoki and captured a battalion of Austrian infantry. The Russian report sums up thus: "We seized Height 909 (909 meters=3,030 feet) with the result that the enemy was repulsed along the entire length of the principal chain of the Carpathians in the region of our offensive."

For the next three days Brussilov attempted to work his way to the rear of the Uzsok position with his right wing from the Laborcz and Ung valleys, while simultaneously continuing his frontal attacks against Boehm-Ermolli and Von Bojna. Cutting through snow sometimes more than six feet deep, the Russians approached at several points within a distance of three miles from the Uzsok Valley. But the Austrians still held the Opolonek mountain group in force. Severe fighting then developed northwest of the Uzsok on the slopes between Bukoviec and Beniova; the Russians captured the village of Wysocko Nizne to the northeast, which commands the only roads connecting the Munkacz-Stryj and the Uzsok-Turka lines. Though both sides claimed local successes, they appear to have fought each other to a deadlock, for very little fighting occurred in this zone after April 14, 1915. Henceforth Brussilov directed his main efforts to the Virava and Cisna-Rostoki sector. From here and Volosate, where there had been continuous fighting since the early days of April, the Russians strove desperately for possession of the Uzsok. They were now only two or three days' march from the Hungarian plains.

Between April 17 and 20, 1915, a vigorous Austrian counterattack failed to check the Russian advance. Between Telepovce and Zuella, two villages south of the Lupkow, the Russians noiselessly approached the Austrian barbed-wire entanglements, broke through, and after a brief bayonet encounter gained possession of two heights and captured the village of Nagy Polena, a little farther to the east. During the night of April 16-17, 1915, the Russians took prisoners 24 officers, 1,116 men, and 3 machine guns.

On April 18, 1915, the Austrians directed several fierce attacks against the heights south of Telepovce, but were compelled to evacuate the approaches to their positions. Here, also, an Austrian battalion was cut off and forced to surrender. Meanwhile the fighting was gradually decreasing in intensity; the great Carpathian campaign had reached the end of another chapter. The Austro-German offensive had failed in its purpose. From Uzsok eastward there had been but little fighting after the Russian recapture of Stanislawow.

CHAPTER XL

CAMPAIGN IN GALICIA AND BUKOWINA—BATTLE OF THE DUNAJEC

WHILE the struggle for the passes was raging in the central Carpathians an interesting campaign was being conducted in Eastern Galicia and the Bukowina between Von Pflanzer-Baltin and Lechitsky. There we left the Russians in possession of Stanislawow, which they had reoccupied on March 4, 1915. Two days before, an Austrian detachment of infantry and two divisions of cavalry attempted a raid into Russian territory near the Bessarabian frontier. Within forty-eight hours they were hurled back. Beyond local skirmishes and maneuvering for positions, nothing of importance happened from March 4 till the 15th, when the Russians attacked the main Austrian forces southeast of Czernowitz. Crossing the River Pruth opposite Ludihorecza, which lies about 600 feet high, and where the Czernowitz waterworks are situated, the Russians occupied the place and threatened the Austrian position in the town, around which pressed laborers were digging trenches night and day for the defenders. Along the line between Sadagora and Old Zuczka the Russians had been settled for over six months. The Austrians attacked this position on March 21, 1915, with the aid of reenforcements and compelled the Russians to evacuate Sadagora.

While falling back in the south the Russians endeavored to advance in the north, from the direction of Czerniavka, and outflank the Austrians. Violent fighting raged for several days, especially northeast from Czernowitz to beyond Rarancze, with the result that the Russians were compelled to withdraw toward Bojan, near their own frontier, on March 27. Three days later some Hungarian Honved battalions, who had penetrated into Russian territory near Szylowce, were surrounded by Cossacks and severely handled. Besides many killed and wounded the Austrians lost over 1,000 prisoners, and by April 2, 1915, the Russians had thrown the remainder back across their borders. On April 10, 1915, the Russians withdrew from Boyan, but returned on the 14th. Here, at the close of April, they concentrated large reenforcements and recovered most of the ground they had lost since the middle of March.

Some twenty miles northwest of Czernowitz, sheltered in a loop of the Dniester, lies an important fortified town called Zaleszczyki. It had a population of over 76,000, and is a station on the branch line connecting Czortkow junction with the Kolomca-Czernowitz railway. From the dense forests east of the town an Austrian column commanded by Count von Bissingen had attempted during the night of March 22-23, 1915, to turn the adjacent Russian positions, held by Cossacks and Siberian fusiliers. A furious fight developed, and the Austro-Hungarian column, which included some of the finest troops, was repulsed with heavy loss. Two other attempts were made here, on April 10 and 17, 1915. On the latter date a detachment of Tyrolese sharpshooters were trapped in the wire entanglements and annihilated.

One more battle on a big scale remains to be chronicled from the far eastern sector; it may also serve to illustrate the wide divergence that not infrequently exists between official communiqués recording the same event. Early in April, 1915, a Russian force threw a bridge across the Dniester near the village of Filipkowu and moved along the road running from Uscie Biskupie via Okna and Kuczurmik on to Czernowitz, the intention being to turn the Austrian positions south of Zaleszczyki from the rear. We will let the rival communiqués relate what happened:

Austrian Version	*Russian Version*
Annihilated two battalions of Russian infantry belonging to the Alexander Regiment; took 1,400 prisoners, and drove Russians back beyond the Dniester.	Annihilated two battalions of the Honveds; captured 21 officers, over 1,000 rank and file, and 8 machine guns.

The curtain was about to rise for the next act, wherein will be played one of the most terrific reversals of fortune ever produced in military history.

For quite a month it had been an open secret that considerable masses of German troops were being transported to the Carpathian front. What was not known, however, was the magnitude or the plan of these preparations. Never was a greater concentration of men and machinery more silently and more speedily accomplished. All along the south of the range, on the great Hungarian plains, there assembled a gigantic host of numerous nationalities. But it was away to the west, in that narrow bottle neck where the Dunajec flows from the Polish frontier down to the Tarnow Pass, that the mighty thunderbolt had been forged. Thousands of heavy guns were here planted in position, and millions of shells conveyed thither under cover of night. Countless trains carried war materials, tents, pontoons, cattle, provisions, etc. Finally the troops arrived—from the different fronts where they could be spared, and new levies from Germany and Austria-Hungary. Smoothly and silently men and machines dropped into their respective places: All was ready; not a detail had been overlooked; German organization had done its part. The commander was Von Mackensen, nominally Commander of the Eleventh German Army, but in reality supreme director of the whole campaign.

During April, 1915, a number of changes had taken place among the commanding officers of the Austro-German armies; the new dispositions of groups along the battle line differ considerably from those which obtained during the fighting for the passes. The line was now enormously strengthened, and more compact. This applies only to the Germanic side; there is little change on the Russian. At this stage the Russian front on the west of Galicia extended from Opatovie on the Polish frontier along the Dunajec, Biala, and Ropa Rivers by Tarnow, Ciezkovice, and Gorlice down to Zboro in Hungary; from here it runs eastward past Sztropko, Krasnilbrod, Virava, and Nagy Polena to the Uzsok Pass, a distance of about 120 miles. Ewarts commanded the army on the Nida; the Dunajec-Biala line was still held by Dmitrieff, Commander in Chief of the Eighth Russian Army; Brussilov still commanded the main army of the Carpathians, and Lechitsky in the Bukowina in the place of Alexeieff, who had succeeded General Russky in the northern group. The whole southern group, from the Nida to the Sereth inclusive, was under the supreme command of General Ivanoff. Facing Dmitrieff on the Dunajec front stood now the Fourth Austro-Hungarian Army under the Archduke Joseph Ferdinand, about five army corps, including a German cavalry division under General von Besser; then the Ninth and Fourteenth Austrian Army Corps; to their right, several Tyrolese regiments; the Sixth Austro-Hungarian Army Corps of General Arz von Straussenburg, with the Prussian Guards on his left and Bavarian troops under Von Emmich on his right; the Eleventh German Army Corps under Von Mackensen; the Third Austro-Hungarian Army under General Boroyevitch von Bojna; the Tenth Army Corps under General Martiny. This formidable combination now confronted the Dunajec-Biala positions, which Dmitrieff had held without exertion for four months. Only a mile or two away he still inspected his trenches and conducted his minor operations, totally unconscious of the brewing storm specially directed against him. The Laborza district was held by the Archduke Joseph with the Seventh Army Corps; on his left stood a German corps under Von Marwitz, and on his right the Tenth Army Corps, north of Bartfeld, with some additional forces in between. Around the Lupkow and Uzsok passes the Second Austro-Hungarian Army under Boehm-Ermolli was stationed where it had been since

February, 1915. Next, on the right, the Austro-Hungarian army corps under Von Goglia; in the Uzsok lay an army under Von Szurmay, nearly all Magyars, of whom the chief commander was Von Linsingen. Farther eastward stood a Prussian corps, embodying a division of Prussian Guards and other regiments commanded by General Bothmer, a Bavarian, who had been reenforced with a Hungarian division under Bartheldy; then followed the corps of Generals Hofmann and Fleischman, composed of all Austrian nationalities, intrenched in the mountain valleys. More German troops held the next sector, and, finally, came Von Pflanzer-Baltin's army groups in the Bukowina and Eastern Galicia. Against this huge iron ring of at least twenty-four Germanic corps (about 2,000,000 men) and a great store of reserves, the Russians could not muster more than about fourteen of their own corps. As has already been pointed out, the greatest disparity of strength existed on the Dunajec line, where Dmitrieff stood opposed to about half of the enemy's entire force with only five corps of Russian troops. The Austro-German forces, moreover, were infinitely better equipped with munitions and heavy artillery. The lack of big guns was undoubtedly the reason why the Russians had not attempted an invasion of Hungary. Hence they stuck to the mountain passes where their opponents were unable to carry their artillery, although they were amply supplied with the same. It is true that the Russians could have produced an equal—or even greater—number of men, but they had not the arms and accouterments.

Speaking from safe knowledge after the event, it is possible to indicate with moderate accuracy at least one of the ingenious stratagems adopted by the Germans to disguise their tremendous preparations against the Dunajec line. For months the fighting in this region had never been severe. When, therefore, local attacks and counterattacks on a small scale started on the Biala, as far back as April 4, 1915, Dmitrieff and his staff regarded this activity on the Austrians part as merely a continuation of the sporadic assaults they had grown accustomed to. Besides holding his own, Dmitrieff had on several occasions been able to assist Brussilov on his left. Until the big German drive commenced they had only been opposed to three Austro-German army corps and a Prussian division; now there were twelve corps on their front, supplied with enormous resources of artillery, shells, and cavalry. Most serious of all, Dmitrieff had neglected to construct second and third lines to which he could retire in an emergency. Of the rivers that lay behind him—the Wisloka, the Wistok, and the San—the first would be useful to cover Brussilov's position at the western passes, but beyond that he could not retreat without imperiling the whole Carpathian right flank. It was on this very calculation that the German plan—simple but effective—was based. The Russian grip on the Carpathians could only be released either by forcing a clear road through any pass into Galicia, or by turning one of the extreme flanks. Had the Austrians succeeded in breaking through as far as Jaslo, Dmitrieff would have been cut off and Brussilov forced to withdraw—followed by the whole line. The same result would follow if a thrust from the Bukowina succeeded in recapturing Lemberg. Both methods had been attempted, and both had failed. Germany's overwhelming superiority in artillery could not be effectively displayed in mountain warfare, but Dmitrieff's position on the Dunajec offered an easy avenue of approach.

At the eleventh hour Dmitrieff grasped the situation and applied to Ivanoff for reenforcements. Owing to some blunder the appeal never reached the Russian chief, and Dmitrieff had to do the best he could. Nothing now could save his small force from those grim lines of gaping muzzles turned against his positions. The overture began on April 28, 1915, with an advance on the Upper Biala toward Gorlice, by Von Mackensen's right. Here some minor attacks had been previously made, and the gradually increasing pressure did not at first reveal the intent or magnitude of the movement behind it. Meanwhile the German troops about Ciezkovice and Senkova—respectively northwest and southeast of Gorlice—were moving by night nearer to the battle line. The Russian front line extended from Ciezkovice in a southeasterly direction. Hence it soon became clear that Gorlice itself was to be the main objective of the attack. A Russian official announcement of May 2, 1915, boldly states:

"During the nights of April 30 to May 1 strong Austrian forces opened an offensive in the region of Ciezkovice. Our fire forced the enemy to intrench 600 paces in front of our trenches." Furthermore, the Germans at the same time had directed artillery fire and bayonet attacks against various points on the Rava, Pilica, Nida, and the Dunajec. These, however, were merely movements aiming at diversion, meant to mask the intentions of the main attack and to mislead the Russians. On the evening of May 1, 1915, the German batteries began experimenting against the Russian positions. This was kept up all night while the engineers attempted to destroy the first line of the Russian wire entanglements. During the same night the Austrians dragged several heavy howitzers across the road from Gladyszow to Malastow, and got them into position without the knowledge of the Russians. In the morning of May 2, 1915, the great batteries began to roar against the Russian line—a fire such as had perhaps never been witnessed before. A spectator thus describes the scene: "In one part the whole area was covered with shells till trenches and men were leveled out of existence." It was reported that 700,000 shells had been fired in the space of four hours, for which period this preliminary bombardment lasted. The Russian line was turned into a spluttering chaos of earth, stones, trees, and human bodies. The German and Austrian batteries then proceeded to extend the range, and poured a hurricane of shells behind the enemy's front line. This has the effect of doubly isolating that line, by which the survivors of the first bombardment cannot retreat, neither can reenforcements be sent to them, for no living being could pass through the fire curtain. Now is the time for the attacker's infantry to charge. Along the greater part of the Ciezkovice-Walastow line this stage was reached by ten o'clock in the morning of May 2, 1915.

A German writer tells us that "in this part of the front infantry fighting has given place for the time being to the action of our heavy artillery, which is subjecting to a terrible fire the positions of the enemy. These positions had been carefully reconnoitered during the lull in the fighting which prevailed during the last few months. Only after all cover is destroyed, the

Grand Duke Nicholas

enemy's infantry killed or forced to retire, we take up the attack against the positions; the *élan* of our first attack now usually leads to a favorable result."

At Ciezkovice the Germans pushed bridges across the Biala under cover of a furious cannonade. Troops were thrown over, and after a very short struggle the village was taken. The huge oil tanks soon were in flames and Ciezkovice a heap of smoldering ruins. The Russian defense crumpled up like smoke; their position blown out of existence. Their guns were toys compared with those of the Germans and Austrians. North of Ciezkovice the Prussian Guard and other German troops under General von François fell upon the Russians and forced them to retire toward the Olpiny-Biecz line. The ground of the Russian positions on Mount Viatrovka and Mount Pustki in front of Biecz had been "prepared" by 21-centimeter (7-inch) Krupp howitzers and the giant Austrian 30.5-centimeter (10-inch) howitzers from the Skoda-Werke at Pilsen. The shells of the latter weigh nearly half a ton, and their impact is so terrific that they throw the earth up 100 feet high. Whatever had remained of the town of Gorlice in the shape of buildings or human beings was meanwhile being wiped out by a merciless spray of shells. Being the center of an important oil district, Gorlice possessed oil wells, great refineries, and a suphuric-acid factory. As the flames spread from building to building, streets pouring with burning oil, huge columns of fire stretching heavenward from the oil wells in full blaze, and, over all, the pitiless hail of iron and explosives pouring upon them, the horror of the situation in which the soldiers and civilians found themselves may be faintly imagined. Gorlice was an inferno in a few hours. When the German infantry dashed into the town they found the Russians still in possession. Fighting hand to hand, contesting every step, the Russians were slowly driven out.

We have mentioned that German troops were moving on Senkova, southeast of Gorlice, by night. During the last two days of April the Bavarians captured the Russian position in the Senkova valley. A further move was made here during the night of May 1-2, 1915, preparatory to dislodging the Russians from the ground they still held. At seven o'clock in the morning the big howitzers started to "prepare" that ground. By ten o'clock it was deemed that every living thing had perished, when the "fire curtain" was drawn behind the Russian position. Infantry were then thrown forward—some Bavarian regiments. To their intense astonishment they were received with a most murderous fire from Russian rifles, and machine guns. The first attack failed and many were killed, few getting beyond the wire entanglements. Cautiously other troops advanced to the battered Russian trenches cut off from the rear by the artillery screen behind. Yet here again they met with strenuous resistance in the Zamczysko group of hills. The Austrian artillery shelled the heights, and the Bavarians finally took possession. The Tenth Austrian Army Corps had meanwhile conquered the Magora of Malastow and the majority of the heights in the Ostra Gora group. On Sunday, May 2, 1915, the Austro-German armies pierced the Dunajec-Biala line in several places, and by nightfall the Russians were retreating to their last hope—the line of the Wisloka. The operations round Gorlice on that day resulted in breaking the Russian defenses to a depth of over two miles on a front of ten or eleven miles. Mr. Stanley Washburn wrote from the battle field at the time: "The Germans had shot their last bolt, a bolt forged from every resource in men and munitions that they could muster after months of preparation." Of the Russian army he said, "it was outclassed in everything except bravery, and neither the German nor any other army can claim superiority in that respect."

With the center literally cut away, the keystone of the Rus sian line had been pulled out, and nothing remained but to retire. Ten miles north of Ciezkovice lies the triangle formed by the confluence of the Dunajec and Biala rivers and the Zakliczyn-Gromnik road. Within this triangle, commanding the banks of both rivers up to the Cracow-Tarnow line, the Russians held the three hills marked 402, 419, and 269 which figures express their height in meters.

During February and March, 1915, the Austrians attempted to dislodge the enemy, but without success. It was now necessary to take those positions before advance could be made against Tarnow, and the Fourth Austro-Hungarian Army, commanded by the Archduke Joseph Ferdinand, undertook the task. At six A. M. on May 2 the Austrian artillery opened fire against Hill 419 from Mount Val (also within the triangle), and the opposite bank of the Dunajec. After three hours' bombardment some regiments of Tyrolese fusiliers, who had crossed the valley between Mt. Val and 419 and had taken up positions at the foot of the latter, about 400 yards from the Russian trenches, were ordered to charge. Dashing up the open, steep slope the fusiliers were suddenly enfiladed from their right by a spray of machine gun and rifle fire, killing many and driving back the survivors. Next day Hill 419 was again fiercely shelled, this time with deadly effectiveness; but even then the Russians still clung to their battered ground.

The Austrians now charged the trenches on Hill 412, whence the fusiliers had been ambushed the previous day. A desperate hand-to-hand encounter, in which they had to force their way step by step, finally gave the position to the attackers. The few Russians still left on 419 could not hold out after the loss of 412. They retired northward on to Height 269, but subsequently followed the general retreat of the line. Still farther north, almost at the right flank of Dmitrieff's line, the Austrians effected a crossing of the Dunajec opposite Otfinow, thus breaking the connection between the West Galician Army of Dmitrieff, and the neighboring Russian Army on the Nida—the left wing of the northern groups commanded by Alexeieff.

Just below Tarnow, however, the Russians still held out; losing the three hills had not quite broken their defense on the Biala. The right wing of Von Mackensen's army, which had smashed the Russian front around Gorlice, rapidly moved east in an almost straight line to reach the Dukla Pass and cut off the retreat of the Russian troops stationed south of the range between Zboro and Nagy Polena, in northwest Hungary. The left wing, on the other hand, advanced in a northeasterly direction, ever widening the breach made in the enemy's domain. This clever move brought the Germans to the rear of Tarnow and onto the lines of communications of the Russians holding it. It also prevented reenforcements from reaching the truncated end of Dmitrieff's right—or what had been his right—wing. By pushing on to Dembica and Rzeszow, along which route assistance could otherwise have been sent to the Russians, Von Mackensen opened a wide triangle into Western Galicia, by drawing an almost horizontal line from Gorlice to Radymno, between Jaroslav and Przemysl, and from there perpendicular down to the Uzsok Pass.

From Uzsok to the Lupkow westward stood the Second Austro-Hungarian Army under Boehm-Ermolli on the north of the Carpathians. To his left, southwest of the Magora of Malastow, and adjoining the formidable Germanic array facing the Dunajec-Biala line lay the Third Austro-Hungarian Army under General Boroyevitch von Bojna. These two armies, it will be remembered, took part in the first offensive in January, and had been there ever since. Both of these armies now began to advance into the triangle, and the brilliant simplicity of Von Mackensen's geometrical strategy becomes clear. Let one imagine Galicia as a big stone jar with a narrow neck lying on the table before him, neck pointing toward the left hand, and he will obtain an approximately accurate idea of the topographical conditions. That side of the jar resting on the table represents the Carpathian range, solid indeed, but with numerous openings: these are the passes. The upper side of the jar represents the Russian frontier, across which the invaders had swarmed in and taken possession of the whole inside, lining themselves right along the mouths of the passes at the bottom and across the neck upwards.

For months the Austrians vainly endeavored to force an entrance through the thickest walls—from the lower edge, and from the base or bottom of the jar (the Bukowina), apparently overlooking the rather obvious proposition that the cork was the softest part and *that* was Dmitrieff's Dunajec-Biala line. Here at least no mountain range stood in the way. It may also be regarded as a mathematical axiom that, given sufficient artillery power, the strongest defense the wit of man could devise can be smashed. What Mackensen did, therefore, was to blow a hole through the cork, push in a pair of scissors up to the rivet, meanwhile opening the blades to an angle of about forty-five degrees. From the lower or southern shoulder of the jar the Third Austro-Hungarian Army pushes forward inside, supported on its right by Boehm-Ermolli, who had been just inside a long time, but could get no farther. They began to shepherd the Russian troops around and in the western passes toward the lower double-edged blade of Von Mackensen's terrible scissors. The Russian retreat to the Wisloka was a serious disaster for Dmitrieff; he had been caught napping, and had to pay dearly in men and guns for not having created a row of alternative positions. His force had been a cover for Brussilov's operations on both sides of the western passes as well as for the whole Russian line in the Carpathians. Now that Von Mackensen had pried the lid off, Brussilov's men in the south encountered enormous difficulties in extricating themselves from the Carpathian foothills, suddenly transformed from comparative strongholds into death-traps and no longer tenable. They suffered severely, especially the Forty-eighth Division.

Besides the menace from the northwest of Von Mackensen's swiftly approaching right, a third blade was gradually growing on the deadly scissors, in the shape of Boehm-Ermolli's and Von Bojna's forces, threatening to grind them between two relentless jaws of steel. It is Sunday, the second day of May, 1915; to all intents and purposes the battle of the Dunajec, as such, was over, and the initial aim of the Germanic offensive has been attained. The Russian line was pierced and its defense shattered. Von Mackensen's "Phalanx" was advancing two mighty tentacles guided by a master mind, remorselessly probing for the enemy's strongest points. Its formation comprised, in the northeastern tentacle, the Sixth Austro-Hungarian Army Corps and the Prussian Guards; in the southern, the Bavarians under Von Emmich and the Tenth Austro-Hungarian Army Corps under General Martiny.

On May 3, 1915, Dmitrieff's troops were falling back farther every hour, continuously fighting rear-guard actions and compelling the pursuers to conquer every foot of ground. There was a powerful reason for this stubborn retirement: it was to gain time for Brussilov to get his men out of their perilous positions and to join the main line again with Dmitrieff's receding ranks. If this could be effected, the fatal gap between them—made by Von Mackensen's battering-ram—would be repaired, and they could once more present a united front to the enemy. It was mentioned a little farther back that the Austrians had pierced the Dunajec line at Otfinow, north of Tarnow, by which was cut in two the hitherto unbroken Russian battle front, from the Baltic to the Rumanian frontier (900 miles); the "scissors" at Gorlice had made it three; if Boehm-Ermolli's drive from the Uzsok upward along the "triangle line" to Jaroslav succeeds, there will be four separate pieces of Russian front. But from Tarnow southward to Tuchow, a small twenty-mile salient on the Biala, the Russians are still in possession on May 4, 1915, defying the Fourth Austro-Hungarian Army.

CHAPTER XLI

RUSSIAN RETREAT

IT is a matter for speculation whether the numerous successes achieved by the Russians against the Austrians and Germans in Galicia and the Carpathians during the first seven months of the war had begotten a spirit of overconfidence among the Russian commanders, or whether it was not in their power to have made more effective preparations than they had done. We have seen that Dmitrieff had not provided himself with those necessary safety exits which were now so badly needed. As no artificially prepared defenses were at hand, natural ones had to be found. The first defense was irretrievably lost; the second line was a vague, undefined terrain extending across the hills between Biala in the west and the River Wisloka in the east. Between Tuchow and Olpiny, the Mountain Dobrotyn formed one of the chief defensive positions, being 1,800 feet high and thickly covered with woods.

Southward, the Lipie Mountain, about 1,400 feet, formed another strong point. Just below Biecz, close to the road and railroad leading to Gorlice, a mountain of 1,225 feet, called Wilszak, is the strategical key to the valley of the lower Ropa. Between Biecz and Bednarka, the line of defense followed the heights of the Kobylanka, Tatarovka, Lysa Gora, and of the Rekaw; hence to the east, as the last defense of the Jaslo-Zmigrod road, lay the intrenched positions on the Ostra Gora, well within Brussilov's sector. Southward of the Gorlice-Zmigrod line lay the mountain group of the Valkova, nearly 2,800 feet high, the last defense of the line of retreat for the Russian forces from Zboro.

The Wisloka was the third line of defense, only a river, and without intrenchments. From Dembica to Zmigrod it runs roughly parallel with the Dunajec-Biala line; its winding course separates it in places from fifteen to thirty-five miles from the latter river. Strong hopes were entertained that the Russians would be able to stem the Germanic torrent by a firm stand on the Wisloka.

A fierce battle raged on the third and fourth of May, 1915, for the possession of the wooded hills between the Biala and the Wisloka. The Prussian Guard stormed Lipie Mountain and captured it on the third; on the fourth they took Olpiny, Szczerzyny and the neighboring hills at the point of the bayonet.

The Thirty-ninth Hungarian Division, now incorporated in the Eleventh German Army under the direct command of Von Mackensen himself, had advanced from Grybow via Gorlice on the Biecz railway line, and were making a strong attack on the Russian positions on Wilczak Mountain with a tremendous concentration of artillery. It seems the Russians simply refused to be blown out of their trenches, for it required seven separate attacks to drive them out. That accomplished, the fate of Biecz was decided and the road to Jaslo—the "key" to the Wisloka line of defense—was practically open to General Arz von Straussenburg. Lying at the head of the main roads leading into Hungary through the Tilicz, Dukla, and Lupkow passes, Jaslo is the most important railway junction in the whole region between Tarnow and Przemysl. It was at Jaslo that Dmitrieff had held his headquarters for four months.

Just south of him, barely fifteen miles away, General von Emmich and General Martiny, with the "Bayonet Bavarians" and the Tenth Austro-Hungarian Army Corps, went pounding and slashing a passage along the Bednarka-Zmigrod road and the auxiliary road from Malastow to Krempna. They were striving hard to reach the western passes before Brussilov had time to withdraw. He began that operation on the fourth. On the same night Von Emmich and Martiny reached Krempna, and the last line of retreat for the Russians around Zboro was imperiled. They have yet to cross the range from Hungary back into Galicia. So subtly potent and effective was the pressure on a flank that the whole line—be it hundreds of miles long—is more or less influenced thereby, as witness:

On the same night, May 4, 1915, the retreat spread like a contagion to the entire west Galician front, compelling the Russians to evacuate northern Hungary up to the Lupkow Pass; in that pass itself preparations are afoot to abandon the hard-earned position. It is not fear, nor the precaution of cowardice that prompted this wholesale removal of fighting men: the inexorable laws of geometry demanded it. The enemy was at Krempna; as the crow flies the distance from Krempna to the northern debouchment of Lupkow is eighty miles; yet Lupkow was threatened, for the "line" or "front" is pierced—the vital artery of the defense is severed. The strength of a chain is precisely that of its weakest link.

The course of events become complex; fighting, advancing and retreating occurred over a widespread area. Apparently disconnected movements by the Austro-Germans or the Russians fall into their proper places in accordance with the general scheme or objective either side may have in view. It is necessary to follow the scattered operations separately. We will therefore return now to the Tarnow-Tucho sector, where we left a small Russian force holding the last remnant of the Dunajec-Biala

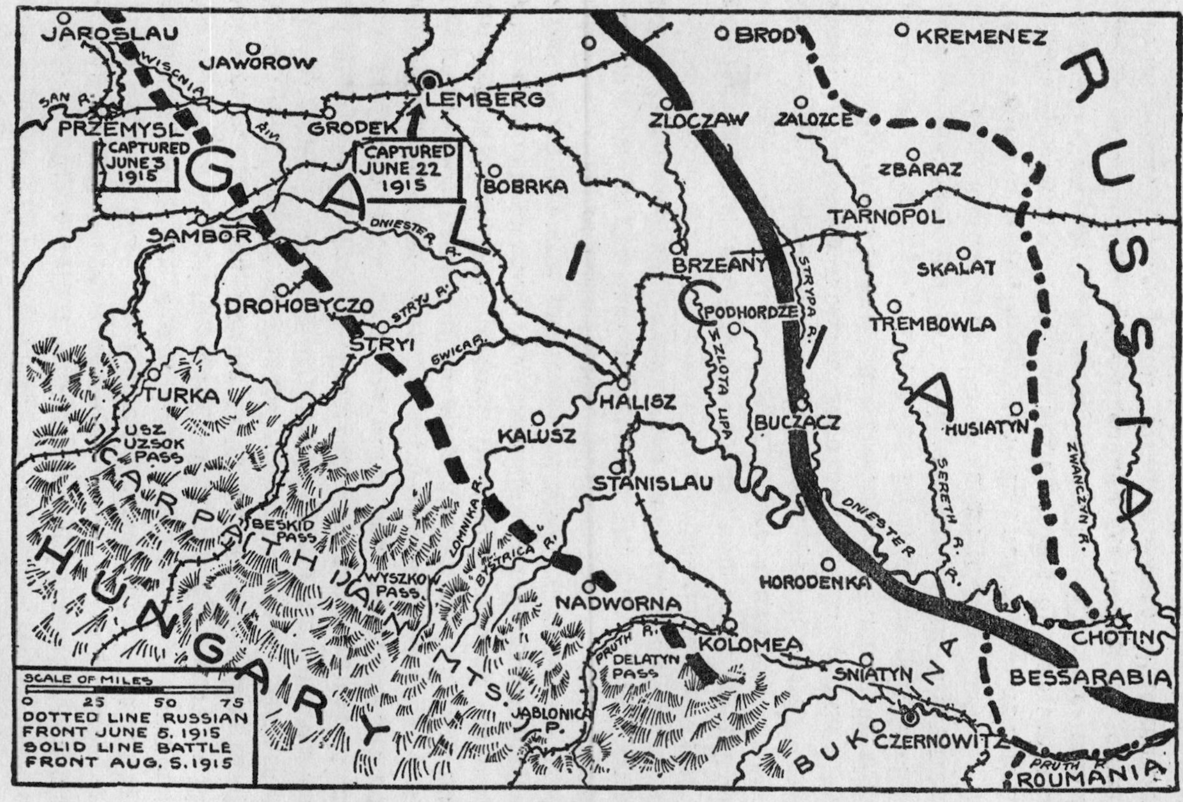

GALICIAN CAMPAIGN FROM TARNOW TO PRZEMYSL

front. Tarnow had been the supply base for that front, and great stores of provisions and munitions still remained in the town. These the Russians succeeded in removing entirely. The main forces had already withdrawn in perfect order and fallen back beyond the Wisloka. During the night of May 4-5, 1915, two regiments of the Ninth Austro-Hungarian Army Corps crossed the Biala near Tuchow and moved northward in the direction of the road leading from Tarnow to Pilzno, along which the remainder of the garrison would have to pass in order to retreat. On the hills west of Pilzno the Russians still held a position to protect that road. By the morning of the sixth everything had gone eastward, and the Austrians had surrounded the town.

The small cavalry detachment that had been left behind as rear guard cut through the Austrian lines and rejoined the main forces on the Wisloka. The Austrians had been bombarding Tarno for months with their heaviest artillery, destroying parts of the cathedral and the famous old town hall in the process.

On May 7 the Russians withdrew from the Pilzno district, and the Dunajec-Biala Russian front had ceased to exist. From the hour that the Austro-Germans had broken through the line at Ciezkovice, on May 2, 1915, the Russian retreat on the Wisloka had begun. Yielding to the terrible pressure the line had increasingly lost its shape as the various component parts fell back, though it gradually resumed the form of a front on the Wisloka banks, where most determined fighting continued for five days.

The Russians lost much of their artillery; they had to reverse the customary military practice of an army in retreat. If the retreating army is well equipped with artillery and munitions, its guns cover the retreat and are sacrificed to save the men. During their retreat the Russians had often to sacrifice men in order to save their guns for a coming greater battle at some more important strategic point. Many prisoners fell to the Germanic armies; according to their own official reports they took 30,000 in the fighting of May 2-4, 1915. What the Austro-German side lost in that time was not made public.

CHAPTER XLII

AUSTRO-GERMAN RECONQUEST OF WESTERN GALICIA

BY the time the retreating Russians had reached the Wisloka they had to some extent recovered from the first shock of surprise, and were better able to attempt a determined stand against the overwhelming onrush of the Austro-Germanic troops. Ivanoff hurriedly sent reenforcements for Dmitrieff and Ewarts which included the Caucasian Corps of General Irmanoff from the Bzura front. The heavy German guns belched forth with terrible effect, and the Russians could not reply at the same weight or distancc. Bayonets against artillery means giving odds away, but the attempt was made. With a savage fury that seems to belong only to Slavs and Mohammedans—fatalists—the Russians hurled themselves against the powcrful batteries and got to close quarters with the enemy. For nearly twenty minutes a wild, surging sea of clashing steel—bayonets, swords, lances and Circassian daggers—wielded by fiery mountaineers and steady, cool, well-disciplined Teutons, roared and flowed around the big guns, which towered over the lashing waves like islands in a stormy ocean. A railway collision would seem mild compared with the impact of 18,000 desperate armed men against a much greater number of equally desperate and equally brave, highly-trained fighters. But machinery, numbers and skillful tactics will overcome mere physical courage. The Russian avalanche was thrown back with terrific slaughter; the Caucasian Corps alone lost over 10,000 men, for which, it is estimated, they killed and wounded quite as many. More remarkable still was the fact that they captured a big battery and carried off 7,000 prisoners. For five days the storm raged backward and forward across the river; during the more violent bombardments the Russians left their trenches to be battered out of shape and withdrew into their shelter dugouts; when the enemy infantry advanced to take possession, the Russians had returned to face the charge. Whereas cool, machinelike precision marks the German soldier in battle as on the parade ground, an imperturbable obstinacy and total disregard of mortal danger characterizes the Russian.

During the night of May 6-7, 1915, the Austrians sent two regiments across the Wisloka, north and south of Brzoctek, about midway between Pilzno and Jaslo, under cover of artillery posted on a 400-foot hill near Przeczyca on the opposite bank, *i.e.*, the left. Austrian engineers constructed a bridge across the river, and on the morning of May 7 the Austrian advance guard were in possession of the hills north of the town. Infantry were then thrown across to storm Brzostek. Here, again, they met with resolute opposition from the Russian rear guards covering the retreat of the main armies, which had already fallen back from the Wisloka. Desperate bayonet fighting ensued in the streets, each of which had to be cleared separately to dislodge the Russians—the civilians meanwhile looking out of their windows watching the animated scenes below. Hungarian troops in overwhelming masses poured across the river and finally captured the town. Once more on the backward move, the Russians established themselves along the western and southern fringe of the forests by Januszkovice, only eight miles away, and prepared to make another stand. More fighting occurred here, and during May 7 and 8, 1915, the Russians fell back farther toward Frysztak, on the river Wistok.

We left Von Emmich and General Martiny with the Bavarians and the Tenth Austro-Hungarian Army Corps on their arrival at Krempna on the night of the 4th, during which time the Russians were making desperate efforts to evacuate northern Hungary and the western passes. The main forces of Von Mackensen's "phalanx" were meanwhile pushing on toward Jaslo, still in Russian possession. On the hills west of the Wisloka the Russian rear guards had intrenched themselves and held their positions till nightfall on May 5, 1915, all with the object of delaying the Germanic advance sufficiently for their comrades to clear the passes. Then they fell back again and made a stand near Tarnoviec, about six or seven miles east of Jaslo, where they dominated an important strategic position. Between them and Jaslo two railways ran along the valley of the River Jasliska, forming a serious obstacle to Von Mackensen's advance so long as the Russians could hold it. It was imperative that they should be cleared out, but the task of carrying it through was a difficult one. The undertaking fell to the Hungarian troops of the Thirty-ninth Honved Division, who advanced to the attack again and again only to be driven back each time by the Russian fire from the heights. Big howitzers were called into play and soon demolished the positions.

The Russians retired east of the Wistok, followed by Von Mackensen's Austro-Hungarian corps, while the Prussian Guards moved on toward Frysztak, where the Russian troops from the Tarnow sector had taken up positions after the retreat from Brzostek.

On May 7, 1915, the Prussian Guards had passed over the railway at Krosno, and at night fell upon the Russian lines east of the Wistok. Particularly fierce encounters took place near Odrzykon and Korczina, ten to fourteen miles southeast of Frysztak. A little farther westward Von Mackensen delivered his main attack against the railway crossing at Jaslo, which fell on the same day, May 7. The Russians retreated in confusion with Von Mackensen close upon their heels. The whole defense on the Wisloka collapsed, and nothing apparently could now save the Dukla and those troops struggling through to escape from the net that was gradually being tightened around them. Meanwhile, General Ewarts's Army of the Nida, which formed the connecting link between the Russian northern and southern armies, had fallen back above Tarnow to the River Czarna in order to keep in touch and conformity with Dmitrieff's shrinking line, which was now actually broken by the Wisloka failure. The Russian position was extremely critical, for it seemed that the German general would roll up the two halves and thereby inflict a crushing and decisive defeat. General Ivanoff appears to have recognized Von Mackensen's intentions in time to devise measures to counteract the peril and save his left (Brussilov's army) from disaster. By pushing forward strong columns from Sanok on the Upper San to impose a temporary check upon the advancing tide, he gained a brief respite for the troops entangled in the passes. To that sector we will now turn to review the course of events.

On May 4, 1915, the Russians began to evacuate the positions they held south of the range when Von Mackensen's extreme right approached Krempna. Forging along at high speed the Germans and Austrians occupied the towns of Dukla and Tylava, and arrived at Rymanow—still farther east—on the following day. The town of Dukla lies some fifteen miles due north of the Galician debouchment of the pass of that name, and Rymanow is about another fifteen miles east of that. Hence the German strategic plan was to draw a barrier line across the north of the Carpathians and hem the Russians in between that barrier and the Austro-Hungarian armies of Boehm-Ermolli and Von Bojna. It must distinctly be borne in mind that these two forces are also north of the passes: that of Von Bojna being stationed at the elbow where the Germanic line turned from the Carpathians almost due north along the Dunajec-Biala front, or across the neck of our hypothetical jar. The Dukla and Lupkow passes were still in Russian hands; these were the only two that the Germanic offensives of January, February, and March, 1915, had failed to capture; all the others, from Rostoki eastward, were held by the Austrians and Germans. It was through the Dukla and Lupkow that the Russians obtained their foothold in northern Hungary, and it was the only way open to them now to get back again. Around the Laborcza district stood the Seventh Austro-Hungarian Army Corps under the command of the Archduke Joseph, who now began to harass them, aided by the German "Beskid Corps" under General von Marwitz. This was the only section in the range where the Russians held both sides. Boehm-Ermolli had forced the Rostoki and Uzsok, but hitherto had been unable to get very far from their northern exits—not beyond Baligrod. During the fighting on the Dunajec these three armies merely marked time; it was their object to keep the Russians in Hungary and in the two passes until Von Mackensen had thrown the right of his "phalanx" across their only avenue of escape. That time was now rapidly approaching, and Von Bojna was gradually squeezing Brussilov from the west, while Boehm-Ermolli was following from the east and south. It appears that the commanders of the Twelfth Russian Army Corps and the Third Russian Army, which stood on Hungarian soil from Zboro to Nagy Polena, did not grasp the full significance to them of the Dunajec catastrophe.

Germanic troops were building a wall against their exits before they had seriously thought of withdrawing. Escape was impossible for many of them; some had managed to get across the Dukla in time, while those left behind would either have to surrender or fight their way through the lines across their path in the north. At the same time they would have Von Bojna and Boehm-Ermolli on their tracks. To make matters worse, they were also being pressed severely from the Hungarian plains by the troops which hitherto stood inactive. The Second Austro-Hungarian Army (Boehm-Ermolli) was fighting on both sides of the range. Through Rostoki they attempted to separate the Russians around Zboro from those situated farther east at Nagy Polena. We have stated elsewhere that the Forty-eighth Division was severely handled. They were surrounded in the Dukla by an overwhelming superior force, but General Korniloff, the commander, with a desperate effort and no little skill, succeeded in hacking his way through the enemy's lines and bringing a large portion of his force safely out of the trap. Inch by inch the Russian rear guards retreated, fighting tooth and nail to hold the pass while their comrades escaped. No less brave were the repeated charges made by the Austrians—clambering over rocks, around narrow pathways hanging high in the air, dizzy precipices and mountain torrents underneath. On Varentyzow Mountain, especially, a fierce hand-to-hand battle was fought between Hungarians and Cossacks, the latter finally withdrawing in perfect order. To conduct a successful retreat in the face of disaster is a no less difficult military achievement than the gaining of a decisive victory, and Brussilov's retreat from the passes deserves to rank as a masterly example of skillful tactics.

On May 8, 1915, the Third Russian Army and the Forty-eighth

Division had reunited with Brussilov's main army in the neighborhood of Sanok, twenty miles north of the Lupkow. When the commanders of a retreating army lose their heads the rank and file will inevitably become demoralized and panic-stricken. The retreat became a rout, and the possibility of making a stand, and to some extent retrieving the lost fortune of war, was extremely remote. A deeper motive than the mere reconquering of Galicia lay behind Von Mackensen's plan—he aimed at nothing less than the complete overthrow and destruction of the Russian armies. It was a gigantic effort of the Germanic powers to eliminate at least one of their most dangerous enemies. Once that was accomplished it would release some millions of troops whose services were needed in the western theatre of war. The original plan had fallen through of crushing Russia quickly at the beginning of the war, before she would have had time to get ready, and then to turn against France in full force. The Austro-German Galician campaign was planned and undertaken with that specific object, and now, although defeated and in full retreat, the Russian troops still formed an army in being, and not a fugitive, defenseless rabble. So long as an army is not captured or annihilated, it can be reorganized and again put in the field. It is on this consideration that so much importance attaches to the handling of an army in retreat. The Russians did not, of course, run away; on the contrary, they fought desperately and stubbornly throughout the retreat, for their pursuers did not average more than six miles per day—a fact which testifies to the steady and orderly character of the Russian retirement. They suffered from the consequences of inadequate preparation and lack of foresight on the part of their leaders.

The Russian troops on the Lower Wisloka held their positions longest, but they also fell back about May 8, 1915, and for the next two days engaged the enemy near some villages southwest of Sanok. Here a strong force had collected, which not only offered a powerful resistance, but even attempted a counter-attack against their pursuers. Over a front of 145 miles, extending from Szczucin near the Vistula north of Tarnow, down almost to the Uzsok Pass, a fierce battle progressed between

May 8 and 10, 1915. In the region of Frysztak, where the Russian line was weakest, the main German offensive was developing its strongest attack. Reenforcements were on the way, but could not arrive in time. For the moment disaster was averted by an aggressive Russian counteroffensive halfway between Krosno and Sanok, from the Besko-Jacmierz front, by which move sufficient time was gained to enable the main forces to retreat. The Russian defense in the Vistok Valley collapsed on May 10, 1915; the German center had almost arrived within striking distance of the important railway line from Tarnow via Dembica and Rzeszow to Jaroslav north of Przemysl. At Sanok the battered remnants of the Russian troops who had escaped from the passes maintained themselves with the greatest difficulty. Heavy German artillery followed the Bavarians to Rymanow, five miles from the Russian line at Besko, and were now playing fiercely upon the positions west of Sanok. The Tenth Austro-Hungarian Army Corps as well as the Seventh were making their presence felt from the southwest against Odrzechova and from the south, whence Von Marwitz with the German Beskid Corps was rapidly advancing. To the southeast, Boehm-Ermolli was battering the Baligrod-Lutoviska front, almost in the same position he occupied at the end of January in the first attempt to relieve Przemysl.

The battle was practically over by the night of May 10, 1915; the Russians could hold out no longer against the ever-increasing flood of Austrians and Germans pouring across every road and pathway against their doomed line. Blasted and scorched by artillery, machine-gun and rifle fire; standing against incessant bayonet and cavalry charges; harassed by the Austrians from the south, the Russians were indeed in sore straits. Yet they had fought well; in the losing game they were playing they were exhausting their enemies as well as themselves in men and munitions—factors which are bound to tell in a long, drawn-out war. Above all, they still remained an army: they had not yet found their Sedan. No alternative lay before them—or rather behind them—other than retreat to the next possible line of defense—toward Przemysl.

Between May 11-12, 1915, the Germanic troops occupied the districts of Sendziszow, Rzeszow, Dynow, Sanok, Lisko, Lancut, and Dubiecko. Przevorsk was deserted by the Russians on the 13th. The Seventh Russian Railway Battalion, under Captain Ratloff, brought up the rear of the retreat to the Dembica-Jaroslav line. From Rzeszow onward this battalion were employed in destroying stations, plants, tunnels, culverts, rolling stock, and railway bridges, to hamper as much as possible the German advance. It took the Austro-Hungarian engineers between two and three weeks to repair the road and put it into sufficient working order to transport their heavy siege artillery. With uninterrupted labor and the most strenuous exertions they could only reconstruct about four miles per day. Repairs and renovations other than those of the railway system were necessary. The wounded had to be sent back to hospital, and fresh troops had to be brought up to fill the gaps torn in the Austro-German ranks during all the severe fighting since May 2, 1915. It is not known exactly what the series of victories cost the Germanic armies in casualties, but it is known that their successes were dearly bought. One fairly competent authority places the loss at between 120,000 to 130,000. From May 2 to May 12, 1915, the forces of Von Mackensen, the Archduke Joseph Ferdinand, and Boroyevitch von Boyna claim to have captured 103,500 men, 69 guns, and 255 machine guns. A retreating army must inevitably lose many of their number as prisoners, besides their wounded must also be abandoned. Furthermore, the Russian line of retreat led through rough and mountainous country, where large bodies of troops could not be kept in touch with each other. Thus it frequently happened that isolated detachments were captured *en bloc* without being able to offer any resistance. In the neighborhood of Sanok and the watering places of Rymanow and Ivonicz some of the biggest Russian base hospitals were situated. These, of course, could not have been evacuated in time, and the patients consequently swelled the number of prisoners. Most of the guns captured by the Austro-Germans were those of the Russian troops whose retreat from northern Hungary and the passes had been intercepted.

They often sacrificed large bodies of troops to save their guns. The lack of artillery was the main cause of their defeat; what little they could save from the wreck was therefore husbanded with jealous care. The German staff accurately calculated on the preponderance of heavy artillery, and that Russia would be compelled to bow low before the superior blast of cannon fire. Though it involved the sacrifice of many miles of territory, it was now the Russian object to draw the enemy's line out to the fullest extent. After the retreat from the Wistok the Russian Generalissimo, Grand Duke Nicholas, was concerned only to save the most for his country at the greatest expense to her enemies. It meant continual retreat on a gigantic scale. Przemysl, captured ten weeks ago, lay behind Ivanoff's line, and Lemberg was but sixty miles beyond. Two hundred miles northward the Germans were hammering at the gates of Warsaw. A retreat such as the grand duke contemplated might involve the loss of all three of these places, but it would stretch the Germanic lines enormously and enable the Allies in the west to strike with better effect. No territorial considerations must stand in the way against the safety of the Russian armies. It was the same policy that had crippled Napoleon in 1812.

CHAPTER XLIII

CAMPAIGN IN EASTERN GALICIA AND THE BUKOWINA

IN order to keep the narrative abreast of the steadily advancing Austro-German line, we must change occasionally from one sector to another to watch the progress of operations over the huge battle field. In accordance with the details laid down in the great strategic plan, each of the different Germanic forces had a distinct task to perform. Turning then to eastern Galicia and the Bukowina, we find that on May 1, 1915, the Austro-Hungarian and Russian armies were facing each other along almost the same front where we left them in the middle of March. That front extended to the north of Nadvorna and Kolomea, by Ottynia across to Niczviska on the Dniester, and from there eastward along the river toward Chotin on the Russian frontier of Bessarabia.

By the beginning of May, 1915, the spring floods had subsided, when operations became again possible. General Lechitsky, on the Russian side, probably aimed at recovering the Pruth Valley, while the Austrian commander, General von Pflanzer-Baltin, directed his efforts to establishing himself on the northern bank of the Dniester. He would then be able to advance in line with the Germanic front that was pressing on from the west, and northward from the Carpathian range between Uzsok and the Jablonitza passes; otherwise his force would lag behind in the great drive, a mere stationary pivot. At that time he held about sixty miles of the Odessa-Stanislau railroad (which runs through the valley via Czernovice and Kolomea) with the Russians only twenty miles north of the line. If that position could be taken the Austrians would have the South Russian line of communications in their hands, for it was along this line that supplies and reenforcements were being transported to Ivanoff's front on the Wisloka from the military centers at Kiev and Sebastopol. Thus the railway was of tremendous importance to both belligerents. What it meant to the Austrians has been stated; to the Russians its possession offered the only opportunity for a counteroffensive in the east that could possibly affect the course of the main operations on the Wisloka, San, and later the Przemysl lines. But however successful such a counteroffensive might prove, it could not have exerted any immediate influence on the western front. With the Transylvania Carpathians protecting the Austro-German eastern flank, there would still be little hope of checking the enemy's advance on Lemberg even if Lechitsky succeeded in reconquering the whole of the Bukowina and that part of eastern Galicia south of the Dniester. Every strategic consideration, therefore, pointed to the Dniester line as the key to the situation for the Austrian side, and Von Pflanzer-Baltin decided to stake all on the attempt.

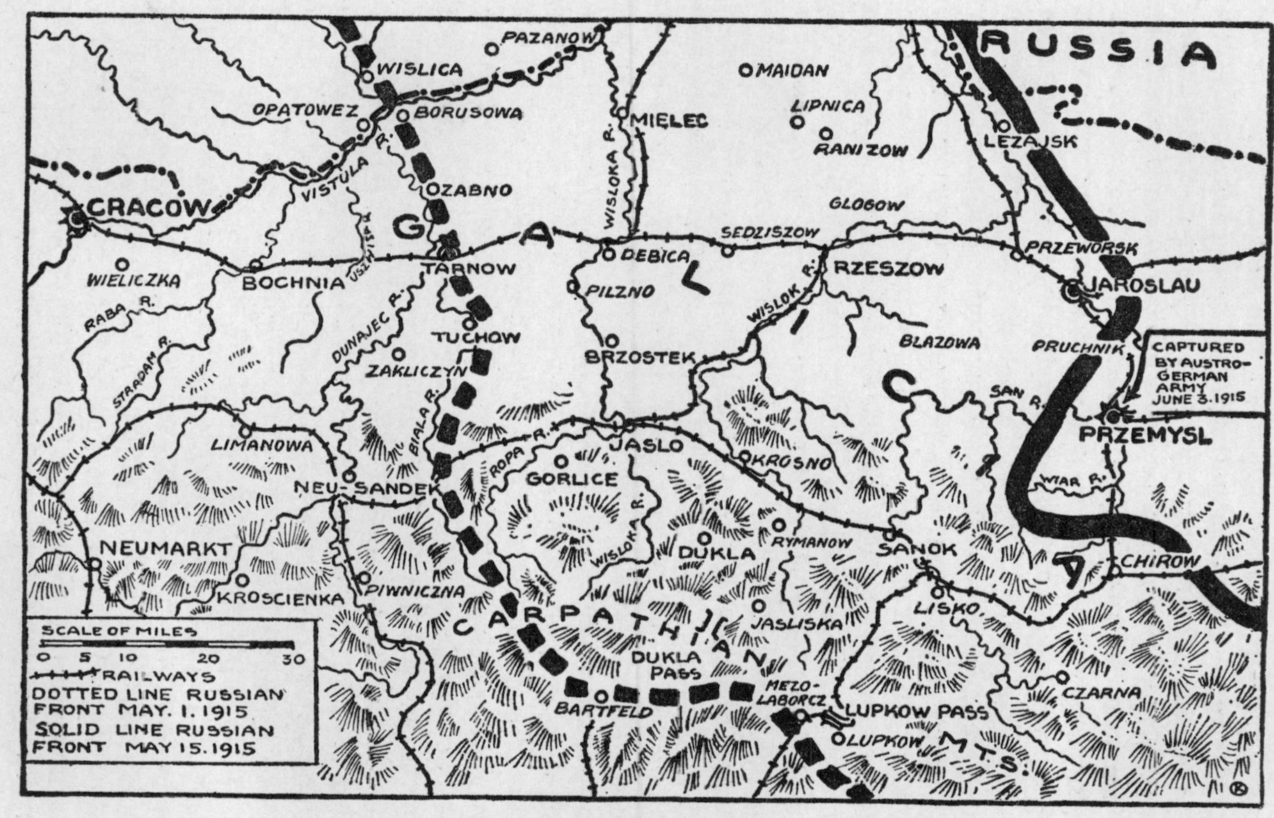

GALICIAN CAMPAIGN FROM PRZEMYSL TO BESSARABIA

On May, 6, 1915, the machine was set in motion by a violent bombardment. By the 8th the Austrians captured the bridgehead of Zaleszczyki; on the 9th the Russians drove them out again, capturing 500 men, 3 big guns, 1 field gun, and a number of machine guns. On May 10 the Russians took the initiative and attacked a front of about forty miles, along the entire Dniester line from west of Niczviska to Uscie Biskupic, crossed into the Bukowina and advanced to within five miles of Czernowitz from the east. A little stream and a village both named Onut are situated southwest of Uscie Biskupic. Here a detachment of Don Cossacks distinguished themselves on May 10, 1915. Advancing toward the Austrian wire entanglements in face of a terrific fusilade, they cut a passage through in front of the Austrian's fortified positions. Before the latter realized what was happening the Cossacks were on top of them, and in a few minutes a ferocious bayonet struggle had cleared out three lines of trenches. Russian cavalry poured in after them, hacking the Austrian's rear, and compelling them to evacuate the entire district. The Cossacks charged into the hurriedly retreating masses—on horse and on foot, with saber, lance, and bayonet, capturing 4,000 prisoners, a battery of machine guns, several caissons and searchlight apparati.

The entire northern bank of the Dniester was in Russian possession by the night of May 10, 1915; several desperate counterattacks attempted by the Austrians on the 11th completely failed to recover the lost ground. Two days later a Russian official reported: "In this operation the Austrian units which led the offensive were repulsed near Chocimierz with heavy losses. Our artillery annihilated two entire battalions and a third surrendered. Near Horodenka the enemy gave way about seven o'clock in the evening of the same day and began a disorderly retreat. We again captured several thousand prisoners, guns, and some fifty ammunition caissons." Being a junction of six roads and a railway station on the curved line from Kolomea to Zaleszczyki, Horodenka is considered to be the most important strategic point along the Dniester-Czernowitz front. It was undoubtedly a severe blow to the Austrians.

During the night of May 11, 1915, and the next day they evacuated a front of about eighty-eight miles, and retired south of the Pruth. General Mishtchenko led his Cossacks on the Austrian trail, taking several towns on their way to Nadvorna, which they captured after a fierce fight. From here they took possession of part of the railway line from Delatyn to Kolomea, and completely severed the connection between Von Pflanzer-Baltin's forces and those of Von Linsingen lying along the north of the range. Larger bodies of Russian troops were on the way to Kolomea; on May 13, 1915, they stormed and carried some strongly fortified Austrian positions eight miles north of the town, in front of which the Austrians had placed reenforcements and all their last reserves. By dint of great efforts they held their position here, but from May 9 to May 14, 1915, the Russians drove them back elsewhere on a front of over sixty miles for a distance of about twenty miles, also capturing some 20,000 prisoners with many guns and valuable stores of munitions. About the middle of May matters quieted down in the eastern sector; the only fighting of importance consisted of severe artillery combats around Czernowitz and Kolomea. The issue of the conflict hung in the west with Von Mackensen's armies; fighting in the Bukowina at this stage became an unnecessary expenditure of strength and energy. The fate of eastern Galicia was being decided 140 miles away, on the banks of the River San, to which region we will now direct the reader's attention.

CHAPTER XLIV

RUSSIAN CHANGE OF FRONT—RETREAT TO THE SAN

AFTER the Russian troops retreated from the Lower Wisloka northward toward the confluence of that river with the Vistula they held the two important bridgeheads of Sandomierz and Rozvadov.

On May 14, 1915, Ivanoff's right was being forced toward the Vistula in the vicinity of Opatow. This right wing was the army under General Ewarts, which since December, 1914, had been stationed in strongly fortified positions on the Nida in Russian Poland. The front extended across the frontier into western Galicia and joined on to the right wing of Dmitrieff's Dunajec-Biala front, which was shattered between Otfinow and Gorlice. The retreat of Dmitrieff's army was in an easterly direction along Tarnow, Pilzno, Dembica, Rzeszow, and Lancut to Przevorsk on the San; from the region of Gorlice and Ciezkovice along Biecz, Jaslo, Frysztak, Krosno to Dynow, Dubiecko, and Sanok, the latter also on the San. The troops that Brussilov extricated from the passes and those with which he held the northern part of the western Carpathians against Boehm-Ermolli were now likewise concentrated on the San. A glance at the map will show that the Russian front on the San from Przevorsk down to Sanok forms a shield between the Germanic advance and the two towns of Jaroslav and Przemysl. It will also be observed that General Ewarts's forces about Rozvadov are on the west side of the San, that is to say, nearer toward the advancing Austrians under the Archduke Joseph Ferdinand.

The retreat in Galicia necessitated modifications in the Russian front in Poland on the way to Warsaw. The line south of the Pilica had to be withdrawn and positions on the Nida abandoned to conform with the retreating line in Galicia. New positions were taken up along Radom and across the Kamienna River. The pivot or hinge from which the line was drawn back was the town of Ivanlodz, about fifty-five miles southwest of Warsaw. North of Ivanlodz the front remained unaltered. While this line shifting was in progress (in Poland) the German troops hung closely to the heels of the retiring Russians, evidently mistaking the motive behind the change of position. Mr. Stanley Washburn thus summarizes the results of these retreating battles:

"Regarding the movement as a whole, suffice it to say that in the two weeks following the change of line one (Russian) army inflicted upon the enemy a loss of nearly 30,000 in killed, wounded, and prisoners. The Russian losses were comparatively trifling." The Austro-German forces were following up leisurely the retreating Russian corps, not expecting any serious fighting to occur until the lines behind the Kamienna were reached.

Instead of that, however, on May 15, 1915, the Russian commander suddenly halted the main body of his troops in front of his fortified positions on a line extending from Brody by Opatow toward Klimontow. Between May 15-17, 1915, a battle developed on this front, which is the more notable as it is one of the few in this war fought in the open without trenches. To quote Mr. Washburn: "In any other war it would have been called a good-sized action, as from first to last more than 100,000 men and perhaps 350 to 400 guns were engaged."

The Austro-Germans came on in four groups. The Third German Landwehr was moving from the southwest by Wierzbnik against Ilza, slightly to the north of Lubienia. Next to it, coming from the direction of Kielce, was the German Division of General Bredow, supported by the Eighty-fourth Austrian Regiment. This body was advancing against Ostroviec, the terminus of a railway which runs from the district of Lodz to the southeast by Tomaszow and Opoczno, and crosses the Ivangorod-Olkusz line halfway between Kielce and Radom. Farther to the south three Austro-Hungarian divisions were also advancing—namely, the Twenty-fifth Austrian Division against Lagow, and the Fourth Austrian Landwehr Division, supported by the Forty-first Honved Division, against Ivaniska; they moved along roads converging on Opatow. The Twenty-fifth Austrian Division, commanded by the Archduke Peter Ferdinand, was composed of crack regiments, the Fourth Hoch and Deutschmeisters of Vienna, and the Twenty-fifth, Seventeenth, and Tenth Jäger battalions. The Russians were outnumbered about 40 per cent. The supposedly demoralized Russians were not expected to give any battle short of their fortified line, to which they were thought to be retiring in hot haste. The Russian general selected the Austrians on whom to spring his first surprise, but commenced by making a feint against the German corps, driving in their advanced guards by vigorous attacks which caused the whole force to halt and begin deployment for an engagement.

This occurred on May 15, 1915. On the same day, with all his available strength, he swung furiously with Opatow as an axis from both north and south, catching in bayonet charge the Twenty-fifth Division on the road between Lagow and Opatow. Simultaneously another portion of his command swept up on the Fourth Division coming from Ivaniska to Opatow. "In the meantime a strong force of Cossacks had ridden round the Austrians and actually hit their line of communications at the exact time that the infantry fell on the main column with a bayonet charge, delivered with an impetuosity and fury that simply crumpled up the entire Austrian formation. The Fourth Division was meeting a similar fate farther south, and the two were thrown together in a helpless mass, losing between 3,000 and 4,000 casualties and nearly 3,000 in prisoners, besides a large number of machine guns and the bulk of their baggage. The remainder, supported by the Forty-first Honved Division, which had been hurried up, managed to squeeze themselves out of their predicament by falling back on Uszachow, and the whole retired to Lagow, beyond which the Russians were not permitted to pursue them, lest they should break the symmetry of their own line." It is admitted by the Austrians themselves that their losses were very severe in this battle. An Austrian source at the time stated that on May 16, 1915, not a single officer and only twenty-six men were left of the entire Fourth Company, First Battalion of the Tenth Austrian Infantry Regiment. By the 17th of May the Austrians had withdrawn more than twelve miles from the scene of the disaster.

During the following night, May 25, 1915, an Austrian division was moving from the line of advance of General Bredow's troops along the Lagow-Opatow road where it is separated by a spur of the Lysa Gora, the highest mountain group in Russian Poland. The Russians, elated over their recent victory, crossed the mountains by a forced march, and fell on the right flank of the German formation, while other troops opened a general frontal attack against it. Bredow was compelled to fall back in haste in the direction of Bodzentyn and to call for assistance from the adjoining Fourth German Landwehr Division. The sudden withdrawal of that division had the effect of weakening the German line southwest of Radom near the Radom-Kielce and the Konsk-Ostroviec railway crossings. The opportunity of thinning the enemy's line in that sector was too good to be lost, for a Russian communiqué of May 17, 1915, states that "near Gielniow, Ruski-Brod, and Suchedniov our sudden counterattacks inflicted severe losses on the enemy's advance guards." Having thus checked the German advance for the time being, the Russians ceased from further troubling to await developments on the San.

CHAPTER XLV

BATTLE OF THE SAN

WHEN the Austro-German armies reached the line of the San on May 14, 1915, the battle for mid-Galicia was over, and a fresh chapter of the campaign opened with the battle of the San, which might more fittingly be described as the battle for Przemysl. The position of Ivanoff's right has been shown; his right center lay west of the Lower San; the center east of the river covered Przemysl; his left center extended along the Upper Dniester, while his left, under Lechitsky, was keeping Von Pflanzer-Baltin employed. Von Mackensen's "phalanx" was slowly coming into action again, directing its course toward the Russian center. The "phalanx" was compelled to travel slowly, for it carried about 2,000 pieces of artillery with ample munitions, and the railroads had been wrecked by the retreating Russians. What has been described by military writers as "Von Mackensen's phalanx" was a concentration of troops along the lines on which the strongest resistance was expected or where the quickest advance was intended. No special group of forces appear to have been set apart for that purpose; there was very little shifting about or regrouping necessary during the campaign, and so well was the plan arranged that the concentrations occurred almost automatically wherever and whenever they were most needed. The infantry marched in successive lines or echelons, about forty yards apart, while in the ranks the men were allowed about four feet elbow room apiece. For frontal attacks this might be considered fairly close formation, but Von Mackensen calculated more upon the disintegrating effect of his artillery to first demoralize the enemy and wreck his position, after which the infantry came into play to complete the destruction. Without an overwhelming supply of artillery the "phalanx" plan would have been unworkable—machine guns would exact too heavy a sacrifice of life.

Ivanoff's chief object for the moment was to hold the enemy in check long enough to allow Przemysl to be cleared of ammunitions and supplies, and to withdraw the troops in possession of the place. Already, on May 14, 1915, the German troops of Von Mackensen's army had occupied Jaroslav, only twenty-two miles north of the fortress. Ivanoff had concentrated his strongest forces on the line between Sieniava, north of Przevorsk, and Sambor, thirty miles southeast of Przemysl. Here he had deployed the three armies which had held the entire front from the Biala to Uzsok in the beginning of May, 1915, nearly twice as long as the line they were now guarding. These were to fight a holding battle on the center while he adopted a series of vigorous counterthrusts on his right and left wings. By the retirement of the center Ewarts had been compelled to fall back from the Nida to the Vistula with Woyrsch's Austrian army against him. When Ewarts dropped behind Kielce in Russian Poland, Woyrsch seized the junction of the branch line to Ostroviecs in front of the Russian line. Ivanoff decided to venture a counterattack which would at the same time relieve the pressure on his center and also check the move on Josefov, dangerously near to the Warsaw-Ivangorod-Lublin line. The result of this plan was the brilliant surprise attack on the Austrians and Germans previously described. Along the San the troops just south of Ewarts delivered a fierce attack and drove the Archduke Ferdinand back to Tarnobrzeg on the Vistula. Ivanoff next drew as many reenforcements from that flank to strengthen his center as was compatible with safety. What had happened meanwhile on Ivanoff's extreme left—in eastern Galicia and the Bukowina—has already been stated. These counterattacks may be regarded as merely efforts to gain time, but the hour of another great battle was at hand.

The battle of the San, one of the greatest of the war, opened on May 15, 1915. Jaroslav was in German hands; the Fourth Austro-Hungarian Army (Archduke Joseph Ferdinand) reached the western side of the San on the 14th; by the 16th the Austro-German armies held almost the entire left bank of the river from Rudnik to Jaroslav, about forty miles. They crossed at several points on the same day and enlarged their hold on the right bank between Jaroslav and Lezachow near Sieniava, which they captured. A German division arrived at Lubaczovka, due north of Jaroslav, and half of the Germanic circle around Przemysl was now drawn. The German plan was an advance in force from the Sieniava-Jaroslav front against the Przemysl-Lemberg railway, the most vulnerable point of the Russian line of retreat from the fortress. Fifteen bridges were accordingly erected over the San in that sector between May 20-24, 1915, across which the German battering ram was to advance on Przemysl. South of the town mounted patrols came into touch with Russian cavalry; four Austro-Hungarian and one German army corps were standing prepared between Dobromil and Sambor; Sambor was occupied by them. The Russians held the left bank close to the river from Sieniava to Jaroslav, and northward of the former and to the west as far as Tarnobrzeg. From Jaroslav their front ran in almost a straight line for thirty miles southeastward to the outer and northern forts around Przemysl, described nearly a complete circle around the western and southern forts to Mosciska on the east, thence south to Sambor, and from Sambor to Stryj. From Stryj eastward to the Bukowina the line remained unaltered. In that region Lechitsky and Von Pflanzer-Baltin had been conducting a campaign all by themselves; they were now resting, waiting, watching.

While great Germanic preparations for the capture of Przemysl were proceeding north of the town, the battle opened on Saturday, May 15, 1915, in the south, against the Russian front between Novemiasto and Sambor. Here the Austro-German troops were thrown against Hussakow and Krukenice to hack their way through trenches and barbed-wire entanglements in order to reach the Przemysl-Lemberg railway and thereby complete the circle. "At the cost of enormous sacrifices the enemy succeeded in capturing the trenches of our two battalions."

But on May 17, 1915, these trenches near Hussakow were recaptured by the Russians. The Austrians returned to the charge, however, and by May 19 were within six miles of Mosciska. By May 21 they had overcome the main Russian defenses to the east of Przemysl and were threatening the garrison's line—their only line—of retreat to Grodek, for other Germanic forces were advancing upon Mosciska from the north.

On May 21, 1915, the Russians opened a sudden counteroffensive along the whole line in a desperate effort to save, not the fortress, but the garrison. The Austrians had destroyed most of the forts before they surrendered the town on March 22; and forts cannot be built or reconstructed in a few weeks. Besides, the Austrians knew the ground too well. Von Mackensen's "phalanx" was meanwhile advancing against the Jaroslav-Przemysl front with Von Bojna's corps on his right; Boehm-Ermolli deserted the passes which had so long occupied him and was now pressing against the south of the town while Von Marwitz on his right attempted to seize the railway between Sambor and Dobromil. Von Linsingen was forging ahead toward Stryj and the Dniester; he had finally worked through the ill-fated Koziova positions, and was now able to rest his right upon Halicz. From there his connection with Von Pflanzer-Baltin had been broken by Lechitsky, and was not repaired till June 6, 1915.

The Russian counteroffensive was a homeopathic remedy, on the principle of "like curing like:" an enveloping movement against being enveloped themselves at Przemysl; but the case was hopeless. Yet they met with some successes of a temporary nature. Between the Vistula and the San they captured some towns and villages; they also got very close to Radava, north of Jaroslav, and forced the Austro-German troops to fall back on to the left bank of the river on a considerable line of front north of Sieniava, where they captured many prisoners and guns.

The counteroffensive reached its zenith on May 27, 1915, when Irmanow's Caucasian Corps stormed Sieniava and captured something like 7,000 men, six big guns, and six pieces of field artillery. Von Mackensen resumed the offensive on May 24, by advancing due east of Jaroslav, capturing Drohojow, Ostrov, Vysocko, Makovisko and Vietlin all in one day. Radymno was occupied by the Austro-Hungarians under General Arz von Straussenburg, still further narrowing the circle and compelling the Russians to fall beyond the San. On the twenty-fifth the Austrians followed them over, captured the bridgehead of Zagrody, the village of Nienovice and the Heights of Horodysko, while Von Mackensen's troops farther north captured Height 241. South of the village of Naklo, between Przemysl and Mosciska, a hill 650 feet high was violently attacked; it commanded the only line of retreat from the fortress still left open. To the south of the town the Russian counteroffensive tried to outflank the Austrian troops which had approached close to the fortress and the railroad to Lemberg. With the assistance of strong reenforcements the Russians were able to check the advance here and make 2,200 prisoners, besides capturing ammunitions and machine guns.

CHAPTER XLVI

RECAPTURE OF PRZEMYSL

THE counteroffensive ended—of necessity—on May 24, 1915. The Russians could still offer an effective resistance between Krukienice and Mosciska, but the pressure of continuous attack against their positions around Hussakow grew fiercer every hour. The enemy was knocking at the outer ring of the forts; from the west the heaviest cannons were pouring shot and shell with such violence that the fall of Przemysl could no longer be prevented. Most of the troops had already been withdrawn, as well as the supplies and munitions; only a small garrison remained behind to man the guns of the forts to the last moment; the little avenue to safety on the east was still open.

On May 30, 1915, the Austrian batteries began their deadly work on the Grodek line near Medyka. The exit was under fire; since May 17, Przemysl had been invested from three sides, and the fourth was all but closed. From the northern side, guarded by the Bavarians under General Kneusel, twenty-one centimeter Krupp howitzers bombarded the Russian positions round Korienice and Mackovice, drawing ever nearer the forts commanding the road and railway to Radymno. The Tenth Austro-Hungarian Army Corps, approaching from Krasiczyn, endeavored to rush some of the outer works, but paid heavily for the venture. They settled down before the forts of Pralkovice, Lipnik, Helicha and Grochovce, and those round Tatarovka mountain. General Artamoff, the Russian commander of Przemysl, had laboriously reconstructed some of the old Austrian forts and equipped them with Russian 12-centimeter howitzers. As the Austrians had brought only their 15-centimeter howitzers, they were obliged to wait until their 30.5 batteries arrived before they could undertake any serious attack.

These batteries came on the scene about May 25, 1915, it took five days' preparation, and the final bombardment began on the 30th. It was an ironical circumstance that the Austrians and Germans were in numerous places sheltering themselves behind the very earthworks which the Russians had constructed when they were besieging the place two months earlier. There had been no time to destroy them on the retreat.

The northern sector of the outer ring of forts fell on May 30, 1915, when the Bavarians captured the Russian positions near Orzechovce. A terrific bombardment was directed against the entire northern and northwestern front; great columns of infantry were pushed forward to finish the cannons' work—still the Russians hung on, ever bent on doing all possible damage to the enemy.

The triumphal entry of the Austrian uhlans and artillery into Przemysl.
Their horses are decorated with sprays of leaves

During the night of May 30-31, 1915, the enemy succeeded in approaching within 200 paces, and at some points even in gaining a footing in the precincts of Fort No. 7, around which raged an obstinate battle that lasted until two in the afternoon of the 31st, when he was repulsed after suffering enormous losses. The remnants of the enemy who had entered Fort No. 7, numbering 23 officers and 600 men, were taken prisoners.

Since the 20th of May, 1915, the clearing of the road had been going on; Von Mackensen battering the western forts and the river line as far as Jaroslav, and Boehm-Ermolli struggling to force the southern corner to get within range of the Lemberg railway. On his right, Von Marwitz had become stuck in the marshes of the Dniester between Droholycz and Komarno. The Bavarians on the north again let fly their big guns against the forts round Dunkoviczki on May 31, 1915. At four in the afternoon they ceased fire; the forts and defenses were crumpled up into a shapeless mass of wreckage. Now Prussian, Bavarian and Austrian regiments rushed forward to storm what was left. They still found some Russians there, severely mauled by the bombardment; but they could no longer present a front. They retreated behind the ring. The Tenth Austro-Hungarian Army Corps now made another attempt on Pralkovice and Lipnik. Von Mackensen's men captured two trenches near Fort No. 11—"they had to pay a heavy price in blood for every yard of their advance." Heavy batteries are also spitting fire against Forts Nos. 10 and 12. When the curtain of night fell over the scene of carnage and destruction, two breaches had been made in the outer ring of the forts.

June 2, 1915, dawned—a bright, warm summer's day; the sun rose and smiled as impassively over the Galician mountains, and valleys, and plains as it had smiled through countless ages before the genius of man had invented even the division of time. From all sides of the doomed fortress eager, determined men were advancing; Fort No. 10 was captured at noon by the Twenty-second Bavarian Infantry Regiment; later in the day the Prussian Grenadier Guards took possession of Fort No. 12;

during the night the besieger's troops marched into the village of Zuravica, within the outer ring. Austrian troops had broken through from the southwest and also penetrated the inner circle.

June 3, 1915, dawned and again the sun smiles over Galicia and sees the same iron belt of machinelike men still nearer the fortress; but the haggard defenders, where are they? Gone! Flown! They have vanished during the night. Austrians and Bavarians march into the town early in the morning. The only enemies they meet are the dead.

Przemysl has fallen again—fallen before twenty times as powerful a blow as that which struck it down seventy-two days earlier.

Before proceeding with the progress of Von Mackensen and his mighty "phalanx," let us briefly trace the progress of Von Linsingen, whom we left on the road to Stryj and the Dniester, or rather, attempting to force that road. While the forts of Przemysl were being smashed in the north, Von Linsingen was pounding and demolishing the Russian positions between Uliczna and Bolechov. Heavy mortars and howitzers were at the same time being placed into position in front of the Russian trenches between Holobutow and Stryj.

On May 31, 1915, they began to roar, and before long the trenches were completely pulverized—the very trenches that thousands of Germans and Austrians had died in in vain attempts to carry by assault. The Thirty-eighth Hungarian Honved Division were sent to finish the work of clearance and take possession of Stryj. The entire Russian line withdrew to the Dniester, step by step, ever fighting their favorite rear guard actions, killing and capturing thousands of their enemies. They retired behind the Dniester, but maintained their hold on any useful strategical position south of the river, so far as was possible without imperiling the continuity of their line.

We must also consider two more Austro-German sectors in order to bring the combatants stationed there into line with the Germanic advance—the Uzsok Pass and the Bukowina-*cum*-Eastern Galicia sectors. In the former the army of Von Szurmay stood beside that of Von Linsingen opposite the Ninth

Russian Army. Von Szurmay led his men out of the pass and advanced northward on May 12, after the fall of Sanok had forced the Russians away from their positions in the vicinity of it. Their line of retreat was threatened by the Austrian approach to Sambor.

On May 16, 1915, Von Szurmay moved across the upper Stryj near Turka and passed along secondary roads in the direction of the oil districts of Schodnica, Drohobycz and Boryslav, arriving on May 16-17, 1915. Von Linsingen's troops had started their advance on the same day as those of Von Szurmay, when the Russians round Koziowa had to retire for the purpose of keeping in touch with their line: the same pressure that Sambor exerted on the Uzsok. Here again the Russians adopted rear-guard tactics and considerable fighting occurred during their retreat to Stryj and Bolechow, both of which were eventually captured by Von Linsingen.

In Eastern Galicia and the Bukowina matters had come almost to a standstill between Lechitsky and Von Pflanzer-Baltin about the middle of May, 1915. When the former had cut the latter's connection with the main line, the brigade of General von Blum and other adjoining German troops on the extreme right of Von Linsingen tried hard to relieve the pressure of Lechitsky on the Austrian forces. Not till after the fall of Przemysl was the connection restored, when the Russians had to fall back from Kalusz and Nadvorna; on June 9 they evacuated Obertzn, Horodenka, Kocman and Sniatyn. Lechitsky was also compelled to withdraw from the Bukowina between Zaleszczyki, Onut, and Czernowitz, where the Austrians were moving along the Dniester in the north, the Pruth in the south, and over the hills in the center against the village of Szubraniec. Here the Russians once more inflicted servere losses on the Austrians, but being in danger from a flanking movement by the Forty-second Croatian Infantry through the Dniester forests, they retired from the Bukowina on to Russian territory on June 12, 1915.

CHAPTER XLVII

CAPTURE OF LEMBERG

THE capture of Przemysl and of Stryj terminates the second stage of the Austro-German offensive in Galicia. The third stage may be described as the battle for Lemberg, or Lwow. Lemberg is the ancient capital of Galicia, and formerly bore the name of Lwow. The Austrians many years ago had changed it to "Lemberg." When the Russians captured the town on September 3, 1914, they had given it back the old Slavonic name, which, however, was destined soon to be transformed back again into the more pronounceable appellation of "Lemberg."

It is estimated that between April 28, 1915, and the recapture of Przemysl the Russian forces in Galicia had been diminished by at least a quarter of a million casualties. The heaviest losses occurred among Dmitrieff's troops in the first days of May, 1915, but in the battles on the San, at the close of the month, the forces of Von Mackensen's "phalanx" were also greatly reduced. Along the entire Galician front, it is computed that quite 600,000 Austro-German troops were put out of action.

While the fight for Przemysl was in full swing an important event of the war occurred—Italy joined the enemies of Austria on May 3, 1915; the Dual Monarchy had now to defend her western frontier as well. Dankl and Von Bojna were transferred to the Italian front with a considerable portion of their Galician troops. A general redistribution of units was effected among the Austrian and German armies. The army of the Archduke Joseph Ferdinand was held along the lower San as far as Sieniava. Von Mackensen was advancing east of Jaroslav along the railway toward Rawa-Ruska. Boehm-Ermolli was fighting on the road to Lemberg from Mosciska. An army under Count Bothmer was operating near the Dniester marshes, beyond which, farther south, a group of armies under Von Linsingen (mainly German) had forced the passage of the Dniester at Zuravno, and was trying to advance on Lemberg and catch

Ivanoff's main forces on the flank. This last movement, if successful, would be the most effective method of crushing the retreating Russian armies: being thus outflanked, some of their lines of retreat would be cut and a dissolution of a large portion of the retiring forces could hardly have been avoided. However, all attempts in this direction failed. The Russians gradually rolled up their line on the Dniester from west to east, keeping step with the retreat of the armies which were facing west. With strong reenforcements from Kiev and Odessa Brussilov commanded the Dniester front under the direction of General Ivanoff. If only the ponderous advance of Von Mackensen could have been arrested, Brussilov would have had little difficulty in sweeping Von Linsingen back to the Carpathian barrier. A somewhat similar condition existed in the north, where the Austrians were at the mercy of Ivanoff's strong right wing.

The archduke's front was smashed at Rudnik early in June, 1915; his forces were driven back a day's march and lost 4,000 men in prisoners, besides many guns. The Second, Third and Fourth Tyrolese regiments were almost annihilated. German troops were hurried to the rescue. Boehm-Ermolli also got into serious difficulties at Mosciska, where the Russians held him up for a week with a furious battle. Ivanoff was scoring points against all his individual opponents excepting only Von Mackensen. The "phalanx," always kept up to full strength by a continuous influx of reserves and provided with millions of high-explosive shells, not only pursued its irresistible course eastward, but had to turn now right, now left, to help Austrian and German commanders out of trouble. Heavy howitzers lumbered along the way to Rawa-Ruska—not to Lemberg, but to the north of it, on the flank of the Russian army still holding the Lower San. This army had therefore to retire northward to the river line of the Tanev stream, cautiously followed by the archduke's forces. The "phalanx" had again saved them from disaster. Similarly, at Mosciska, when Boehm-Ermolli tried to storm the Russian position by mass attacks, his infantry was driven back with such terrible punishment that they could not be induced to make another advance. There was nothing to be done here, but wait till Von Mackensen turned the flank of the Russian position for them, which he did in one of the most stubborn conflicts of the war—the battle of the Lubaczovka, a tributary of the San between Rawa-Ruska and Lemberg. Never were the fighting abilities of Slav and Teuton more severely tested. For over a week the struggle raged; a half million men were brought up in groups and flung against the Russian front. Shell, shrapnel, bullets and asphyxiating bombs finally wore down the Russian resistance.

Incapacitated by physical exhaustion and outnumbered by three to one, the Russian infantry gave way on June 13, 1915. The "phalanx" drove into their ranks and advanced rapidly in a northerly direction on its great flanking movement. But the Russian spirit was not broken, for at this critical moment General Polodchenko rode out with three regiments of cavalry—the Don Cossacks, the Chernigov Hussars, and the Kimburn Dragoons. They dashed into the unbroken lines of the triumphant German infantry like a living hurricane, sabered the enemy, and put thousands on the run. Swerving aside, they next charged deep into the German rear, mauled the reserves into confusion, hacked their way out again and captured several machine guns. The most remarkable feature about this extraordinary exploit was the fact that the losses sustained by the cavalry amounted only to 200 killed and wounded. The effect on the "phalanx," however, was such that no more attacks were made that day, and the Russians were able to retire to the hills near Rawa-Ruska. Ivanoff was now compelled to draw reenforcements from other parts of the line to strengthen his front at Rawa-Ruska. This meant weakening Ewarts's against the archduke and Brussilov against Boehm-Ermolli. The downfall of the Dunajec-Biala front had been attributed by the Russian War Staff to overconfidence or neglect on the part of General Dmitrieff, who was subsequently relieved of his command and replaced by General Lesch. At an official inquiry Dmitrieff was exonerated and reinstated on the reasonable ground that, whatever precautions of defense he might have taken, they would have proved ineffective against the preponderance of the German artillery.

After the battle of Lubaczow the Russian line drew back about twenty miles. For the defense of Lemberg the front ran in a concave form from along the River Tanev, five miles from Rawa-Ruska, down to Grodek and Kolodruby; then eastward behind the Dniester to Zuravno and Halicz. The marshes of the Dniester, then swollen by heavy rains, formed a good natural defense; the intrenchments on the hills north of Grodek to Rawa-Ruska protected the approaches to Lemberg from that direction. The weakest spot lay around Janov, fifteen miles north of Grodek, where the level ground would permit the easy transport of heavy artillery. This position had been fortified with trenches and wire entanglements. Here also were concentrated the troops withdrawn from other parts of the line, and four armored trains with quick-firing guns from the depot at Rovno. General Ivanoff had no intention of making any decisive stand against the "phalanx"; neither did he think of risking his armies in a battle for Lemberg. That town was certainly of great military and political importance — worth a dozen Przemysls — and worth fighting for. But for that he would need artillery in enormous quantity. Von Mackensen carried 2,500 guns with him, as well as siege trains of heavy howitzers. Ivanoff possessed none of these, and could therefore hope only to fight rear-guard actions while retiring before Von Mackensen. In any other part of the Galician line except the center he had little to fear. We left Von Linsingen forcing the Dniester at Zuravno. He got the bulk of his army across, the main advance commanded by Von Bothmer, who captured the northern heights and penetrated the forests near the Stryj-Tarnopol railway. They were less than fifty miles from Lemberg.

The "retreating" Brussilov suddenly turned round and fell on Von Bothmer's advance. The fight lasted three days, with the result that the Austro-Germans were obliged to fall back across the Dniester, leaving behind 2,000 killed and wounded, besides 17 guns, 78 machine guns, 348 officers and 15,430 men as prisoners, June 8-10, 1915.

On June 11, 1915, however, the Germans renewed the attack on Zuravno, recaptured the town, and on June 12 were five miles north of it. By June 13 they had made ten miles, when Brussilov lashed out again. Within two days the Germans were back on the Dniester. Von Mackensen had meanwhile concentrated a new series of heavy batteries around Jaroslav and formed a new "phalanx" (with reenforcements) west of the San between Piskorovice and Radymno. Another attempt was preparing to break through Ivanoff's right wing.

A violent bombardment began on June 12, 1915, and Austro-Hungarian troops crossed the river and occupied both Sieniava and Piskorovice. Next day the advance spread along the whole line, extending from Tarnoviec on the Zlota to the Radymno Javorov road, pressing north and eastward against the Russian front. Pivoting on Sieniava, Von Mackensen swung his right toward Mosciska, which Von Marwitz captured on June 14, 1915. The same night the Archduke Joseph Ferdinand's entire army was slowly wheeling from the San toward the Tanev, facing due north.

On June 16, 1915, the left of this line was already inside the borders of Russian Poland, and its right wing along the entire Tanev front. By June 16 numerous towns and villages were taken by the Germans. The Wolff Telegraphic Bureau announced that Von Mackensen's army had captured 40,000 men and 69 machine guns, which undoubtedly referred to all the Galician groups, for on June 12, 1915, Von Mackensen had "replaced" the Archduke Frederick as generalissimo of the Austro-Hungarian armies. The "phalanx" was pressing against Rawa-Ruska, Magierow, and Janov; Boehm-Ermolli against Grodek, part of which he captured by a midnight assault on June 16. In five weeks the Russian line or front in Galicia had shrunk from 300 miles to about 100. Before Dunajec, when it was united with the northern groups, it had represented the longest battle line in the history of the world.

The Russians began to evacuate Lemberg about June 17, 1915, the day Von Mackensen's right entered Javorov. On the 19th his advance guard was approaching Rawa-Ruska. Boehm-Ermolli was meanwhile undergoing severe punishment near Komarno, where an Austrian advance force endeavored to get through the

Grodek Lakes. The Russian artillery drove them back; for three days there were furious bayonet and cavalry charges and counter-charges; despite the most terrific bombardments the Austrian attacks were broken by the desperate Russians. On this occasion, at least, the Russians were well supplied with shells hurriedly sent by rail from Kiev, which enabled them to repulse the Austrians on the lakes. Boehm-Ermolli is said to have lost half of his effectives in his attempt to penetrate through Grodek and Dornfeld, fifteen miles south of Lemberg.

Von Mackensen again came to the rescue by making a great turning movement in the district of Zolkiev, about sixteen miles north of Lemberg, and attacking the Russian positions about Janov, forcing the Russians over the hills and the Rawa-Ruska railway to Zolkiev. His left wing, resting on Lubaczov, swung northward in a wheeling movement to envelop Rawa-Ruska. But the Russians intercepted the move; ferocious encounters and Cossack charges threw the Germans back to their pivot with heavy losses on both sides. Von Mackensen's center, however, was too strong, and Ivanoff desired no pitched battle—the only way to check its advance. He therefore fell back between Rawa-Ruska and Lemberg, yielding the former to Von Mackensen and the latter to Boehm-Ermolli, who was able to lead his battered troops into the town on June 22, 1915, without further resistance. Brussilov now had to withdraw from the Dniester. As at Przemysl, the Russian garrison departed with all stores and baggage before the victors arrived. Lemberg had been in Russian possession for 293 days.

A German attack near Rawa-Ruska was repulsed by the Russians on June 25, 1915. For two days the "phalanx" rested to replenish its stock of shells; when these had arrived along the Przemysl line, Von Mackensen turned northward in the direction of Kholm on the Lublin-Brest-Litovsk railway. On his left marched the Austro-Hungarian army of the Archduke Joseph Ferdinand. These two armies drop out of the Galician campaign at this stage and become part of the great German offensive against the Polish salient. The gigantic enveloping movement had failed in the south; it was now to be attempted against the Russian line in front of Warsaw, conducted by Von Hindenburg and Von Gallwitz in the northern sector, and by Von Mackensen, assisted by General Woyrsch and Archduke Joseph Ferdinand, in the southern. These operations are described in the pages following.

More than three-fourths of Galicia had now been reconquered, and it was left to the Austrians and the Germans to complete the conquest. The campaign was one of the greatest operations of the war. An English military writer thus describes the achievement: "Only a most magnificent army organization and a most careful preparation, extending to infinite detail, could execute a plan of such magnitude at the speed at which it was done by the Austrian and German armies in May, 1915."

Not yet, however, were the Russian armies destroyed; to the German War Staff it was not now a question of taking or retaking territory, but of striking a final and decisive blow at the vitals of Russia. The continuous series of reverses suffered by Boehm-Ermolli and Von Linsingen exerted an important effect on the end of the Galician campaign: it frustrated the plan of eliminating the Russian forces. The battle lines in France and Flanders could wait a while till the Russian power was annihilated.

After the fall of Lemberg, Ivanoff withdrew the main body of his troops toward the river line of the Bug, Boehm-Ermolli following up behind. Again that unfortunate general was roughly handled—another of his divisions was annihilated southeast of Lemberg in a rear-guard action. Von Linsingen directed his efforts against the Gnila Lipa and Halicz, while Von Pflanzer-Baltin still operated on the Dniester. For many months the Russians and Austrians faced each other in eastern Galicia; they were still skirmishing at the end of the year. Both Russia and Austria had more important matters on hand elsewhere: the former against Germany in the north, and the latter with her new enemy—Italy. Galicia became a side issue.

The Galician campaign will rank as one of the most instructive episodes in military history, an example of unparalleled calculation, scientific strategy, and admirable heroism, involving, it is computed, the terrible sacrifice of at least a million human lives.

PART VII—RUSSO-GERMAN CAMPAIGN

CHAPTER XLVIII

WINTER BATTLES OF THE MAZURIAN LAKES

THE battle known in the German official accounts as the "Winter Battle in Mazurian Land" is sometimes described as the "Nine Days' Battle." In this sense it is to be considered as beginning on the 7th of February, 1915, and ending on the 16th, when the German Great Headquarters reported that the Tenth Russian Army, consisting of at least eleven infantry and several cavalry divisions, had been driven out of its strongly fortified positions to the east of the Mazurian Lake district, forced across the border, and, having been almost completely surrounded, had been crushingly defeated. In fact, however, fighting continued as part of the same action until the 21st of February, 1915, when the pursuit of the defeated army ended.

The forces engaged in this titanic conflict were the Russian Tenth Army, consisting, according to the Russian version, of four corps, under General Baron Sievers, and the German East Prussian armies, under General von Eichhorn, operating on the north on the line Insterburg-Lötzen, and General von Bülow on the line Lötzen-Johannisburg to the south of Von Eichhorn. Sources favorable to the Allies represent the strength of General Sievers's army as 120,000 men. They assert that the total German force consisted of nine corps, over 300,000 men. These are said to have included the Twenty-first Corps, which had been with the Crown Prince of Bavaria in the west; three reserve corps, also from the west; the Thirty-eighth and Fortieth Corps, new formations, from the interior of Germany; the equivalent of three corps from other sections of the eastern front; and a reserve corps of the Guard. The German official description of the battle credits the Russians with having had in this sector of the battle front in East Prussia at the beginning of February six to eight army corps, or about 200,000 men.

For months the heavy fighting in the east had centered on other sections of the immense battle line, running from the Baltic to the Carpathians. The second general Russian offensive, the great forward thrust of the Grand Duke Nicholas toward Cracow in the direction of Berlin, aimed through the center of the German defense, had been met, and the German counterthrust toward Warsaw had come to a standstill in the mud of Poland and before the stone-wall defensive of the Russians on the Bsura and the Rawka. Attacks launched by the Russians against the East Prussian frontier, centering at Lyck, in January, 1915, seemed to forebode a fresh Russian offensive intended to sweep back the German armies in this section whose position on the Russian right wing was a continual threat to the communications of the Russian commander in chief.

The Germans, disposing of comparatively weak forces, estimated at three army corps, were compelled to yield a strip of East Prussian territory, and had fallen back to positions of considerable natural strength formed by the chain of Mazurian Lakes and the line of the Angerapp River. They reported their forces standing on the defensive here as 50 per cent Landwehr, 25 per cent Landsturm, and only 25 per cent other troops not of the reserve. Repeated attempts of the Russians to gain possession of these fortified positions had, however, broken down. They had been directed especially against the bridgehead of Darkehmen and the right wing of the German forces in the Paprodtk Hills. Wading up to their shoulders in icy water, the hardy troops of the Third Siberian Corps had attempted in vain to cross the Nietlitz Swamp, between the lakes to the east of Lyck.

At the beginning of February, 1915, finally Von Hindenburg had been able to obtain fresh German forces and to put them in position for an encircling movement against the Russians lying just to the east of the lakes, from near Tilsit to Johannisburg. With the greatest secrecy the reenforcements, hidden from observation by their fortified positions, and the border forces maintaining the defense, were gathered behind the two German wings. The Russians apparently gained an inkling of the big move that was impending about the time the advance against their wings was under way. The first news of the opening of the battle came to the public in a Russian official announcement of the 9th of February, 1915, to the effect that on the 7th the Germans had undertaken the offensive with considerable force in the Goldap-Johannisburg sector. The northern group of Germans began its movement somewhat later from the direction of Tilsit.

Extensive preparations had been made by the German leaders to meet the difficulties of a winter campaign under unfavorable weather conditions. Thousands of sleighs and hundreds of thousands of sleigh runners (on which to drag cannon and wagons), held in readiness, were a part of these preparations for a rapid advance. Deep snow covered the plain, and the lakes were thickly covered with ice. On the 5th of February, 1915, a fresh snowstorm set in, accompanied by an icy wind, which heaped the snow in deep drifts and made tremendously difficult travel on the roads and railways, completely shutting off motor traffic.

The Germans on the south, in order to come into contact with the main Russian forces, had to cross the Johannisburg Forest and the Pisseck River, which flows out of the southernmost of the chain of lakes. The attacking columns made their way through the snow-clad forests with all possible speed, forcing their way through barriers of felled trees and driving the Russians from the river crossings.

Throughout the 8th of February, 1915, the marching columns moved through whirling snow clouds, the Germans driving their men forward relentlessly, so that, in spite of the drifted snow which filled the roads, certain troops covered on this day a distance of forty kilometers. The Germans under General von

Falck took Snopken by storm; those under General von Litzmann crossed the Pisseck near Wrobeln. The immediate objectives of these columns were Johannisburg and Biala, where strong Russian forces were posted.

On the 9th the southern column, under Von Litzmann, was attacked on its right flank by Russians coming from Kolna, to the south of them. The German troops repelled the attack, taking 2,500 prisoners, eight cannon, and twelve machine guns. General Saleck took Johannisburg, and Biala was cleared of the Russians. The advance of these southern columns continued rapidly toward Lyck.

The German left wing at the same time fell overwhelmingly on the northern end of the Russian line. On the 9th they took the fortified Russian positions stretching from Spullen to the Schorell Forest and nearly to the Russian border. They had here hard work to force their way through wire entanglements of great strength. Having noticed signs of a retreat on the part of their opponents, these German forces had on the preceding day begun the attack without waiting for the whole of their artillery to come up. The Russians retreated toward the southeast.

Swinging forward toward the Russian border, the German left wing now exerted itself to the utmost to execute the sweeping encircling movement for which the strategy of Von Hindenburg had become famous. The Russian right wing had been turned and was being pressed continually toward the southeast. The German troops rushed forward in forced marches, ignoring the difficulties which nature put in their way. By the 10th of February these columns reached the Pillkallen-Wladislawow line, and by the 11th the main highway from Gumbinnen to Wilkowyszki. The right wing, up to the capture of Stallupohnen, had taken some 4,000 prisoners, four machine guns, and eleven ammunition wagons. The center of this army, at the capture of Eydtkuhnen, Wirballen, and Kibarty, took 10,000 prisoners, six cannon, eight machine guns, numerous baggage wagons, including eighty field kitchens, three military trains and other rolling stock, a large number of gift packages intended for the

Russian troops, and, of chief interest to the fighting men, a whole day's provisions.

On the afternoon of February 10 some one and a half Russian divisions had come to a halt in these three neighboring villages: Eydtkuhnen, Kibarty, and Wirballen. Although it was known that the Germans were approaching, it was apparently regarded by the Russians as impossible that pursuers would be able to come up with them in the raging snowstorm. So certain were they of their security that no outposts were put on guard. Only thus could it happen that the Germans, who had not allowed the forces of nature to stop their advance, arrived right at the Russian position on the same day, though with infantry alone and merely a few guns, everything else having been left behind, stuck in the snowdrifts.

CHAPTER XLIX

THE RUSSIANS OUT OF GERMANY

IT was evening when the Germans made their surprise attack on Eydtkuhnen and midnight when they fell upon Wirballen. On the roadway stood two Russian batteries with twelve guns and a considerable number of ammunition wagons. The German infantry approached without firing a shot until they were within fifty yards. Then all the horses were shot down and the guns and ammunition seized. The men of the battery fled. In both these towns there was street fighting in the night, lit up by burning houses which had been fired by the Russians in their retreat.

One of the captured trains was the hospital train of the czar. This was utilized as headquarters for the night by the staff of General von Lauenstein.

By the 12th of February, 1915, the German troops of the left wing, sweeping down from the north and pressing the Russians back from village to village, were entirely on Russian soil. Wizwiny, Kalwarja, and Mariampol were occupied on this day. The number of guns taken by these troops had been increased by seventeen, according to German reports. The German Headquarters Staff declared that by this time the Russian Seventy-third and Fifty-sixth Divisions had been as good as annihilated, and the Twenty-seventh division nearly destroyed. The Russians lying before the Angerapp line and the defenses of Lötzen had in the meantime also begun to retreat toward the east. German troops, consisting chiefly of reserves of the Landwehr and Landsturm which up to this time had been held back within the German fortified line, now advanced to attack the yielding army, whose long marching column could be observed by the German flyers. While General von Eichhorn's troops, coming from the neighborhood of Tilsit and making their way through snow and ice, were advancing upon Suwalki and Sejny, and the German right wing was fighting its way through Grajewo, toward Augustowo, the center of the troops of General von Bülow for several days fought the Russians in furious battle in the vicinity of Lyck. From all sides the Germans were closing in. To protect the withdrawal of this main army to Suwalki and Augustowo, the Russians endeavored by all means to hold the narrows of the lakes before Lyck, where they were favored by the nature of the ground and aided by strong defensive works, for the most part well provided with wire entanglements. The best of the Russian troops, Siberian regiments, here fought with great energy under a determined leadership, and the Russians, in fact, at some places took the offensive. By the 12th of February, 1915, however, the Germans had taken these positions and the Russians had withdrawn to the narrow passages among the lakes before Lyck. The battles around this town were carried on under the eye of the German Emperor. The German soldiers were still occupied in hunting through the houses for scattered Russians as the emperor stepped from his motor car. He was received with hurrahs, and the soldiers surrounded him, singing "Deutschland, Deutschland über Alles." The emperor, standing amid the blackened ruins of burned homes, delivered a short address to the soldiers gathered about him, giving special recognition to Infantry Regiment No. 33, an East Prussian unit which had especially distinguished itself and suffered great losses. On the same day the Germans advanced beyond Lyck, and by the 15th of February no Russian remained on German soil.

CHAPTER L

TIGHTENING OF THE NET—REPORT OF THE BOOTY

THE Russian right, retiring to avoid envelopment, sought the natural line of retreat along the railway to Kovno. In executing this movement it turned toward the northeast, and exceeding in speed of movement the corps to the south of it, the Twentieth, under the command of General Bulgakov, the latter was left out of the line. In consequence its right wing was turned and it was pressed down toward the south with the enemy on three sides of it. It speedily became a broken force in the forest north of Suwalki. The Russians endeavored to reach the protection of their great fortress of Grodno. It was the task of the German division coming down from the north in forced marches to cut off this way of escape and prevent the Russians coming out of the forest toward the southeast.

The march of these German troops carried them through great woodlands, amid frozen lakes, when suddenly a thaw set in. The sleighs which had been used had to be abandoned and wagons requisitioned on the spot wherever possible.

An officer with these troops relates that infantrymen were sent forward on wagons, and on the night following the 15th of February took Sopozkin, to the east of Augustowo, on the line of the Russian retreat, capturing the baggage of an entire Russian army corps. "The morning," he writes, "presented to us a unique picture. Hundreds of vehicles, baggage carts, machine guns, ammunition, provision and ambulance wagons stood in a vast disorder in the market place of the town and in the street

In between were hundreds of horses, some harnessed, some loose, dead Russians, dead horses, bellowing cattle, and sounding over it all the words of command of our troops endeavoring to create order in this mad mix-up, and to take care of the rich booty. Many an interesting find did we make—'mementos' which the Russians had taken with them from Prussia and which now were to find their way back."

A German commander tells how, in their efforts to cut off the Russian retreat, the artillery were compelled to cross many brooks running through deep gullies, so that it was necessary frequently to lower guns and wagons by means of ropes on one side and pull them up on the other.

One of the German leaders, describing this encircling movement to the southeast from the north in which he played a part, says: "The roads and the weather were beyond all description—twelve to fifteen degrees Reaumur, with a cutting wind and driving snow, with nothing to eat, as the field kitchens on these roads could not follow. During pauses in the march one could but lean against the wall of a miserable house or lie down in the burned-out ruins, without straw to lie on and no covering. Men and horses sank to their hips in the snow, and so we worked our way forward, usually only about two kilometers an hour. Wagons and horses that upset had to be shoveled out of the drifts. It was a terrible sight, but we got through. We had to go on without regard for anything, and the example of the higher officers did much."

Two Russian corps from the southern wing of the army retreating by the Suwalki-Sejny causeway and by the Ossowetz Railway, according to accounts from Russian sources, made their way out of the trap under heavy rear-guard fighting.

The escaped portions of the Russian army crossed the Bobr toward Grodno. From the direction of this Russian stronghold a desperate effort was made to relieve the four corps which were endeavoring to escape toward the fortress from the forest southeast of Augustowo into which they had been pressed by the Germans from the west and north. On the 21st of February came the final act in the great drama. The German troops pushed forward at their best speed from all directions toward the forest. The help that had been intended for them came too late. Concerning the captures of this day, the German Great Headquarters reported: "On the 21st of February the remnants of the Tenth Army laid down their arms in the forest of Augustowo after all attempts of the Russian commander of this army, General Sievers, to cut a way out for the encircled four divisions by means of those parts of his army which remained to him after escaping over the Bobr to Grodno failed with extremely heavy losses."

Summarizing the results of the entire battle in an announcement of the 22d of February, the German Great Headquarters said: "The pursuit after the winter battle in Mazurian Land is ended. In cleaning up the forests to the northwest of Grodno, and in the battles reported during the last few days in the region of the Bobr and the Narew, there have been captured to date one commanding general, two division commanders, four other generals, and in the neighborhood of 40,000 men, seventy-five cannon, a quantity of machine guns, whose number is not yet determined, and much other war material.

"The total booty of the winter battle in Mazurian Land, therefore, up to to-day rises to seven generals, more than 100,000 men, more than 150 cannon, and material of all sorts, inclusive of machine guns, which cannot yet be approximately estimated. Heavy guns and ammunition were in many cases buried by the enemy or sunk in the lakes; thus eight heavy guns were yesterday dug out or hauled out of the water near Lötzen and Lake Widmin.

"The Tenth Russian Army of General Baron Sievers may, therefore, now be considered as completely annihilated."

This summary was corrected in a later announcement, which stated that the number of guns taken as booty in the pursuit after the winter battle in Mazurian Land had risen to 300, including eighteen heavy guns. This was published on the 23d of February. In an announcement of the 26th of February the Great Headquarters amplified its account of the victory with this statement:

"In the Russian official report the extent of the disaster in the winter battle of Mazurian Land is either concealed or an attempt is made to obscure it. It is unnecessary to go further into these denials. As evidence of the extent of the defeat, the following list of the positions held by the captured generals, however, may serve:

"Of the Twentieth Army Corps: the commanding general, the commander of the artillery, the commander of the Twenty-eighth and Twenty-ninth Infantry Divisions, and of the First Brigade of Infantry of the Twenty-ninth Infantry Division. The commander of this latter division succumbed to his wounds soon after being made prisoner.

"Of the Third Army Corps: the commander of the Twenty-seventh Infantry Division and the commander of the artillery and of the Second Infantry Brigade of this division.

"Of the Fifty-third Reserve Division: the division commander and the commander of the First Infantry Brigade.

"Of the First Siberian Cossack Division: a brigade commander."

This brought the total of Russian generals captured up to eleven.

This account of one of the greatest battles of the European War is necessarily based to a large extent on reports of the Germans, owing to the fact that material from this source is virtually the only official account available of the operation as a whole. The Russian General Staff has contented itself with the following announcement, made public on February 21, 1915:

"When the Germans, after a series of extraordinary obstinate and persistent attacks which caused them heavy losses, had recognized the impossibility of pressing in our front on the left bank of the Vistula, they turned at the end of January to the execution of a new plan. After the creation of several new corps in the interior of the country, and the bringing up of troops from their west front, the Germans threw important forces into East Prussia. The transportation of troops was made easier by the extraordinarily developed net of railways which Germany has at its disposal.

"The task of the new troops sent to East Prussia was to defeat our Tenth Army, which held strongly constructed positions along the Angerapp. To assure the success of the undertaking the Germans brought a portion of their forces from the Bzura and Rawka fronts to the right bank of the Vistula. A movement of the Germans in East Prussia already became noticeable on the 4th of February, 1915. But the extent of this movement could only be recognized a few days later. As our leaders, because of the lack of railroad lines, could not collect the necessary forces on the East Prussian front with the necessary speed to meet the hostile attack adequately, they decided to take back the abovementioned army of East Prussia to the border. In this movement of the right wing the Tenth Army, which was pressed by heavy hostile forces and threatened with being surrounded from the right, was forced to make a rapid change of alignment in the direction of Kovno. In this rapid movement a corps was separated from the rest of the army. The other corps which continued the battle obstinately without interruption, slowly drew back in the prescribed direction, bravely repelling the enemy and inflicting upon him heavy losses. Our troops overcame unbelievable difficulties, which were caused by the snow which filled all roads. As the streets were impassable, automobiles could not run. Trains were delayed and frequently failed to arrive at their destination. Our corps which formed the left wing of the Tenth Army held the enemy, while drawing back step for step for nine days on a stretch of territory which ordinarily is covered in four days. On the 19th of February these corps withdrawing by way of Augustowo left the battle field and took the position assigned to them. Further battles developed in the region before Ossowetz, on the roads from Lomza to Jedwabno and to the north of Radislow, also halfway between Plozk and Plonsk. These battles were in places very intense."

An English authority says: "The chief Russian loss was in General Bulgakov's Twentieth Corps, which the German staff asserted they had completely destroyed. But during the fortnight which ended on Saturday the 20th, at least half of that corps and more than two-thirds of its guns safely made their way through the Augustowo and Suwalki woods to the position which had been prepared for the Russian defense. The total Russian losses may have been 80 guns and 30,000 men; they were no more. The two southern corps, in spite of their stubborn action at Lyck, crossed the woods between Augustowo and Ossowetz without serious disaster."

CHAPTER LI

BATTLES OF PRZASNYSZ—BEFORE MLAWA

THE shattering of the Tenth Russian Army in the "winter battle" of the Mazurian Lakes was part of a greater conflict which in February, 1915, extended far down the armies on the right flank of the great Russian battle line which ran from the Baltic to the Dniester. A "new gigantic plan" of the Slavs was involved. As interpreted by the German General Staff it meant that while the extreme northern wing of the Russian armies was to sweep westward through the projecting section of Germany, East Prussia, along the Baltic another Russian army was to advance in force from the south against the corner formed by West Prussia and the Vistula. With vast masses of cavalry in the van, it was to break through the boundary between Mlawa and Thorn, and pushing northward, come into the rear of those German forces which were facing eastward against the attack aimed at East Prussia from the northeast. For operations in this section the Russians had favorable railway connections. Two railways terminating at Ostrolenka permitted the rapid unloading of large masses of troops at this point, and the line Warsaw-Mlawa-Soldau led straight into the territory aimed at by such an invasion. It seemed easily credible that the Russian commander in chief did, as reported, give orders that Mlawa should be taken be the cost what it might.

The northern Russian armies based upon the fortresses of Kovno and Grodno on the Niemen had not fully started on their part of this great, well-planned undertaking when the German counteroffensive was suddenly launched with tremendous strength from the Tilsit-Insterburg-Mazurian Lakes line. The disaster which followed, and which banished all hope of an advance of the Russians on this wing, has been described on a preceding page. While the Germans, using to the best advantage their net of railroads for the swift accumulation of troops, had gathered large forces on the Mazurian Lakes line, they had at the same time strengthened the troops standing on the southern boundary of West and East Prussia. An artillery officer, General von Gallwitz, was placed in command of this army with orders to protect the right flank of the German armies attacking in Mazurian Land, and to prevent the expected Russian attempt at invasion in his own sector of the front.

While the "winter battle" was raging to the east of him, Von Gallwitz in the characteristic German fashion of defense by a strong offensive moved forward up the right bank of the Vistula to Plozk. A cavalry division and regiments of the Guard at Sierpe and Racionz, February 12-18, 1915, won well-earned laurels for themselves by driving an enemy of superior strength before them. At Dobrin, according to German report, they took 2,500 prisoners.

General von Gallwitz's plan, however, was of more ambitious scope. It was his intention, by encircling the Russians in the territory before him from both wings, to sweep clear of enemies the entire stretch of country in the Polish triangle between the Vistula and the Orczy rivers. The right wing of his troops that had come down the bank of the Vistula was to swing to the eastward in behind the Russians. German troops which had arrived at Willenberg inside of the East Prussian boundary, one of the German concentration points on the line of railroad lying behind their front, on the other hand, received orders to descend the valley of the Orczy and to come in behind the Russian right flank from the east. These troops, making a wide detour, swept past Przasnysz on the east, and swinging round to the south of the city attacked the Russians holding the place from this direction. The Germans had understood that only small Russian forces were in the city. Anticipating the German movement, however, a Russian division, as the Germans learned later, had hastened to Przasnysz. The Russians also had collected large forces on the Narew, and were hurrying them toward Przasnysz on roads covering a wide front. Two full Russian corps from this line were flung upon the German left wing.

The forces of Von Gallwitz which had carried out the encircling movement from the east and south of Przasnysz now found themselves caught between two Russian armies. However, they were unwilling to relinquish the booty which they had planned to seize. A part of the German forces was disposed in a half circle as a defense against the Russians coming up from the south, and a division of reserves, February 24, stormed Przasnysz. The German Great Headquarters announced that the Germans captured 10,000 prisoners, including 57 officers, and took 36 cannon, 14 machine guns, and much war material of various sorts. However, the Russian troops were now pressing forward from the south with irresistible force. The Germans, in consequence, slowly fell back, fighting under great difficulties, and moving northward toward their defensive lines, carrying with them their prisoners and booty.

The Russian General Staff on the first of March, 1915, devoted an explicit account to the fighting about Przasnysz which differs but slightly from the narrative by the German Great Headquarters which has in general been followed in the preceding description. Both sides apparently considered the operation of special importance, and as reflecting credit upon their respective troops. The Russian story emphasizes the attacks made by their force on the line Lyssakowo-Chainovo simultaneously from north and south, that is, both in the flank and in the rear of the Germans to the west of Przasnysz. They represent their troops in the city as having consisted of only a brigade of infantry and some insignificant cavalry units. On the 25th of February, when the Germans had established themselves in the town, the Russians, according to their account, were pressing their enemies hard upon a long front from Krasnoseltz through Vengerzinovo, Kolatschkowo to Voliaverlowska.

On the evening of this day they drove the Germans into positions close to the city. The Thirty-sixth German Reserve Division on the same evening is said to have met serious disaster after a determined resistance at the crossings of the Anetz. On the evening of the next day the Russians began to reenter Przasnysz, but did not completely occupy the town until the night after the 27th. "The Germans," the Russian account continues, "hereupon began a disorderly retreat, endeavoring to withdraw in the direction of Mlawa-Chorgele. Regardless of the exhaustion consequent upon the marching they had undergone and four days of battle, our troops energetically took up the pursuit of the enemy. On the 28th of February they inflicted serious losses upon his rear guard. In these battles we seized a large amount of booty. The total number of prisoners amounts to at least 10,000." The Russians maintain that they had defeated no less than two German army corps and thrown them back to the border.

On the 12th of March, 1915, the German Great Headquarters protested against this version of the affair, and pointed to the fact that within a few days their troops were again threatening Przasnysz, and that since giving up the city they had captured on the battle fields between the Vistula and the Orczy no less than 11,460 Russians.

The city of Przasnysz itself suffered heavily in these attacks and counterattacks. For days and nights it had lain under bombardment and repeatedly fierce, hand-to-hand combats had been fought in its streets. Most of the houses of the place were left mere heaps of smoking ruins.

From the German point of view this offensive just north of the Vistula which included the temporary capture of Przasnysz was a success, especially in this, that it had prevented the big Russian forward movement against the West Prussian boundary which the impending great Russian offensive had foreboded. It had been impossible for the Russians seriously to endanger the German flank in this section, while the Germans had struck to the east in the "winter battle," and had definitely spoiled the Russian appetite for invasion from the Kovno-Grodno line.

As though determined to avenge their defeat to the east of the lakes, the Russians now continued to direct a series of fierce attacks in the direction of Mlawa, intending apparently to break through the German line of defense between Soldau and Neidenburg. It was said that the Russians believed General von Hindenburg in person to be in charge of the German forces in this sector. In consequence the German troops for the most part were forced to stand upon the defensive. In the beginning of March the Russian attacks increased steadily in violence. They broke against the German positions to the east and south of Mlawa, according to German reports, with enormous losses. At Demsk, to the east of Mlawa, long rows of white stones mark common graves of masses of Russians who perished before the German barbed-wire entanglements. The Germans point to these as dumb witnesses of the disaster that overtook forty-eight Russian companies that assaulted ten German ones. The cold weather at this time had made possible the swampy regions in which the Orczy rises, and had enabled the Russians to approach close to the German line of defense.

The Russian attack at this point in the night of the 7th of March, 1915, was typical of the fighting on this line in these weeks. After a thousand shells from the Russian heavy guns had descended upon and behind Demsk, a seemingly ceaseless series of infantry attacks set in. They were carried close up to the lines of wire of the German defense. Enough light, however, was shed by the searchlights and light balls shot from pistols to enable the Germans to direct a destructive infantry and machine-gun fire on the approaching lines. Those of the Russians who did not fall, fled to the next depression in the ground. There they were held by the beams of the searchlights until daybreak. Then they surrendered to the German patrols. Of another attack a few kilometers farther to the north, at Kapusnik, the Germans reported that after the enemy had penetrated into their trenches and had been driven out in a desperate bayonet fight, they buried 906 Russians and 164 Germans.

On the 8th of March, 1915, General von Gallwitz again tried an offensive with fresh forces which he had gathered. It was thwarted, however, on the 12th, to the north of Przasnysz. The Germans estimated the Russian forces which here were brought up for the counterattack at some ten army corps and seven cavalry divisions. The Russians in advancing this time, instead of directing their thrust at Mlawa, pushed northeastward of Przasnysz along the rivers Orczy and Omulew. In this sector the Germans counted from the 13th to the 23d of March forty-six serious assaults, twenty-five in the daytime and twenty-one at night. With special fury the battles raged in the neighborhood of Jednorozez. This attempt to break into Prussia was also unsuccessful, and in the last week of March the Russian attacks slackened, quiet ensuing for the weeks following Easter.

For six weeks the armies had struggled back and forth in this bloody angle, fighting in cold and wet, amid snow and icy rains. The Germans asserted that in these six weeks the troops of General von Gallwitz had captured 43,000 Russians and slain some 25,000. They estimated the total losses of the enemy in this sector during the period at 100,000. Countless graves scattered about the land, and the ruins of cities and villages were left to keep awake the memory of some of the fiercest fighting of the war in the east.

CHAPTER LII

FIGHTING BEFORE THE NIEMEN AND BOBR—BOMBARDMENT OF OSSOWETZ

THE winter battles of the Mazurian Lakes had forced the armies at the northern end of the Russian right flank back into their great fortresses Kovno and Grodno, and behind the line of the Niemen and the Bobr. A great forest region lies to the east and north of Grodno, and between the Niemen and the cities of Augustowo and Suwalki which the Germans, after their successful offensive, used as bases for their operations. A strip of country including these forests, and running parallel to the Niemen was a sort of no-man's land in the spring of 1915. Movements of troops in the heavily wooded country were difficult to observe, and the conditions lent themselves to surprise attacks. This resulted in a warfare of alternate thrusts by Russians and Germans aimed now at this point, now at that, in the disputed territory. Several actions during the spring stand out beyond the rest in importance, both because of the numbers engaged and their effects. In what follows will be described a typical offensive movement in this district undertaken by the Russians, and the way it was met by the Germans.

A new Russian Tenth Army had been organized by the end of February, 1915, with Grodno for its base. General Sievers, his chief of staff, and the general in command of the Third Russian Army Corps had been demoted from their commands, and three new army corps (Two, Three, and Fifteen) had been brought to Grodno. The ranks of the remaining corps that had suffered in the "winter battle" had been filled up with fresh recruits. Hardly had the German pursuit in the forest of Augustowo come to an end when the freshly strengthened Russians moved forward from their defensive lines in a counterattack. The Germans had been engaged in the task of gathering and carting away their enormous booty which lay scattered about the forest. They now drew back from in front of the Russian fortified lines to prepare positions close to Augustowo, and on a line running roughly north and south from this place, with the forest in front of them.

The Third Russian Army Corps advanced from Simno toward Lozdsisjo, their Second Army Corps from Grodno by way of Kopiewo and Sejny toward Krasnopol and other Russian corps advanced through the forest of Augustowo. Here they soon struck strong German resistance, and for several days vainly attacked German fortified positions.

On the 9th of March, 1915, a German offensive began against the Russian Third Corps which held the right wing of the advancing army. When this corps suddenly found itself threatened in the flank from the north and in danger of being surrounded it hastily began to retreat toward the east and southeast, leaving several hundred prisoners and several machine guns in the hands of the Germans. This withdrawal exposed the right flank of the adjoining Second Army Corps, which by this time, March 9, 1915, had reached Berzniki and Giby. The German attack was now continued against this corps. It was cold weather, the thermometer was considerably below the freezing point, and the roads were slippery with ice, so that dozens of horses fell, completely exhausted, and the infantry could march only two or three kilometers an hour.

On March 9 and 10, 1915, the battle flamed up at Sejny and Berzniki, the Russian corps, which had developed its front toward the west, being forced to swing about and face the north, whence the Germans were driving down upon it. At Berzniki two Russian regiments made up entirely of young troops were, according to the German account, completely annihilated, and the commanders of the regiments captured. It seemed as though the leader of the Russian armies saw approaching a repetition of the encircling movements that had proved fatal to the Russians in the Mazurian "winter battle," for on the 10th of March he gave orders for the withdrawal of his entire army. The German airmen on this day reported the Russian columns on the march through the forest in full retreat toward Grodno all along the line from Giby to Sztabiz, far to the south.

On the 11th of March, 1915, the German troops vigorously pushed the pursuit. They occupied Makarze, Froncki, and Giby. On the same night a German cavalry division took Kopciovo by assault. At this place alone they counted 300 dead Russians, and more than 5,000 prisoners, 12 machine guns, and 3 cannon, fell into the hands of the Germans.

The threatened envelopment of this Russian army was typical of the method employed by the leaders under Von Hindenburg in local operations, as it was of German method in general when applied to operations extending over the entire field of action. It could be applied with special success where the German information service was superior to that of the Russians, as it usually was, and the movements of German troops were facilitated by good railway connections. In the Augustowo forests, however, rapidity of movement had to be achieved by the legs of the German soldiers to a large extent, and on this they prided themselves not a little. The operation just described was regarded by the German Great Headquarters as being of great significance, valuable for its moral effect in establishing in the German troops a sense of superiority, and confidence in their leadership, and for its infliction of material losses of considerable moment on the Russians.

The Russians likewise claimed advantages from their forward thrust from Grodno. As represented by the Russian General Staff the withdrawal of the Germans from a front close to the line of the fortress in the first place was not a voluntary one, as it is pictured in the German account, but was forced by the strong pressure exerted by the Russian attacks following upon their retreat after the "winter battle." Thus they report the complete defeat of two German army corps, resulting in the seizure by the Russians of Height 100.3, which they described as dominating the entire region of the operations before Grodno. "In this battle," says the Russian report of March 5, 1915, "we took 1,000 prisoners and six cannon and a machine gun. Height 100.3 was defended by the Twenty-first Corps, the best of them all which lost during the battle 12,000 to 15,000 soldiers, as can be estimated from the dead left behind. After the shattering of the German counterattack at Height 100.3 the operations of the enemy became entirely passive. We, on the other hand, took village after village, and everywhere made prisoners."

The fortress of Ossowetz on the Bobr River proved inconquerable by the 42-centimeter mortars which had worked such terrific effects on the forts of Belgium and France. It was continually under German artillery fire through the months of February and March, 1915, without suffering appreciable damage. The great mortars were brought up within range of the fortress with much difficulty, owing to the fact that the place is almost completely surrounded by swamps. The Germans apparently had counted seriously at first on making a breach in the Russian defensive lines at this place. After persistent attempts to make an impression on the fortress with their heaviest guns they were obliged, however, to content themselves with keeping the garrison in check so as to forestall offensive moves.

A German artillery officer who took part in the bombardment relates that the chief obstacle to the pressing home of an attack were several heavily armored batteries which lay concealed outside the visible works of the fortress itself in the broad strip of swampland surrounding it. These were built deep into the ground, protected by thick earthworks, and very effectively screened from observation. They were a constant menace and apparently could not be destroyed by the German fire. Even though the main fort itself had been destroyed they would have prevented the approach of the enemy's troops, for they commanded the only causeway leading through the swamps to the fortress and would have blown to pieces any infantry that ventured to push along this road.

Furthermore, even the intense cold did not make the swamp passable except by the roadway because warm springs here and there prevented the ice from freezing sufficiently strong to bear the troops. The German gunners noted too that their shots fell practically without effect, plunging quietly into the mud to a great depth so that they did not even throw up earth or mud.

The result was that the 42-centimeter monsters were hastily withdrawn after a few trial shots and the bombardment was continued with a battery of 28-centimeter coast defense guns, an Austrian motor battery, a 30.5-centimeter mortar and some other heavy batteries. The fire rose to considerable intensity in the last days of February and the first days of March.

On the 3d of March the Russians in their official report dwelt on the fierceness of the bombardment and its ineffectiveness. On the 16th they reported that the Germans were pushing several of their batteries up into closer range, as they had recognized the uselessness of shooting from a greater distance and on the 18th they stated that the fire was falling off. On the 22d, finally, they reported that beginning with the 21st the Germans had been withdrawing their heavy batteries. They added that a 42-centimeter mortar had been damaged by the Russian fire, and that "not a single shot of these mortars has reached the fortress, not a redoubt has been penetrated. The superiority of the artillery fire evidently rests with us. The German attack was not only far removed from placing the fortifications of Ossowetz in a critical position, it did not even succeed in driving our infantry out of the field works."

On the 27th of March there was a resumption of the bombardment on a small scale and another effort began on April 11 with some heavy guns, ending in an attempted advance which was repulsed without difficulty by the Russians.

CHAPTER LIII

RUSSIAN RAID ON MEMEL

AN event in which no great number of troops were concerned, but which is of importance, because of the feeling which it aroused in Germany and because it was the first of a series of operations in what was practically a new theatre of the war was the Russian invasion of the very northernmost tip of East Prussia. On Thursday, the 18th of March, 1915, the Russians coming simultaneously from the north and the east across the border of Courland, moved on the Prussian city of Memel in several columns. Their troops included seven battalions of militia with six or eight guns of an old model, several squadrons of mounted men, two companies of marines, a battalion of a reserve regiment, and border defense troops from Riga and Libau, a total of some 6,000 to 10,000 men. The German Landsturm troops at the Prussian boundary fell back on Memel, not being in sufficient force to resist the advance. They were finally driven through the city and across the narrow strip of water known as the Kurische Haff to the dunes along the shore of the Baltic. The Russians burned down numerous buildings along the roads on which they approached, according to the German report, inflicting heavy damage on fifteen villages. A considerable number of the inhabitants, including women and children, were removed to Russia, and a number of civilians were killed. The troops entered the city on the evening of March 18 and took the mayor and three other men of the town as hostages. Apparently the Russian commander made some efforts to restrain his men, but plundering of stores and dwellings nevertheless occurred. On the 20th of March, 1915, the city was for a time cleared of Russian troops, but on Sunday, the 21st, other soldiers entered the town from the north. These were met by German patrols, which were followed by stronger German forces that had come up from the south to drive back the invaders. Street fighting followed, and the Russians were finally thrown out, losing about 150 dead.

The Russians were pursued on March 22 and 23, 1915, and in passing through Polangen, close to the shore of the Baltic, came under the fire of German cruisers. They lost some 500 prisoners, 3 guns, 3 machine guns, and ammunition wagons. With the German troops which cleared the Russians out of Memel was the son of the emperor, Prince Joachim of Prussia.

Concerning this raid the following official announcement was made by the Germans on March 18, 1915: "Russian militia troops have gained a cheap success in the northernmost corner of East Prussia in the direction of Memel. They have plundered and burned villages and farms. As a penalty, we have ordered the cities occupied by us in Russian territory to pay considerable sums in damages. For every village or farm burned down by these hordes on German soil three villages or farms of the territory occupied by us in Russia will be given over to the flames. Each act of damage in Memel will be answered by the burning of Russian Government buildings in Suwalki and other capitals of governments."

To this the following Russian official reply was made on March 21, 1915: "The official communiqué of the German Great Headquarters of the 18th of March concerning the movement of Russian troops against Memel contains a threat of reprisals to be exacted on Russian villages and cities held by the enemy on account of the losses which might be suffered by the population in the neighborhood of Memel. The Russian General Staff gives public notice that Memel was openly defended by hostile troops, and that battle was offered in the streets. Since the civil population took part in this fight our troops were compelled to reply with corresponding measures. If, therefore, the German troops should carry out their threat against the peaceful inhabitants of the Russian territory which they hold, such acts should be considered not as reprisals but as independent acts. Responsibility for this, as well as for the consequences, would rest upon the Germans."

The move against Memel was apparently part of a Russian operation which was intended also to strike at the city of Tilsit. The German Great Headquarters reported that for operations intended to seize the northern regions of East Prussia a so-called Riga-Shavli army group had been formed under the command of General Apuchtin. While portions of these troops were active in Memel on March 18, 1915, the fourteen German Landsturm companies holding Tauroggen, just to the north of the East Prussian boundary, were attacked by superior forces and practically surrounded. They fought their way through to Langszargen with some difficulty, and were being pressed back on the road to Tilsit when on March 23 German reenforcements came up and General von Pappritz, leading the Germans, went over to the offensive.

A heavy thaw made movement of troops anywhere except on the main roads extremely difficult. Guns were left stuck in the mud, and the infantry waded to the knee in water, and sometimes to the waist. It is reported that one of the horses of the artillery literally was drowned on the road. Germans attacked Tauroggen, where the enemy had intrenched himself, under an artillery fire directed from the church tower of the place. On the 28th the town was taken, after a difficult crossing of the Jura River in front of it, on the ice. The Germans then exulted in the fact that not a Russian was left on German soil.

CHAPTER LIV

GERMAN INVASION OF COURLAND—CAPTURE OF LIBAU

ON the 20th of April, 1915, an announcement was made by the German Great Headquarters which took the Russians and the world in general more or less by surprise. It gave the first glimpse to the public of a group of operations which caused no little speculation in the minds of strategists. It read:

"The advance troops of our forces operating in northwestern Russia yesterday reached on a broad front the railway running from Dunaburg (Dvinsk) to Libau. Thus far the Russian troops present in that region, including also the remnants of those which took part in the raid against Memel, have attempted no serious resistance anywhere. Fighting is now in progress near Shavli."

The advance into Courland here announced had been made by the German troops at high speed. The forces were under the command of General von Lauenstein. They had begun to move early on the 27th of April, in three columns. One of these crossed the Niemen at Schmalleningken, forming the right wing of the troops engaged in the movement. The columns of the left wing broke out of East Prussia at its northernmost point, and moved along the dunes of the Baltic. On the second day of the forward march it was learned by the leaders of the advancing troops that the Russians had hastily left their position at Skawdwile, on the main road from Tilsit to Mitau, to escape being surrounded on their left flank, and had withdrawn to Shavli by way of Heilmy. On the third day the German right column crossed the Windawski Canal under the enemy's fire, and on the afternoon of the 30th of April this column entered Shavli, which had been set on fire by the Russians.

The Germans had now crossed at several points the Libau-Dunaburg railway. They were in Telsche and Trischki. Their cavalry pushed ahead at full speed with orders to destroy the

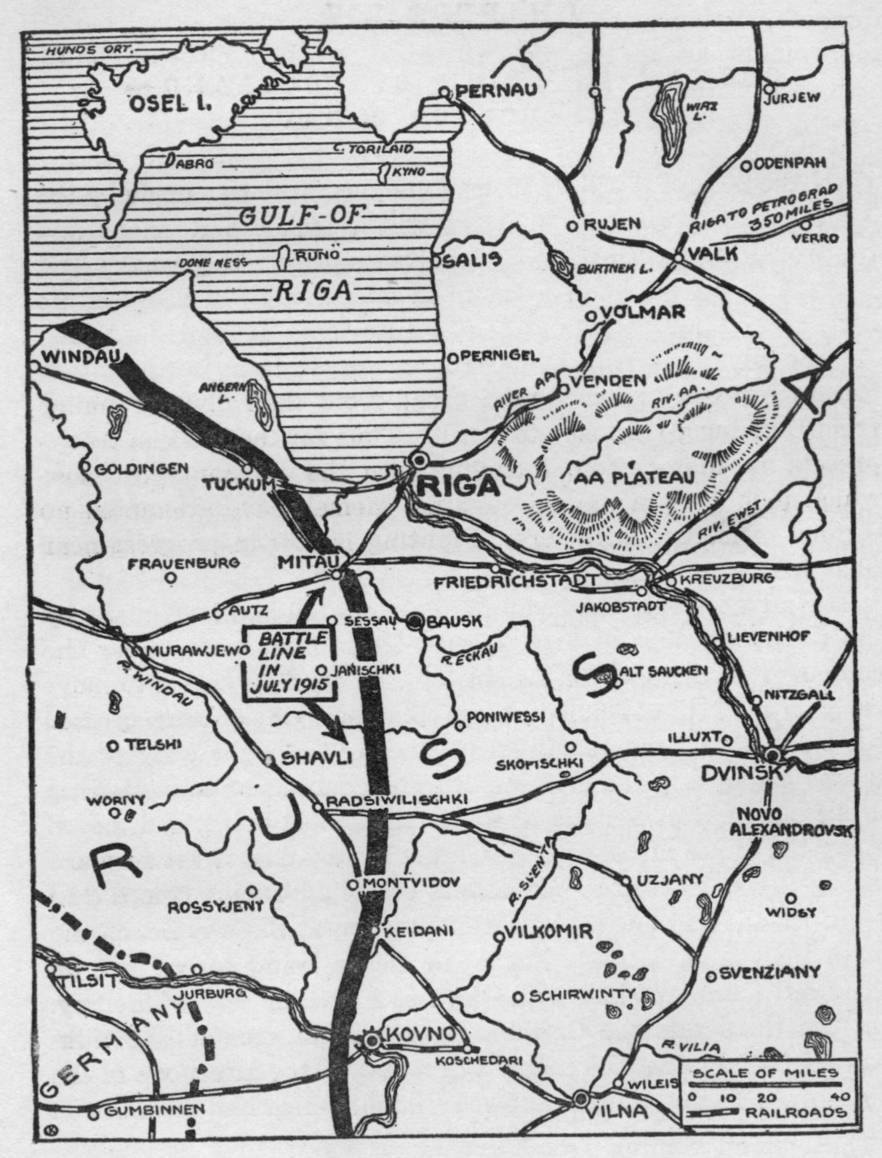

GERMAN ADVANCE ON RIGA

railways wherever it found them. On the road to Mitau they captured Russian machine guns, ammunition wagons, and baggage, and broke up the railway tracks to the southwest and northwest of Shavli. The Russians who had been taken by surprise by this movement had apparently only weak forces in Courland, and these had retired while reenforcements were being rushed up by railway. The German infantry, upon the receipt of reports that the Russians were moving up by rail from Kovno on their right flank, was ordered to stop its advance and prepare to hold the Dubissa line, taking up a front running a little east of south. Cavalry moving forward in the center of the German advance on the 3d of May, 1915, got within two kilometers of Mitau, going beyond Grünhof and capturing 2,000 Russians. At Skaisgiry on the day before 1,000 prisoners had been taken, and Janischki and Shagory had been occupied far beyond the Libau-Dunaburg railway. By this time Russian reenforcements were arriving at Mitau in huge numbers. The German cavalry ultimately fell back after indicting all possible damage to the communications in their reach.

The Germans prided themselves a good deal on the marching of their troops in this swift advance. They pointed out that the roads were in extremely bad condition, the bridges for the most destroyed, and the population to a large extent hostile. A military correspondent figured that for a daily march of fifty kilometers, such as was frequently made in Courland, 62,000 steps of an average of eighty centimeters were required. This for a day's march of from nine to ten hours gives an average of five to six kilometers per hour, some 6,000 to 7,000 steps. That makes in the neighborhood of 100 steps per minute, which the correspondent regarded as a considerable accomplishment when allowance is made for the fact that this was kept up hour after hour in full marching equipment.

The column coming from Memel, directed along the Baltic shores, had been steadily moving on Libau. In preparation for the land attack German naval vessels on the 29th of April had bombarded the forts defending the town. On the 6th of May the Russians themselves blew up one of the forts on the eastern front. The shore batteries were soon after silenced by German fire. The German troops advancing from the land side took the forts on the south almost without opposition. Russian troops which had been unloaded at Mitau and sent forward toward the southwest were unable to come up in time to offer any obstacles to the German advance, and on the 8th of May, at six o'clock in the morning, the German soldiers marched into Libau, where they took about 1,500 prisoners, twelve guns, and a number of machine guns.

The Germans immediately turned the metal-working plants of the city to their uses in the manufacture of chains, barbed wire, etc. They also found here a large supply of tools for intrenching work. Most of the Russians of the city had fled. One motive for the German advance into Courland advanced by their enemies was that it was an attempt to include a rich section of country in foraging operations, and it is a fact that the German authorities gave expression to their satisfaction at seizing a region that was of considerable economic value. It is apparent, however, in regarding these operations in the retrospect that they had no small bearing on the German plan of campaign as a whole. It was at the time that the inroad into Courland was started that the signal was about to be given for the great onslaught far to the south on the Dunajec, as described in the account of the Austro-Russian campaign. As the vast campaign along the whole eastern front developed, it became more and more apparent that the position of the German troops in Courland placed them advantageously for taking the Russian line of defenses, of which the fortress of Kovno represented the northern end in the flank in this carrying out of an important part of the vast encircling movement which took all Poland in its grasp. They were a constant threat to the all-important Vilna-Petrograd Railway.

In hostile and neutral countries the Courland invasion provoked comment indicating astonishment at the resources of the Teutonic powers in being able to extend their lines while already fully engaged on an enormous front.

The Russians, awakening from their first astonishment, made vigorous attempts to obtain permanent possession of the Dubissa line. Along this line the German troops were for a time forced to yield ground and to go into the defensive and to resist heavy Russian attacks. Shavli was given up under Russian pressure. By May 14, all the territory east of the Dubissa and Windau (Vindowa) was reported free of Germans.

Especially noteworthy among the struggles for the Dubissa was the fight at Rossiennie, a town which was of special importance because of its command of the roads centering in it. On the 22d of May, 1915, an attack was delivered against this place by the First Caucasian Rifle Brigade with artillery and assisted by the Fifteenth Cavalry Division. On the 23d the German cavalry which had resisted their crossing the river drew back, and the Russians here crossed the Dubissa, approaching Rossiennie from the north. The Germans during the night moved the greater part of their troops around the western wing of their opponents and placed them in position for attack.

At daybreak heavy artillery fire was poured upon the Russians from the German position to the north of Rossiennie, while at the same time the German infantry fell upon the Russian flank and rolled it up, with the result that the Russians were compelled to recross the Dubissa. In the crossing numerous wounded were drowned in the river. The Germans took 2,500 prisoners and fifteen machine guns. Similar counterattacks were delivered by the Germans on the River Wenta. Then, on the 5th of June, 1915, a general offensive was entered upon by the whole German line on orders from the General Staff, which carried it beyond the Dubissa, and after heavy fighting finally secured for the Germans the Windawski Canal, which they had had to relinquish before. Their troops now slowly pushed their way back toward Shavli until the city came within reach of their heavy guns, and took Kuze, twelve kilometers to the northwest of Shavli on the railway. On the 14th of June, 1915, this series of operations came to a temporary halt. German official reports pointed to the fact that among 14,000 prisoners which they had taken there were only a few officers, and that with these not a single cannon was captured. They regarded it as showing that the Russians were getting very cautious in the use of their artillery and were short of officers.

CHAPTER LV

RUSSIAN OFFENSIVE FROM KOVNO—FOREST BATTLES IN MAY AND JUNE

OFFENSIVES on a large scale such as that which had been prevented by the "Winter Battle of the Mazurian Lakes" were not attempted by the Russians on their northern wing after the short counterattack that had pushed their lines into the Mlawa angle in the corner of the Vistula and the Prussian boundary beyond Przasnysz, to the east of Thorn. They virtually remained in their strongly fortified positions along the Narew, the Bobr, and the Niemen, except for the sending out of occasional attacking columns against the German lines lying opposite to them.

These forward thrusts were made especially from the fortresses Grodno and Kovno, and the fortified place Olita. We have already dealt with one such operation which came to grief in the forest of Augustowo in March. The German invasion of Courland had taken place, and the extension of the German lines to the north invited a thrust at their communications when, in the middle of May, the Russians attempted to break through the German lines with columns starting from the great forest to the west of Kovno. Here German troops under General Litzmann, acting under the command of General von Eichhorn, stood on guard. When Litzmann received information that the Russians were advancing in force he was obliged hastily to gather such troops as he could find to stem the Russian attack. Troop units from a large variety of different organizations were freshly grouped practically on the battle field. At Szaki and Gryszkabuda, on May 17-20, they struck the Russians with such force that the Slavs were driven back into the forests.

The German general now decided to clear this territory of his enemies, as it had given them a constant opportunity for the preparation of moves which could not be readily observed, because of the protection of the thick woods. Again he executed the favorite maneuver of Von Hindenburg's armies. He gathered as heavy a weight of troops as possible on his left wing and pushed them forward in an extended encircling movement. From the south a strong column from Mariampol and the line of the Szsczupa moved upon the fortified position of the Russians and the southern corner of the great forest, meeting with strong resistance at Dumbowa Ruda. The troops moving down from the northern part of the woods swung to their right to cut off the Russians from their retreat toward Kovno. By the time the operations had reached this stage it was the second week in June, 1915, and in the great pine forests extending for miles there was an oppressive heat with perfect absence of breeze. Three Russian positions lying in the river valleys in the forest were encircled one after another from the north and had to be given up.

The Russians recognized the danger of the concentric attack directed at them and fought with great bravery. They strove to keep open the road of their retreat toward Kovno as long as possible. However, the ring of the German troops closed swiftly. At Koslowa Ruda, in the southern part of the forest, they found at night a sleeping army; something like 3,000 Russians had lain down exhausted in order on the next day to find the last opening through which to make their escape. They were now saved the trouble and were led away prisoners. The great forest was cleared of Russians. The German move had served to insure the safety of the lines connecting the troops in Courland with their bases to the south of the Niemen.

In an official announcement of the 18th of March, 1915, the German Government sketched the line held in the east by the German troops northward of the front covered by joint German and Austrian forces. It read: "The line occupied by us in the east runs from the Pilica, along the Rawka and Bzura to the Vistula. North of the Vistula the line of our troops is continued from the region to the east of Plozkz by way of Zurominek-Stupsk (both south of Mlawa). From there it runs in an easterly direction through the region to the north of Przasnysz—south of Mystinez, south of Kolno—to the north of Lomza, and strikes the Bobr at Mocarce. From here it follows the line of the Bobr to northwest of Ossowetz, which is under our fire, and runs by way of the region to east of Augustowo, by Krasnopol, Mariempol, Pilwiszki, Szaki, along the border through Tauroggen to the northwest. This is from beginning to end entirely on hostile soil." This long line, it appears, was under the supreme command of Von Hindenburg, while Von Mackensen had charge of the great drive to the south.

The statement here quoted was issued as reassurance to Germans who had been made nervous by reports of a Russian invasion of East Prussia, and was connected with the Russian raid on Memel.

Until June there was practically no change in this great line, except that on its northern end it was swung outward into Russian territory to include a large part of Courland, the River Dubissa roughly forming the dividing line until the front swung eastward toward Libau, in the line of the Libau-Dunaburg Railway.

The tasks of both German and Russian troops were similar. Comparatively weak German forces held the front in the region of the Niemen, the Bobr, and the Narew, safeguarding such Russian territory as had been seized by the Germans, and protecting East Prussia against invasion. Opposed to them lay considerable Russian forces whose task it was, supported by the fortresses of the Narew and the Niemen, especially Grodno, to protect the flank and rear of the Russians standing in Warsaw and southward in the bend of the Vistula, with the Warsaw-Vilna Railway behind them, while great decisions were fought for in the Carpathians and Galicia.

In Poland, between the lower and the upper courses of the Vistula, the Germans about the middle of February, 1915, having occupied the Rawka-Sucha ridge of upland, had developed fortified positions along the rivers Bzura, Rawka, Pilica, and Nida. The bad weather of the winter and early spring, which had turned the roads of Poland into pathless morasses, made against extensive operations, and the momentous undertakings carried out on the wings of the eastern front led the German General Staff to refrain from important movements in this section, where the Russians had strongly fortified themselves for the protection of Warsaw. It was not until the Teutonic allies had gone over to the offensive in the Carpathians and in western Galicia, and the Russians had withdrawn to the Polish hills of Lysa-Gora early in May, that, favored by improved weather conditions, operations in this part of Poland again took on larger scope. Especially along the Bzura the German attacks again became violent in an effort to hold the Russian forces in the district to the west of Warsaw while thrusting at their wings from the south and north. However, fighting was not of great consequence in this middle sector until the middle of June, 1915.

CHAPTER LVI

CAMPAIGN IN SOUTHERN POLAND—MOVEMENT UPON WARSAW

BY the 1st of July, 1915, the stupendous enveloping campaign of the Teuton armies on the eastern front had advanced to a point where the Allies were forced to recognize the imminence of a catastrophe, which could be averted only by the most decisive action of the Russian armies.

Far in the north, on the extreme right wing of the Russians, the army of General von Bülow was hammering at the defenses of the Dubissa line. Off and on fighting was taking place in the neighborhood of Shavli. Russian counterattacks, reported from day to day through June, with difficulty had held in check this army, which evidently was aiming at the Warsaw-Petrograd

Railway on the sector between Vilna and Dvinsk. On the right flank of these forces operated the troops of General von Eichhorn, with the line of the Niemen for their objective. Next to these on the south, aiming at the Bobr River and the Upper Narew, were the forces of General von Scholtz, and on their right the army of Von Gallwitz, based on Mlawa with Przasnysz in front of it. Below the line of the Vistula, before the Bzura and down to the middle course of the Pilica, operated the Ninth German Army, commanded, at least in the later stages of the Warsaw campaign, by Prince Leopold of Bavaria. The whole group of northern and central armies was acting under the general direction of Field Marshal von Hindenburg.

The armies to the south of this group, cooperating in the drive under Field Marshal von Mackensen which had gained the Teutons Przemysl and Lemberg, had as their left flank the forces of Generals von Woyrsch and Kövess between the Pilica and the Vistula mouth of the San. The troops of Archduke Joseph Ferdinand were pushing forward on the right of these, and the army directly under Mackensen himself came next in line to the eastward, joining up with the armies still operating in Galicia at the extreme right of the great German battle line.

The chief danger to the Russians at this stage still threatened from the south, where the archduke and Mackensen had pushed forward irresistibly in their advance to the east of the Vistula toward the railway running from Warsaw through Ivangorod, Lublin, Cholm, and Kovell to Kiev and Moscow.

The advance of these Austro-German armies, which had operated in the neighborhood of Lemberg, was extremely rapid in the last days of June, 1915. In four days they covered from thirty to forty miles in pursuit of the Russians. By the 1st of July, having swept out of Galicia, their right, under Mackensen, entered the upper valley of the Wieprz, a marshy country which presented considerable difficulty to the advance of troops where a tributary of the Wieprz, the Por, afforded the Russians a natural line of defense. Drasnik, on the Wyznica, which here extended the Russian defensive line westward, was occupied by the archduke's forces on Mackensen's left on the 1st of July, 1915.

The drive of the Austro-German armies through Galicia has been dealt with in the account of the Austro-Russian campaign. As we carry forward the account of the activities of the greatest part of the forces concerned in that series of operations from the point where they crossed over the boundary between Galicia and Poland out of Austrian territory, it will be well to glance backward a moment to enumerate here briefly the gains of these armies on Polish soil up to the 1st of July.

On June 16, 1915, the Teutonic allies forced the Russians to fall back upon Tarnograd from north of Siemandria, thus pushing this section of the front across the boundary into Poland about to the line of the Tanev. Tarnograd itself was occupied by the Teutons on the 17th, and on the 18th the Russians retreated behind the Tanev. There was little change in this particular sector during the fighting which was crowned for the Austro-Germans by the capture of Lemberg on June 22, 1915. Further to the east, however, to the south of the Pilica and west of the Vistula, Von Woyrsch was exerting pressure, and on the 20th of June Berlin announced the capture of several Russian advance posts by these troops. By the 24th the Slavs had begun to retreat before Von Woyrsch in the forest region south of the Ilza on the left bank of the Vistula; thus rear guards had been thrown across the Kamienna, and Sandomir was occupied by the Austro-Hungarians. On the 25th the fighting developed on the line Zarvichost-Sienno-Ilza, to which the Russians had fallen back.

Defeats of the Russian rear guards on June 29, 1915, to the northeast and west of Tomaszow, where Teutonic forces had now also crossed into Poland, caused the Slavs to begin the relinquishment of the Tanev forest district and the lower San. Tomaszow itself was occupied by the pursuing troops. By the 30th the Teutonic allies had swept forward beyond the Tanev region to Franpol, Zamoez, and Komarovo, and on the same evening they threw the Russians out of their strong defenses on the Zavichost-Ozarow-Sienno line, west of the Vistula. The pursuit was pushed energetically on both sides of the Kamienna.

The important bridgehead on the Vistula, Josefovo, was taken on the 1st of July.

The Russians between the Bug and the Vistula were now offering strong resistance with large forces on the line Turobin-Krasnik-Josefovo, the rivers Por and Wyznica forming roughly their defensive front, as previously pointed out.

In its daily bulletins of July 1, 1915, the German Great Headquarters made this announcement for the eastern theatre of war (from the Baltic to the Pilica): "The booty for June is: Two colors, 25,595 prisoners, including 121 officers, seven cannon, six mine throwers, fifty-two machine guns, one aeroplane, also a large amount of war material." For the southeastern theatre of war (from the Pilica to Bukowina) the headquarters announced: "The total booty for June of the allied troops fighting under the command of General von Linsingen, Field Marshal von Mackensen, and General von Worysch is 409 officers, 140,650 men, 80 cannon, 268 machine guns." The Austro-Hungarian General Staff on the same day reported: "The total booty for June of the troops fighting under Austro-Hungarian command in the northeast is 521 officers, 194,000 men, 93 cannon, 364 machine guns, 78 ammunition wagons, 100 field railway carriages, etc."

CHAPTER LVII

BATTLE OF KRASNIK—CAPTURE OF PRZASNYSZ

ON July 2, 1915, the forces of the Archduke Joseph Ferdinand which had passed through Krasnik, on the Lublin road, struck serious resistance from the Russian army of General Loesche which held strong positions across the highway, just to the north of the town, and was now evidently determined to stop once for all the Teuton advance toward the railway at its back, connecting Warsaw with Kiev, through Lublin and Cholm.

On July 3, 1915, the Austrian report, however, announced that 4,800 prisoners and three machine guns had been taken in the neighborhood of Krasnik and along the Por stream, and the next day they reported that they had occupied the heights which run along to the north of the city, having pierced the enemy's main position on both sides of Studzianki, and taken more than 1,000 prisoners, three machine guns and three cannon.

The Russian front was turned to such an extent that they had to fall back some three miles on the Lublin road. The Austrians on the 5th of July summed up their enemy's losses as twenty-nine officers, 8,000 men, six cannon, five ammunition wagons, and six machine guns. As the result of this Austrian advance the adjoining enemy forces to the eastward along the Wieprz River had been obliged to fall back beyond Tarnograd, and by the 6th of July Vienna summarized the Austrian captures in these battles as having grown to forty-one officers, 11,500 men.

The Austrians, however, could make no further headway. On July 5, 1915, they were heavily attacked, being forced back to their intrenched lines on a ridge of hills to the north of Krasnik. The Russians now reported that they had taken 15,000 prisoners and a large number of machine guns. Two thousand bodies were reported by the Russians to have been found before their front. More prisoners were taken by the Russians on the 7th and it was only on the afternoon of July 9 that the Austrians were able to stem the tide. The total loss of the Austrians in this action was given by their opponents as 15,000 men.

The Austrian explanation of their retirement in front of Krasnik issued on July 11, 1915, pointed out that the relative subsidence of activity of the Teutonic allies was due to the fact that the goal set for the Lemberg campaign had now been attained. This, they explained, was the taking of the city and the securing of strong defensive positions to the east and north. The ridge to the northward of Krasnik was a natural choice for this purpose on the north, while the line of the Zlota Lipa and Bug rivers served the purpose toward the east (see Austro-Russian campaign). The Austrian explanation pointed out further that some of their troops had rushed beyond the positions originally selected to meet heavy reenforcements brought up by the Russians from Lublin, and that these had to withdraw to the ridge, where they were successfully resisting all attacks.

The battle of Krasnik was regarded by the Russians as an effective victory, for it seemed to have halted the advance on Lublin. The army of Von Mackensen had now also come to a stop about halfway between Zamosc and Krasnostav, an artillery duel on July 7, 1915, being the last activity noted on the front of this army for some time.

Their comparative quiet in the region between the Vistula and the Bug where the main advance of the Teutonic forces on the south had been under way with great vigor for several weeks until the check at Krasnik was not interrupted until July 16, 1915. Day after day the Teutonic headquarters reported "nothing of importance" in this quarter. When the quiet was finally broken it appeared that it had been the lull before the storm. Before taking up again the activities on this section of the front, it will be necessary to take a glance toward the northern half of the great arc that enveloped the Warsaw salient on two sides.

In these early days of July, 1915, considerable uncertainty prevailed among those who were watching the progress of the campaign in Poland as to where the heaviest blow of the Teutons would fall, whether from the south or the north. The decisive stroke came with lightning suddenness. A tremendous attack was launched in the direction of the Narew by the army of General von Gallwitz.

A laconic announcement of the German General Staff on July 14, 1915, bore momentous news, although its modest wording scarcely betrayed the facts. It read: "Between the Niemen and the Vistula, in the region of Walwarga, southwest of Kolno, near Przasnysz and south of Mlawa, our troops have achieved some local successes." The Russian report referring to the beginning of the same action was equally noncommittal, though possibly more misleading. This states: "Considerable enemy forces between the Orczy and the Lidynja adopted the offensive and the

Russians declining a decisive engagement retreated during the night of the 13th to the second line of their positions."

On July 15, 1915, the Germans announced that the city of Przasnysz, for which such hot battles had been fought in February, and which had since been strongly fortified by the Russians, had been occupied by them. The German summary of this action given out a few days later stated that three Russian defensive lines lying one behind the other northwest and northeast of Przasnysz had been pierced and taken, the troops at once rushing forward to Dzielin and Lipa, respectively west and east of the town. Under attack from these two points the Russians after yielding Przasnysz, on the 14th, retired to their defensive line Ciechanow-Krasnosielc which had been prepared long beforehand. On the 15th the German troops pressing closer upon the retiring Slavs stormed this line and broke through it to the south of Zielona on a breadth of seven kilometers, forcing the Russians again to retire. General von Gallwitz's troops in this assault were supported by the forces of General von Scholtz, on their left, who were pressing the Russians from the direction of Kolno. On July 16, 1915, the Russians were retreating on the whole front between the Pissa and the Vistula, toward the Narew.

The German summary of the fighting during these days reported the capture by the army of General von Gallwitz of eighty-eight officers, 17,500 men, thirteen cannon (including one heavy gun), forty machine guns, and seven mine throwers; and by the army of General von Scholtz of 2,500 prisoners and eight machine guns.

This great attack in the north, to which may be ascribed the final breaking of the lines that had so long protected Warsaw, had been carefully planned and undoubtedly was timed in coordination with the movements of Mackensen's armies on the south, striking the Russians just when Mackensen and the Archduke Josef, having had time for recuperation and preparation for another push forward after the check administered at Krasnik, were in readiness to inflict a heavy blow on their side of the Warsaw salient. When it began the German lines all along the front burst into fresh activity. It was the signal for a simultaneous assault along nearly a thousand miles of battle front.

In the Mlawa sector to the north of Przasnysz the Russians had developed an exceedingly strong system of fortified positions between their advance lines and the Narew fortresses. For miles, to a depth of from fifteen to twenty kilometers, there ran some three or four and at certain points even five systems of trenches, one behind the other. Hundreds of thousands of thick tree trunks had been worked into these defensive works and millions of sand bags piled up as breastwork. Bombproof dugouts had been constructed deep in the ground. Everywhere there were strong wire entanglements before the front, sometimes sunk below the level of the earth, arranged in from two to three rows. Projecting bastions and thoroughly protected observation posts gave these systems of trenches the character of permanent fortifications.

The country in this region is hilly, with here and there steep declivities and peaks of considerable elevation. The Russians had cut down whole stretches of forest in order to afford them a free field for their fire and an opportunity to observe the advance of their opponents. Enveloping tactics on the part of the Germans were here quite excluded as the two lines ran uninterruptedly close to one another. Przasnysz which had become a heap of ruins had been converted virtually into a fortress by strong defensive works built while the Germans and Russians lay opposite each other in front of it throughout the spring. The country round about had been drenched with much German and Russian blood.

General von Gallwitz, to capture a place with the least possible loss, decided to break through the Russian defenses at two points at both sides of the town sufficiently close to each other so that the intervening lines would be immediately affected. His attacks were therefore directed at the first line Russian positions, which formed projecting angles to the northwest and northeast of Przasnysz so that instead of taking the city directly from the front he would seize it as with a gigantic pair of pincers from both sides and behind. The plan succeeded to the full. The Russian lines were broken on both sides of the city and the German troops, rushing through, met behind it, forcing the Russian defenders hastily to evacuate the place to avoid being caught within the circle.

Strong infantry forces were collected opposite the points of attack, and enormous masses of artillery were placed in position with abundance of ammunition in readiness. The preparations had been made with all possible secrecy and even when the German batteries had begun gradually to get their range by testing shots no serious assault seems to have been expected by the Russians. On the morning of the attack they were just to inaugurate service on a small passenger railway line they had constructed behind their front.

On the morning of July 13, 1915, soon after sunrise, a tremendous cannonade was let loose from guns of all calibers. Although the weather was rainy and not well fitted for observation the German guns seem to have found their marks with great accuracy. When the German infantry stormed the first line of works which had been shattered by the artillery fire they met with comparatively little resistance and their losses were small. The bombardment apparently had done its work thoroughly. The German infantry rushes were started in successive intervals of a quarter of an hour, line following line. Swarms of unarmed Russians could be seen coming out of the trenches seeking to save themselves from the terrible effect of the shell fire by surrendering. During the course of the forenoon the sun came out and illuminated a scene of terrific destruction. The Russian positions on the heights northwest of Przasnysz had been completely leveled. In their impetuous forward rush the German troops did not give the enemy time to make a stand in his second line of trenches and overrunning this, by night began to enter the third Russian defensive line. Przasnysz was flanked in the course of twenty-four hours and could no longer be held. A fine rain was falling as the German columns marched through the deserted, smoke-blackened city, a melancholy setting for a victory.

On July 14, 1915, the German troops had broken through on both sides of the city, met to the south of it and forming a mighy battering ram, on the next day, forced the next Russian line, the last, to the north of the Narew. This ran through Wysogrod-Ciechanow-Zielona to Kranosiele. The Russians here made a desperate defense and the German advance pushed forward but slowly. The effect of the German artillery fire seems not to have been as striking as on the first day of battle. The German report of the attack on this line points out that the regiment of the Guard holding the right wing of a division which was to attack the heights to the south and southeast of Zielona was impatient to go forward, and was allowed to advance before the reserves which were to be held in readiness to support the move had come up.

However, confident of the accuracy with which the "black brothers" (shells from the big guns) struck the enemy's trenches, the riflemen leapt forward through fields of grain as soon as they saw that a gust of their shells had struck in front of them. By means of signs which been agreed upon they then signaled their new positions and the guns laid their fire another hundred meters farther forward. The infantrymen then stormed ahead into the newly made shell craters. Thus they went forward again and again. Neither Russian fire nor the double barbed wire entanglements were able to check their assaults.

As the German shouts rolled forth the Russians ran. A neighboring division consisting of young men who had enlisted in the course of the war, in a brilliant charge took a bastion at Klosnowo. The effect of this first penetration of the Russian main position made itself felt in the course of the afternoon and night along the whole front. Further German forces were thrown into the breach and strove to widen it.

The Russians at many points resisted obstinately, but under the pressure from the front and in the flank they were finally unable to hold their ground. The German account speaks with admiration of the ride to death of a Russian cavalry brigade which attacked the German infantry southeast of Opinozura without achieving any results. Cossacks and Hussars were mowed down in an instant.

The German advance taking several intermediate places did not halt until it stood before the fortification of the Narew line itself. As a result of this stroke the German troops had advanced some forty to fifty kilometers into hostile territory on a breadth of a hundred and twenty kilometers and had captured some 10,000 prisoners and much war material. By the 18th of July, 1915, German trains were running as far as Ciechanow.

Advances were likewise made by the Germans to the right of the attack on the Przasnysz positions on both sides of the Mlawa-Ciechanow Railway, rolling up the Russian positions as far as Plonsk. On the left progress had also been made and heavy fighting done, but the German great headquarters pointed out that in times to come history will assign the important place to the central feature of this great offensive by General von Gallwitz, that is the enveloping attack at Przasnysz and the ramming thrust at Zielona.

The report issued by the Russian General Staff on July 19, 1915, admitted that to the west of Omulev their troops had withdrawn to the Narew bridgeheads on the 17th. The points of some of the German columns on this day, in fact, came within the range of the artillery of the fortress of Novo-Georgievsk and the army of General von Scholtz reached the line of the Bobr and the Narew between Osowice and Ostrolenka. The action at Przasnysz had been decisive. It resulted ultimately in the relinquishing by the Russians of the lines of the Rawka and Bzura which had been so stubbornly held against the Germans in the long defense of Warsaw. The troops directly charged here with defending the capital fell back to the Blonie lines about fifteen miles from the city.

CHAPTER LVIII

GRAND OFFENSIVE ON THE WARSAW SALIENT

THE great stroke at Przasnysz was the most dramatic feature of a grand offensive all around the German lines that were endeavoring to close in upon the Russian armies. On July 16, 1915, the Archduke Joseph struck hard at the Russians on the Krasnik-Lublin road in an endeavor to carry the fortified positions at Wilkolaz. His men, however, were thrown back after ten furious assaults. Krasnostav, on the road to Cholm, was attacked on the same day by the army of General von Mackensen, and after a series of desperate rear-guard actions had been fought by the Russians was swept over by the German Allies. By the close of the day the Germans had taken twenty-eight officers, 6,380 men, and nine machine guns.

The Germans, prepared in the recent pause in the fighting, by the bringing up of their artillery on the long lines of communication which now stretched behind them, with troops reenforced by such fresh forces as they could muster, were hurling themselves upon the Russian defensive positions everywhere along the line. Thus, on the forenoon of July 17, 1915, the army of General von Woyrsch, whose objective was the mighty fortress Ivangorod, operating just to the west of the upper Vistula, broke through the Russian wire entanglements and stormed the enemy's trenches on a stretch of 2,000 meters. The breach was widened in desperate hand-to-hand combat. The Teutons by evening inflicted a heavy defeat on the Moscow Grenadier Corps at this point and the Russians were forced to retreat behind the Ilzanka to the south of Swolen. Some 2,000 men were taken prisoners by the Germans in this battle and five machine guns were captured.

Far in the northeast in Courland the army of General von Bülow, on July 17, 1915, defeated Russian forces that had been rushed up at Alt-Auz, taking 3,620 prisoners, six cannon and three machine guns, and pursuing the Slavs in an easterly direction. Desperate fighting was also taking place to the northeast of Kurschany.

Notes of anxiety mixed with consoling speculations had begun to appear in the press of the allied countries when the vast German offensive had thus become plainly revealed and had demonstrated its driving force. A Petrograd dispatch to the London "Morning Post" on the 15th of July, 1915, said of the German plan that it was to catch the Russian armies like a nut between nut crackers, that the two fronts moving up from north and south were intended to meet on another and grind everything between them to powder. The area between the attacking forces was some eighty miles in extent, north to south, by 120 miles west to east. The writer offered the consolation that this space was well fortified, the kernel of the nut "sound and healthy, being formed of the Russian armies, inspired not merely with the righteousness of their cause, but the fullest confidence in themselves and absolute devotion to the proved genius of their commander in chief."

The dispatch pointed out that it was all sheer frontal fighting, that the Germans had been twelve months trying frontal attacks against Warsaw on a comparatively narrow front and in vain. What chance had they, he added, "of success by dividing their forces against the united strength of Russia." This sort of argument is typical of the endeavor to sustain the hopes of Russia's friends during these days. Doubts, however, began to creep in more strongly as to the possibility of holding Warsaw.

In Berlin the announcement of the Teutonic victories that began with the successful assault at Przasnysz was received with general rejoicing, and the appearance of flags all over the city. The Russian retreat toward the Narew River in particular was regarded by the military critics as threatening momentarily to crumble up the right flank of the positions of the Russians before the capital of Poland.

Cholm and Lublin on the southern line of communication of the Russian armies were now in imminent danger. On July 19,

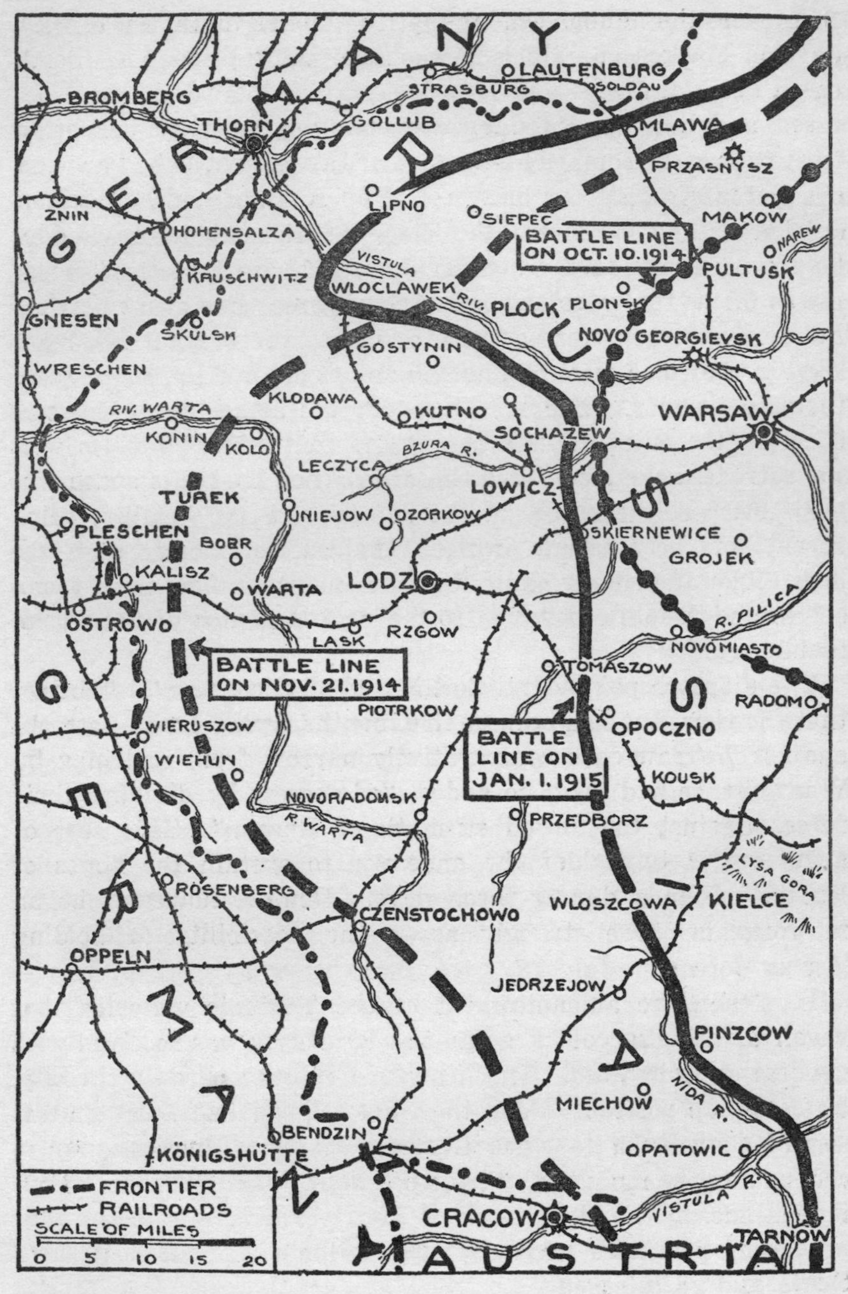

GERMAN ATTEMPTS TO REACH WARSAW IN 1914

1915, came the announcement that the troops under Field Marshal von Mackensen, which had pierced the Russian line in the region of Pilaskowice and Krasnostav, had increased their successes, and that the Russians were making the most desperate effort to prevent complete defeat. All day the battle had swayed in a fierce struggle for mastery. The Russians threw a fresh division of the Guards into the fight, but this too had to yield to the overwhelming force of the Teuton onslaught. Farther to the east as far as the neighborhood of Grabowiec, Austro-Hungarian and German troops forced the crossing of the Wolica, and near Sokal in Galicia Austro-Hungarian troops crossed the Bug. (See Austro-Russian Campaign.) In consequence of these Teuton successes the Russians on the night of the 18th to the 19th of July retreated along the whole front between the Vistula and the Bug—practically the last line of defense, for the Warsaw-Kiev railway had been broken down. The German troops and the corps under the command of Field Marshal von Arz alone from the 15th to the 18th of July, 1915, took 16,250 prisoners and 23 machine guns.

It was announced by the Germans that according to written orders captured during this action the Russian leaders had resolved to hold the positions here conquered by the Germans to the utmost, regardless of losses.

The same day that brought the report of this Russian retreat on the south brought the news that in the adjoining sector to the west of the Upper Vistula the army of General von Woyrsch had met resistance from the Russians behind the Ilzanka after the Russian defeat on July 13, 1915, that, however, Silesian Landwehr on the 18th had captured the Russian defenses at Ciepilovo by storm, and that the Russian line at Kasonow and Barenow was beginning to yield. The army of General von Gallwitz had now taken up positions along the whole Narew line from southwest of Ostrolenka to Novo Georgievsk. The Russians, however, as already indicated, were still holding fortified places and bridgeheads on the right bank of the river. In this sector the number of prisoners taken by the Germans had risen to 101 officers and 28,760 men.

In the sector next adjoining, passing onward around the enveloping lines, that lying between the Pissa and the Szkwa, the Russians likewise had retreated until they stood directly on the Narew. Here the Slavs had been favored by forests and swampy land which made pursuit difficult.

At the extreme left end of the German line a magnificent success had been achieved in the occupation of Tukkum and Windau. This capture brought the Germans to within fifty miles of Riga, seat of the governor general of the Baltic provinces. They were, however, destined not to make any substantial progress in the direction of that city for many months to come.

Blow fell upon blow. The question "Can Warsaw be held?" began to receive doubtful answers in the allied capitals. The colossal coordinate movement of the Teutonic forces in these July days had received so little check from the Russian resistance that the British press had begun to discount the fall of the Polish capital. Shortness of ammunition and artillery was ascribed as the cause of Russia's failure to make a successful stand against the onrushing Teutons.

On July 20, 1915, Berlin announced the capture of those fortifications of Ostrolenka lying on the northwest bank of the Narew River. This was one of the strong places designed to protect the Warsaw-Grodno-Petrograd railway. The threatened fall was highly significant. To the south of the Vistula the Teuton troops had advanced to the Blonie-Grojec lines. Blonie is some seventeen miles west of Warsaw and Grojec twenty-six miles south of the city.

Farther eastward and to the south troops of the army of General von Woyrsch had completely turned the enemy out of the Ilzanka positions, having repulsed the counterattacks of the Russian reserves which had been quickly brought up, and captured more than 5,000 prisoners. Von Woyrsch"s cavalry had now reached the railway line from Radom to the great fortress of Ivangorod, the objective point of this army, and Radom itself had been seized.

CHAPTER LIX

BEGINNING OF THE END

So uncertain had grown the positions of Lublin on the southern railway line leading to Warsaw that the Russian commander in chief had issued an order that in case of a retreat the male population of the town was to attach itself to the retiring troops.

On July 21, 1915, the Russians throughout the empire were reported to be joining in prayer. "Yesterday evening," telegraphed the London "Daily Mail's" Petrograd correspondent on the 21st, "the bells in all the churches throughout Russia clanged a call to prayer for a twenty-four hours' continual service of intercession for victory.

"To-day, in spite of the heat, the churches were packed. Hour after hour the people stand wedged together while the priests and choirs chant interminable litanies. Outside the Kamian Cathedral here an open-air Mass is being celebrated in the presence of an enormous crowd."

The chronicle of the closing days of July, 1915, is an unbroken narrative of forward movements of German armies on all parts of the great semicircle. The movement now, however, was slow. The Russians were fighting desperately, and the Germans had to win their way inch by inch. By the 21st the Russians were withdrawing in Courland to the east of the line Popeljany-Kurtschany, and the last Russian trenches westward of Shavly had been taken by assault. To the north of Novgorod the capture of Russian positions had yielded 2,000 prisoners and two machine guns to the Germans on the 20th.

Farther south on the Narew a strong work of the fortress Rozan defending an important crossing was stormed by the Germans, and desperate fighting was going on at Pultusk and near Georgievsk. Already the Russians were beginning to yield their positions to the west of Grojec, which meant that the Teuton armies were about to push into the opening between

Warsaw and Ivangorod and divide the Russian forces. The armies of Von Woyrsch on July 20, 1915, seized a projecting bridgehead to the south of Ivangorod, and captured the lines that had been held by the Russians near Wladislavow.

In the positions defending the railway between Cholm and Lublin, Russian resistance was once more marked, and was checking the progress of the armies of Von Mackensen and Archduke Joseph Ferdinand.

By noon of July 21, 1915, the Silesian troops of Von Woyrsch had stormed the bridgehead on the Vistula between Lagow and Lugawa-Wola, with the result that Ivangorod was now inclosed from the south, while to northwest of the fortress Austro-Hungarian troops were fighting on the west bank of the Vistula. Austro-Hungarian troops too were battling their way close up to the fortress directly from the west. Line after line was giving way before the Teutons. The Russian retreat over the bridge at Novo Alexandria to the south of Ivangorod was carried on under the fire of German artillery. Numerous villages set afire by the Russians were now sending great clouds of smoke into the sky over all this region.

The troops of the Archduke Joseph Ferdinand, after a stubborn resistance on the part of the Russians, seized enemy positions on July 21, 1915, near Chodel and Borzechow, advancing another step toward Lublin. Eight thousand Russian prisoners, 15 machine guns, and 4 ammunition wagons were taken.

By the 23d of July, 1915, the Teutonic troops were close up to the encircling forts of Ivangorod and stood on the Vistula all the way between the fortress and the mouth of the Pilica. On the 24th the Teutons announced a victory over the Fifth Russian Army by General von Bülow at Shavli. The report read: "After ten days of continuous fighting, marching, and pursuit, the German troops yesterday succeeded in brmging the Russians to a stand in the regions of Rozalin and Szadow and in defeating them and scattering their forces. The booty since the beginning of this operation on the 14th of July consists of 27,000 prisoners, 25 cannon, 40 machine guns, more than 100 loaded ammunition wagons with their draft animals, numerous baggage wagons and other material."

This day brought the announcement also of the capture of the fortresses of Rozan and Pultusk on the Narew, after violent charges by troops of General von Gallwitz. The crossing of the Narew between these places was now in German hands, and strong forces were advancing on the southern shore. The Russians had been resisting obstinately in this quarter, and the Germans had made their way only by the most heroic efforts. German headquarters announced at this time that in the battles between the Niemen and the Vistula covering the ten days since July 14, 1915, more than 41,000 prisoners, 14 cannon, and 19 machine guns had been captured. The German troops now also attained the Vistula to the north of the Pilica. In their summing up of results since the 14th of July the Teutons recounted further on this day, the 24th, that some 50,000 prisoners had been taken by the armies of General von Woyrsch and Field Marshal von Mackensen during the period.

The army of Archduke Joseph Ferdinand had been making rapid progress. On July 24, 1915, under the attacks of these troops the Russians retreated on a front of forty kilometers, between the Vistula and the Bistritza, from eight to ten kilometers northward to prepared lines, their attempts to halt in intermediate positions being frustrated by the onrush of the victorious Teutonic forces in pursuit.

By July 25, 1915, the Narew had been crossed by the Germans along its whole front, southward from Ostrolenka to Pultusk, and by the 26th they had gained the farther side of the Narew above Ostrolenka likewise. The troops moving southeast from Pultusk now approached the Bug, getting toward the rear of Novo Georgievsk and Warsaw, and threatening to close the Russians' line of escape, the Warsaw-Bielostok railway.

On July 26, 1915, the Russians made a determined counteroffensive from the line of Goworowo-Wyszkow-Serock in an effort to remove the threat to the rear of Warsaw. This, however, had little success, the Russians losing 3,319 men to the Germans in prisoners.

To the south of Warsaw the Germans had seized the villages of Ustanov, Lbiska, and Jazarzew, which brought them nearly to the Vistula, just below the capital.

The great attacks of the Germans on the troops defending Warsaw were being hampered to some extent by the laying waste of the country by the retiring Russians. Difficulty in moving heavy artillery on roads had also interfered with their progress, but on the morning of July 28, 1915, Von Woyrsch crossed to the eastern shore of the Vistula between the mouth of the Pilica and Kozienice at several places, and was threatening the Warsaw-Ivangorod railway.

Novo Georgievsk was steadily being inclosed. The Russian counterthrusts in the neighborhood of Warsaw both on the north and the south of the city were repelled by night and day. To the south near Gora-Kalvaria a desperate attempt of the Russians to push forward toward the west on the night from July 27th to the 28th, 1915, was shattered.

The armies of Field Marshal von Mackensen, breaking through Russian positions to the west of the Wieprz, captured thousands of prisoners and many guns, and once more thrust back the Russian front between the Vistula and the Bug. On the evening of the 29th they attained the Warsaw-Kiev railway at Biskupice, about halfway between Lublin and Cholm, thus crowning their efforts to get astride their important line of communications. The Russians were destroying everything of value in the country as they retired, even burning grain in the fields.

On the afternoon of July 30, 1915, Lublin at last was occupied by the army of the Archduke Joseph Ferdinand, and on the 31st the Germans of Von Mackensen passed through Cholm. Thus the Teutonic armies were now across the important railway from Warsaw and Ivangorod to Kiev, on a broad front, running all the way down to the Vistula at Novo Alexandria. In Courland the Germans continued to push forward, so that on the 12th of August they were enabled to seize the important railway center Mistan.

Hope in Russia died hard. Press correspondents up to July 29, 1915, still spoke of the possibility of the Russians standing a siege in their principal fortress on the Warsaw salient. On the 29th, however, reports came from Petrograd that the fortresses of the Warsaw defense were to be abandoned and the capital of Poland given up to the army.

The correspondent of the New York "Times" on July 29, 1915, in a special cable summed up the situation in an announcement that the fate of Europe hung on the decision that Russia might make on the question: "Shall Russia settle down to a war of position in her vast fortifications around Warsaw, or shall she continue to barter space against time, withdrawing from the line of the Vistula and points on it of both strategic and political importance, in order to gain the time which Germany has already stored in the form of inexhaustible gun munitions?" The reply was the evacuation of Warsaw.

The decisive blow to Russia's hopes came with the crossing of the Vistula about twenty miles north of Ivangorod on July 28, 1915, already noted. It showed that Warsaw was being rapidly surrounded. The Russian communiqué of the 30th of July told of the crossing over of the Teutons on both sides of the Radomka, a tributary of the Vistula, to the right bank of the Vistula on pontoons, and of attempts to throw bridges across the great rivers. Von Woyrsch's troops that had crossed over were irresistibly pursuing still farther east on the 30th, defeating troops hastily brought up to stop their advance. By August 1 two entire German army corps reached the right bank of the Vistula. Ivangorod, now threatened from all directions, could evidently not be held much longer.

The fortress surrendered on August 4, 1915, after a violent bombardment of the outer forts had taken place, beginning on the first of the month. Austro-Hungarian troops under General von Koevess especially distinguished themselves in the attack on the west front.

CHAPTER LX

WARSAW FALLS

THE retreat from Warsaw began during the night of August 3 and 4, 1915. Already the city had been stripped as far as possible, to judge by reports from Petrograd, of metals, such as church bells and machinery that might possibly be of use to the Germans. A portion of the civilian population left the city. The Blonie line just to the west of the capital was given up under pressure from the Teutons on the 3d. While the retreat was taking place the Russians gave all possible support to their forces defending the Narew lines, so far as they still were maintained.

Desperate charges were hurled by the Russians against the Germans moving forward all along the front Lowza-Ostrow-Wyszkow. The bravery of the Russians, especially in their counterattacks on both sides of the road from Rozan to Ostrow on the 4th of August, won the admiration of the Germans.

The correspondent of the London "Times" reports that on August 4, 1915, there was probably not over one Russian corps on the west side of the Vistula. "Half of that crossed south of Warsaw before 6 p. m.," he writes, "and probably the last division left about midnight, and at 3 a. m. on August 5 the bridges were blown up. The Germans arrived at 6 a. m." The formal entry of the Polish capital was made by Prince Leopold of Bavaria as Commander in Chief of the army which took the city.

The formal announcement issued by the German Great Headquarters on the 5th of August read: "The army of Prince Leopold of Bavaria pierced and took yesterday and last night the outer and inner lines of forts of Warsaw in which Russian rear guards still offered stubborn resistance. The city was occupied to-day by our troops."

In the capture of Warsaw seven huge armies had been employed. The German northern army, operating against the double-track line which runs from Warsaw to Petrograd, 1,000 miles in the northeast, via Bielostok and Grodno; the army

The central figure is Prince Leopold of Bavaria, who led the victorious Teutons into Warsaw, August 6, 1915. The Prince with his staff are posed before Warsaw's magnificent cathedral

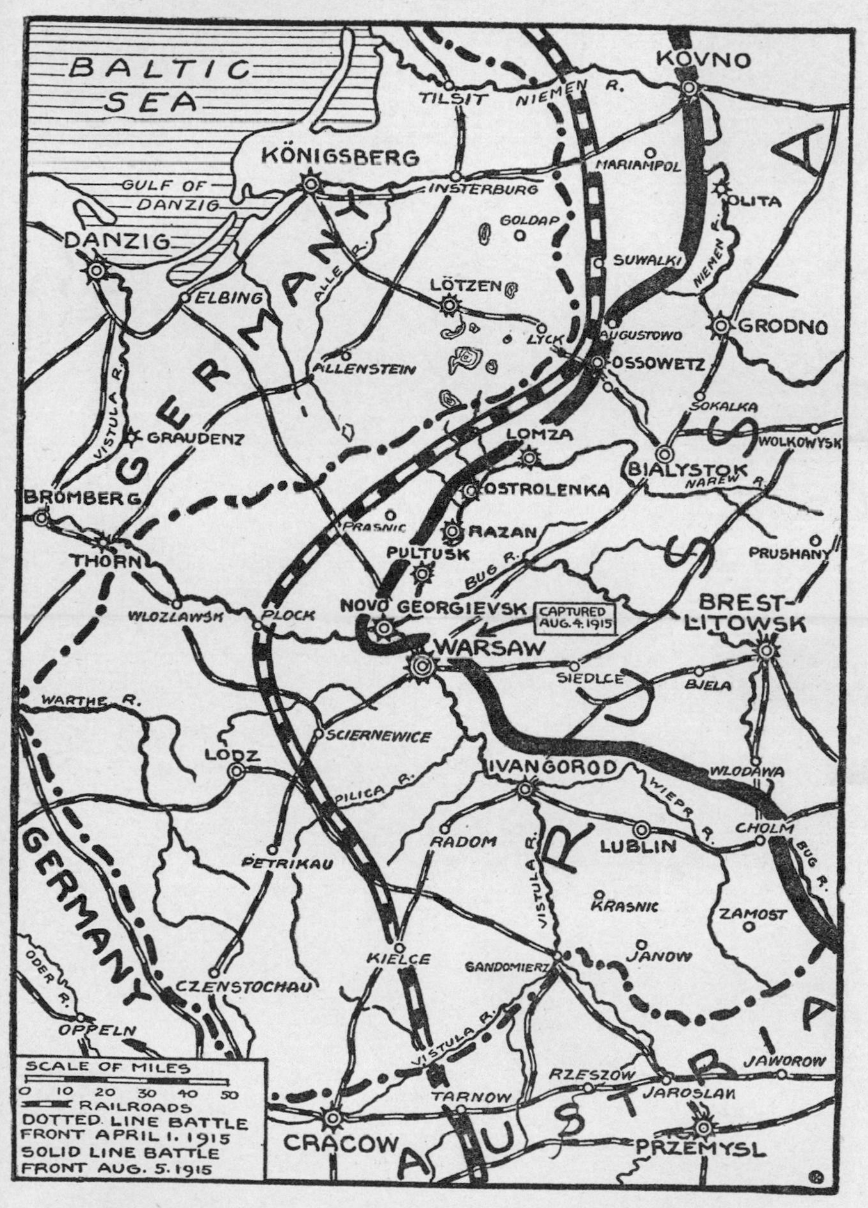

ADVANCE AND CAPTURE OF WARSAW

operating in the Suwalki district, threatening the same line farther west; the army aimed at the Narew based on Mearva; the army directly aimed at Warsaw, north of the Vistula; the (Ninth) army directly aimed at Warsaw, south of the Vistula; ten or twelve Austrian army corps attempting to reach the single- and double-track railway from Ivangorod to Brest-Litovsk and Moscow, and the line from Warsaw to Kiev via Lublin and Cholm, which is for the most part a single track, and, finally, the army of Von Linsingen, operating on the Lipa east of Lemberg.

The campaign for Warsaw had been fought along a front of 1,000 miles, extending from the Baltic to the frontier of Rumania. An estimate which lays claim to being based upon authoritative figures placed the number of men engaged in almost daily conflict on this long line at between 6,000,000 and 7,000,000. The attacks upon the sides of the lines on which the defense of Warsaw depended had been the most furious in the course of the war on the eastern front. The losses on both sides undoubtedly were enormous, though they can be ascertained only with difficulty, if at all.

The following summary of captures was issued by the German Great Headquarters on August 1, 1915: "Captured in July between the Baltic and the Pilica, 95,023 Russians; 41 guns, including two heavy ones; 4 mine throwers; 230 machine guns. Taken in July in the southeastern theatre of war (apparently between Pilica and the Rumanian frontier): 323 officers; 75,719 men; 10 guns; 126 machine guns."

PART VIII—THE BALKANS

CHAPTER LXI

DIPLOMACY IN THE BALKANS

IN discussing the causes of the Great War in Vol. I we have already shown how important a part the little Balkan States played in the long chain of events leading up to the final catastrophe. The tragedy at Serajevo had served to precipitate a long-threatened conflict between Great Powers. One of the prizes at stake was the control of the natural highways between Europe and Asia, occupied by the Balkan countries. It would hardly be possible for one of these states to escape war. Defeat, however, might bring not only the terrors of invasion but perhaps the overthrow of the state as an independent power. Naturally, the government would delay plunging into war.

This was, in fact, the situation of all the Balkan States when the Great War began, with the exception, of course, of Serbia, which had been directly attacked. Rumania, Bulgaria, and Greece very hastily announced their complete neutrality to each other as well as to the world at large, though Greece was in the very awkward position of having signed a defensive treaty with Serbia.

Though the Balkan situation has always been considered very complicated, certain broad facts may be laid down which will serve as a key to a fair understanding of the motives behind each of the various moves being made on the Balkan chessboard.

First of all, it must be realized that popular sentiment plays a much smaller part in Balkan politics than it does in such countries as England, France, and our own country. Though each is more or less democratic in form, none of these governments is really controlled by its people in matters requiring such quick decisions as war. At the head of each of the Balkan States is a monarch surrounded by a governing clique who have full authority in military matters. Each of these cliques has only one aim in mind: How shall it increase the area of its territory, or at least save itself from losing any of what it already controls?

Rumania, being largely of Latin blood, has no strong natural affinity to range her by the side of either of the big fighting powers that concern her—Austria and Russia. She believes, however, that Transylvania, an Austrian province with a large Rumanian population and with grievances against the Austrian Government, should become a part of Rumania.

Bulgaria, like Russia, is Slavic. Added to that, Bulgaria owes her freedom to Russian arms. Because of these two reasons there is a very strong sentiment among the people in favor of Russia. Russian political intrigues during the past thirty years have done a great deal, however, in undermining this kindly feeling among the more intelligent Bulgarians. And then Russia's ambition to possess herself of the Bosphorus as an outlet into the Mediterranean is directly contrary to the ambitions of the governing clique of Bulgaria, which also has its eyes on Constantinople.

Toward the Austrians the Bulgarians feel nothing but dislike: "Schwabs," they call them contemptuously. Moreover, Austria's contemplated pathway to Saloniki would cut down through Macedonia, another territory coveted by Bulgaria. Ferdinand, King of Bulgaria, however, is a German by birth and training.

Greece, like Rumania, is also racially isolated. She fears Russia for the same reason that Bulgaria does; Greece is determined that Constantinople shall one day be hers. And she fears Austria because Austria's pathway would even take Saloniki from her. And finally she fears Italy because Italy has ambitions in Asia Minor and Albania. All the belligerents seem to be treading on the toes of Greece.

It will be seen, therefore, that the diplomatic game was an especially delicate one in the Balkans. If the Second Balkan

War had not occurred, they might be defending themselves in alliance against any aggressor. But each of them has its own ambitions which conflict with those of the other states and create fear and suspicion where there might be cooperation.

During the first half year of the war there was very little for the Balkan diplomats to do but lie low and watch events. To be sure, Turkey threw in her lot with the Teutons during this period, but German control of the Turkish machinery of government and the army appears to have been so strong that it seems doubtful whether Turkish initiative was much of a factor in the move.

One of the first moves by the Teutonic Powers through Austria-Hungary was the attempted invasion of Serbia, by which they hoped to eliminate her from the field and also to swing the other Balkan States, especially Bulgaria, over to their side. And had Austria succeeded in penetrating the peninsula through Serbia, there can hardly be any doubt that the effect would have been immediate.

But the invasion by Austria, attempted three times, was an abject failure. At the end of five months a whole Austrian army corps had been annihilated by the Serbians and the rest of the huge invading armies had been driven back across the Danube and Save. Following close upon this came the extraordinary success of the Russians in Bukowina and in the Carpathians, which placed Hungary in immediate danger of being invaded. The cause of the Allies began to look promising and the machinery of Balkan diplomacy began slowly to revolve.

Meanwhile the principal efforts of the Entente statesmen had been directed toward effecting a reconciliation between Bulgaria and the other Balkan States which, she maintained, had robbed her of Macedonia. Indeed, it may well be said that the Treaty of Bucharest, whereby the Macedonian Bulgars were largely handed over to Serbia, and Greece was, and continued to be, the main stumblingblock in the path of the Allies to bring Bulgaria around to a union with Serbia and Greece and Rumania, for Rumania had increased her territory in the Second Balkan War, by taking a strip of territory at the mouth of the Danube. In

January, 1915, Rumania began to show signs of shaping a definite policy that might later lead her to take the side of the Allies. Her king, Carol, a Hohenzollern by blood, had died shortly after the war began and his nephew, Ferdinand, ascended the throne on October 11, 1914. It became evident that his sympathies were with the Entente, and it was noteworthy that in January, Rumania received a loan of several millions from Great Britain and that a large part of the money was spent on the Rumanian army, already partly mobilized.

During the year, negotiations of a tentative nature were opened by the Rumanian Foreign Office with Russia, the purpose being to arrange for the throwing of the Rumanian military power on the side of the Allies. In return Rumania would expect to acquire from Austria-Hungary the provinces of Transylvania and Bukowina and a part of the province of Banat; and from Russia a part of Bessarabia peopled by Rumanians.

The reason for such demands lay in the fact that many Rumanians lived in these territories. But for the time, the negotiations were held in abeyance, for the year proved unpropitious for the abandonment of Rumanian neutrality. There occurred the terrible defeat of the Russians in the Carpathian Mountains in the spring of 1915, followed by the advance of the Teutons toward Warsaw. These events may have influenced the Rumanian Government. At any rate, guided by her premier, Bratiano, she remained for the time being neutral while the tide of war swept by on the eastern front. But it seemed likely that Rumania might eventually join the Entente.

Bulgaria had, at about the same time, accepted a loan from Germany. Attempts were made at the time to explain away the political significance of the transaction by representing the advance as an installment of a loan the terms of which had been arranged before the beginning of the war, but the essential fact was that the cash came from Germany at a time when she was herself calling in all the gold of her people.

Bulgaria now plainly let it be understood under what conditions she would join a union of the Balkan neutrals against the Teutonic Powers. Her premier, Radoslavov, head of the Bulgarian Liberal Party, whose policy has always been anti-Russian, is one of the most astute politicians in the Balkans, and this description is equally true of King Ferdinand as a monarch. These two stated definitely Bulgaria's price; that part of Macedonia which was to have been allowed to her by the agreement which bound her to Serbia and Greece during the first Balkan War; the Valley of the Struma, including the port of Kavalla, that part of Thrace which she herself had taken from Turkey, and the southern Dobruja, the whole of the territory Rumania had acquired from her while her back was turned during the two Balkan wars.

The Entente Powers held council with the other Balkan States, each of which had taken its share of booty from Bulgaria. In order to persuade them to consent to Bulgaria's terms, they suggested certain compensations for the concessions they were asked to make. To Serbia, which, in spite of her very precarious situation at the time, was very averse to returning any part of her Macedonian territory, they pointed out that she could find compensation in adding to her territory Bosnia, Herzegovina and the other Slav provinces of Austria, where the population was truly Serb. To Rumania, which was already willing to meet Bulgaria half way, they promised Transylvania and Bukowina. To Greece, which had done less and gained more than any of the other states during the two Balkan Wars and so could afford to be generous, they held out the prospect of gaining a considerable area in Asia Minor, thickly populated by Greeks.

These changes naturally all depended on the complete defeat of the Teutonic Powers, but Bulgaria demanded that at least some, and especially Serbian Macedonia, should be handed over to her at once.

This latter demand brought about strong opposition. The other Balkan States considered that, granting even that all these concessions were to be promised to Bulgaria, she should not expect their fulfillment until she had earned them by helping to defeat the Teutonic Powers.

Venizelos, the premier of Greece, and probably the most broad-minded statesman in the Balkans, stated that, on the part of

Greece, concessions to Bulgaria were possible, though, as developed later, in this he did not have the backing of the king and the rest of the governing clique. In February no progress in the negotiations had been made, though a special French Commission, headed by General Pau, visited all the Balkan capitals and tried to bring about a mutual agreement.

At about that time another important military event occurred, especially affecting the Balkans; the warships of the Entente began bombarding the forts in the Dardanelles and it seemed that Constantinople was presently to fall into their hands. Not long after Venizelos stated, in an interview, that he was privy to this action and proposed to send 50,000 Greek soldiers to assist the Allies by a land attack on the Turks.

The Greek General Staff, however, immediately declined to support Venizelos. Such a campaign, it declared, was impossible unless Greece first had strong guarantees that Bulgaria would not take the opportunity to invade Greek Macedonia and fall on the flank of the Greek army operating against the Turks. Venizelos thereupon approached Bulgaria and was told that Bulgaria would remain neutral if Greece would cede most of her Macedonian conquests, which would include Kavalla, Drama, and Serres.

Venizelos attempted to compromise, and here he was caught between two obstacles. Bulgaria absolutely refused to recede one inch from her demand; and, on the other hand, the Greek governing clique suddenly refused to consider any proposal that would mean the cession of any territory at all to the hated Bulgars. What probably stiffened the opposition of the other members of the Greek Government to the Turkish campaign was the realization on their part that Italy would probably come into the war on the side of the Allies. Now Italy and Greece were rivals in southern Albania and in their ambitions for power in the Ægean and in Asia Minor. Even more than in the case of the Balkan countries, their historic boundaries and their modern ambitions overlap. The powerful aid Italy could bring the Allies might render her claims for power far more likely to be heard than those of Greece. What deepened these suspicions was the fact that the Allies refused to indicate definitely just what territory Greece was to have in return for her support against the Turks. Their promise of "liberal compensation" was not at all definite enough. Only Venizelos was satisfied with this promise; he was in favor of trusting implicitly to Anglo-French gratitude.

To bring this deadlock to a conclusion King Constantine called a Royal Council, and by this body the matter was thoroughly discussed during the first few days of March. The Council, together with the king, decided against supporting the Allies actively on such terms. On the morning of March 6 Venizelos called at the British legation in Athens to say that the opposition of the king made it impossible to fulfill his promise. That night he resigned.

The fall of Venizelos was, naturally, a heavy blow to the Allies. He was succeeded by Gounaris, an ex-Minister of Finance, who announced his policy as one of strict neutrality. Venizelos was so deeply mortified that he declared that he would withdraw permanently from public life, and then left Greece.

April, 1915, opened with an occurrence that seemed to throw a strong light on the attitude of Bulgaria. On the night of the second day of the month a large force of Bulgar Comitajis made a raid over the southeastern frontier of Serbia, and, after attacking successfully the Serbian outposts and blockhouses, in an attempt to cut the railroad, by which Serbia was getting war supplies from the Allies, they were repelled by the Serbians, though only after severe fighting.

Serbia and Greece both protested loudly, but Bulgaria affirmed that she had had nothing to do with the matter.

As has developed since, Bulgaria had by this time definitely decided to strike for the Teutonic allies when the right moment should come. Already back in January, 1912, a secret treaty had been negotiated between Bulgaria and Germany. This was signed a little later by Prince Bülow and M. Rizoff at Rome. There were more reasons than one for keeping this secret. For within the Bulgarian Parliament there was a strong opposition to the German policy of Ferdinand and Radoslavov, led by

Malinoff, chief of the Democratic party, and Stambulovski, chief of the Agrarian party, an opposition so bitter and determined that the king had good reason to fear an open revolution should he openly declare himself for the Germans.

On May 29, 1915, the Allies again sent a note to Bulgaria, making proposals which comprised the results of their efforts to obtain concessions from the other Balkan States. On June 15 Radoslavov sent a reply, asking for further information, obviously drawn up in order to gain time.

Meanwhile, on June 11, Venizelos had again appeared in Athens, where he received a warm welcome from the populace, with whom he was the prime favorite. Within a few days he resumed the leadership of the Greek Liberal party and, at a general election, which was held shortly after, he showed a popular majority support of 120 seats in the Popular Assembly, nothwithstanding a determined opposition made by his opponents. Before the Balkan wars the Greek Parliament had consisted of 180 members, but by according representation to the districts in Macedonia annexed after the wars the number was brought up to 316. Venizelos and his policy in favor of the Allies were emphatically indorsed by the Greek suffrage. Naturally this expression of the people's voice was a smart blow at the king and his councillors. On the other hand, they were encouraged by an unfavorable turn that was now taking place in the military operations of the Allies.

The attack on the Dardanelles by the warships had been a decided failure. Nor were the operations of the British troops on the peninsula of Gallipoli meeting with any real success. The Austrians and the Germans had driven the Russians back from the Carpathians and had retaken Przemysl and Lemberg. In fact, the situation of the Austro-German armies had now become so favorable that it was possible for the Teutonic allies to make proposals to the Balkan States with a fair chance of being listened to.

During July, 1915, Serbia was approached by Germany with an offer of a separate peace, but Serbia would not even consider the terms.

On July 8 Austria delivered a note to Rumania, through the Austrian Minister in Bucharest, Count Czernin, which contained two sets of proposals. One was contingent upon the continued but "friendly" neutrality of Rumania, the other on her active participation in the war on the side of Austria-Hungary.

In the first proposal Rumania was promised all of Bukowina south of the Seret River, better treatment of the Rumanian population of Austrian territory, the establishment of a Rumanian university in Brasso, large admissions of Rumanians into the public service of Hungary, and greater liberty of administration to the Rumanian churches in Austria.

The second proposal specified that Rumania should put five army corps and two cavalry divisions at the disposal of the Austro-Hungarian General Staff to operate against the Russians. In return Rumania should receive all of Bukowina up to the Pruth River, territory along the north bank of the Danube up to the Iron Gate, complete autonomy for the Rumanians in Transylvania and all of Bessarabia that the Rumanian troops should assist in conquering from the Russians.

Just a week after this note was received in the Rumanian capital, Prince Hohenlohe-Langenburg, whose wife was a sister of the Queen of Rumania, arrived in Bucharest and tried to induce King Ferdinand to come to terms with Austria, or at least to allow the transportation of war munitions through the country to the Turks, who were then running short of ammunition. The king refused this concession. How important it would have been, had it been granted, may be judged from the many efforts the Germans had made to smuggle material down to Turkey. In one case the baggage of a German courier traveling to Constantinople had been X-rayed and rifle ammunition had been found. Again, cases of beer had been opened and found to contain artillery shells.

Rumania, however, was not yet ready to make the momentous decision for war. For this reason, she did not choose, either to hasten her refusal of the Austrian proposals, since that would seem to range her definitely on the side of the Allies in the opinion of the Central Powers. The attitude of her nearest neighbor, Bulgaria, also caused her uneasiness. She was not strong enough to resist attack from the Austro-Hungarians on one side and from the Bulgarians on the other, unless Russia could give her powerful support. And one of the chief ambitions of the Bulgarians was to acquire the southern part of the Dobrudja, taken from them in the Second Balkan War. At length, however, it became evident even to the Austrian agents that Rumania would not decide to join their country in the war.

Having failed at Bucharest, the German agent, Prince Hohenlohe-Langenburg, moved on to Sofia. At that moment King Ferdinand of Bulgaria was endeavoring to get Turkey to sign a treaty, for which negotiations had been going on secretly for some months, by which Bulgaria was to obtain all the Turkish land on the west side of the Maritza River, and so free the Bulgarian railroad to Dedeagatch from Turkish interference. On July 23 this treaty was finally signed, and Bulgaria acquired a full right of way along the line.

Bulgaria was now frankly asking bids for her support from both sides. In an interview which the Premier, Radoslavov, granted to the correspondent of a Budapest newspaper on August 3, 1915, and who remarked to the premier that it was at least strange for a nation to carry on such negotiations simultaneously with two groups of powers, he replied:

"It is these negotiations which give us the chance to make a decision. Our country seeks only her own advantages and wishes to realize her rights. We have decided to gain these in any case. The only question is: How can we achieve this with the least sacrifices? As regards the internal situation of Bulgaria, I may proudly say that our conditions have improved, and that everybody in the country looks forward to the great national undertaking we are about to embark on with immense joy and enthusiasm."

PART IX—ITALY ENTERS THE WAR

CHAPTER LXII

SPIRIT OF THE ITALIAN PEOPLE—CRISIS OF THE GOVERNMENT

THE crystallization of popular opinion in favor of intervention kept pace with the trend of diplomatic negotiations. Italy, especially the northern provinces, was a great beehive, humming with patriotic fervor. Evenings in almost any northern town might be seen companies of young men in civilian dress marching in companies and maneuvering with military precision. At first the organizers of these "training walks," as they were called, maintained reticence regarding their purpose. The youths, they said, were merely undergoing voluntary training to be ready "in case they should be needed." But the purpose of these volunteer drills was unmistakable. At times, when the drill grounds were rather isolated, the marchers would burst into patriotic songs—the hymn of the Garibaldians, or, perhaps, "Trieste of My Heart." Soon the neutralists began to organize counterpreparations. Encounters between bands of the rival factions became increasingly frequent, in fact daily occurrences. From jeers they passed to scuffles, in which missiles and clubs were the weapons. As a rule these encounters took place far enough from the city limits to avoid interference by the police, and only vague reports of them reached the main body of home-loving citizens.

Milan was the center of these demonstrations. During April, 1915, the Socialists proclaimed a "general strike," which left a large part of the working population idle to attend gatherings addressed by the neutralist orator. These meetings generally wound up with a parade, and perhaps a hostile demonstration in front of the office of some interventionist newspaper, or cheers outside the German Consulate. The next day the Piazza would be thronged with a gathering of interventionists wearing the national colors entwined with the flag of Trieste, and, perhaps, with the "honorable red shirt" of the Garibaldians. During the period just before the entrance of Italy into the war these rival processions were held on different days by order of the police, who ruthlessly broke up any attempt to interfere with assemblies entitled to the right of way. As the war party began to gain, their opponents adopted the custom of attacking the demonstrants after they had disbanded.

As it was, a mob attacked the Milan branch of the Siemens-Schuckert works, the great Berlin electrical machinery factory, battered in the main entrance, and exchanged shots with some young German employees left in charge. The timely arrival of the armed police stopped this riot, and removed the Germans to safe quarters.

At this juncture, or before, the influence of the "Garibaldi" movement became widely apparent. Early in the war the Garibaldians had launched a movement to recognize the aid received from France by Italy during her War of Independence. A special corps of Garibaldi volunteers was enrolled in France, and its valiant service in the Alsace campaign, where one of the members of the Garibaldi family fell, had a telling effect in Italy. Volunteers for this corps at once sprang up from all parts of the country.

On May 10, 1915, Germans and Austrians throughout Italy were advised by their consulates to leave the country. The exodus proceeded rapidly, and during the next ten days nearly all the citizens of the two Central Powers who were able to leave had taken refuge in Switzerland. Italy seemed ripe for war; but still the Government delayed. There was now no doubt of the popular mind; but events ouside the country were not encouraging. Perhaps the weightiest of these deterring factors was news of the Russian retirement in the north and information reaching the Italian Minister of War that the Entente Allies were short of ammunition.

Then came the crisis in the Government. Baron Sonnino's denunciation of the Alliance caused a change in the attitude of the Austro-Hungarian Foreign Office. Prince von Bülow and the Austrian Ambassador, Baron von Macchio, were authorized to conclude a new agreement on the basis of further Austrian concessions. Sonnino refused to accept the new terms and the German and Austrian representatives played their last trump. Baron von Macchio telegraphed to Vienna accusing the Italian Foreign Minister of concealing information of the Austrian concessions both from the king and the majority of the cabinet. The concessions were printed and circulated widely among the people. Signor Giolitti, Salandra's predecessor, and at one time all but dictator of Italy, hurried to Rome and rallied his followers. The neutralists hailed him as the man to save Italy from a ruinous war.

Parliament was to meet on May 20, 1915. It was clear that the supporters of Giolitti, in majority both in the Senate and the Chamber of Deputies, could, if they chose, overthrow the Government. Popular anxiety was intense.

On the evening of May 13, 1915, came the announcement that the Salandra ministry had resigned. If there had been any doubt of the state of things throughout Italy up to that point, this news cleared the situation. The whole country burst into a flame of indignation. The next day Italy learned for the first time that the Triple Alliance had been denounced early in the month.

It became clear that whatever the fate of Salandra and his cabinet, his foreign policy was bound to be continued.

On May 15, 1915, announcement that the king had declined to accept Salandra's resignation caused a great popular outburst of joy. In Rome an immense gathering called to protest against the Giolittians and German influence was transformed into a demonstration of triumph; more than 150,000 persons took part in a procession a mile long that moved from the Piazza del Popolo to the Quirinal.

The next morning, May 16, 1915, there was nobody in Rome who doubted what Italy would do. That day Giolitti left Rome, and his departure marked the end of his active influence during the opening months of the war. His party crumpled.

When Parliament met on May 20, 1915, Salandra received an overwhelming vote of confidence in the passage of a bill conferring extraordinary powers upon the Government in the event of war. Miles north of Rome, word came to the Austrian commanders, working feverishly to strengthen their forts in the fastnesses of the Alps, to brace themselves for the assault.

CHAPTER LXIII

THE DECISION MADE—ITALIAN STRATEGIC PLAN

ON the night of May 24, 1915, little groups of the Alpini, Italy's famous mountain troops, moved silently. They passed from San Giorgio, Cividale and Palmanova on the eastern frontier, from Paluzza and San Stefano and Pieve on the north, from Agordo, Feltre and Asiago, from Brentino and Malcesine toward Lake Garda, from Garganano the western shore of the lake and from other positions all along the mountain frontier up to the Stelvio Pass.

Marching silently and in single file, by three o'clock in the morning of May 25, 1915, one detachment reached a deep trench. "Our frontiers," said their officers. "We advance to make new ones." Then began a long, steep climb up narrow mountain paths, through snow lying in patches knee-deep, and through a storm of sleet and rain that broke along the Trentino boundary before dawn. As dawn broke they hurled themselves upon an Austrian shelter trench excavated the autumn before on the plateau. It was empty. The enemy had retired only a few hours before. The camp-fire ashes were still warm. As the sun began to throw the long shadows of the Alpine peaks to the west Austrian guns crashed out their first salute from the rocky fortresses beyond. Italy and Austria-Hungary were at war.

To comprehend the task before the Italian army it is necessary to examine the Italian-Austrian frontier. Austria's problem was one only of defense. Her warning had been ample and when war was declared she was prepared to the last detail. Being the challenged party hers was the choice of weapons, and she had equipped herself with an almost impregnable line of fortifications. The grievance was Italy's, and hers the duty of assault. Every advantage of position lay with Austria.

The strategic plan of the Italian generals was determined by hard geographical facts. The Italo-Austrian frontier is about 480 miles long, divided naturally into three sections. On the west the Austrian province of Trentino indents Italian territory like a wedge; next comes the great wall of the Dolomites and the Carnic and Julian Alps; then, on the east, a boundary line running north and south between the main Alpine chain and the Adriatic Sea. Steep mountain heights dominated by Austrian troops guarded the first two parts of this frontier. Only on the eastern border, from Pontebba to the Adriatic was Italian offensive on a large scale at all feasible; but before offensive operations could be started here it was necessary for the Italians to close the open gates to the north.

Here in the north lay Italy's problem at the opening of the war; and here her armies confronted an almost impossible task. In a word, they had to fight uphill. A salient, such as that formed by the Trentino, may offer dangers for the side that holds it—an example of which is the Russian position in Poland at the opening of the war; but the Trentino situation was quite unlike that in Poland. The sides of the Trentino were buttressed with mountains. The most tempting avenue of invasion was the valley of the Adige River. An enemy advancing by this route would find himself confronted with the strongly fortified town of Trent, which long resisted attacks from Venice in the Middle Ages. Having forced his way past Trent the enemy would be in a wilderness of lateral valleys with the main ridge of the Alpine chain, at the Brenner, still before him.

On the western side of the Trentino is the lofty Stelvio Pass, leading from the Upper Adige to the valley of Adda. This pass is 9,000 feet high and its narrow defiles were easily defended. To the south lies the pass of Tonale over which runs the road from Noce to the Oglio, but this offers similar difficulties. The road pass of Cornelle, close to Lake Garda, is too narrow for any considerable force. On the eastern side of the salient conditions for invasion are still worse. The railway from Venice to Innsbruck crosses the Valsugana at Tezze, but the Brenta valley through which it runs is a difficult road to Trent. Summed up, the salient of the Trentino was an ideal position for those who held it, both offensive and defensive. The few breaches by which invasion could come were a source of strength rather than weakness, because they compelled attack from the Italian plain to be made on divergent lines from different bases.

The second part of the frontier is the ramparts of the Dolomite and Carnic ranges through which an important offensive was possible for neither belligerent. The main pass, at Ampezzo, 5,000 feet high, makes a sharp detour toward the west to circumvent the mass of Cristallo, and here the road is a narrow defile commanded by a hundred points of danger. The adjacent passes of Misurina and the Monte Croce are no better, and the defiles to the east contain little more than bridle paths. The lowest pass, which leads from the valley of the Fella by Pontebba to the upper streams of the Drave and carries the railway from Venice to Vienna is only 2,615 feet high at its greatest elevation. Although this is the easiest of the great routes through the mountain barrier, it is still narrow and difficult. A modern army given the advantages of time and preparation should be able to close and hold it with ease.

Although the maps show few natural difficulties on the third section of the frontier to compare with those farther west, it is not the obvious avenue of attack a hasty survey would seem to suggest. It is only twenty miles wide and behind it is the line of the River Isonzo with hills along its eastern bank. The upper part of this stream, above Salcana, is a ravine; then comes six miles of comparatively level ground in front of Gorizia; then the hills begin again and sweep round to the seacoast by Monfalcone. What this front lacks in natural defenses had been amply supplied before the war opened by Austria with artillery and men. Toward this narrow twenty-mile stretch, and especially toward the plain before Gorizia, tended, in a sense, however, all the operations of the Italian strategists. The engagements fought during the first of the Italo-Austrian struggle all had their bearing upon the great offensive launched later against Gorizia.

But the natural lay of the land was by no means the only consideration with which the rival generals had to deal. In respect to lateral communications Italy had the advantage. Behind her invading armies stretched an elaborate system of railways through her northern provinces. Austria had a railway running through the whole curve of the frontier, but owing to the difficulty of breaking through from the hill valleys this system had few feeders. This lack of branch lines meant that Austria had to concentrate any offensive at certain definite places—Trent, Tarvis, and Gorizia. Italy aimed at these points and one more, Franzensfeste, the junction of the Pusterthal line with the railway from Innsbruck to Trent. If she could take this point she could cut Austria's communications in the whole Trentino salient. But Franzensfeste was the most difficult of any of these local points for Italy to reach, for south and east of it lay the bristling system of the Dolomites.

The successive revelations of Italian strategy during the first months of the war brought few surprises. Austria had her hands full in the Carpathians just then and was unable to take advantage of the opportunities for swift offensive which her frontier positions offered. It was a foregone conclusion that the first advance would come from the Italian side and the direction of that movement was not long in doubt. Its objective was Trieste, the Austrian peninsula, and the hills of Styria which sweep to Vienna. There lay the country where modern armies could maneuver. At the same time the whole northern boundary must be watched to prevent Austrian forces from the Trentino cutting the communications of the invader and attacking him in the rear. Therefore General Cadorna, the Italian commander in chief, resolved to attack at all the salient points. Such a plan led to a series of movements—toward Trent, across the Dolomite passes against the Pusterthal railway, at the Pontebba Pass, and across the Julian Alps to threaten the line between Tarvis and Gorizia. Meanwhile the main Italian army was to strike at the Isonzo and the road to Trieste.

The same conditions which made the Austrian frontier lines easy to defend also would have given the Central Power a big advantage in offensive operations, but for excellent reasons the Austrian staff did not attack. In the first place, Austria lacked men. The Teutonic war councils concluded that Austro-Hungarian troops were of more value in the great drive then in progress against the Russians than they would have been in offensive operations against the cities of the northern Italian plains. Had the Austrians debouched from their mountain strongholds and forced the Italians to concentrate against them in Italian territory, as they undoubtedly could have done, the benefits of such an enterprise from the standpoint of the alliance powers would have been small in proportion to the risks. Only a combined drive by both Austria and Germany, it is believed, could have gained any telling advantage in northern Italy; and Italy, it must be remembered, had not declared war on Germany. Ensconced in their mountain fastnesses, the Austrians believed they could maintain a successful defensive indefinitely. Then, after the Italian armies had exhausted themselves beating against the mountain barrier, an opportunity might arise for Austrian reprisals. At the time few believed that Italy would long be able to maintain her attitude of neutrality regarding Germany—an opinion, by the way, which was not supported by the developments of the first year of the war.

The Austrians had months in which to prepare, and they had made good use of their time. The natural difficulties confronting an Italian assault had been enormously increased by trenches of steel and concrete. The Austrian engineers had connected their elaborate systems of wire entanglements with high-power electric stations, and dug mines at all vulnerable points. Heavy guns had been moved, at great expenditure of labor, to the frontier forts and rails laid on which to move them from place to place. The broken nature of the ground afforded ideal opportunities for the concealment of artillery positions. It is safe to say that nowhere in the whole theatre of the Great War was there a line better adapted by nature and equipped by man for purposes of defensive warfare. The Austrian Archduke Eugene, who was in charge of the Italian operations, revealed his plan of campaign during the first few days after the beginning of hostilities. His aim was to risk nothing until Field Marshal von Mackensen had finished his operations in Galicia, where Austria's best troops were fighting with their German allies. To meet the Italians he had only the Landsturm and a few reserve divisions, but these were considered enough. The archduke resolved to hold the crests of the passes along the Trentino frontier and the line of the Carnic Alps, withdrawing his outposts before the enemy's advance. On the Isonzo he would abandon the country west of the river line and make his stand on a fortified line to the east which touched the Isonzo only at Gorizia, where the Austrians held the bridgehead on the western bank.

It has been pointed out in preceding pages that not a little of Italy's delay in entering the war, and of the tortuous diplomatic negotiations which for several months kept the outside in doubt as to her ultimate intentions, was due to the state of military unpreparedness confronting the country in the summer of 1914. But by May, 1915, the country had had nine months in which to get ready. Moreover, she had been able to profit by the lessons of the war. When Italy started to get ready there was no waste motion, although the task to be accomplished entailed enormous labor and expense.

CHAPTER LXIV

STRENGTH OF ITALIAN ARMY AND NAVY

AT the head of the Italian army and navy was the king, Victor Emmanuel, a monarch whose gallantry and simplicity had made him a popular idol. Popularity with the people meant also popularity with the army. The chief of the General Staff was General Count Luigi Cadorna. At the outbreak of the war General Cadorna was sixty-five years old. As a young man he had seen service under his father, Rafaele Cadorna, who, in September 1870, led an army into papal territory and blew in the Porta Pia. He had been a corps commander at Genoa. In 1914 he had succeeded General Pollio as chief of the General Staff.

Cadorna was the Von Hindenburg of Italy. As the German commander had studied the bogs of East Prussia, so he had devoted a large part of his life to becoming familiar with the broken line of Italy's northern frontier. He was known throughout Europe for his writings on military science.

The beginning of the war found the Italian navy far better equipped than the army. For the task of holding Austria in the Adriatic, which Italy now took over from France, she possessed four dreadnoughts and two more almost ready. She possessed also ten battleships of the predreadnought class and a number of older vessels. Compared with those of Great Britain and Germany, her armored cruisers were slow, none of them being capable of a speed exceeding twenty-two knots; but she had twenty submarines, forty destroyers and a large number of torpedo boats. Compared with the Austro-Hungarian fleet, the Italian navy showed on paper a distinct superiority. Its admiral in chief, the Duke of the Abruzzi, ranked among the most brilliant men of his time, not only as a naval man, but as a scientist, explorer, and man of affairs. He was first cousin of the king.

By May, 1915, General Cadorna virtually had remade the Italian army. Nine months earlier Italy's military forces were anything but prepared. There was a shortage in every kind of munitions, stores, and equipment. This was plainly evidenced when General Porro had refused an offer of the portfolio of Minister of War in the spring of 1914 because he was unable to obtain a pledge for the adoption of a program of reequipment that demanded a great expenditure of money. The late Government had not made good the expenditure of material caused by the Lybian War, and great quantities of stores had been allowed to deteriorate until they were almost valueless. There was a certain number of guns of medium caliber, but no heavy artillery of the modern type which the Teutonic allies soon showed they possessed in abundance. Of machine guns Italy had a lower proportion than any other of the great powers. All this had been realized, but the money to repair these deficiencies was not forthcoming until the Italian statesmen knew that they were on the brink of war.

Filling the gaps in the army, raising it from a peace to a war footing, was an easier matter. The Italian military law provided automatically for this increase. Every Italian citizen able to bear arms is liable to military service. Recruits are called in the year during which they become twenty years old, although volunteers are accepted as young as eighteen. The last Italian census, in 1911, gave Italy a population of 34,686,683 and the levy lists of that year totaled 487,570. By the close of the year 1914, when the mobilization began, it is reasonable to suppose that the population had grown to something like thirty-six or thirty-seven million, with a corresponding increase in the number available for military service. The peace strength of the army was 14,000 officers and 271,000 men. Mobilization added to each of the twelve corps a division of Mobile Militia bringing its strength up to 37,000 men and 134 guns. The army's war strength was about 700,000 in the first line—from the two classes of the regular army—and 320,000 in the Mobile Militia with a reserve of more than 2,000,000 in the Territorial Militia. The force of trained men that Italy put into the field at the beginning of hostilities, therefore, numbered something over 1,000,000 men. The reservoir of the Territorial Militia contained twice as many more untrained men who for some reason or other were exempt from military service in times of peace, although physically fit to be soldiers. This class was designed primarily for garrison duty, guarding railways and bridges, but in war time was liable to any service. When the mobilization began the men of this class immediately went into training. Each of the twelve army corps consisted of two divisions of line infantry, a regiment of Bersaglieri (light infantry corresponding to the French Chasseurs and the German Jaegers), a regiment of cavalry, a section of Carabinieri (military police), thirty-six field guns and from two to three heavy howitzer batteries. In addition there was the ammunition column, telegraph and engineer parks, ambulance and supply sections, reserve store and supply sections, and a section of field bakery.

The famous Alpine troops ("Alpini") and the mountain artillery were not within the organization of the twelve permanent army corps. These numbered seventy-eight companies, each of 256 officers and men on a war footing. The rest of the Italian infantry units at normal war strength were as follows: Company, 255 officers and men; Battalion, 1,043 officers and men; Regiment, 3,194 officers and men. Five of the cavalry regiments contained six squadrons, the rest five. The war strength of a squadron was 142 officers and men.

The infantry were armed with a magazine rifle of very small caliber, .256-inch. The magazine held six rounds and was loaded with a clip. The length of this piece was 4 feet 2¾ inches, with bayonet 5 feet 2½ inches. It weighed without bayonet 8 pounds 6 ounces, and was sighted up to 2,200 yards. The outbreak of the war found a process of rearmament going on in the artillery. Italy at that time had no adequate siege train and her heaviest mobile weapons were 210-millimeter howitzers and 149-millimeter guns. While the details of the final artillery equipment were not made public by the War Department, events showed that the Italians were well supplied with modern guns of both medium and heavy caliber. The mountain artillery, of which there were thirty-nine batteries, was especially efficient, not only in guns, but in men and transport animals. It was said that the Italian artillery mules could drag a gun wherever there was room for its emplacement.

Italy was one of the first countries to use aeroplanes in war, and her aviation corps had had experience in Tripoli. Although handicapped by lack of money, the Italian military aviators were well abreast of their opponents, at least in the theoretical and mechanical development of the science. During the winter of 1914 a considerable increase was made in the personnel of the corps and in the number of machines.

There is reason to believe that at the beginning of the war the Italian soldier was not highly regarded by Austrian and German military authorities. As a whole the army's reputation had been injured by the Adowa disaster and by the slowness of the campaign in Tripoli. But the developments of actual warfare in the spring and summer of 1915 proved that Italian apologists were correct in their claim that in the former war the army was handicapped by political causes. Physically the Italian troops were equal to any in Europe. The Alpini were perhaps the best mountain soldiers in the world. The Italian soldier is not impressive as to stature, but he is tough and enduring. He is cheerful and obedient under discipline and hardship, and the relations between officers and men were such as to produce the best results in a hard campaign.

All these qualities were requisite for the difficult task to which General Cadorna now turned his first line troops, numbering about 700,000 men. To oppose this advance the Austrians mustered on the frontier about half that number. General von Hofer was chief of staff under Archduke Eugene and General Dankl was in command in the Tyrol.

Two reasons have been advanced to explain the succession of small victories with which the Italians opened their campaign. The first, already mentioned, is that it was part of the Austrian plan to yield their outpost positions with slight resistance and protect their numerically inferior forces in the main strongholds of the mountains. The other is that the archduke and his generals made the mistake of underestimating the enemy. For centuries Italy had supplied the Austrian Court with its poets and musicians, until in the Dual Monarchy the Italians were regarded as an effete race, fit only for the politer pursuits of art, literature and song. Italy's successful War of Independence in the latter half of the nineteenth century had not altogether destroyed this impression. This idea, it may be said, was not shared by the Germans, whose military men had made a closer study of world conditions and had learned to respect the virility of the men of modern Italy.

CHAPTER LXV

FIRST ENGAGEMENTS

OWING to the nature of the scene of hostilities the first days of the Austro-Italian campaign brought a series of engagements between small groups of combatants. Artillery played a large part, and here the Austrians, with their big guns already in carefully studied positions, had a decided advantage. Viewed as a whole only does the campaign at this stage take on an importance and dignity that ranks with the great battles on other fronts of the Great War. Never before had two great powers fought in territory so absolutely ill adapted to the movement of large bodies of troops. For the same reason the story attains a picturesqueness absent from the dreary plains of Galicia and Poland and Flanders. Austrians, Hungarians and Italians fought in a land known throughout the world to tourists for its grandeur of scenery, its towering, snow-clad peaks, and idyllic lakes and valleys. It was warfare where the best soldier was the man most able to surmount the natural difficulties and take advantage of the natural protection of the ground. The official statements of the Italian and Austrian war offices told of feats of mountaineering, and of hand-to-hand struggles, of dripping bayonets and of combatants locked in last embrace with hands clutching each other's throats.

On both sides of the boundary were thousands of men who had spent their lives exploring the trackless mountainsides, climbing with ropes and ice axes and staves. Both nations had encouraged the formation of Alpine clubs.

Soon after midnight on May 23, 1915, the Alpini and Bersaglieri of the Italian army, supported by a few battalions of first line troops and gendarmes, crossed the mountain frontier. Soon the peaks resounded with the popping of rifle fire and the louder detonations of the Austrian mountain guns. Along the whole Trentino front that night a hundred skirmishes drove back the Austrian outpost. Only a few thousand men in all were engaged. The Italian cyclist sharpshooters advanced swiftly up the steep mountain roads until greeted by musketry fire. Then they sought shelter, pushing forward from rock to rock and from tree to tree. Often the light infantry and Alpini foot soldiers were able to skirt the enemy's posts and catch them in the rear.

By May 26, 1915, all Italy was thrilled by the news that all the lower passes of the Dolomites were won and breaches made at Tonale Pass along the northwest and in the Carnic and Julian Alps along the northeast front. Among the points occupied were the Montozzo Pass, 9,585 feet high, Ponte Caffaro, running into southwestern Trentino, the ridge of Monte Baldo, extending northward fifteen miles toward Arco and Roverto in southern Trentino, some of the heights looking westward toward Trento, all the valleys in the labyrinth of the Dolomites, and several footholds in the Alps of Carinthia. The eastern army was well inside Austrian territory, its left at Caporetto on the Isonzo just under Monte Nero, its center looking down on Gorizia from the heights between Indria and the Isonzo, and its right between Cormons and Terzo. Losses on both sides were surprisingly small considering the extent of territory covered by the fighting. The Austrians, after slight resistance, withdrew into their fortresses and waited behind their guns, grimly conscious that the real struggle was still before them.

Then, through the holes pierced by the mountain troops, the Italian engineers began to move forward their artillery and building emplacements and constructing trenches. Skirmishing on the mountain frontier continued until the end of May, 1915. By that time Italian forces attacking Trentino had crossed the Lessini Mountains north of Verona, captured the Austrian town of Ala on the Adige, and penetrated nearly ten miles into Austrian territory. They held high ground on the south commanding the forts of Roverto, and had begun to bring up their heavy guns against this important stronghold. Roverto is one of a number of strongly fortified places girdling Trent and commanding the converging routes to this center of the Austrian defensive. Other lesser fortresses in this girdle are Laredo on the Chiese, Levico on the Brenta, and Riva at the head of Lake Garda. Upon these the Italians closed in, and there they consolidated their positions awaiting the support of the first-line troops advancing in heavy detachments, and of their artillery.

While Italy struck the first blow on land, the first offensive operation of the Italo-Austrian conflict by sea came from Austria. This was an extensive raid on Italy's Adriatic coast. Its object was to delay the Italian concentration by attacking vital points on the littoral railway from Brindisi to the north.

The Austrian fleet began its attack early on the morning of Monday, May 24, 1915. The ships engaged were a squadron from Pola, consisting of two battleships, four cruisers, and eighteen destroyers, strongly supported by aircraft. The assault extended from Brindisi to Venice, and covered a large extent of coast territory hard to defend. At Venice the Austrian air raiders dropped bombs into the arsenal and the oil tanks and balloon sheds on the Lido. The priceless relics of art and architecture, all that remained to recall the city's proud position as ruler of the Adriatic, were uninjured, but the attack from the air caused an outcry from the nations of the Entente almost equal to that which rang through the world when the Germans shelled the cathedral at Rheims and destroyed Louvain. The Austrians replied that the attack was a serious military operation, and by

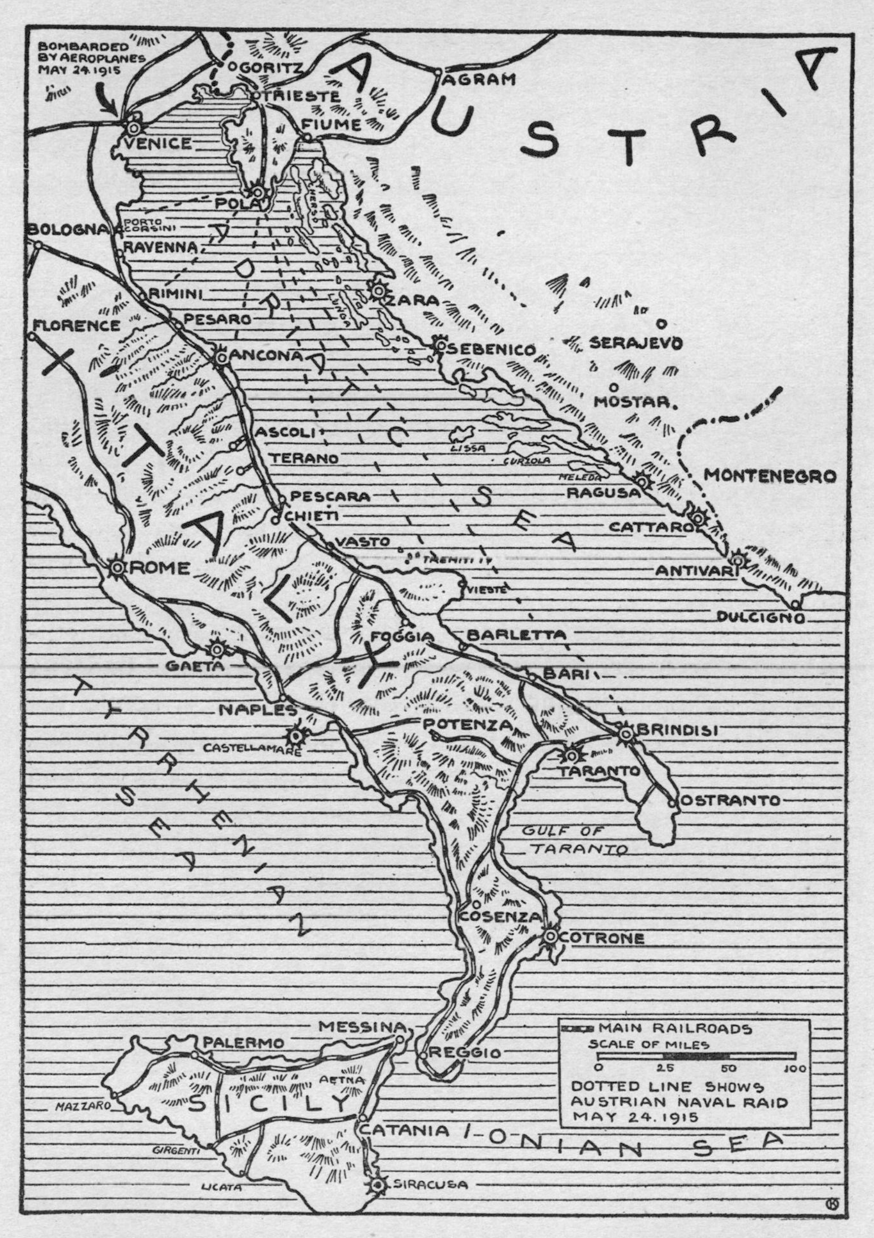

THE COASTS OF ITALY AND AUSTRIA, SHOWING THE NAVAL RAID MAY, 1915

no means the wanton outrage their enemies had tried to make it appear.

The Austrian naval raid lasted barely two hours, but in that time the cruiser *Novara* and several destroyers attacked Porto Corsini, north of Ravenna, in a vain effort to destroy the Italian torpedo base; the cruiser *St. Georg* shelled the railway station and bridges at Rimini; the battleship *Zrinyi* attacked Sinigaglia, and wrecked the railway station and bridge; south of Ancona the battleship *Radetzky* destroyed a bridge over the River Potenza. In the south the cruisers *Helgoland* and *Admiral Spaun* with destroyers shelled a railway bridge and station and several signal stations in the neighborhood of Manfredonia and Viesti, and caused some damage in small coast towns. The raid was well planned and swiftly executed, and it accomplished much of its purpose. The Italian fleet was taken by surprise, and the marauders were back in safety at Pola by six o'clock in the morning, unharmed.

While Italian Alpine troops were driving in the Austrian outposts on the frontiers of Trentino and the Tyrol, General Cadorna advanced his main infantry force, the Third Army, across the Friuli Plain through Udine, Palmanova, and St. Georgio toward the Isonzo. Here the covering troops on May 24 and 25 had captured nearly all the small towns and villages between the frontier and the river from Caporetto in the north just below Monte Nero to Belvedere in the south on the Gulf of Trieste. Cadorna feared lest his opponent, General von Hofer, would launch his main attack from Gorizia against the Italian city of Palmanova, fourteen miles to the west. But Von Hofer, so it developed, had a subtler plan of campaign than a direct attack through Gorizia. What he did was to place a strong force on the mountain of Korada between the Isonzo and the Judrio. This height commanded the middle course of the Isonzo, and it had been transformed into a network of permanent trenches, protected by strong wire entanglements.

The Austrian general believed that by the time the Italians could bring up their heavy artillery and begin to smash the entanglements with their field guns, supports could be pushed across the river. Realizing that Korada must be captured, if at all, by dash and surprise, the Italian brigadier in charge of the attack gathered a herd of fierce bulls, which are numerous in that part of Venetia, and penned them in a hollow out of sight of the enemy, while his artillery began to bombard the hostile trenches. When the animals were wrought to a frenzy of rage and fear by the noise of the guns, they were let loose and driven up the mountain against the Austrian positions. Their charge broke through many strands of the wire entanglements, and before the last of them fell dead under the Austrian rifle fire, Italian troops with fixed bayonets had crowded through the gaps in the wires and captured the position.

By the end of May, 1915, the Third Army had reached the Isonzo River, but had not crossed. Its advance was slow and cautious. Operations were hampered by the heavy rains, which caused the river to overflow its banks and added greatly to the difficulties put in the path of the advancing army by the Austrians, who, as they withdrew, left not a bridge behind them.

Grado, a fishing town of about 5,000 inhabitants, but important on account of its strategic situation, was occupied by the Italians with no great difficulty. Grado lies at the head of the Adriatic, and is twelve miles from Trieste and sixty from Pola. The waters of the lagoons in this neighborhood were valuable to the Italians as a safe shelter for submarines and other small war-craft, and as a base for a prospective attack later upon Pola itself. The inhabitants, most of whom preserved their Italian traits and sympathies, although the town had been under Austrian rule since 1809, hailed the conquerors enthusiastically. Cannon and military carriages were decorated with flowers. Thousands of Italian flags appeared as if by magic. The entering troops were greeted with shouts of "All our lives we have been waiting for this moment when we can cry 'Viva Italia!'" The possession of Grado gave the Third Army virtual control of the mouth of the Isonzo, but the main Austrian position of defense at Gorizia remained apparently unweakened.

Scenes like those at Grado were witnessed at Ala, the first Austrian town of any size and the first railroad center captured by the Italians in the Trentino. Ala was occupied May 27, 1915. Three days before this the Italian light infantry had massed behind the boundary line, and when they began their advance along the main highway their first act was to pull down the yellow and black pole that marked the frontier.

The next day, May 28, 1915, the commanding general with his chief of staff and two guards motored to the spot, cut a passageway through the barricade, and, encountering no opposition, kept on until they reached Ala, seven miles beyond.

The Italian troops were ordered to advance next day, May 29, 1915, and as they marched into the town, officers shouted: "Open your windows. Long live Italy!" The Mayor of Ala called out his townsmen and set them at work removing the barricades on the main road.

In the midst of these rejoicings the sharp rattle of musketry was heard, and the Italians rushed to cover. A reconnoitering party reported that the Austrians were intrenched in a large villa beyond a stream outside the town. The Italian troops began an attack upon this position, and a skirmish party sought to take a position in a house on a near-by hill commanding the villa held by the enemy. Although the way to this house was exposed to the Austrian fire, the Italian officer decided to risk an attempt to reach it. But as he raised his sword to signal an advance, a young girl ran to his side and told him of a path sheltered from the Austrian fire. This girl, Signorina Abriani, whose name will go down in Italian history as one of the first heroines of the war, guided the detachment safely. The Austrians holding the villa were strongly intrenched, and they held out against superior forces until late in the afternoon, when four shells crashed into the building, bringing it down about their ears. The Italians had brought up a battery on the opposite side of the Adige River and opened fire at long range. The Austrians made good their retreat, leaving all their ammunition and three dead. Later fifty-seven Austrians were taken prisoners.

That night the Italian general took the precautions, usual on entering a newly occupied town, of ordering that all the windows in town be kept open and illuminated, and kept patrols about the town. The mayor was reconfirmed, and his first act was to announce to the citizens that "the royal military authorities, knowing the needs of the inhabitants, have with affectionate solicitude and great generosity placed 5,000 rations of bread and 2,000 of rice at the disposal of the poor." Thus Ala became Italian.

The incidents of these first advances into Austrian territory were reported in detail in Italy, and are set down here as typical of events that accompanied the irruption of Italian troops over the border into the country which once had been Italian and where, despite more than a century of Austrian occupation, a large proportion of the inhabitants in spirit was Italian still. Such reports spread through Italy naturally increased enthusiasm for the restoration of the "unredeemed" provinces.

Although, as a rule, the Austrians retired before the first Italian advance into Trentino, they did not depart until they had left every possible obstacle. Roads were barricaded, bridges destroyed, and mines were laid, cleverly concealed on hillsides where it was intended their explosion would overwhelm the Italians under masses of rock and earth. But this was just what the Alpini and Bersaglieri had been trained to anticipate. According to the official Italian accounts, their scouting was so excellent that the wires connecting these mines with Austrian hiding places were discovered and cut, and hardly a mine was exploded. All this took place while the Austrians were drawing in their outposts and consolidating their forces in the great strongholds where later they held the Italians in absolute check. The Italians advanced cautiously in small groups, and the Austrians abandoned the frontier villages soon enough to avoid serious encounters, but not a minute sooner.

In the Alps in these days of May, 1915, the Great War was fought much as wars have been fought in times we are accustomed to regard as the age of true romance. The Italian King visited the Alpine troops and surprised his men and redoubled their devotion by showing his skill as a mountain climber. "You forget," he told an officer who remonstrated with him as he was about to scale a particularly difficult position to examine a gun. "chamois hunting is my favorite sport."

If certain portions of the Italian population seemed lukewarm toward the war during the period of diplomatic negotiations, there was no doubt of the temper of the nation after hostilities actually began. The chord of national feeling was struck by King Victor Emmanuel in an order issued upon taking supreme command of the army and navy.

"Soldiers on land and sea," said the order, "the solemn hour of the nation's claims has struck. Following the example of my grandfather, I take to-day supreme command of Italy's forces on land and sea, with the assurance of victory which your bravery, self-abnegation, and discipline will obtain.

"The enemy you are preparing to fight is hardened to war and worthy of you. Favored by the nature of the ground and skillful works, he will resist tenaciously, but your unsubdued ardor will surely vanquish him.

"Soldiers, to you has come the glory of unfurling Italy's colors on the sacred lands which nature has given as the frontiers of our country. To you has come the glory of finally accomplishing the work undertaken with so much heroism by our fathers."

The stormy scenes which followed the resignation of the Salandra cabinet gave way to a confident calm. From his seclusion in the Vatican the pope addressed a letter to Cardinal Vannutelli, breathing a spirit of resignation and faith, but carefully refraining from any expression of partisanship in the great struggle.

"The hour which we are traversing is painful," he said, "but our prayers will go out more frequently and more fervently than ever to those who have in their hands the fate of nations." The pope recalled that in his first Encyclical issued at the beginning of the war he exhorted the belligerent nations to make peace, but his voice was unheeded and the war continued "until the terrible conflagration has extended to our beloved Italy. While our hearts bleed at the sight of so much misery," he wrote, "we have not neglected to continue our work for relief and the diminution of the deplorable consequences of war. I wish that the echo of our voice might reach to all our children affected by the great scourge of war, and persuade all of them of our participation in their troubles and sorrows. There is little of the grief of the child that is not reflected in the soul of the father."

The greatest enthusiasm, naturally, was manifested in the cities of the north nearest the scene of war. The Master Workers' Guild of Milan voted unanimously to give up one day's pay each month to be devoted to the relief of the families of men at the front. Many business houses carried soldiers' names on their payrolls and remitted their wages to their families.

In all cities within range of the enemy's aircraft precautions were taken to guard public buildings, and especially the famous objects which for centuries had made Italy the Mecca of lovers of art. In Venice the bronze horses of St. Mark's were taken down from their pedestals and hiddden in the subterranean caverns of the cathedral. The gilded statue of the Virgin surmounting the celebrated white marble cathedral at Milan was covered with cloth, so that it might not serve as a guide to Austrian raiders. The stained glass windows of the edifice were removed as a precaution against possible bombardment. After the first Austrian sea and air raid along the Adriatic coast orders were issued that lights should be darkened in all Adriatic ports. This order was extended also to certain inland cities, such as Milan, Bologna, Verona, Brescia, and Udine. A special watch for aeroplanes was kept at Bologna on account of the location there of an important factory for the manufacture of explosives. Watches were set on the crests of the Appenines ready to notify Rome of approaching danger from the air.

The attitude of Germany toward Italy at this period of the war is best indicated by the speech delivered at the session of the Reichstag by Dr. von Bethmann-Hollweg, the Imperial Chancellor. He imputed the Italian declaration of war to a combination of mob dictation, bad faith on the part of the cabinet of Premier Salandra, and, to a certain degree, to the money of the powers of the Entente. The greater part of the Italian people, the chancellor asserted, and a majority in the Italian Parliament had not wanted war, and were even kept in ignorance of the extent of the concessions which Austria-Hungary was willing to make for the sake of peace. The Salandra cabinet, he declared, long before the Triple Alliance had ceased to exist, aligned itself with the Triple Entente and "unchained the mob spirit and intimidated the advocates of peace."

On the eve of leaving Rome, Prince von Bülow gave out a statement in which he declared that Italy was led into the war by a "noisy minority," and that even if in the end she obtained what she asked she would not get much more than what Austria already had offered. "It should be understood," he explained, "that it was impossible to deprive the central empires of Trieste, their only outlet to the Adriatic in the Mediterranean."

Turkey regarded the entrance of Italy into the war on the side of the Entente with apparent equanimity. "We will not declare war on Italy," announced Talaat Bey, the Turkish Minister of the Interior. "We can wait. What can Italy do to us?"

CHAPTER LXVI

FIGHTING IN THE MOUNTAINS

WHILE the world hears little about strategic plans that fail to work out, it is believed that the Austrians in May, 1915, had in mind to let the enemy obtain a good start in his advance against Trieste. Then, when the Italian operations were well under way, and the two railroads from Venice were choked with their supplies, the Austrians probably intended to launch a swift attack upon Verona and the rich cities of Lombardy, thus cutting off the chief centers of Italian industry. At the same time, they undoubtedly meant to send an invading army through the passes of the Carnic and Julian Alps from their base at Tarvis, and by a sudden swoop southward take the Italian forces on the Isonzo in the flank. At least this is what the Italian staff believed was their plan, and they arranged their own forces accordingly.

This was the reason for the extensive Italian drive during the third week of May, 1915, at all the mountain passes of the long frontier. For almost any of these passes might prove to be the gateway of invasion, whereas, once captured, they could be held by a few battalions. But behind each force that occupied the passes won in the first Italian dash was a large reserve ready to lend support wherever the enemy tried to break through. The Italians were not kept long in suspense as to where this thrust from the north first would come.

On May 29, 1915, under cover of a heavy fog, the Austrians concentrated a strong force from Villach, brought them to Mauthen, and from that point launched five successive attacks in an effort to win back the pass of Monte Croce in the Carnic Alps. The Alpini met the attacks with musketry and machine-gun fire, then, after the last attempt had failed, leaped from their trenches and drove the Austrians down the valley.

Thus began the battle of Monte Croce, an engagement described in the official bulletins of both countries in a way that gave the world its first intimation of the peculiar features of this mountain warfare. Each side had large reserves, and the struggle for the pass continued day and night, the Italians pushing over the neighboring passes and gathering their strength for a counterattack when the Austrians were exhausted.

On June 8, 1915, the Italians stormed Freikofel, a height commanding the Plocken Plateau, and took the Pass of Valentina and the Pass of Oregione, 7,500 feet high, and overlooking the wooded valley of Gail. The Alpini won Oregione by climbing through ice and snow over Paralba Mountain and fighting their way downward. Undaunted, General Dankl called up a fresh corps.

On the night of June 14, 1915, the Austrians made a supreme effort to break through the Italian line and put into effect his plan of pouring an army through the Carnic Alps to attack the flank of the main Italian army. Although 100,000 men were engaged in this battle, the ground permitted no massed movements. For miles the saddle of Oregione, the snow-clad sides of Paralba, and every smaller peak and ravine extending to Monte Croce and Freikofel were speckled with fighting men. After the two sides came to grips, the big guns held their fire, and it was man to man and bayonet against bayonet. At one point only did the Austrian thrust reach Italian soil. For a short time the Austrians were on Paralba at an elevation of 8,840 feet, but threatened both in the flank and in the rear they were forced to retreat and take refuge in their prepared positions on Steinwand, a huge limestone mountain overlooking the Gail Valley.

The strategic idea of General Cadorna is more easily understood when one studies the railway map of the Austrian territory north of the Carnic border. Here their railway line through the Drave Valley passed closer to the boundary line than did the Italian system on the south, and they could bring up fresh troops with more speed. In the Gail Valley they had a wide region in which they could mass hidden from the enemy, and they had a good road up the mountains from Mauthen, while the Italians had to depend upon rough tracks through the valley. Although Cadorna had the hard task of keeping the doorway to Venice closed while he attacked the enemy on both flanks, he accomplished his purpose.

The Italian army operating in the province of Cadore won its next success in an attack upon the village of Cortina, situated in a salient of the frontier, 4,000 feet high, amid some of the most beautiful scenery in the world. Cortina was taken on May 30. The Austrians had barricaded the famous road winding up through the Dolomites, and dug elaborate trenches; but the Italians, by superhuman efforts, moved up their mountain guns, while the Alpini scrambled over the mountains by the glaciers of Serapis and the tarns of Croda da Lago, and descended into Cortina on either side. Then, holding the enemy on the east, they advanced into the Tyrol westward to Falzarego.

In this region they had an experience which illustrated the foresight of the Austrians in preparing for the attack they believed would come. Some years before an Austrian had built a hotel in a deep ravine shut in by walls of limestone and very difficult of approach. Tourists had commented upon the lack of practicability of the man who placed a hostelry in so inaccessible a spot. But when the war came it developed that the hotel builder probably had a subsidy from the Government. For sandbags, machine guns, and quick-firers quickly converted the hotel into an excellent fort, which dominated the famous ravine. Thanks to the hardiness and ingenuity of their picked Alpine troops, the Italians, after a week of hard fighting, cleared the mountains above the ravine and dropped upon the hotel fort.

By June 9, 1915, the Italians had won the Falzarego Pass. At times the fighting raged on summits 10,000 feet high, where the thin air exhausted the combatants far quicker than their physical exertions. In the last battle of this engagement the Italians obtained a footing upon a point of great strategical importance three miles beyond the pass on the Sasso d'Istria, close to where the Dolomite road bends southward through the ravine and penetrated the mountains in two tunnels.

This victory gave the Austrians cause for anxiety regarding the western defenses of Tyrol, for by a double flanking movement along the Cordevole River and the Dolomite road the Italians in Cadore had extended like two arms around one of the principal systems of defense. General Dankl hurried reenforcements to the Cadore front to check the thrust up the Cordevole Valley. At the end of this valley was the focal point of the system of railways that carried food and munitions to both the Trentino forces and those in southern Tyrol. If the Italians had succeeded in cutting the railway at this point the enemy would have had great difficulty in maintaining his armies on the Trentino and Tyrol fronts. The Italian effort was not pushed to success; but it at least had the effect of discouraging any plans General Dankl might have formed of invading the plains of northern Italy at the foot of the frontier mountains.

Only twenty miles south of the Austrian outposts was the important city of Verona, famed for its memories of Romeo and Juliet. Nearer still was Brescia with the fertile lands of Lombardy surrounding it. But by his maneuvers at the opening of the war, General Cadorna effectively protected Italian territory and forced the enemy to devote all his attention to resisting the attacks of active light infantry and mountain artillery. The great 12-inch Skoda howitzers, upon which Austria depended to batter down the defenses of these Italian cities, were needed elsewhere, behind the Julian and Carnic Alps, and especially in the corner of the frontier near Predil Pass, by which Napoleon invaded Italy, and on the Isonzo front between Tolmino and the Adriatic.

Thus with his infantry, Cadorna overcame the artillery handicap under which Italy labored during all the first months of the war. The Skoda gun was reputed to be the best in the world. It had proved its worth in Belgium and Russia, and the fact that the Austrians were able to lend guns to their ally proved their wealth of big-gun power. Now, even after ten months of war, when thousands of the great howitzers were busy in Galicia and along the Danube, the Skoda works could still produce an armament superior to that of Italy. Much of the effectiveness of the Skoda gun lay in the fact that it could be separated into two parts for easier transportation. In addition to these 12-inch mortars, Austria had a 6-inch steel Skoda, designed in the summer of 1914, for use in the Carpathians and well adapted to fighting in the Alps. Due in part to their realization of this superiority of Austria in big guns, the Italians remained neutral for ten months, but meanwhile they had created a new armament for their own armies at full speed. For the attack on the Austrian infantry in the field they adapted the French 75-millimeter quick-firer, and for siege work they manufactured 6- and 12-inch howitzers. But it takes time to build heavy artillery, and at this time every armament firm in the world was pushed to its full capacity, while the Italians, being without coal fields, were handicapped in the development of armament resources at home. For political reasons also General Cadorna would not risk sacrificing his men to overcome this artillery handicap. His problem was to conserve his forces as much as possible in readiness for a defensive campaign against combined Teutonic armies, winning what small victories he could, and meanwhile keeping down his casualty lists, while fighting heavy howitzers with light mountain guns and 3-inch quick-firers.

After the Italians had established their hold upon the frontier points there was an apparent relaxation of effort while the infantry of the line waited for the heavy siege artillery to issue from the armament factories and come into action. This movement of artillery was slow, especially on the Isonzo front where engineering operations were delayed by the summer floods caused by the melting snows from the mountain tops. To transport heavy pieces of ordnance across the floods the Italian engineers had to build strong bridges, often under heavy fire from the enemy, who, even after their retirement from the east bank of the river, continually harassed the Italian advance guard holding the bridgeheads. The Austrians aided the work of the mountain floods by breaking down the high embankment used to carry off the snow water, and thereby inundated the plain. Working under a plunging fire from the enemy's batteries on the foothills, the Italian sappers built light pontoon bridges over the floods upon which the first Italian contingent crossed at night and occupied the first line of Austrian trenches near the river.

This much the Italians accomplished by the first week in June, 1915; but there they were forced to pause for the reasons already described. Active hostilities during the first part of June on the Isonzo front centered around Monfalcone, a seaport just below the dominating Carso headlands. Taken from Venice by the Austrians during the Napoleonic era, Monfalcone had become the third most important port in the empire. In its yards warships were being constructed.

On June 9, 1915, the Italians made their swift stroke in a southwesterly direction from their Isonzo line. The port was bombarded on June 7, 1915, by a light Italian cruiser squadron, and the Castle of Duino, standing at the sea edge near Trieste and defended by three artillery batteries, was shattered and set afire apparently to prepare for the operations against Monfalcone from the southwestern side of the Gulf of Panzano. Archduke Eugene hastily collected a strong force above Duino ready to resist an attempt by the Italians to land, but the attempt never was made. It developed that the bombardment of Duino was a feint.

The real movement against Monfalcone was launched from another quarter straight across the Isonzo. The Bersaglieri cyclist corps and grenadiers broke through the Austrian line at the river, and since the Austrians had neglected to prepare a reserve line, the Italians advanced by a swift, running fight through the villages around the Isonzo delta. Near the historic town of Aquileia, now a mere hamlet, the Italians forced a passage of the river at the point of the bayonet and flowed in two streams around the enemy's positions, depending for their rapid movements upon their cyclists with machine guns and their fast-marching light infantry. The Austrians set fire to the pine-clad mountain slopes, but were unable to stem the rush of the Italians who, under the flare of the forest fires, broke into the open town of Monfalcone after storming the promontory of Rocca.

Here, however, the Italian advance guard was in a dangerous position, for the Austrian batteries posted on the limestone bluffs rising 1,000 feet on the northern side of the town still dominated the streets occupied by the Italians near the water's edge. The situation was critical, not only because the troops in the lower town were in danger of annihilation if they held their ground, but because the Italians were anxious to save the town from bombardment, and preserve the warships under construction in the shipyards. So a brigade of light troops scaled the limestone cliffs dragging their mobile 3-inch guns, and forced the Austrians to retire, taking their heavy howitzers with them. Monfalcone now rested securely in Italian possession. The Italians in all this engagement lost only about 100 killed and wounded, while the enemy's casualties were estimated at 2,000. The loss stung the Austro-Hungarian Government deeply.

CHAPTER LXVII

ATTACKS IN GORIZIA

AFTER the Italian success in June, 1915, certain readjustments were manifest in the Austrian forces in the Italian theatre. Although there was no declaration of war between Italy and Germany, it was reported that German officers were sent to aid the Austrians, and that the forces of Archduke Eugene were progressively strengthened from this time on. German soldiers who joined the Austrian detachments were supposed to have volunteered in an irregular individual manner. In this manner Germany preserved the appearance of neutrality.

The latter part of June, 1915, found Austria occupied with the siege of Lemberg, and the archduke, apparently, was content to hold his own on the Italian front until a decision had been obtained in the more important operations against the Russians. Satisfied with their initial successes, General Cadorna on land and the Duke of Abruzzi at sea settled down to a slow, patient chess play, not unlike that worked out by General Joffre in France. Cadorna issued a statement to the Italian people in which he warned them that the preliminary successes which, he said, had made good the strategical defects of their frontier, would be followed by a long stage of gradual approaches against the enemy's second line.

The attrition of the Austro-Hungarian forces would be carried on by long-range artillery and sappers and local trench warfare with hand grenades. The Italian commander in chief resolutely refused to divert any part of his forces to the Dardanelles. Possible danger to Italian dominion in Tripoli, pointed out by the leaders of the Entente Powers, did not change his purpose to maintain a single concentrated front and not diffuse his efforts. The war with Austria, he believed, would be won or lost on the Italian frontier. His theory as to the best way to meet advances by the Teutonic allies in new fields was to increase pressure on their home frontiers where their interests were most vital. The Italian army in the field was increased to a million men, and, after the fall of Lemberg, Austria gradually moved more and more troops to the Alpine passes and the Isonzo, until by August she had 600,000 men facing the Italians, double the number arrayed on this front when Italy declared war. Had the Russians been able to hold out longer in Galicia, there is little doubt that Cadorna would have had something to show for the month of July besides a few local victories which did not vitally affect the main campaign.

On June 9, 1915, the capture of Gradisca completed the Italian control of the lower Isonzo, and Cadorna prepared for a general

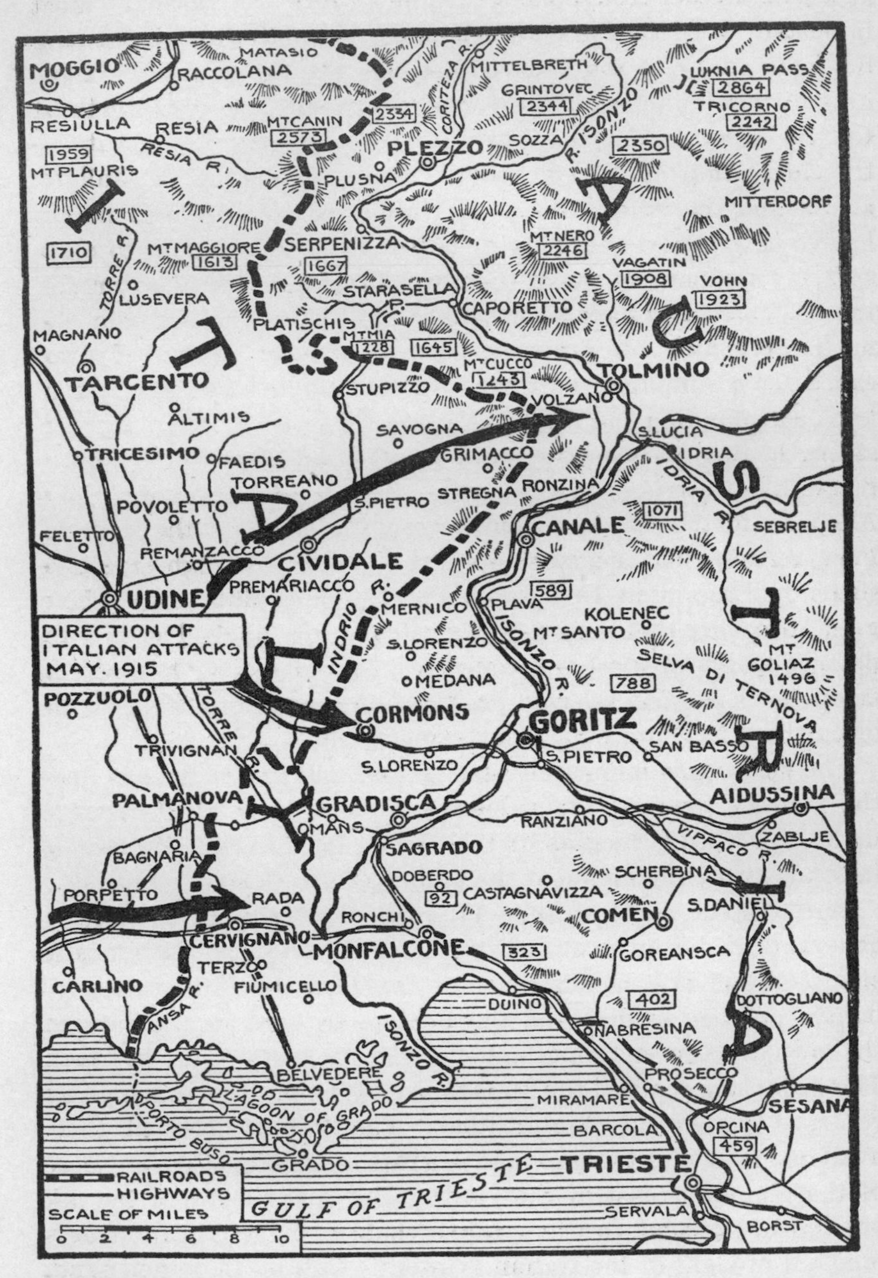

ITALIAN ATTACK ON AUSTRIA

attack on all the strongholds guarding Trieste. Of these the most important were the Carso tableland on the south, Gorizia barring the river-valley of the Vipacco between the Carso and the foothills of the Julian Alps, the fortified system of heights north of Gorizia surrounding the town of Tolmino, and the great intrenched camp of Tarvis above Tolmino extending to Malborghetto and the other Alps of Carinthia. These fortified points had to be attacked generally or not at all. Any attempt to mass an army against any one of them would have spelled disaster, for the Italians would have been flanked by Austrian forces from the north or south. A properly defined advance against Trieste called for a simultaneous thrust at Tolmino and the Tarvis fortress commanding the road to Vienna. The Austrians had been strengthening Tarvis ever since 1859, after Napoleon III overthrew the Austrians in the battles that freed Lombardy. The Austrian fortresses were again strengthened after the siege of Port Arthur had demonstrated the power of high-explosive shells, and again in 1910 when the Teutonic allies made their great discovery that their new giant howitzers laughed at modern defense works of steel and concrete. In remodeling her Alpine strongholds Austria selected positions on the plateau for systems of earthworks containing mobile siege guns.

The key to this immensely strong Austrian line of defense was the railway town of Plava on the eastern bank of the Isonzo under the wooded heights of the Ternovane Forest. Plava was in a salient occupying about the middle of the Austrian line.

Here, on the night of June 17, 1915, the Italians began their general offensive by an attack from Mount Korada on the opposite side of the river. Under cover of darkness the Italian sappers built a pontoon bridge, and the Bersaglieri crossed and carried the town and the surrounding heights at the point of the bayonet. The Austrians realized the importance of the position and quickly returned to a violent counterattack. The Italians threw all their available men into the gap, and a great battle raged on the edge of the highlands east of the river. The Austrians had the advantage of position, for their forces could be massed in the woodland out of sight of the Italian aviators. But, on the other hand, the Italian batteries on Mount Korada were able to pour a plunging fire into the lower tableland; and due mainly to the aid of their artillery the Italian troops drove back the enemy and maintained the ground won by the first dash.

General Cadorna was now in a position to begin a direct attack upon Gorizia. He assailed the Hill of Podgora, forming the barbican of the city's system of defenses and advanced a reconnoitering force toward Mount Fortin. Meanwhile he massed 500 pieces of artillery on the heights commanding the city. But the defenses of Gorizia had been well planned, and they proved their completeness by a long resistance covering a period that brought successive reports that the fortress had fallen. All these reports proved false. South of the city the Austrian intrenchments covered a front of more than ten miles, from the Mount of San Gabriele below Plava to Mount San Michele on the Carso tableland. The trenches were built in the most modern style, of concrete more than a yard thick covered with steel armor, against which ordinary shrapnel had no more effect than so much hail, and even high-explosive shells of medium power did little damage. The Italian weapons of attack were hand grenades and short knives, in the use of which the infantry were expert. Four army corps operating under the Duke of Aosta between Gorizia and the sea were beaten back by the Austrians with heavy losses. This victory so encouraged the archduke and chief lieutenant, General Boroevics, that they decided upon a counter-offensive in force. Therefore, as soon as the Italian attack slackened, the main Austrian army advanced across the Carso Plateau.

The series of battles that now followed were the first engagements of any size between the Italians and the Austro-Hungarians in the open field. They began June 22, 1915, and lasted until the close of July, with a short let-up at the end of the first week in July. The theatre included the whole Carso front, the Vipacco Valley, and the southern part of the Ternovane Forest. After his first repulse General Boroevics brought up fresh corps and renewed the attack, but in the end he was driven back to his main line with shattered forces.

In the Carso tableland the Austrians had as nearly perfect a position of natural defense as a general could choose. On the east of the Isonzo plain the broken, rocky wall rises in places to 1,000 feet, seamed with gullies and ravines, and bristling with forest growth which afforded ideal cover. The action of the rain has pitted the limestone with funnel-shaped holes which form natural redoubts for machine guns; and there are larger depressions and caves where heavier pieces of artillery may be placed in excellent shelter.

But while the Italians were unable to capture this position, when General Boroevics took his troops out of their defenses and sent them charging across the open ground, he found that the enemy had made good use of his precarious hold on the edges of the tableland. Although they occupied barely more than the rim of the plateau, with the flooded Isonzo a third of a mile broad beneath them, the Italians had strengthened their positions with sandbag intrenchments and hauled up a few pieces of light artillery.

The chief support of the infantry holding these sandbag defenses was the heavy guns across the river, which searched out the Austrian columns whenever they left cover. In weight of artillery the Italians had the advantage, for most of the Austrian 12-inch howitzers were busy in the Alps, and they had to depend mainly upon 6-inch pieces.

By the second week in July, 1915, the Austrians relaxed their efforts, and the Italians began a slow advance, working up the hills overlooking Gorizia by a variety of methods. In the places, comparatively few, where there was cultivated ground, they practiced the siege method of sapping forward, but generally their advance was over bare rock, where trenches could be excavated only by the use of dynamite, and when a charge was made the troops had to carry sandbags to build temporary cover from machine-gun fire. This method of warfare, in fact, was general throughout the whole mountain front, where the hard rock carried a mere veneer of earth, and sandbags had to serve for defense until the engineers could blast trenches and galleries in the flintlike face of the slopes.

The repulse of the Austrian counterattack in the middle of July, 1915, ended the first phase of the battle of Gorizia. On July 18th, 19th and 20th, General Cadorna delivered a fierce assault aided by knowledge gained in the first stage of the battle, which, for the Italians, was little more than a reconnaissance in force. For three days and nights he drove the troops of his combined Second and Third Armies against the enemy's lines all along the Isonzo. His system was to attack by day and then at night resist the enemy's couterassaults on his newly won positions. The Italians retained all the ground they won during these days of terrific fighting, and captured 3,500 prisoners.

By the 20th of July their confidence had increased to such an extent that they determined upon a night assault. But next morning Cadorna received word from his aeroplane scouts and his spies that the enemy was massing for a supreme effort. The Italian advance was stayed and every man was set at work helping the engineers strengthen the trenches.

On July 21, 1915, there came a complete lull. The next day the Austrians opened their attack with a concentrated bombardment. During the period of Italian advance the railways had been piling up the Austrian shells and German gunners had been sent by the Crown Prince of Bavaria to help serve the heavy howitzers rushed to the Carso from the Julian Alps and the Tyrol and Trentino salients. With the design to cut the Italian line of communication, the main Austrian infantry attack was delivered toward Gradisca where the Italians had constructed their principal bridges across the Isonzo. The infantry massed behind the neighboring hills and under cover of a tremendous artillery bombardment advanced in close formation. The first line of Italian troops seemed about to be swept away when the gunners on the heights across the river got the range and poured into the advancing Austrians a massed fire from all their 500 pieces. General Boroevics's advance was pounded to pieces; the Italians brought up reenforements and charged and captured the lines from which the Austrians had delivered their assault, taking 2,000 prisoners.

A cloud of poisonous gas released by Italian troops from tanks concealed in the thicket

On July 23, 1915, the archduke ordered another attack upon the Italian positions near the sea on the edge of the Carso tableland. This was really an effort to recapture Monfalcone; but it failed, although the Italians did not dare risk pursuit over the rough ground. Later two Austrian divisions, advancing from San Michele and San Martino against Sagrado were repulsed with heavy losses.

By July 25, 1915, the Italians were able to attack and capture some of the intrenchments on the slopes of San Martino and to storm Sei Busi. This hill of Sei Busi witnessed some of the most sanguinary fighting of the whole series of engagements. On a single day it was won, lost and won again by the Italians, both sides bringing up strong reenforcements and concentrating against the summit all the artillery within range. Over the crest of San Michele which dominated a large part of the tableland the battle surged for many days.

On July 27, 1915, the Italians, attacking with bombs and bayonets were able to occupy the summit, but could not establish themselves there in the face of the enemy's bombardment. The lower slopes they were able to hold behind their sandbag intrenchments, but the crest, swept by the enemy's heavy artillery and offering no shelter, was absolutely untenable. In all this fighting artillery played the major rôle. The Italians charged that Archduke Eugene, realizing that any infantry advance against this terrific gunfire was a certain sacrifice of men, placed in his van regiments of men from the Italian-speaking provinces and from Old Serbia and Croatia. In this position these troops were exposed to fire from their own batteries with the knowledge that any attempt at treachery meant annihilation by their own guns in the rear. No figures as to the number of men from the "unredeemed" provinces forced to fight against their kinsmen on the frontier are obtainable. Italian writers, however, maintain that during the first months of the war Austrian infantrymen of Latin and Slav origin were sacrificed by the hundred thousand around Gorizia and Trento.

Like other great drives of the Allies on the French front, the Italian offensive on the chain of forts guarding Gorizia failed to break the enemy's resistance. The fighting, however, seasoned the untried troops of General Cadorna and won them praise even from the veterans of General Boroevics and from Boroevics himself. "I cannot refrain from saying," declared the Austrian General in an interview published in a Hungarian newspaper, "that the bravery of the Italian regiments was almost incredible, for even if certain regiments lost all their officers, this did not deter them from advancing with the greatest contempt for death."

CHAPTER LXVIII

FIGHTING IN THE ALPS—ITALIAN SUCCESSES

LEAVING the situation on the Isonzo where it rested at the close of July, 1915, in a condition virtually of stalemate, we return to the still more picturesque struggle in the Alps. While the Italian Third Army in massed assault was making its unsuccessful fight for possession of Gorizia with Trieste as its ultimate objective, warfare was in progress in a hundred places in the Julian, Carnic, Dolomite, Trentino and Tyrolean mountains. Although along this part of the frontier the Italians inflicted no vital harm upon the enemy during the first two months of the war, they were successful in a multitude of minor enterprises, each of which furnishes its stirring tale of hand-to-hand fighting, individual heroism and novel expedients in a country singularly adapted to some of the methods of primeval warfare. Being on the defensive, the Austrians frequently made use of the primitive ambush of mountain tribes. Loose, heavy bowlders were lashed to the edge of a precipice and masked with pine branches. Then when the enemy passed along the mountain path beneath, the wires holding the rocks in place were cut, releasing a deadly avalanche upon the advancing foe.

Any description of the fighting on this Alpine front becomes by necessity a catalogue of apparently isolated operations, for the nature of the ground negatived any great battle in force such as that along the Isonzo River. In the Julian Alps the Italian mountaineers gained a lucky success early in June. General Rohr, the Austrian commander, had set two companies to guard a rampart of rock between Tolmino and Monte Nero. The position was so strong that a few hundred men with Maxims and quick-firers could have held it against an army corps. Its strength, in fact, was so apparent that the Austrians took their duties too lightly. Leaving only a few sentries on watch, both companies enjoyed plenty of sleep at night. But one night the Italian Alpinists climbed silently over the mountain, killed the enemy's sentries with knives before they could make an outcry and coming upon the two companies from the rear captured them with scarcely a struggle.

The peak of Monte Nero, a stump-shaped mountain 7,370 feet high at the headwaters of the Isonzo, proved important to the Italians, for it gave them a fire-control station from which 12-inch shells were dropped into the forts of Tolmino and the southern forts of Tarvis. North of Monte Nero, where the boundary turns to the west, is the important pass of Predil, the gateway to Tarvis, guarded on the southeast by the fortress of Flitsch and on the west by Malborghetto. These two positions were the strongest points in a great ring of fortified heights protecting the pass and the highway and railroad running through an angle of the Julian Alps into the heart of Austria. The forts of Malborghetto projected into Italian territory and its chief works, Fort Hensel, a great white oblong of armored concrete, was visible miles away in the Italian mountains. Against this system of fortifications the Italians brought their heaviest howitzers and demonstrated, as satisfactorily as the Germans had shown months earlier at Liege, that the strongest forts were no match for modern artillery. Fort Hensel and the other permanent forts were shattered and the ground around them was pitted with great craters from explosions of the 12-inch shells.

The final ruin of Fort Hensel was accomplished by a shell which penetrated through the thickest of its steel and concrete layers and exploded in its ammunition magazine. This bombardment of Malborghetto necessitated firing mortar shells at a high angle completely over mountains which hid the target from the Italian gunners. The work of destruction was slow owing to the fact that mists often curtained the mountain tops and forced the gunners to cease operations, because to fire while the observers were unable to watch every shot and telephone the results would have been only a waste of ammunition.

But the Austrians already knew that their forts were no match for 12-inch howitzers, once these great guns could get into position, and they had prepared another method of defense which they put into use as soon as the forts were destroyed. Batteries of Skodas, hidden in a stretch of pasture land below the summit of the mountain, were brought up and placed in pits concealed by tufts of grass and brush from reconnoitering airmen, while at a safe distance dummy guns were displayed to draw the Italians' fire. Thus one of the greatest artillery duels of the whole front continued day after day, neither side being able to see the enemy and relying for information upon observers posted on mountain tops and in aeroplanes. These 12-inch guns were not intended for such work. They had been laboriously hauled to their lofty emplacements five and six thousand feet above sea level to destroy 6-inch batteries, as these 6-inch guns had been brought up to overpower the lighter 3-inch mountain guns, some of which the Italians worked from peaks as high as 10,000 feet. When both sides got these monster howitzers into position the natural sequence was a deadlock. The most the infantry could do was to drive the enemy's troops from summits valuable as observation points in the service of the heavy artillery.

Thus the official reports issued by the Austrian and Italian staff headquarters reiterated the names of peaks hitherto unknown to the traveler and tourist mountaineer, peaks which became of immense importance now, not so much on account of their height as because they commanded the best views of the surrounding territory. One of these was Freikofel. The Alpini captured it early in the war with scarcely a struggle and then or weeks the Austrians sacrificed regiments and even brigades n vain attempts to recover it.

The loss of Freikofel by the Austrians was followed, on June 4, 1915, by the loss of Cresta Verde, and then in the first week f July the Italians captured the important observation peak of ;ellenkofel. This mountain was held by the Austrians with a orce of only forty men, but in view of its extraordinary position his squad was considered sufficient. The slopes below them vere swept by a battery of their mountain guns, in telephonic ommunication with the more distant howitzer battery upon vhich it could call for assistance if necessity arose, and a large nfantry reserve was stationed in the wooded valley below. But ne night twenty-nine Alpini crept up the almost sheer precipice , thousand feet high that separated them from the Austrian lefenders. They carried ropes and a machine gun and just as he moon rose they attained the summit, set up their Maxim and pened fire. Every man in the observation station was shot down.

Then followed a desperate fight with the Austrian mountain attery on the reverse slope. But thanks to their machine gun he Italians were able to break up the enemy's charge and as lay broke they captured the Austrians' guns and drove the men who served them down the mountain. When the Austrian eserves arrived the Italians had intrenched themselves on the outhern slope and were able to make use of the captured guns. The attacks of the reserves were repulsed and the Italians held he mountain.

CHAPTER LXIX

MORE MOUNTAIN FIGHTING—RESULTS OF FIRST CAMPAIGN

AT the western end of the rugged battle front, the Italian mountain troops, after the first advance, were less successful than the troops of Cadorna in the Carnic and Julian Alps. Here the fighting mountaineers of Tyrol redeemed their reputation by a daring stroke. The scene of this brilliant operation was close above the Tonale Pass, the site of one of the greatest glaciers in Europe. From Presanella to Care the ice extends in a gleaming crescent for more than twenty miles. Its broadest part stretches for six miles to Monte Adamello, 11,640 feet high. The paths over or by these glaciers had been seized and fortified by the Italians and their line along this front lay mostly within Italian territory. In mid-July a force of Tyroleans found a new track through the ice and before the Italians, engrossed with operations elsewhere, knew what they were doing they had penetrated several miles into Italian lands. The Italians met the invaders at the famous Garibaldi Hut owned by the Italian Alpine Club just beneath Mount Adamello and checked the advance, although the Austrians retained some of the peaks commanding the Hut.

Just north of the Adamello group of peaks in the upper part of the Giudicari Valley extending to Lake Garda the Italians took one of the northern passes by surprise and advanced toward the forts defending Riva and Arco. Eventually they won all the country south of the Ledro Valley with a series of fierce artillery duels. A similar advance was made east of Lake Garda and down the Lagarina Valley. The forward movement was signalized by engineering feats comparable, in their mastery of the human hand over the forces of nature, only to the building of the Pyramids. The great siege guns weighing many tons were hoisted to the top of cloud-piercing summits solely by man power. Every bit of ammunition and supplies had to be brought up by the same laborious method. At Col di Lana the Austrians had an intricate series of works excavated deep in the solid rock. High explosive shells and hand bombs were useless against this defense, but Colonel Garibaldi, a grandson of the great Italian Liberator, found a way to drive the Austrians out of their position. He mustered a corps of engineers who had helped drill the great railway tunnels on the Swiss frontier and under his direction they tunneled right through the mountain into the Austrian galleries on the reverse slope. When the fumes of the last charge of blasting dynamite cleared away a letachment of bomb carriers leaped through the jagged hole, lrove the enemy from their galleries, and, constantly fed by supporting troops, cleared their way up and down the mountain.

The first of August, 1915, found the Italians holding the Ausrian outpost positions they had taken during June and July; out the Austrian main defenses from one end of the frontier to he other, a distance of more than 300 miles, were virtually intact. t must be borne in mind, however, that the Italian General Staff at this period of the war never contemplated any general offensive except on the Isonzo River. Although their attack along the Isonzo did not attain its object of reducing the main lefenses of Trieste and Gorizia, proved too hard a nut to crack, he Italians here won a series of minor victories against great odds and, to the Italian mind at least, demonstrated the valor of the army and the effectiveness of the new artillery which boded well for the future.

It has been pointed out that in these operations General Cadorna had to consider other things besides the immediate problems facing his troops. The Italo-Austrian warfare was but a small factor in the great plan of the Entente allies, who as the war progressed, realized more and more the importance of cooperative action. All that happened in Galicia, Poland, Lithuania and Courland had a direct influence upon Cadorna's plans. Russian reverses and the failure of all attempts by the French and British to break the German line in France and Belgium made the Italian commander cautious. The series of Teutonic victories made it possible that at any time he might have to face an overwhelming host of Austrians and Germans equipped with artillery which he could not hope to equal and backed by an apparently limitless supply of ammunition. For political reasons, also, he could not risk, even in the hope of reaching Trieste, sacrificing his men in an offensive costing anything like the quantities of human material being used up each day in other theatres. His preponderance of troops at the opening of operations in May was gradually reduced. But the enemy's positions and his superior artillery offset the Italian's greater numbers. On the whole it may be said that the Italians accomplished quite as much as any of their allies. They penetrated farther into the Alps and the rugged tableland west of Trieste than the British and French with their colonials did into the hills of Gallipoli or into the ridge of the Lille region, and the length of their thrusts was greater than the French advances in Artois and Champagne.

The Italians were more successful in concealing the extent of their losses than most of the other belligerents. A conservative estimate places their total casualty list between the last week in May and the first of August, 1915, at 25,000. The Austrians in the same period on the same front lost about 15,000 dead, 50,000 wounded and 15,000 prisoners. The slight Italian losses compared with their enemy's is remarkable in view of the fact that they were almost constantly on the offensive. By far the greater portion of the casualties were suffered in the east, during the two assaults on the defenses of Gorizia.

Measuring the territory gained during these two months and comparing it with the concessions offered by Austria as the price of Italy's neutrality—on this basis the Italians had no cause to regret their decision. On the Venetian Plain by the lower Isonzo a few thousand men in two days with comparatively small loss conquered all the territory which the Italian nation had been offered for keeping out of war. This conquered territory, however, was far less than the prize the Italian King and his Cabinet set before the eyes of the people when they declared war.

PART X—THE DARDANELLES AND TURKEY

CHAPTER LXX

BEGINNING OF OPERATIONS

DURING the month of January, 1915, the British and French naval authorities came to a decision to attempt a naval attack upon the Dardanelles. It was decided, too, to lose no time in the matter, but to push the campaign with all speed. Undoubtedly, behind this decision there were many political factors of a grave kind because, on the face of it, there were many reasons why the attack should have been delayed until fine weather. Once having come to a decision, no time was lost. The Island of Tenedos was seized, and under an agreement with Venizelos, the Greek Premier, the island of Lemnos was occupied. In the latter the large harbor of Mudros offered an ideal naval and military base for operations against the Dardanelles, overcoming one of the chief original handicaps of the allied command, distance of base from scene of operations. Lemnos was less than fifty miles from the tip of the Gallipoli Peninsula, while Tenedos was but twenty-two miles away, lying close to the Turkish coast. At these two depots a considerable Anglo-French naval squadron was rapidly collected. They came from all parts of the world.

The elimination of the German commerce raiders from the high seas, and the obvious intentions of the main German and Austrian fleets to avoid a general action against overwhelming odds, freed a large number of allied, and especially British, warships of secondary fighting value.

By the middle of February, 1915, the rendezvous was complete. Besides the ships belonging to the British and French Mediterranean fleets, there had arrived, fresh from the battle of the Falkland Islands, the *Inflexible*, a dreadnought battle cruiser. The *Queen Elizabeth*, too, arrived, the newest and strongest of the ships of the whole British navy. It is evident that great reliance had been placed on the enormous gun power of this vessel, it being hoped that her great 15-inch pieces would blow the Dardanelles defenses to pieces, somewhat in the way the gigantic German land guns had blown the Belgian forts into fragments. In no other way is it possible to explain the risking of this capital ship in the highly dangerous operations in the Ægean sea.

In addition to the *Queen Elizabeth* and the *Inflexible*, the British force included the *Agamemnon*, the *Irresistible*, the *Vengeance*, the *Triumph*, the *Albion*, the *Lord Nelson*, the *Ocean* and the *Majestic*. The French ships numbered the *Charlemagne*, the *Gaulois*, the *Suffern*, and the *Bouvet*.

Early in the morning of February 19, 1915, these vessels, under the supreme command of Vice Admiral Sackville Carden, and with Rear Admiral Guépratte in command of the French division, arrived off the Gallipoli Peninsula. At 8 a. m. they opened an intense bombardment of the several forts. At first they battered away at the Turks at long range but finally, about the middle of the afternoon, the *Vengeance*, *Cornwallis* and *Triumph* of the British forces, and the *Suffern*, *Gaulois* and *Bouvet* of the French fleet, closed in upon the Turkish forts which were still replying. It was not until darkness that all the land batteries had been apparently silenced.

At this time, and throughout the various attempts to reduce the Dardanelles forts by naval bombardment, there was considerable difficulty in making the demolition permanent. On the following morning a detachment of the Naval Flying Corps made a reconnaissance and discovered that the damage was not as great as had been hoped. Accordingly, preparations were made to give the Turks another dose of the 12-inch guns. Before this could be done bad weather intervened.

On February 25, 1915, there was a further bombardment and by five o'clock in the evening all the forts again had been silenced. Mine sweeping operations were then begun. For this work English-Scotch trawlers from the North Sea had been brought down and the crews of these little unprotected boats added many pages of heroism to the book of great deeds of the Dardanelles operations.

The following day a division of the battleship fleet entered the straits for a distance of four miles, the mine sweepers having cleared the channel for that distance. The *Albion, Vengeance* and *Majestic* opened fire with their 12-inch guns on Fort Dardanos, a battery mounting nothing but 5.9-inch guns, situated on the Asiatic shore some distance below the Narrows. Fort Dardanos bravely replied, however, until put out of action, as did several concealed batteries, the presence of which the British and French had not suspected.

With the completion of this operation the allied command believed they had not only permanently silenced the forts guarding the entrance to the Dardanelles but had, as well, made both sides of the straits then too warm for the Turkish troops. Accordingly forces of marines were landed to complete the work of demolition. They were successful except at Kum Kale where the Turks proved to have maintained a large force. The British landing party was driven back to its boats in a hurry after suffering a score of casualties.

The apparent success of these naval operations raised high hopes in Great Britain and in the other allied countries. The British Government, which had established a censorship for all news that might tend to depress the British public, saw no reason for interfering to prevent the publication of news that might tend unduly in the other direction. The newspapers and the so-called military experts gave the public what they evidently wanted. The attack upon the Dardanelles, according to the majority of these, was practically over. A few voices of warning were raised, but they were immediately silenced as "croakers" and "pessimists" and even "pro-Germans." Absurd reports of consternation and panic in Constantinople were sent broadcast throughout Great Britain, and thence to the whole world. Thousands of Turks, in abject fear, were pictured as spending most of their days and nights on the housetops of the sacred city, anxiously awaiting the first glimpse of the victorious allied fleet sailing up the Golden Horn. Hundreds of thousands were said to be fleeing into Asia Minor and preparations were being made by the sultan and his government to follow suit.

Meanwhile, nothing of the kind was happening, either in Gallipoli or in Constantinople. The German and Turkish authorities, confident in their ability to hold the straits against all the forces that could be brought against it, were quietly perfecting their plans. Bad weather again interrupted the Allies' operations, and it was not until March 1, 1915, that the *Triumph*, *Ocean* and *Albion* again entered the straits, and bombarded Fort Dardanos (once more active), and the concealed shore batteries. The same night the mine sweepers, under the protection of destroyers, cleared an additional five miles of the channel, and the waters were safe up to within a mile and a half of the entrance to the Narrows.

About the same time the two French squadrons bombarded the Bulair lines, where the Gallipoli Peninsula connects with the mainland, in an attempt to interrupt the Turks' supply of troops and ammunition.

On the following day, March 2, 1915, the *Canopus*, *Swiftsure* and *Cornwallis* drew close into Fort Dardanos and opened fire. By so doing they got within range of the Turkish batteries in the pine woods just below the Kilid Bahr plateau and all three boats were hit.

For the next few days the bombardment of various Turkish positions and batteries was continued. On the afternoon of March 4, 1915, a large landing party was put ashore at Kum Kale and Sedd-el-Bahr to complete the demolition of the works. That on the Asiatic shore again had a hard time and was driven off by a Turkish force after doing only small damage. The force on the European side also found that the Turks had quickly returned to the tip of the peninsula as soon as the fire of the warships had ceased.

On the following day there occurred at Smyrna an incident that is hard to explain. Even British experts have not made any attempt to solve the puzzle. Vice Admiral Peirse with a British and French fleet, appeared off the city and opened a bombardment. The Turkish command did not reply and, after doing considerable damage, Peirse and his ships sailed away. He made no attempt to land, indeed he is not believed to have had a force for that purpose with him. The only reasonable explanation of the bombardment is that it was in the nature of a diversion intended to keep as many troops as possible from Gallipoli.

In the Dardanelles the operations were rapidly coming to a head. The Anglo-French command believed the time had now arrived for an attack in force upon the forts at the Narrows, the real defenses of the straits. Accordingly, on March 6, 1915, the *Albion, Prince George*, the *Vengeance*, the *Majestic* and the *Suffern* steamed well up the straits and opened a direct fire on the big forts. It was not upon the work of these ships, however, that great hopes rested. A new experiment was being tried from the Gulf of Saros on the other side of the Peninsula of Gallipoli, at the same time. With their long range guns the *Queen Elizabeth*, the *Agamemnon*, and the *Ocean* stood well out and, by indirect fire, threw shell after shell over the heights of the peninsula into the land works. All the while circling aeroplanes, under the constant fire of the Turkish antiaircraft guns, watched and corrected the firing, while a captive balloon, sent up from the *Agamemnon*, did additional and valuable service in this respect.

It was found that, because of the angle of fire of the big naval guns, it was not possible to score any hits from the Gulf of Saros on the Turkish forts on the European side of the straits and the attempt was soon abandoned. Modern big gun ammunition was too expensive to be lightly thrown away. Furthermore, the life of one of the big guns of these battleships is strictly limited, especially if full charges are being used. Ultimately, the three battleships in the Gulf shifted their fire to the forts near Chanak, on the Asiatic side, where the works were on low ground, almost at sea level.

It was confidently hoped that, by means of this indirect fire, it would be possible to put the 14-inch guns of these forts out of action, without giving them a chance to reply. The idea of trying to force a way past these great guns, exposing the relatively frail sides of precious battleships to their direct fire, was not relished by the allied command.

But if the Turks could not reply to the fire of the three battleships in the Gulf of Saros with their 14-inch guns, they could and did do effective work with smaller guns concealed on the heights of the peninsula overlooking the gulf, and the *Queen Elizabeth* was hit three times.

On the following day, March 7, the attack was renewed. The four French battleships, the *Charlemagne, Gaulois,* the *Bouvet* and the *Suffern* took the post of greatest danger inside the straits and finally again silenced the Dardanos fort. The *Agamemnon* and the *Lord Nelson,* behind them, made a long range attack upon the forts fringing the Narrows. Three of the allied battleships, the *Gaulois,* the *Agamemnon* and the *Lord Nelson* were hit by Turkish shells but, as an offset, it was believed that the great forts at Chanak, as well as the works at Dardanos, had been permanently silenced.

This confidence, as we shall see later on, was not justified. Inside the great forts, it is true, the Turks and their German officers were suffering terribly from the bombardment. That they stood it in some cases for periods of seven hours at a stretch, and continued firing effectively for the whole of that time, is testimony to their courage and devotion to duty. As the great shells of the *Queen Elizabeth* landed in the forts they did frightful havoc. The shrapnel shells contained something like 12,000 separate bullets and it is on record that one of these shells wounded or killed no less than 250 Turkish soldiers. As the high explosive shells struck the works and exploded they threw up tons of earth and cement a hundred feet in the air, plainly visible to the allied observers on the warships in the straits.

But this was not the worst that the defenders had to endure. The exploding shells gave off poisonous gases that filled the underground passages of the redoubts. The heroic Turks worked under such conditions as long as it was humanly possible, but eventually their German officers were compelled to withdraw their men from each fort in turn to allow the gases to clear away. These circumstances undoubtedly account for the fact that almost every one of the forts was reported permanently silenced, only to resume action a few days later, much to the surprise and consternation of the allied command.

Furthermore, there is abundant evidence that the Turks were economizing ammunition, especially big gun shells. They had made up their minds that there would be a direct naval attack upon the forts sooner or later, and their instructions were to reserve their fire "until they saw the whites of the enemy's eyes," so to speak.

From March 6 to March 18, 1915, there was a lull in activity at the straits. Momentous events were transpiring in London and at the island of Lemnos, and upon the outcome of these events depended the future course of the operations at the Dardanelles. While the individual ships of his fleet conducted minor bombardments intended to harass the Turks, Vice Admiral Carden, pleading ill health, had been allowed to relinquish the command of the allied fleet, and Vice Admiral John de Robeck, newly promoted to his rank, succeeded him. Almost immediately the latter steamed away to Mudros to engage in a fateful conference.

CHAPTER LXXI

PREPARATIONS FOR LANDING—COMPOSITION OF FORCES

IT had evidently been the intention of the Allies to force the Narrows by naval power, and then follow up the success by an occupation of Gallipoli by a land force. For this purpose the troops solicited of Venizelos, the Greek Premier, were undoubtedly to be used, but sole reliance was not to be placed upon them. For one thing, the Allies had no intention of allowing Greece to assume too great an importance in the campaign against Constantinople, well knowing that the Greek people had large ambitions in that part of the world—ambitions that clashed with those of more important powers.

In early March, 1915, the French were busy concentrating an expeditionary force in North Africa, under the command of General d'Amade. By March 15 the French force had been gathered together at Bizerta, in the Ægean Sea. At the same time the British Government had been undertaking a similar concentration, and by the third week in March a force estimated at about 120,000 men had arrived in transports at Mudros in the island of Lemnos. This English force consisted of the Twenty-ninth Division, the Royal Naval Division, a special force formed by Winston Churchill, British Secretary to the Admiralty, and used in the attempt to relieve Antwerp, the Australian and New Zealand divisions originally brought to Egypt, a Territorial division, and some Indian forces.

These troops, with the comparatively small French force under General d'Amade, were placed under the command of one of the most popular of British officers—General Sir Ian Hamilton.

Sir Ian Hamilton and his staff were hurried from London by special trains and a fast cruiser steaming upward of 30 knots an hour. By the time he reached Mudros the French troops had also arrived from Bizerta.

The island of Lemnos presented a strange and picturesque spectacle when all these troops, drawn from so many distant parts of the world, were gathered in the sheltering bay. The blue and red of the Frenchmen's uniforms, the khaki of the British, the native costumes of the Indian and North African troops contrasted strangely. Mixing freely with them and driving hard bargains, were the native Greek tradesmen. All over the little town thousands of temporary huts and shops and tents sprang up for the supply of the needs of the troops.

Out in the harbor hundreds of ships of every description were moored. There were battleships, cruisers, torpedo boats, submarines, transports, supply boats, barges, picket boats, and dozens of Greek trading vessels. Into all this mess and chaos came the British commander.

Then followed a long conference with General d'Amade, Admiral de Robeck, and Admiral Guépratte. There does not seem to be any reason for doubting that the plan was to launch a land attack upon the Gallipoli defenses immediately. But General Hamilton demurred. He inspected the loading of the transports, and refused to give the order for an attack until grave defects had been remedied. Of this period he wrote subsequently:

"I knew that nothing but a thorough and systematic scheme for flinging the whole of the troops under my command very rapidly ashore could be expected to meet with success."

The slightest delay in landing, Sir Ian Hamilton realized, would prove terribly costly, if not absolutely fatal. He and his troops were embarking on a campaign opening with a feat of arms for which there was no precedent in history. He did not intend that there should be the slightest chance of failure if forethought and intelligent preparation could prevent it.

The prime obstacle to an immediate descent of the allied land forces upon Gallipoli Sir Ian Hamilton found to be the manner in which the British transports had been loaded. The only consideration that seems to have been present in the minds of the military authorities who superintended the work was the question of getting the material and men aboard the ships. The supplies, artillery, and ammunitions had all been loaded without any consideration as to which was to come off the boats first. Material absolutely necessary for the protection of the troops once they had landed on hostile shores, and vital in any attempt to press home the advantage thus gained, was buried under tents, hut parts, cooking material, etc.

"I cannot go ahead with a transport fleet in this condition," said General Hamilton in substance to his French and English colleagues. "The whole fleet must return to Egypt and be reloaded."

"But time," urged Admiral de Robeck. "It will take weeks of valuable time."

"Better lose time than run straight to certain disaster," declared General Hamilton.

And back to Alexandria went the whole fleet of transports, with the exception of a few vessels carrying the Australian Infantry Brigade, which, by some miracle, had been properly loaded.

When General Hamilton and his soldiers sailed out of Mudros Harbor, bound for Alexandria, Admiral de Robeck came to a momentous and historic decision. Acting either on his own responsibility or under orders or advice of some superior authority, he decided not to wait for the troops, but to make a determined attack upon the Narrows with his whole fleet. By sheer weight of guns he would try to run past the great forts that lined the 1,500-yard channel, pounding his way through on the theory that "what will not bend must break."

March 18, 1915, was an ideal day for such an heroic attempt. The sailors of the allied fleet were called to quarters as the morning sun, in a perfect sky, arose over the towering hills that lined the straits. Briefly the officers addressed the men, told them of the work ahead, spoke of the glory that awaited them if successful, and ordered each man to his post.

The reader, in order to gain some definite idea of the defenses that were to be attacked, should take up a map showing the Dardanelles. He will find, about ten miles from the entrance, a narrow channel where the shores of Asia and Europe almost touch. There, at the narrowest point of the channel, the Turks had built their chief defenses. On the south slope of the Kalid Bahr were three powerful works. The Rumeli Medjidieh Battery mounted two 11-inch, four 9.4-inch, and five 3.4-inch guns. The Hamidieh II Battery had two 14-inch, while the Namazieh Battery had one 11-inch, one 10.2-inch, eleven 9.4-inch, three 8.2-inch, and three 5.9-inch guns.

On the Asiatic side of the Narrows, near Chanak, was a system of redoubts of equal strength. The Hamidieh I Battery, south of Chanak, consisted of two 14-inch and seven 9.4-inch guns, while the Hamidieh III Battery possessed two 14-inch, one 9.4-inch, one 8.2-inch, and four 5.9-inch guns.

Besides all these formidable defenses there were many minor positions on the very edge of the Narrows. In fact the whole channel, and the way of the allied fleet to the Sea of Marmora, lay through rows upon rows of high-power guns.

The disastrous naval attack upon the big forts at the Narrows, resulting, as it did, in the loss of three battleships and the disabling of others, convinced the British and French naval authorities that it was hopeless to expect success along that line, except at a price that they could ill afford to pay, and that would have a terribly depressing effect upon public opinion at home.

Admiral de Robeck and his British "bulldogs" were called off to await the coming of Sir Ian Hamilton and his mixed expeditionary force. This force, while the 12- and 15-inch guns of the Anglo-French fleet had been vainly battering the Dardanelles forts, had returned to Alexandria, and, under the careful supervision of Sir Ian Hamilton and General d'Amade, had been reshipped aboard the great transport fleet.

At this point there appears to have arisen a serious misunderstanding between Great Britain and France as to the exact number of troops to be supplied by each. Although the true facts have not yet come to light, it is believed that General Joffre emphatically refused to detach any of the French troops from the western front. The force that France eventually contributed to the allied army at the Dardanelles consisted of units not at that time in view for service in northern France. These numbered a small detachment of Fusiliers Marines, a section of the Armée Coloniale, and the Foreign Legion, a force made up of volunteers from all over the world, enlisted for service anywhere, and generally assigned to a post of unusual danger.

Great Britain was, therefore, under the necessity of providing the bulk of the troops.

The British authorities did not make the mistake of throwing raw troops into the initial struggle at the Dardanelles. The backbone of the force supplied to General Sir Ian Hamilton was the Twenty-ninth Division of Regulars, made up largely of the hardiest of England's youth—the north countrymen. It comprised the Eighty-sixth Brigade of Infantry—Second Royal Fusiliers, First

Lancashire Fusiliers, First Royal Munster Fusiliers, and the First Royal Dublin Fusiliers; the Eighty-seventh Brigade—Second South Wales Borderers, First King's Own Scottish Borderers, First Royal Inniskilling Fusiliers, and First Border Regiment; the Eighty-eighth Brigade—Second Hampshires, Fourth Worcesters, First Essex, and the Fifth Royal Scots, the latter a Territorial battalion. Attached to this force of infantry was a squadron of the Surrey Yeomanry and two batteries of the Fourth Mountain Brigade, a Highland artillery unit.

To the command of these regular troops, Major General Hunter-Weston was appointed. This officer had been through much of the early fighting in the western theatre, originally commanding the Eleventh Brigade of the Third Corps of General French's army. His appointment to the Dardanelles was in the nature of a promotion, it being recognized that his dash and energy would be useful in the style of warfare that would govern the battle for the straits.

In addition to the regular troops brought out from England, there was the Naval Division. This force had seen a bit of action in the attempt to save Antwerp. It consisted of two Naval Brigades and a Royal Marine Brigade.

Also there was a Territorial Division, known as the East Lancashires, under the command of Major General Douglas. Immediately upon the outbreak of war this division had volunteered for foreign service and had been shipped to Egypt, where it had had six months' training. It comprised the Fifth, Sixth, Seventh, and Eighth Lancashire Fusiliers, the Fourth and Fifth East Lancashires, the Ninth and Tenth Manchesters, the Fifth, Sixth, Seventh, and Eighth Manchesters.

These troops, with the inclusion of the Australian and New Zealand forces brought to Egypt at the beginning of the war, under the command of Lieutenant General Birdwood, and a considerable number of Indian troops, made up the force at the disposal of Sir Ian Hamilton. They numbered in all, with the French troops, about 120,000 men.

What had the Turkish authorities to set against this army, supported by the great fleet of battleships and unlimited number of transports and subsidiary vessels? Estimates of the potential strength of the Turkish army available for service in and about the Gallipoli Peninsula at this time vary widely. There were those, for instance, who claimed that, if necessary, the Turks could command at least 600,000 troops for the defense of the straits, and that any attempt to capture the positions with the force supplied to Sir Ian Hamilton was doomed to failure. On the other hand were those who claimed that the Turks were short of equipment and ammunition, and had no means of replenishment; that they had no heart in the fight; that they were already in revolt against their German taskmasters; that the Suez and Caucasus defeats had undermined their morale and depleted their numbers, and that the Turkish high command had decided that it was useless to attempt to defend the position. Evidently, neither of these two extremes represented the situation, and the best evidence points to the conclusion that, for the defense of the Dardanelles, from first to last, the Turks depended upon about 200,000 men with reenforcements brought up from time to time to refill the ranks. Probably when the great landing took place only a small proportion of the Turkish troops were in Gallipoli.

These troops were under the command of the German General Liman von Sanders, although, from time to time in the operations, the picturesque figure of Enver Pasha appeared. Admiral Usedom, a high German naval expert, was placed in command of the purely naval defenses of the straits.

Unfortunately for the allied force the attack upon the Dardanelles lacked the important — and perhaps indispensable — element of surprise. By their early naval attack upon the outer fort, by the gathering of the army at Mudros and its subsequent return to Alexandria, and, finally, by the ill-fated naval attack upon the Narrows' defenses, the Allies had given the Turks ample warning of their intentions. During the many weeks that intervened between the first naval attack upon the outer forts and the approach of Sir Ian Hamilton's army, the Turks, under the supervision of their German mentors, and borrowing largely of the lessons of the trench campaign in Flanders and France, made of the Peninsula of Gallipoli a network of positions which it proved possible, to borrow an expression used of the German concrete trenches in France, "for a caretaker and his wife to hold." This elaborate system of trenches and redoubts was dominated by the three great heights. Every foot of the sides of these major positions had been prepared with barbed wire, monster pits, mines, concealed machine-gun batteries, and the almost endless variety of traps evolved out of six months' experience with the new style of warfare.

Along the many miles of coast of the Peninsula of Gallipoli there were but few places where, even under the most advantageous of conditions, it was possible to effect a landing in the face of a strongly intrenched enemy. The steep slopes of the hills rose from the very water's edge. Even in cases where there was a low, sandy beach, the nature of the country in the immediate vicinity made it impossible to deploy and maneuver any considerable number of troops.

Furthermore the Turks, well aware of the limited possibilities at the disposal of the allied force, had made terrifically strong defensive positions of the few beaches where successful landings were at all possible. Row upon row of barbed wire had been run along the shores and even out into the sea. Mines had been constructed that could be depended upon to blow the intrepid first landing parties to pieces. The ground had been thoroughly studied and machine-gun batteries placed so that every inch of the beaches could be raked with a devastating fire. And finally, the ranges for all the great guns in the hills beyond had been accurately measured so that the ships and the troops would be literally buried under an avalanche of shells.

CHAPTER LXXII

PLANS OF SIR IAN HAMILTON—FIRST LANDING MADE

THE broad outlines of the problem that faced Sir Ian Hamilton and his force were comparatively simple. The assault upon the Gallipoli Peninsula resolved itself into rush attacks upon two major heights, leading up to a grand assault upon the key position to the Narrows.

These three positions formed an irregular triangle. The first was Achi Baba, situated within three and a half miles of the tip of the peninsula. The second was Sari Bair, about eight miles due north of the Narrows. By either taking or isolating these two positions the Allies would be in a position for a grand attack upon the third and most important height, the plateau of Kilid Bahr, or Pasha Dagh. This position not only commanded the Narrows and the adjacent channel but it contained two of the great forts that successfully withstood the grand fleet attack. It was, in the minds of the allied command, the key to the whole situation. With Kilid Bahr in their hands, they believed the way to Constantinople would be open and the elimination of the Turk as a factor in the war and the settlement of the Balkan question or questions in a manner favorable to the allied powers would necessarily follow.

The operations as planned by Sir Ian Hamilton, then, consisted of a number of landings—as many as possible so as to conceal the real objectives of the allied troops and to disperse the Turkish force—and an attempt to rush the position of Achi Baba, and to isolate the position of Sari Bair by advancing through the low country that lay between that position and Kilid Bahr.

On April 7, 1915, Sir Ian Hamilton, with his staff, returned to Mudros and held a conference with the naval commands. By the 20th his plans had been perfected and the great landing was fixed to take place on Sunday, April 25, 1915. During the previous week the Allies had been making feints along the shore of the Gulf of Saros in an attempt to give an element of surprise to the real attack.

As Sir Ian Hamilton subsequently wrote, the question of weather was one of vital importance to the success of the landing. If, after a number of the troops had been thrown upon the beaches, bad weather had intervened, prevented further landings and perhaps driven the fleet and auxiliary vessels to Mudros Harbor, the unfortunate troops ashore would have been wiped out.

Sunday, April 25, 1915, however, was a perfect day. The low mist of the early morning hid the great fleet until it was close to the shore of the peninsula. As the day progressed the mist disappeared, the blue sky presented an unbroken expanse, while no wind disturbed the placid sea. In a setting such as this was enacted one of the greatest battles of all history.

At the tip of the Gallipoli Peninsula were five small beaches. They were subsequently named by the Allies, for identification purposes, Beaches S, V, W, X, and Y. Against these points was to be flung the Twenty-ninth Division, supported by some of the naval division. These troops, once having gained the shore and held it against the enemy counterattacks, were to push on in all haste by the road that led to the village of Krithia, northwest of Achi Baba, turn east before reaching that place, and carry Achi Baba with a rush.

At the same time the Australian and New Zealand troops were to effect a landing at Gaba Tepe, about twelve miles up the Ægean coast of the peninsula and about three and a half miles south of Sari Bair. Running southeast from near Gaba Tepe was a good road connecting with the town of Maidos, on the Dardanelles, above the Narrows. The whole way lay through low country and, once in command of this road, the allied troops would not only sever direct communications between Sari Bair and Kilid Bahr but would be in a position to attack the defenses of the latter on the flank.

Meantime the French were to make a landing at Kum Kale on the Asiatic side of the straits. There is some doubt as to the real purpose of this landing. After the French had reembarked—"driven off with terrible losses," according to the Turkish official

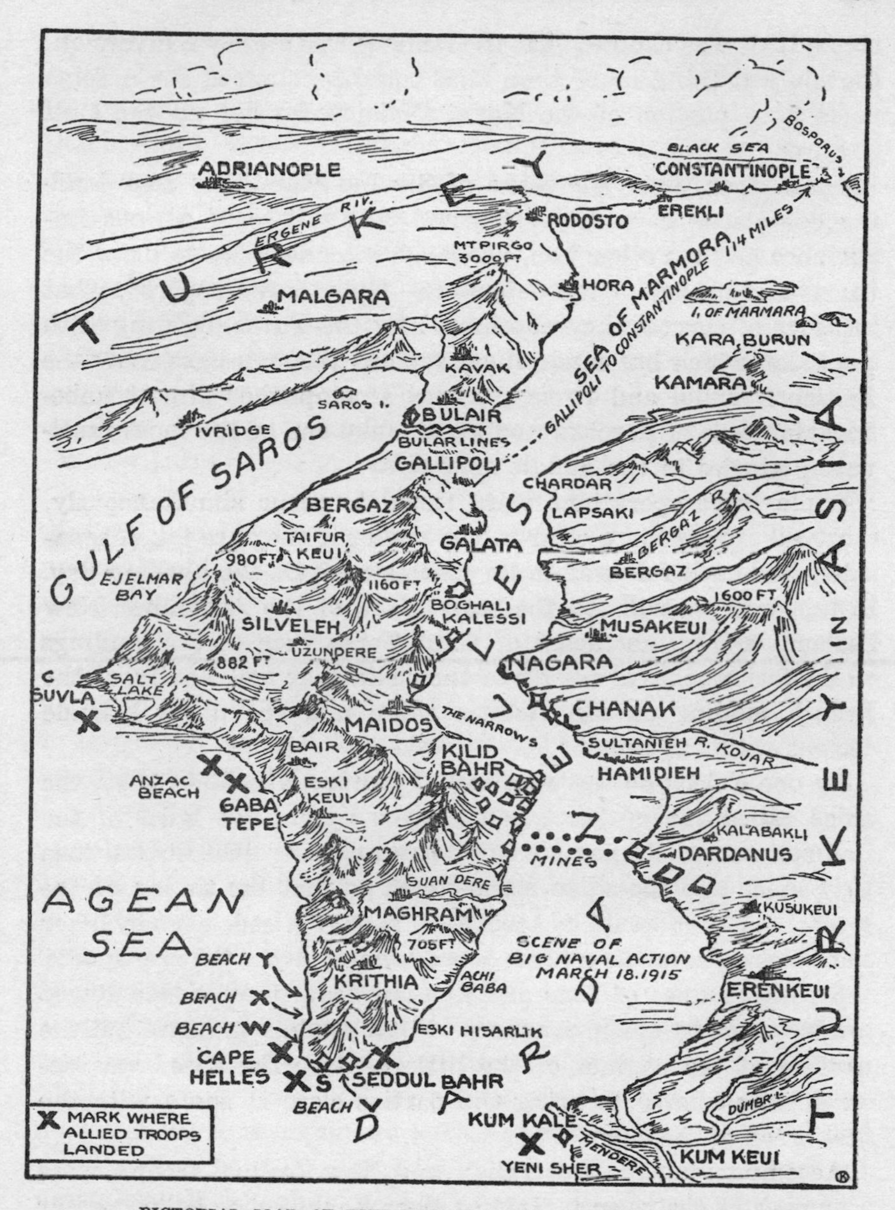

PICTORIAL MAP OF THE DARDANELLES, SHOWING WHERE THE ALLIES LANDED

account—it was claimed that the landing was merely a diversion. Certainly nothing more than that could be claimed for a feint made by a portion of the Naval Division farther up the Gulf of Saros.

These, then, were the plans of Sir Ian Hamilton: four landing operations in widely separated points, two of serious importance and the other two, probably, intended only to draw the troops and energy of the defenders. How they prospered, what measure of success they obtained, how the Turks, fighting with the valor which has made them famous through ages, how the British Colonial and French troops accomplished almost unbelievable deeds of heroism and skill, make one of the most fascinating stories in the annals of warfare.

While these operations were timed to occur simultaneously, they will appear more clear to the reader if they are taken separately and each followed to its conclusion from the opening day. In this way we will tell the story, first, of the Australian-New Zealand landing northeast of Gaba Tepe; then of the landings on the five beaches at the tip of the peninsula; and, finally, of the French landing on the Asiatic shore and the naval brigade demonstration at Bulair.

By one o'clock on the morning of Sunday, April 25, 1915, the allied expeditionary force had arrived within five miles of the Gallipoli shore. Under cover of darkness the final dispositions were made and the ships maneuvered so that the timing of the several landings would be accurately synchronized. Shortly after one o'clock the landing boats were lowered from the transports.

Strung in lines of four and five the boats were slowly towed toward shore by steam pinnaces. Not a sound was heard but the panting of the engines of the little boats. The speed was accurately calculated to bring the parties close in shore with the first break of the dawn.

Accompanying the Australian and New Zealand troops, were a number of destroyers. Just as they reached the shallow water in front of the cliffs of Gaba Tepe, a Turkish lookout spied them in the hazy light of the morning. Instantly he gave the alarm and a flaring searchlight flashed its rays on the little flotilla.

The need for silence had disappeared. With a cheer the British troops leaped from their boats into the shoal water and splashed their way ashore. While many of them were still in their boats, however, the Turks opened fired. The whole ground had been carefully prepared and from every cover on the shore and the cliffs beyond a deadly fire was poured upon the Colonial troops.

Without faltering, however, the Australian and New Zealand troops, supported by a squadron of battleships and destroyers, came on straight at the strongly intrenched Turks. The first of the Australians to reach the shore were the Third Brigade under Colonel Sinclair Maglagan. With a rush they charged the first Turkish lines, bayoneted the defenders, and scrambled up the steep cliffs that rise a hundred feet in the air.

Fortunately for the British troops, as these and subsequent events proved, there had been a slight miscalculation in the landing, and the men had actually gone ashore a mile and a half northeast of Gaba Tepe, instead of at that point. Gaba Tepe is so rugged and uninviting that it was believed that the Turks would not trouble to intrench it. Actually the Turks appeared to have intrenched and prepared every inch of the coast. But at Sari Bair, where the Australian and New Zealand troops actually landed, the character of the ground, although not so advantageous at first, afforded much more protection once the men were ashore. Sir Ian Hamilton, in his graphic account of the operations, subsequently said:

"Owing to the tows having failed to maintain their exact direction, the actual point of disembarkation was rather more than a mile north of that which I had selected, and was more closely overhung by steeper cliffs. Although this accident increased the initial difficulty of driving the enemy off the heights inland, it has since proved itself to have been a blessing in disguise, inasmuch as the actual base of the force of occupation had been much better defiladed from shell fire.

"The beach on which the landing was actually effected is a very narrow strip of sand about 1,000 yards in length, bounded on the north and the south by two small promontories. At its southern extremity, a deep ravine with exceedingly deep, scrub-clad sides, runs inland in a northeasterly direction. Near the northern end of the beach a small but steep gully runs up into the hills at right angles to the shore. Between the ravine and the gully the whole of the beach is baked by the seaward face of the spur which forms the northwestern side of the ravine. From the top of the spur the ground falls almost sheer, except near the southern limit of the beach where gentler slopes give access to the mouth of the ravine behind. Farther inland lie in a tangled knot the under-features of Sari Bair separated by deep ravines which take a most confusing diversity of direction. Sharp spurs, covered with dense scrub and falling away in many places in precipitous sandy cliffs, radiate from the principal mass of the mountain, from which they run northwest, west, southwest and south to the coast."

As fresh British troops came ashore they cast aside their heavy packs and followed their comrades across the forty feet of open beach and into the scrub that covered the side of the cliffs. Halfway up the Turks had prepared a second position. Attacking it in open formation the Third Brigade succeeded in clearing it within fifteen minutes of the time they came ashore, despite the desperate and brave defense of the Turks.

Meanwhile some of the landing boats, subjected to the terrible fire of the Turkish guns, were having a bad time. The towing ropes of three of them were cut by the fire and the boats drifted helplessly about under the withering rain of bullets that rapidly wiped out their cargoes of men. But despite these mishaps the First and Second Brigades were hurried ashore to support the Third. Soon, in the face of terrible difficulties including the narrowness of the beach, there were between 3,000 and 4,000 allied troops ashore.

By this time the Turks, by means of the mobile carriages prepared for them by the Germans, had maneuvered some heavy artillery into position on the heights inland. Also some of their warships, moored in the Narrows, began throwing heavy shells across the peninsula into the allied fleet standing close inshore. So dangerous and accurate became this fire that the transports had to be ordered out to sea and this delayed the operations seriously.

At Gaba Tepe and on the heights to the north of the beach the Turks posted guns and enfiladed the Narrows beach. Thus the troops, as they landed, had to make their way through a rain of shrapnel, machine gun and rifle fire that wiped out hundreds. Despite the success of the Australian Brigades in clearing the beach and the face of the cliff, the Turkish fire never seemed to slacken.

Because of the nature of the country there could be no central control over the advance fighting and no continued communications between the several forces making their way to the top of the cliffs. The battle resolved itself into a series of fights between small parties, or even individual soldiers, whose one object was to kill as many of the enemy as possible and make their way as far inland as possible in the first rush.

By two o'clock about twelve British regiments had been landed and the ground gained consolidated and prepared against counterattack. Thousands of Turkish troops were by this time pouring along the road from Maidos and by the middle of the afternoon it was calculated that there were fully 20,000 of them before the Australian and New Zealand troops. The latter, in the meantime, had been further reenforced by two batteries of Indian Mountain Artillery. The pressure of the constantly increasing Turkish force compelled General Birdwood, who came ashore about this time, to contract his lines and to reach a decision that, at that time at least and until the arrival of more troops, no further advance could be made. The Gaba Tepe landing had not been the surprise that was expected and the Turks had proved to be in unexpected strength.

About three o'clock the Turkish counterattacks began. Absolutely regardless of human life, they threw themselves in dense masses against the Second and Third Brigades. The British battleships, the *Queen*, the *London*, the *Prince of Wales*, the *Triumph* and the *Majestic*, posted close inshore, poured a devastating fire on the advancing Turkish troops as they came into the open.

About five o'clock the Turks, after repeated assaults upon the British lines, massed for a final attempt to drive the invaders into the sea. On and on they came, concentrating on the hard-pressed Third Brigade as the weak spot in the British defense. Fighting gamely against heavy odds, this Australian Brigade which had borne the brunt of the landing attack and which had been almost continually counterattacked all afternoon, gave way slowly, selling every inch of ground dearly. Hundreds of the brave Turkish troops were mown down by the machine guns which the Australians had by this time brought ashore. At nightfall, however, General Birdwood, as a consequence of the persistence of the enemy, had to contract his lines further.

As night settled on the battle field on the ridge above Gaba Tepe and Sari Bair, and the two forces rested from sheer exhaustion, the British troops, who once were well inland toward Maidos, their objective, were barely hanging onto the ridge overlooking the shore of the Gulf of Saros. All their water and food and munitions and reenforcements had to be brought ashore across the exposed beach, while the landing of the necessary artillery in the face of the Turkish fire was a feat to appal the bravest. But though their hold on their position was precarious it was tenacious and, in the end, effective. If they had not won all they expected to win they had at least won a foothold in the face of terrific difficulties.

While the Australians and New Zealanders were fighting desperately beyond Gaba Tepe, the other forces of the allied army were accomplishing similar deeds of heroism at the tip of the peninsula.

Coming down the coast of the peninsula from Gaba Tepe, about three miles from the extreme southwestern tip, was what was known as Beach Y. It was almost due west of the important town of Krithia, and the landing was intended primarily to protect the left flank of the British landing forces from attack by the considerable forces believed to be concentrated there.

The actual landing seems to have been somewhat of a surprise to the Turks. Indeed, subsequent events showed that they were correct in their estimate that a landing at the so-called Beach Y would be a mistake. A narrow strip of sandy beach led to the cliffs, two hundred feet high, that were believed to be almost unscalable. It is easy to be wise after the event, but military writers subsequently declared that if the Turks had been prepared to defend the position, the force that landed at Beach Y would have been wiped out in the preliminary attempt to establish a footing.

The force assigned to this point of attack consisted of the First King's Own Scottish Borderers, and the Plymouth Battalion of the Royal Naval Division, under the command of Lieutenant Colonel Koe. The latter was under orders, if the landing proved successful, to work his way south to effect a junction with the force landing at Beach X, some two miles away.

About five o'clock, Koe's force appeared off Beach Y, on the transports *Braemar Castle* and *Southland,* and escorted by the battleship *Goliath,* and the cruisers *Amethyst* and *Sapphire.* The Turks had posted a large force at Beach Y 2, between Beach Y and Beach X, but half of the Scottish Borderers were ashore before the Turkish command had realized what was happening. As a result Colonel Koe's force was partly established on the cliffs before the Turks had begun to arrive.

But if the initial stages were unexpectedly easy for this force, difficulties soon developed. Once on the heights, Colonel Koe ordered an advance to link up with the force at Beach X. The British troops had not gone far when they ran into the Turkish troops from Beach Y. So large was this force and so determined an opposition did it offer to the British troops that Colonel Koe soon decided it would be impossible, with the two battalions at his disposal, to accomplish the task assigned him.

Early in the afternoon the little British force was dismayed by the approach on its left flank of a large force of Turks from Krithia, which threatened to cut it off from the landing beach. Reluctantly Colonel Koe, just before he received a fatal wound, gave the order to intrench.

CHAPTER LXXIII

THE BRITISH IN DANGER—BITTER FIGHTING

THE British troops were now in a critical position. There was a peculiar spoonlike formation of the ground at the end of the Gallipoli Peninsula. From the high cliffs along the shore the ground fell away. Thus it was impossible for the supporting warships lying offshore to give any effective aid to the little British force once it had left the shore and the edge of the heights. The Turks realized to the full their advantage and attacked the Borderers and the marines with fury. Frequent attacks were launched against the dwindling line of the British force. Guns of large caliber were rapidly brought up from Krithia, while the Turks showed extraordinary daring and cleverness in bomb attacks upon the hastily dug trenches of the enemy.

All night long the Turks attacked. By morning the remnants of the British force were in desperate straits. Sir Ian Hamilton subsequently declared that the losses at this time had been "deplorable." Many of the officers, in addition to Lieutenant Colonel Kee, had been killed or wounded, while 50 per cent of the Borderers had been put out of action. They were no longer able to defend properly their trenches. Food, water, and ammunition were running short. A consultation of the remaining officers was held. The question of trying to hold out until reenforcements arrived was considered, but ultimately it was decided to retreat to the shore and to reembark.

At seven o'clock on Monday morning the order was given. The attending fleet had been strengthened by the arrival of the cruisers *Talbot* and *Dublin,* and, supported by the *Goliath,* the *Amethyst,* and the *Sapphire,* they began a terrific bombardment of the tops of the cliffs. Protected by this screen of fire, the few remaining British troops were able to get away in their boats without molestation save for a long distance bombardment by the Turkish artillery.

The landing at Beach X was more successful. The Eighty-seventh Brigade, under the command of Brigadier General Marshall, was assigned to this part of the field. It was to work its way as far as possible inland and link up with the troops coming ashore at Beach W. At Beach X the Turks were well prepared. They had constructed bomb-proof shelters and trenches on the heights and were well led by German officers.

Before the actual landing the supporting battleships, led by the *Swiftsure* and the *Implacable,* bombarded the Turkish positions for almost an hour with their heaviest guns. The ground was thoroughly swept by the great 12-inch and smaller guns of the warships. Finally, just before the actual landing, the *Implacable* steamed within 500 yards of the shore, dropped her anchor and smothered the near cliffs and the foreshore with her fire.

Subsequent investigation proved that in this affair of Gallipoli, as in Flanders and elsewhere, the British suffered from their lack of foresight in the provision of proper shells. The battleships used shrapnel, which, it was afterward discovered, did little damage to the deep, protected trenches prepared by the Turks under the supervision of the German officers. If the British had had instead the high-explosive shells that were necessary for the work, the story of the Gallipoli landings under the wing of the great fleet of battleships might have made different reading.

After about a quarter of an hour's final bombardment by the *Implacable,* two companies and a machine-gun section of the First Royal Fusiliers were thrown ashore at Beach X. Under cover of the battleships, the landing was safely accomplished and the Fusiliers advanced almost 1,000 yards without much opposition. Hill 114 on their right, where the Turks proved to be firmly intrenched, then proved a serious obstacle to the advance. While the Royal Fusiliers were considering the best method of attacking this position, a Turkish battery, in position near the town of Krithia, opened fire and tore holes in the left wing of the British force. At the same time they were heavily counter-attacked by a Turkish force coming from the east. Gradually the Royal Fusiliers were compelled to give ground. Two battalions of the Eighty-seventh Division were sent ashore and with these reenforcements the British again advanced, this time clearing Hill 114 of the enemy. There they joined hands with the First Battalion of the Lancashire Fusiliers, and although all day long the Turks tried to break the union of the two forces, they did not succeed in doing so.

However, General Marshall's force was hard pressed. Once more the unceasing Turkish counterattacks drove them back to the very edge of the heights overlooking Beach X, where only the intense bombardment of the protecting warships saved them. General Marshall was wounded, but refused to relinquish his command, and a very large proportion of the total force was either killed or wounded in the day's fighting. When night fell the British troops held only half a mile of territory around their original landing place, with their right wing resting on Hill 114, linked up with the force from Beach W.

Here at Beach W, a mile and a half down the coast, midway between Tekke Burna and Hellas Burna, was being enacted a feat of arms which, in the opinion of competent military men, is fit to rank with the great military accomplishments of all time. In speaking of it subsequently Sir Ian Hamilton made use of the following terms:

"So strong, in fact, were the defenses of Beach W that the Turks may well have considered them impregnable, and it as my firm conviction that no finer feat of arms has ever been achieved by the British soldier—or any other soldier—than the storming of these trenches from open boats on the morning of April 25."

At Beach W the Turks, fully foreseeing a landing, had prepared as at no other point. The beach is in a wide bay and leads into a gully flanked on one side by the hills extending to Cape Tekke and, on the other side by the steep cliffs extending to Cape Hellas.

Every inch of the ground had been prepared against attack. Sea and land mines had been profusely laid, wire entanglements had been placed along the shore and stretching out into the water. Deep trenches had been dug on the heights and on the sides of the slopes while strong redoubts had been built at two dominating positions. Every bush and cover contained a sniper while larger covers concealed machine guns trained to sweep the beach and the slopes leading to the Turkish trenches.

As a defensive position Beach W was almost ideal. It had two weak points, however, which in the end turned the scales and made success possible for the attacking force. At either end of the bay were small rock positions from which it was possible to enfilade the elaborate system of defenses.

The landing party at Beach W consisted of the First Battalion Lancashire Fusiliers, under command of Major Bishop. "It was," wrote Sir Ian Hamilton, "to the complete lack of the sense of danger or of fear of this daring battalion that we owed our astonishing success." After a preliminary bombardment by the supporting warships the men of the First Battalion, in thirty-two cutters drawn by eight picket boats, approached the shore. The Turks made no move until the men were in shallow water and were leaping out of the boats. Then they opened fire with a murderous torrent from artillery, machine guns, and rifles. The first line of the First Battalion went down to a man. The second never faltered, but came on bravely into the fire, striving desperately to cut the wire entanglements. So quickly did they fall that observers on the warships wondered why they were "resting" on the bullet swept shore instead of running to cover.

Rapidly the men from Lancashire worked. Finally a remnant of the battalion forced its way through the last line of wire and ran for shelter on the bush covered slopes. Almost at the same moment, detachments that had landed on the rocks at Cape Tekke and under Cape Hellas began to have an important effect upon the struggle. At the latter point, the Eighty-eighth Brigade, under Brigadier General Hare, clambered up the steep side of the cliffs, searched out the machine gun positions of the enemy and swept the ground clear with the bayonet. This and the work of the force at Cape Tekke eased the Turkish fire on the beach and, on the slopes of the Cape Tekke side of the ravine, the few remaining officers of the First Battalion were able to re-form the remnants of their force and advance upon Hill 114.

About nine o'clock reenforcements were landed, this time not on the exposed beach but under Cape Tekke, the heights of which were by now largely in the hands of the British troops. With the help of these fresh troops, three lines of Turkish trenches were carried. Brigadier General Hare was seriously wounded and his place was filled by Colonel Wolley-Dod, who was sent ashore with orders to organize a further advance at all speed. At this point the attacking force ran up against the Turkish redoubt at Hill 138.

The afternoon opened with an intense naval bombardment of the ground around Hill 138 and of that redoubt itself. At two o'clock the Fourth Battalion of the Worcesters was ordered to take the position by assault. Under Lieutenant Colonel D. E. Cayley, they advanced a considerable distance under rifle fire and charged up the heights with a cheer. The Turks fought bravely against a stronger force, but by four o'clock Hill 138 was in the hands of the Worcesters.

Less than a mile down the coast, almost to the old fort and village of Sedd-el-Bahr, was what was known as V Beach. There a landing in great force was attempted. Largely because of the scale of the operations, but also because of the difficulties and the accidents of warfare, this landing was made with great losses.

The beach and the shore in the immediate vicinity form a most regular amphitheatre of a radius of about 400 feet. The beach is about 10 yards wide and 350 to 400 feet long and it runs into a slightly concaved, grassy slope that rises gently to a height of a hundred feet. Little or no real cover was to be found on this slope and the defenders were able to sweep it from all angles with a devastating rain of all kinds of shells. Just at the edge of the strip of sand, however, was a continuous escarpment about four feet high, which afforded a cover in which troops once ashore might be re-formed. As a result of the early naval bombardment of the tip of the peninsula, much of the village of Sedd-el-Bahr and the fort and the barracks had been reduced to ruins. The ruins afforded, however, excellent cover for the Turkish troops and proved a serious obstacle to the advance of the British when they reached the shore.

In addition to the natural disadvantages under which the attacking party had to work, the Turks had constructed two lines of barbed wire obstacles—one at the edge of the beach and the second two-thirds of the way up to the top of the ridge. These two lines of barbed wire were more stoutly constructed than were any others with which the British had to contend. Just beyond the second obstacle the Turks had built their first line of trenches and beyond the ground was scored with innumerable covers for the defenders.

The force assigned to the attack upon V Beach was composed of the Dublin Fusiliers, the Munster Fusiliers, half a battalion of the Hampshire Regiment, the West Riding Field Company and a few minor units. The action opened with a short range bombardment of the enemy's trenches and such parts of the fort, the village and the barracks as were still standing and believed to be affording cover for riflemen and machine-gun batteries. Then three companies of the Dublin Fusiliers were towed ashore. At this point one of the great experiments of the Gallipoli landings was put to the test, and, despite the cleverness of its conception, it did not meet with great success.

A large transport vessel, the *River Clyde,* had been loaded with about 2,000 troops. She had been reconstructed inside and great doors had been cut in one of her sides. The troops were ready on long platforms for instant disembarkation. The ships were to be run ashore, as close as possible to the beach, lighters were to be floated in between her and the shore, the side doors were to be flung open, and the troops were to rush ashore and carry the slopes by sheer momentum. In the front of the vessel, protected by sandbags, was a battery of machine guns which, it was hoped, would be especially effective in protecting the landing force from counterattacks.

As at the other landings, the Turks gave no sign of life until the collier had been beached and the other landing force had almost reached the shore in its tows. Indeed, so long did they hesitate in opening fire that at one time the watchers on the warships thought the landing was going to be unopposed. They were soon disabused of such an idea, however, as the first of the towboats grounded on the sandy beach, the Turks opened fire from a dozen different positions. Many of the Dublin Fusiliers were killed before they were able to get out of their boats. A few scrambled ashore and reached the shelter of the escarpment that rimmed the beach. The Turks concentrated their fire on the boats and their crews. None of them were able to get away, and almost instantly their crews were killed and the boats wrecked.

Meantime the *River Clyde,* had been run ashore. Unfortunately, the operation was not carried out as expeditiously as it was hoped it would be, and the Turks soon became aware of the intentions of the British. They poured a punishing fire on the naval party attempting to get the lighters into position between the ship and the shore. The heavy tide that at this point sweeps around the point of land also seriously interfered with the work. Finally however, by deeds of heroism that received subsequent official acknowledgment, the lighters were got into position and the doors of the *River Clyde* flung open.

At a trot a company of the Munster Fusiliers led the way. It was almost impossible to live for even a short time in the fire that the Turks concentrated upon the lighters, and hardly a man reached the shore. Nothing daunted, a second company of the same battalion followed. As they dropped in scores the lighters began to drift and dozens of the men, in attempting to swim ashore in their heavy kits, were drowned.

Despite the storm of fire, volunteers once more swung the lighters into position. The third company of the Munsters were ordered to attempt to reach the beach. By this time the Turks had been able to concentrate shrapnel fire on the *River Clyde* and her human freight, and the third company suffered even more casualties than had the first two.

There is a limit to human sacrifice, and Brigadier General Napier, in command of the troops, called a halt in the attempt to land. A little later, it was resumed, with General Napier and Captain Costeker and a detachment of the Hampshire Regiment heroically leading the way. When they had reached the lighters the moorings again gave way and they drifted into deep water. In the torrent of bullets that was being poured down upon them by the Turks it was impossible to do anything but lie flat on the exposed decks and wait for the lighters to be swung into position again. Scores of them were killed, including both Brigadier General Napier and Captain Costeker.

With this major disaster, all attempts to make further landings were abandoned for the day. A few hundred British troops had succeeded in reaching the escarpment on the shore and there they huddled, not daring to lift their heads above the four-foot natural cover. Fortunately for them, the machine-gun battery on the *River Clyde* raked the slope, kept the fire of the Turkish defenders down and prevented any counterattacks, which might have ended disastrously for the British troops. The troops still on board the *River Clyde*, numbering about 1,000 were effectively protected from the fire of the Turks, suffering few casualties, although shrapnel tore four great holes in the side of the collier.

Matters had not gone any better at other sections of the beach. Half a company of the Dublins landed east of Sedd-el-Bahr for the purpose of flanking the Turkish defenses, failed to accomplish its purpose and lost all except twenty-five of its men. In the afternoon the landing at V Beach was definitely accepted as a failure and plans made for the diversion of the troops not yet landed to one of the other beaches. It was first thought that Y Beach would be the best point, but it was decided that it would be too late to effect the issue there and the troops were finally diverted to W Beach, where, despite the heavy cost, the Lancashire landing had led to some real results.

As nightfall approached there was a momentary thrill of hopefulness among those who remained on V Beach because of the fact that some of the Worcestershire and Lancashire Fusiliers succeeded in working their way across country from W Beach and threatened to make untenable the Turkish positions. The few hundred men on V Beach and the thousand or more cooped up in the *River Clyde* could hear the fight coming closer and closer and, cheered by their officers, their spirits rose. But the men from W Beach were stopped finally by the frequent lines of barbed-wire obstructions that had been stretched by the Turk at right angles to the shore, between the two beaches, in preparation for just such an eventuality as this.

Night came, but with it not much relief from the constant vigilance of the Turks. There was in the perfect sky not a cloud to screen the moon's rays. A successful attempt was made, however, to land the infantry from the *River Clyde*, and subsequently the force then ashore, numbering close upon 1,500 men, tried to clear the ruins of the fort and the outskirts of the village. All these efforts were in vain, however, and finally the troops returned to the protection of the escarpment along the shore. From there the task of removing the wounded to the protection of the *River Clyde* was proceeded with under a heavy fire.

In comparison with the sanguinary affairs at the four other beaches, the landing at S Beach was a minor affair, costing only about fifty casualties. This beach was located at the extreme eastern end of Morto Bay, close by Eski Hissarlik Point, and the work was delegated to the Second South Wales Borderers under Lieutenant Colonel Casson. The chief difficulty of this landing was found in the powerful current which delayed it for several hours beyond the appointed time. However, the men were finally got ashore and easily drove out the small Turkish force that had been posted in the neighborhood.

CHAPTER LXXIV

FURTHER EFFORTS AT LANDING—FAILURE TO TAKE KRITHIA

MEANWHILE the French were carrying on a disastrous operation at Kum Kale, on the Asiatic shore, directly south of S Beach. About 2,800 men had been landed after a preliminary bombardment by the French fleet. Before they reembarked next morning they had lost more than a quarter of their effectives. After landing they stormed the ruined castle of Kum Kale and then drove inland with the object of clearing the village of

Yeni Shehr. The Turks were in force, however, at that point and held the French midway between Kum Kale and Yeni Shehr. Finally it became apparent that further advance was impossible without reenforcements and the French intrenched for the night. All through the darkness the Turks launched a counterattack upon the landing force and morning found the French preparing to reembark. Under the guns of the French warships this was accomplished without any great further loss.

Thus of the seven landings that had been attempted by the allied forces two, that at Kum Kale and that at Y Beach, had been definitely abandoned. Of the remaining five only two had been successful in linking up—that at Beach X and that at Beach W. Farther up the Gulf of Saros, near the lines known by the name of Bulair, a force of the Royal Naval Reserve made a demonstration but did not effect a landing.

The Australians and the New Zealanders on the cliffs above Gaba Tepe were fighting desperately against the constant Turkish counterattacks, but, assisted by the fleet under Admiral Thursby, successfully resisted all attempts to drive them into the sea. Already the little cove in which the landing had been made had been christened "Anzac Cove," "Anzac," of course, was formed by taking the first letters of the official designation of the colonial forces—Australian and New Zealand Army Corps. The spirits of the men were high, despite the awful experience they had gone through, and they frequently exchanged cheery messages with the gunners of the warships who were pounding away at the Turkish positions, although not accomplishing any great damage in their blind firing.

It had been intended to organize an immediate resumption of the advance from Anzac Cove with daybreak of April 26. But the Turks were constantly bringing up reenforcements. Watchers on the warships could see them creeping over the crest of Sari Bair and although the naval guns were turned on them, their loss was comparatively small because of their open formation and their cleverness in making use of every bit of cover.

During the early morning the Anzacs had hauled heavy field guns up the face of the steep cliffs and had, in many other ways, strengthened their positions. This was all the more necessary as it became apparent that the Turks were massing for a great attack shortly after nine o'clock. About noon the battle reached its height. The Turks attacked bravely and although they suffered great losses, never wavered. Despite their efforts, however, the Anzacs held fast. By this time reenforcements were beginning to arrive and a more permanent character was given to the trenches. An attempt was made to organize for an advance as headquarters were constantly impressing upon the individual commands the necessity of making good as much ground as possible before the Turks were able to bring into action their undoubted superiority in forces.

The constant attacks of the Turks, however, made any real attempt at advance impossible, although a little ground was gained on the 26th by counterattacks. It soon became apparent, too, that, although the operation at Anzac Cove was part and parcel of the general attack, it had, through its inability to make progress, become a separate affair and had been so conducted for the rest of the campaign—or at least until a much greater advance had been made in all quarters.

At the tip of the peninsula the chief events of the second day of the landing, April 26, 1915, occurred at V Beach, where the *River Clyde* had been run ashore. About 1,500 men were left, composed of the survivors of the Dublins and the Munsters and two companies of the Hampshires, under cover of the escarpment on the beach. There Colonel Doughty-Wylie and Captain Walford rallied them on the morning of the 26th and covered by a heavy bombardment by the warships set out to clear the village. Desperate hand-to-hand fighting followed and the casualties were appalling. Most of the houses contained squads of riflemen and the more important machine guns. Each had to be carried separately. By noon, however, the town had been cleared. Captain Walford had fallen, bravely leading his troops in a way that earned him the Victoria Cross.

Colonel Doughty-Wylie called a halt and collected the survivors of the attack. Under cover of some empty houses he rallied them, re-formed them as best he could, called upon them for one last effort and walked out into the open at the head of his troops for the assault upon the old Castle, and Hill 141.

Carrying a light cane, the figure of Colonel Doughty-Wylie was a conspicuous one. Yet he survived almost to the end and to victory. He reached the slope leading up to Hill 141, urging his men forward. He was in the lead when a bullet killed him instantly. Fired by his splendid example which earned him a posthumous Victoria Cross, the Dublins, Munsters, and Hampshires swept on and carried the summit. By two o'clock the commanding position was in the hands of the British.

At the same time the Lancashire Landing force had linked up with the landing at V Beach. Also, the French Expeditionary force, after its hard experience at Kum Kale, was successfully landed at V Beach. Additional troops were landed at S Beach to prevent the South Wales Borderers being wiped out in their isolation.

On the morning of April 27, 1915, Sir Ian Hamilton looked over the positions. He found that, although he had several beaches securely in his grasp, he lacked room in which to maneuver. Also his force was beginning to suffer from lack of water. Accordingly he decided that an immediate advance was necessary.

Sir Ian Hamilton set his men the task of clearing the comparatively low ground at the tip of the peninsula—a distance of about two miles from the extreme southwestern point of the land. He drew a straight line from the position held by the South Wales Borderers near the ruined De Tott's Battery to Y Beach. After some hard fighting this was accomplished with the exception of the extreme left wing, which got only as far as Y 2 Beach, where the Turks were in force.

On the following day, April 27th, despite the fact that his forces were almost exhausted, Sir Ian Hamilton called upon them for a supreme effort. He intended, he said, to capture the Village of Krithia and, from that point, carry Achi Baba, the first main objective in the campaign to open the Narrows.

The advance was ordered for eight o'clock in the morning. The Twenty-ninth Division, under Major General Sir Aylmer Hunter-Weston, was to move on Krithia, the French force was to move along the right flank of the Twenty-ninth to the Kereves Dere, which ran from the base of Achi Baba, and there await the capture of Krithia and the assault upon the main height.

The leading units of the Twenty-ninth Division advanced almost without opposition for a couple of miles, but was then heavily attacked by the enemy. Despite all further attempts the British troops were able to make no further advance at this point and intrenched for the night. A little to the right, other units eventually got within three-quarters of a mile of Krithia, but finally were compelled to fall back in line with the force on its left. Still farther to the right the Eighty-eighth Brigade had been brought to a halt and found itself running short of ammunition.

The Eighty-sixth Brigade, which had been held in reserve, came into action shortly after one o'clock in the afternoon. It was ordered to move through the Eighty-eighth Brigade and carry Krithia. A few units got within sight of Krithia, but the main body of the Eighty-sixth Brigade was unable to force a way beyond the line reached by the Eighty-eighth.

The French, meanwhile, were having an equally hard time. At one time they were within a mile of Krithia, but ultimately they, in company with the whole allied line, had to give way before strong Turkish counterattacks. Masses of Turkish troops advanced against the British center and right and against the whole line of the French and drove them back with the bayonet. An almost successful attempt was made to pierce the allied linc at the point where the French linked up with the British. The French gave way and uncovered the right flank of the Eighty-eighth Brigade. The Fourth Worcesters suffered cruelly and had it not been for the reenforcements of the Eighty-sixth Brigade a serious situation might have ensued.

In speaking of this critical moment Sir Ian Hamilton subsequently wrote:

"The men were exhausted and the few guns landed at the time were unable to afford them adequate artillery support. The small amount of transports available did not suffice to maintain the supply of munitions, and cartridges were running short despite all efforts to push them up from the landing places."

The situation was now becoming serious and it became apparent that Krithia could not be carried. Accordingly, the allied forces were ordered to dig in as rapidly as possible and hold their ground at all costs. Thus ended the Battle of the Landings, extending over three days. The results obtained fell far short of expectations. Krithia and Achi Baba had not been carried, the Australians and New Zealanders had been unable to advance along the road to Maidos and, indeed, were hanging on to a thin strip of shore by their very teeth. It became more apparent with each new attempt that the difficulties before the attackers in the Gallipoli Peninsula were far beyond anything that had been conceived.

In speaking of his failure to reach Krithia, Sir Ian Hamilton said:

"Had it been possible to push in reenforcements in men, artillery and munitions during the day, April 27, Krithia should have fallen, and much subsequent fighting for its capture would have been avoided.

"Two days later this would have been feasible, but I had to reckon with the certainty that the enemy would, in that same time, have received proportionately greater support. I was faced by the usual choice of evils, and although the result was not what I had hoped, I have no reason to believe that hesitation and delay would better have answered my purpose."

CHAPTER LXXV

KRITHIA AGAIN ATTACKED—HEROIC WORK OF "ANZACS"

ON April 28, 1915, Sir Ian Hamilton decided to send reenforcements in force to Anzac Cove. Despite the constant landing of fresh troops there the Australians and New Zealanders, because of their heavy losses and the increasing pressure of the Turkish attacks, had been almost continually in the firing line.

They had been able to enjoy little or no rest or sleep, and things began to look serious. Accordingly four battalions of the Royal Naval Division were sent to General Birdwood. On the following day two more naval battalions were landed and as well a company of the Motor Maxim Section.

These fresh units moved into the Anzac trenches and held them against renewed Turkish attacks. Meanwhile the Australian and New Zealand battalions were being reorganized behind the line and after three and a half days' rest took their places again in the front-line trenches.

From the evening of the 27th of April until May 1 there was comparative quiet on what might be called the Krithia front, at the tip of the peninsula. Fresh forces were landed by the French and the English, the latter bringing into line the Twenty-ninth Indian Infantry Brigade. Heavy artillery was brought ashore and moved up to positions inland, and the whole organization of the allied force was re-formed and strengthened.

At 10 p. m. on the evening of May 1 opened what is known as the first battle of Krithia. It was elaborately organized by the German staff of the Turkish forces and took the allied troops by surprise. Indeed, the first line of the attacking force, creeping up on its hands and knees, got into the trenches of the Eighty-sixth Brigade and bayoneting most of the defenders opened up what Sir Ian Hamilton subsequently described as "an ugly gap." Thanks to the fine conduct of some territorial units, however, the Turks were not able to press home this temporary advantage and the hole was soon closed.

Along the rest of the British front the attack of the Turks was not serious. Instead they concentrated on the left of the French line, held by a Senegalese brigade. After several attacks the African troops began to give way. Realizing the seriousness of the situation, the two companies of the Worcesters moved across from the British right and saved the day. Some hours later, the extreme French right was hard pressed, and it was necessary to bring up a battalion of the Royal Naval Division from the reserves to strengthen it.

The following morning, the allied troops moved out of their trenches in a counterattack. It at first met with great success. As Sir Ian Hamilton wrote in his dispatch to London: "Had it not been for those inventions of the devil—machine guns and barbed wire—which suit the Turkish character and tactics to perfection, we should not have stopped short of the crest of Achi Baba."

By 7.30 in the morning the British left had advanced more than 500 yards, while the center and the right and the French left had also registered promising advances. The rest of the French line, however, was held up by strong Turkish forces posted along the Kereves Dere and the more advanced sections of the British left came under heavy cross-fire. In the end it was necessary to relinquish all the ground gained and to retire to the original trenches.

Although the Turks made night attacks against the French line on May 2 and 3, 1915, and in the end inflicted such heavy losses that it was necessary to shorten the line held by General d'Amade's troops, it was not until May 6, 1915, that heavy fighting occurred again along the whole line. On May 5 the Lancashire Fusilier Brigade of the East Lancashire Territorial Division, which had been training in Egypt, arrived and was placed in reserve, behind the British left.

At this time it was calculated that the British total losses, killed, wounded and missing since the initial operations of the landing, had been just short of 14,000 men. This of course did not include the sick who must have numbered 10,000 or the French losses, which were not revealed. These were heavy and serious and more than counterbalanced the reenforcements that had arrived.

Sir Ian Hamilton decided to make a fresh attempt against Krithia and Achi Baba on May 6, 1915. This battle was important because it marked the turning point in the character of the campaign carried on by the allied troops in Gallipoli. Although an advance was registered none of the main positions of the Ottoman troops were carried or even reached, and it became apparent that the task of reducing the Dardanelles was not one likely to be solved by rush frontal attacks. Rather, as in other fields of the world war, the problem became one of siege tactics, and from the date of the end of this second battle of Krithia the operations in Gallipoli resolved themselves into variations of the methods that were being forced upon the troops of all the belligerent countries in Europe.

For his grand attack upon Krithia and Achi Baba, Sir Ian Hamilton brought down from Anzac Cove the Second Australian Infantry Brigade and the New Zealand Brigade. With two brigades of the Royal Naval Reserve he formed them into a reserve division. The Twenty-ninth Division held the British line, and was ordered forward about 11 a. m. of May 6, 1915, with orders to go as far as Krithia if possible, but at all events to seize as much of the ground around that point as possible. At the same time the French corps were to attempt to wrest from the Turks the crest above the Kereves Dere.

The advance was extremely slow. At the end of two hours the Twenty-ninth Division had progressed less than three hundred yards and had not yet come into touch with any of the main Turkish positions. Three hours more of desperate fighting showed many fluctuations but no more progress. Finally they were ordered to intrench where they were for the night.

The French had succeeded in reaching the crest aimed at, but found it by no means a comfortable position. They could not go forward and they dared not go back. Yet they were subject to a raking fire that cost them hundreds of casualties. Time and time again the Senegalese troops were sent against the Turkish trenches and machine gun positions, but each time they were beaten back with cruel losses. To make matters even worse, the French could not, in the heavy fire maintained by the Turks, intrench until after nightfall, and they had to spend hours in the exposed position.

The following morning May 7, 1915, the allied warships opened a furious bombardment of the ground around Krithia. Every few feet of the difficult country was searched out by the destroying lyddite of the Allies' shells, until it seemed that not a living creature could have survived. But when the Lancashire Fusiliers

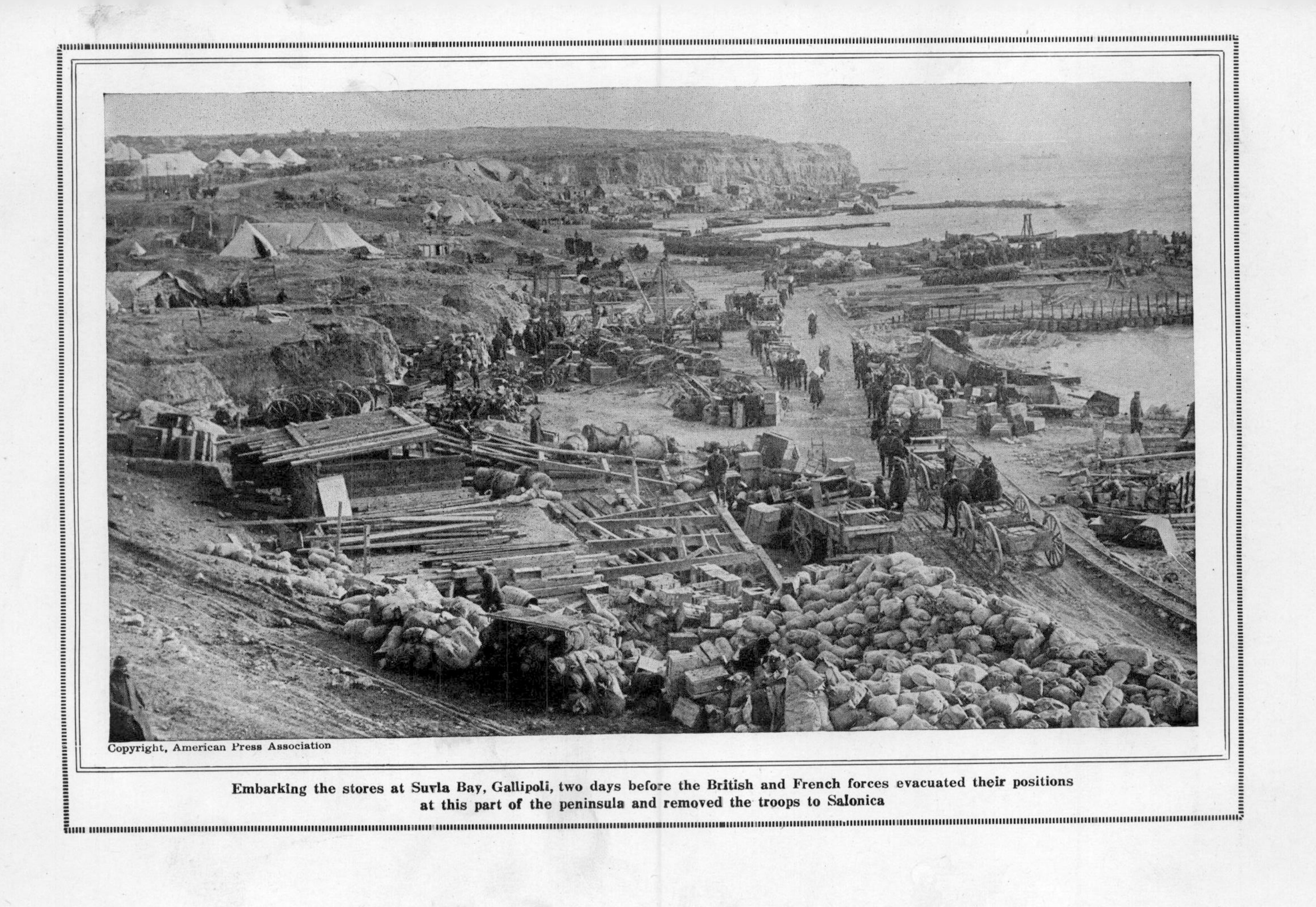

Embarking the stores at Suvla Bay, Gallipoli, two days before the British and French forces evacuated their positions at this part of the peninsula and removed the troops to Salonica

Brigade moved out to the attack a few minutes later it soon became apparent that the naval bombardment had by no means exterminated or demoralized the Turks.

The British troops were greeted by a perfect hurricane of fire from rifles and machine guns. Hundreds of the men went down and, brave as the remainder were, they were compelled to abandon the attempt to cross the open ground that lay between the British front and Krithia. Some progress was made on the right, however, where a clump of fir trees which had been holding up the advance for some time was finally carried by the Fifth Royal Scots. Early in the afternoon the Turks recaptured the firs and such of the ground they had lost and shortly after four o'clock when Sir Ian Hamilton relieved the situation, the British were in the position of being absolutely "stuck." The British commander decided to make another desperate attempt, however, and called upon the French for cooperation. The whole allied line advanced to the attack just as evening was closing in but the Turks by this time had brought up some additional batteries and poured in on the French and the British a smothering fire of deadly shrapnel. So heavy was the punishment of the French that the line literally melted away and General d'Amade was compelled to throw his last reserve into the front line. At nightfall the allied attack subsided.

During the night, word came to Sir Ian Hamilton that heavy Turkish reenforcements were on their way and he decided to make one last attempt to carry Krithia and Achi Baba before they arrived in the morning. Accordingly, the Lancashire Fusiliers Brigade which had been particularly roughly handled was withdrawn from the line, and their places taken by the New Zealand Brigade. After another naval bombardment the New Zealanders were ordered forward shortly after 10 a. m. of May 8, 1915. By 1.30 they were two hundred yards closer to Krithia than any allied troops had been up to that time. There, however, they were heavily checked. Other units were unable to advance, and the French sent word that they were unable to go any farther unless the British line could move.

There was a long pause. Finally word was passed along the line that the final desperate effort was to be made—namely to carry Krithia and Achi Baba by a combined bayonet attack. Every man in the line was ordered to fix bayonets and not to stop short of the objectives. At 5.30 in the afternoon came the order to advance, after a bombardment by the fleet. Almost immediately all central control was lost, and each unit was fighting desperately for itself in the hills and gullies of that difficult, almost uncharted, country. Not for many hours afterward, indeed, in some cases not for days, was it possible to piece the story together.

The New Zealand troops got well past the Turkish machine guns without discovering them, with the consequence that their supports were mown down by a hail of fire from unexpected quarters. Nevertheless, they got within a few yards of the Turkish trenches and proceeded to dig themselves in. The Second Australian Infantry Brigade actually won about 400 yards of ground and stuck to it with a tenacity warmly praised by Sir Ian Hamilton. To the left the Eighty-seventh Brigade had suffered terribly from machine-gun fire while the French had been severely handled. The French troops were steady enough, but the Senegalese broke in. At one point General d'Amade rallied the troops in person.

Nightfall came and still Krithia and Achi Baba were far away. Thus ended the second battle of Krithia, the supreme attempt of the allied troops to carry the Turkish positions by a maneuver battle. Some little ground had been gained, but the losses had been all out of proportion to the advantage wrested from the brave and tenacious Ottoman troops. The only consolation found in the situation by the higher commands was in the assurance that the enemy had suffered equally heavy losses, but as they were largely on the defensive this statement is open to a very large measure of doubt.

While all this fighting was going on at the tip of the peninsula, the Anzacs, or that part of them left on the cliffs overlooking the cove, were having a hard time to maintain their positions. The Turks were aware of the withdrawal of the two brigades to assist in the second battle of Krithia, and they made a heavy demonstration to prevent the departure of any further troops. To understand how vital a matter this was one has only to read the dispatches of the period. Indeed, it has often since been pointed out by military writers that, had the troops landed from first to last at Anzac Cove been available at the tip of the peninsula, Krithia and Achi Baba would undoubtedly have been carried in the early days of the fighting, thus altering the whole course of the campaign. This dispersal of forces would appear to have been one of the major blunders of the Dardanelles campaign.

For five days, beginning May 6, 1915, the Anzacs were in almost constant action. The fortunes fluctuated, gains were made by both forces, but in the end, aside from heavy losses by both, there was practically no change in the relative positions. The allied troops still held a strip of land on the top of the cliffs, of a radius of about 1,100 yards. As illustrating the intense character of the combat at this period, it was calculated that during one bombardment no less than 1,400 Turkish shells fell on this small strip of land in one hour.

It has been said that the task of the Anzacs at this period was to keep open this door to the vitals of the Turkish army and to hold as many of the Turks as possible, and thus relieve the pressure on the Krithia front. It can be said with equal force that the task of the Turks arrayed against them was to hold as many of the Anzacs on this front as possible. Judged from these angles, both Turks and Britons were successful.

In the following week both the British and the French received substantial reenforcements. On May 14 General d'Amade, in command of the French forces at the Dardanelles, was relieved by General Gouraud, who, at the age of 47, was the youngest officer of his rank in the French army. He had enjoyed conspicuous success in northern France, and had been nicknamed by his soldiers, the "Lion of the Argonne." It was believed that his experience in the country of the Argonne and the style of fighting that had developed there would make him especially valuable to Sir Ian Hamilton, who, of course, had had no previous experience with the new style of warfare.

On May 18, 1915, began the second battle of Anzac. Elaborate preparations were made by General Liman von Sanders, the German commander in chief of the Ottoman forces. Fully 30,000 troops are said to have been gathered for the attack upon the Colonial troops. The latter were fully prepared, warned of the concentration by the observers on the warships and the aerial scouts.

About midnight of that day the attack began. After a preliminary bombardment of the British positions, successive infantry attacks in massed formation were launched against the trenches. For six hours the battle waged, but the Anzacs' positions were not shaken. In the end the ground in front of the trenches was literally covered with the dead and wounded. An actual observer wrote of the scene:

"The ground presents an extraordinary sight when viewed through the trench periscopes. Two hundred yards away, and even closer in some places, are the Turkish trenches, and between them and our lines the dead lie in hundreds. There are groups of twenty or thirty massed together, as if for mutual protection, some lying on their faces, some killed in the act of firing; others hung up in the barbed wire. In one place a small group actually reached our parapet, and now lie dead on it, shot at point-blank range or bayoneted. Hundreds of others lie just outside their own trenches, where they were caught by rifle or shrapnel when trying to regain them. Hundreds of wounded must have perished between the lines."

There was a lull after this terrible slaughter, during which the Turks made unsuccessful overtures to obtain an armistice to bury their dead. On May 20, 1915, toward evening, the Turks again attacked, concentrating on Quinn's Point, a strong Anzac redoubt at the outer edge of the Australian trenches. No results were obtained and finally, out of sheer necessity for reasons of health, an opportunity was given the Turks to bury their slain.

There was some additional fighting on this line during the remaining days of May, but nothing of real importance occurred.

It was calculated, at the end of the month, that the total British losses, killed, wounded and missing and not including sick, was just short of 40,000 men. The figures for the sick were not given out, but reports made later make it tolerably certain that they must have numbered between 30,000 and 35,000 additional. The intensity of the struggle at the Dardanelles will be realized when it is pointed out that the total British casualties in the three years of the South African War were only 38,156.

During the last two weeks of May the British and French troops on the Krithia fronts made elaborate preparations for an attack upon the Turkish lines. Miners had been brought out from England and France, and mining and sapping had been conducted on a large scale. On June 4, 1915, Sir Ian Hamilton ordered the attack. It was preceded by the usual heavy naval and artillery bombardment. Finally, at noon, the mines were exploded, and the troops advanced along the whole line with fixed bayonets.

It is calculated that the British had no less than 24,000 men on a front of less than 4,000 yards. Their attack was delivered with tremendous power and was brilliantly successful. At one point, however, where the French line linked up with the British, the Turks discovered a weak spot. By noon about a third of a mile had been gained over a front of four miles, but soon afterward the French began to weaken and subsequently were compelled to retreat. This exposed the right wing of the British, which was enfiladed by the Turkish riflemen and machine gun batteries and suffered terrible losses. The Collingwood battalion of the Royal Naval Reserve, according to Sir Ian Hamilton, having gone forward in support when the right wing was hard pressed, was practically wiped out.

The attack slackened in the afternoon and nightfall found almost all the gains of the morning lost to the heavy Turkish counterattacks. So exhausted were the British and French troops that it was impossible to renew the battle on the following day.

On June 21, 1915, the French force fought probably its most successful action since the landing. About noon of that day, the Second Division stormed two lines of Turkish trenches and captured what had been called the "Haricot" redoubt, a strong Turkish position which had twice changed hands. On the right, the First Division was unable to make corresponding progress until General Gouraud made a last inspiring appeal. Before night the whole of the Turkish first line trenches above Kereves Dere were in the hands of the French troops. The cost had been terrible, no less than 2,500 soldiers of the Republic falling in the assault. More important still, General Gouraud was so seriously injured that he had to return to France. On the way his right arm was amputated. He was succeeded in command of the French Expeditionary force by General Bailloud.

A week of comparative inaction was followed by an action on the British right, which became known as the battle of the Gully Ravine. This was a successful attempt to capture the ground originally included in Sir Ian Hamilton's instructions for the second day of the Battle of the Landings, near Beach Y, where the Turks had maintained themselves in force, on June 28, by a strong British force, including the overworked Twenty-ninth Division, which at this time had but few of the officers who commanded at the landing on April 25, 1915, the 156th Brigade of the Lowland Division, and the Indian Brigade. Several of the Turkish trenches could be easily enfiladed from the sea and H.M.S. *Talbot,* guarded by a ring of destroyers against the German submarines which had given effective evidence of their presence in the Gulf of Saros, did terrible execution and played a large part in the success of the British attack.

By nightfall, five lines of Turkish trenches along the coast had been captured, 200 prisoners had been taken and several guns and much ammunition had fallen to the British troops. The Turks made counterattacks on the two succeeding nights but never regained the ground they had lost.

While this was going on, Enver Pasha directed in person a determined attack upon the troops at Anzac Cove. On the night of June 29, 1915, after artillery preparation, two unsuccessful attempts were made by the Ottoman troops to carry the British lines.

On July 4, 1915, the Turks launched another attack, starting from the neigborhood of Achi Baba, against the whole allied front, concentrating on the point where the French and British lines joined up. They had a momentary success when they penetrated into one of the British trenches, but in the end they were driven out.

On July 12, 1915, Sir Ian Hamilton ordered an attack which won about 400 yards in the direction of Achi Baba, but at heavy loss to one of the Territorial Brigades, which broke through a couple of the Turkish trench lines, but was unable to establish a connection with the French on their right. Finally some local points and a few trenches were carried, but as the Turks had something like fifty miles of trenches in Gallipoli, it became apparent that at this rate the allied troops would be wiped out long before they came within sight of the Narrows.

CHAPTER LXXVI

RUSSO-TURKISH OPERATIONS

THE Russo-Turkish campaign which had developed in Transcaucasia, the Caucasus and Persia at the beginning of 1915, proved to be little more than a futile dissipation of energy for the best part of a year. To Russia it was more of an inconvenience than otherwise, while for the Turks it was the only point besides Egypt where their geographical position permitted them to strike a blow against the enemies of Germany. Her two nearest neighbors—Greece and Bulgaria—were both neutral at the time. The most interesting feature of this campaign is the fact that it largely influenced the allied operations at the Dardanelles.

On August, 1915, Sir George Buchanan, the British Ambassador in Petrograd, published the following statement in an interview which appeared in the Russian press: "When Turkey declared war Russia turned to Great Britain with a request that she would divert a portion of the Turkish troops from the

Caucasus by means of a counterdemonstration at some other point. The operations at the Dardanelles were undertaken with a double object—on the one hand, of reducing the pressure of the Turks in the Caucasus, and, on the other, of opening the straits and so making it possible for Russia to export her grain and receive foreign products of which she stands in need."

The Turkish offensive in the Caucasus, as we found in Volume II, began in the middle of December, 1914, and reached its farthest point toward the end of the year. Although it was subsequently broken by Russia, its renewal was expected when the weather became more favorable. That it was not renewed during the summer of 1915, and that Tiflis was in consequence relieved from further menace, was due entirely to the British attack on the Dardanelles, to which all available Turkish troops were immediately dispatched. Russia had her hands full enough at the time to maintain her long front of 900 miles—from the Baltic through the Polish salient and through the Carpathian line of Galicia. She could therefore ill afford to spare any considerable part of her forces for an extended Transcaucasian campaign.

Turkey's first plan of action in the Great War appears to have been an attempt to recover Ardahan and Kars, both of which places, as well as Batum, had been taken from Turkey and handed over to Russia by the Treaty of Berlin in 1878. To forestall any such aspirations Russian troops had entered Asia Minor on November 4, 1914, and advanced for seventeen miles along the road to Erzerum in Armenia, and on November 8 they successfully resisted an attack by the Turks, armed with heavy German artillery, at Kuprikeui, from which place several mountain paths lead to Erzerum. Further attacks had also been made by the Turks during the rest of the month and in December likewise in the Euphrates Valley without any notable result, until they had reached Ardahan and Sarikamish in an attempt to regain Kars.

In a three days' battle with the Russians, January 1-4, 1915, they were driven back with enormous losses, the whole of one Turkish army corps (the Ninth) surrendering. (See Volume II,

Turkey in the War.) The Turks did not get within thirty miles of Kars. In numerical strength the Turks were estimated at three to one against the Russians. Fighting in the deep snow at altitudes of 8,000 to 10,000 feet in a severe winter is an enormously difficult undertaking for the attacking side, and it is evident that the Turkish forces suffered terrible hardships in their attempt to retain a footing on Russian territory.

At the end of January and the beginning of February furious fighting raged in the neighborhood of Sarikamish, when the Russians inflicted another defeat on the Turks. During a blinding snowstorm the former had crossed a mountain and, after heavy fighting, captured the commanding general and the staff of the Thirtieth Turkish Division and a large quantity of war material. The roaring of the wind was so great that the Russian approach could not be heard, while the thickly blowing snow rendered the troops invisible.

At the same time the Russian squadron bombarded the Turkish barracks at Trebizond and Rizah from the Black Sea, also sinking some Turkish sailing vessels used as transports. Under the superintendence of German engineers the Turks hurriedly set about constructing a branch railroad from Angora to Sivas, Asia Minor, intended to replace the Trebizond water route as a line of communication for the Turkish troops on the Caucasus front. Meanwhile another Russian column pushed out from Julfa along the Tabriz road to force battle upon the Turkish army invading the Persian province of Azerbaijan. The Turks advanced northward from Tabriz to Marand, where a stubborn battle was fought. They were commanded by Djevet Pasha, who was considered one of their best tacticians and most agressive fighters, but after a series of unsuccessful frontal onslaughts his army broke in disorder, abandoning cannon, colors (standards), and all their dead and wounded. To the Russians the victory was more of political than military value, for it dealt a severe blow at Turkish and German influence in Persia.

On February 8, 1915, the Turkish cruiser *Midirli* (formerly the German warship *Breslau*) fired upon the Russian port of Jalta on the Crimean Peninsula, opposite Balaklava. The Russian fleet retaliated by again bombarding Trebizond on the other side of the Black Sea.

About February 20-21, 1915, several small engagements were fought in the vicinity of Chorokh, as a result of which the Turks were driven beyond the river.

On February 22, 1915, news came from Petrograd to the effect that the Turks had indulged in cruel atrocities during their occupation of Ardanuten in Transcaucasia, near the Armenian frontier. The Tiflis correspondent of the "Russkoye Slovo" (the "Russian Word") stated that at first the Turks confined themselves to pillage and killed only fifteen civilians, but that after December 30, 1914, when news of the Russian occupation of Ardaham was received, the local Mussulmans had organized a systematic massacre. A hundred and fifty Armenians were led out into the streets and killed.

Fifty Armenians were removed from prisons, stripped naked, and compelled to leap into the abyss of Jenemdere, the "Devil's Gap," until one victim carried a Turk with him, when the remainder were shot. At Tamvot 250 Armenians were massacred and the women carried into captivity. The Turks did not permit the burial of the corpses, which were left to be devoured by dogs till the arrival of the Russians. Again, it was reported from Urumiah, northwestern Persia, that prior to the evacuation of towns between Julfa and Tabriz the Turks and Kurds, who were retiring before the Russian advance, plundered and burned the villages and put to death some of the inhabitants. At Salnac, Pagaduk, and Sarna orders were said to have been given by the Turkish commissioner for the destruction of the towns. All the Armenian inhabitants of Antvat were collected and, according to this message, 600 males were put to death, and the women, after being compelled to embrace the Islamic faith, were divided into parties and sent to various interior towns.

On March 19, 1915, the Armenian Red Cross fund in London issued some details supplied by an Armenian doctor named Derderian, who testified that the whole plain of Alashgerd was virtually covered with the bodies of men, women, and children. When the Russian forces had retreated from this district the

Kurds fell upon the helpless people and shut them up in mosques. The men were killed and the women were carried away to the mountains. The Armenian Red Cross fund stated that there were 120,000 destitute Armenians in the Caucasus at that time.

As war in itself is not far removed from being a wholesale, organized atrocity on a large scale, it is always advisable to accept such accusations with extreme reserve and to consider the probability of their having been perpetrated. In the case of Turk and Kurd *versus* Armenian, however—and unfortunately —there is little reason to doubt even the most gruesome stories that could possibly be written. It is a feud as old as the hills, and no historic battle field of the world was ever so liberally drenched with human blood as the soil of Armenia.

Having expelled the Turks from the Transcaucasian region toward the end of February, 1915, the Russians again moved forward on the Asiatic front, sweeping aside, destroying and capturing detachments of Turks that opposed their advance.

By March 1, 1915, the Russians were approaching Oltichai along one of the main highroads toward Erzerum from the west. Another column advancing from the east encountered some Turks in the mountain passes south of Alashkort. These they defeated, capturing two guns. On February 28, 1915, the Russian troops operating in the coast region occupied the port of Khopa on the Black Sea, eighteen miles southwest of Batum. This port was of great military value to the Turks.

On March 3, 1915, the Russian Army of the Caucasus, driving the Turkish forces before it, had reached the River Khopachas, the estuary of the Chorokh in Armenia. This move severed the route of Turkish reenforcements and supplies from Constantinople to the Caucasian frontier through Khlopa, Turkish Armenia, thereby isolating a big portion of Turkish territory. From Batum Russian troops advanced near the Turkish border, the Turks opposing them step by step. Russian warships from the Black Sea sprayed their shells over the shore and cleared a fifteen-mile strip of coast of Turkish barracks and troops, successively cutting off several lines of their communications by sea until, after a three days' battle, the last route was effectively closed. A number of Turkish coasting vessels, laden with ammunition and supplies, were also sunk.

According to an official Russian report issued on March 3, 1915, the number of Turkish prisoners who had passed through Pyatigorsk on their way to the interior of Russia (since Turkey entered the war) up to February 13, 1915, amounted to 527 officers and 49,000 men.

During February, 1915, the Turks had been nibbling at Egypt through the Sinai Peninsula. On the 25th of that month the allied squadrons had begun heavy firing on the Dardanelles. This decided the supreme Turkish war council early in March to recall most of the troops from Egypt and the Caucasus to defend the straits. By March 16, 1915, the Turks had lost so many important points in the Chorokh region that they completely abandoned to the Russians what positions they still held on the river.

On March 20, 1915, Petrograd announced that the Russian advance to the sea had deprived the enemy of all means of operating in the Transchorokh region or of transporting troops and munitions to Erzerum, and that the Turks had been put to flight near Olti. The road between Archava and Khopa, to the eastward, was strongly defended by the Turks in a series of stubbornly contested battles. The Russian advance created a panic throughout the Chorokh Valley; the inhabitants fled to the mountains, abandoning farms and villages. The mountain heights in the district of Ardanuch, however, were strongly fortified and still in Turkish possession. These fortifications had been built under German supervision, and the defense thereof was conducted by a German officer.

Hostilities were resumed in Persia during the last week in March, 1915, and on the 25th the Russians defeated the Turks in a violent, sanguinary battle at Atkutur, north of Bilman in northwestern Persia. The Turks were stated to have lost 12,000 in killed, wounded, and prisoners, as well as many guns. Preceding the Russian occupation of Salmac Plains in Azerbaijan province, northwest of Urumiah, hundreds of native Christians were rounded up by the Turks in the village of Haftdewan and massacred. Many of them were dragged out from the homes of friendly Mohammedans, who tried to hide them. The Russians on entering the village found 720 bodies, mostly naked and mutilated. The recovery of bodies from wells, pools, and ditches, and their interment kept 300 men busy for three days. The wailing of women intensified the horror of the scene. Surviving widows who were able to identify the bodies of their husbands insisted upon digging graves and burying the bodies. "Some of the victims had been shot. In other cases they were bound to ladders, and their heads, protruding through, were hacked off. Eyes were gouged out and limbs chopped off."

Messages from Urumiah confirmed earlier reports that more than 800 persons had already been killed in the neighborhood, and that more than 2,000 had died of disease.

A dispatch from Tiflis, Transcaucasia, dated April 24, 1915, stated that refugees who had reached the Russian line reported that the massacre of Armenians was being continued on an even greater scale. All the inhabitants of ten villages near Van were stated to have been killed. On being advised of massacres at Erzerum, Berjan, and Zeitun, and of the conditions at Van, the Katolikos, head of the Armenian Church at Etchmiadzin, near Erivan, cabled to President Wilson an appeal to the people of the United States to act on behalf of the Armenians.

The village governments or relief committees had managed to issue eight pounds of flour to each refugee in six weeks. A journey through Salmac three weeks after the outrages revealed unmistakable signs of the slaughter. Pools of blood still marked the "execution" places in Haftdewan. The caps of thirty-six victims lay where a mud wall had been toppled over them. A young Armenian named Hackatur related the story of his escape from a well in which the bodies of the dead had been crammed. He had fallen with the others and was flung into the well, but he managed to wriggle through the bodies lying on top of him, and escaped at nightfall.

At the end of April, 1915, after a slight lull, fresh activity broke out again in various regions of the Caucasian front. The campaign had almost come to a standstill owing to typhus. On the average, 150 men succumbed daily. The epidemic raged for a while under indescribably awful conditions. Every available doctor was hurried out, and several of them died of the disease. The Russians had cleared the Kurds out of the Alashkart valley and were now pushing forward in the direction of Olti. The fight for the valley centered on the possession of Klichgjaduk Pass, which would have been extremely useful to the Turks could they have held it securely for a few days to enable them to complete a junction with their separated forces. The Russians "lay low" in strongly protected positions. The Turks came on, first obviously for reconnaissance, and were easily repulsed without the Russians making much display of force. Whatever may be said of the Turkish soldier, he is at all times a brave and self-reliant fighter. They advanced to make the real attack, supported by some mountain guns. But the Russian artillery continued to lie silent, and the Turkish attack developed with misplaced confidence and swept boldly up to the line of the Russian wire entanglements. Only sixty yards separated the combatants when, suddenly, a perfect tornado of fire rattled out from the Russian intrenchments. Maxims, mountain guns and rifles poured a deadly shower of shells and bullets into the closely packed thousands of Turks. With extraordinary courage the Osmanli still rushed into the trap, uttering fierce shouts of "Allahoo Akbar!" The Russians then broke from cover and some terrible bayonet work completed the task of securing the pass for the Russians.

By May 10, 1915, the Turks had been driven back to the southwest, leaving a large quantity of tents and munitions behind them. Farther south, from Sarikamish, a number of insignificant conflicts were kept up. Turkish stragglers formed partnerships with local professionals and organized companies of banditti; the Russians were kept busy clearing out the villages where these bands had established their headquarters, driving them into the hills. To the southeast, the pursuit of Halil Bey's defeated army continued during the first week in May. The battle had begun at Hantahta, near Urumiah, on April 29, 1915. Both sides lost heavily. In the beginning the Russians had held the Turks at bay, but the latter received reenforcements and on April 30, 1915, the Russians had to withdraw from Dilman. They intrenched themselves at Magonzhio, the first village on the way to Khori, whence they battered the Turks with their heavy artillery until the arrival of Russian reenforcements.

On May 14, 1915, it was announced from Washington that replies were being prepared at the State Department to a flood of communications from various parts of the country urging that steps be taken to protect Christians in Armenia and other regions under Turkish control. Assurance was given that the Department was doing all in its power to aid the Armenians. Mr. Morgenthau, our Ambassador at Constantinople, was instructed to make representations to the Turkish Government. It was at his request that Turkish regular troops were sent to Urumiah, Persia, to keep order.

The Russian consul at that place reported on May 15, 1915, that 6,000 Armenians had been massacred at Van, which has been the scene of so many similar outrages during the last twenty years. On May 23, 1915, a detachment of Russian soldiers occupied the town of Van, in Asiatic Turkey, thus bringing the eagerly expected relief to the Armenians, who were besieged by the Turks—besieged in their own country by their own countrymen. Upon the arrival of the Russians the Turks retreated in the direction of Bitlis.

The Russian successes in the Van region included the occupation of Baslan; in the capture of Van itself they took twenty-six guns, a great quantity of war materials and provisions, as well as the Government Treasury. A considerable part of the town was destroyed by fire. All the foreigners residing there were reported as safe. By June 6, 1915, the Russians had the whole Van region and part of the Sanjak of Mush in their hands. They had practically annihilated Halil Bey's original corps and cleared the Turkish troops out for many miles around. A Turkish offensive in the Province of Azerbaijan ended in a complete breakdown. On their right wing the Russians occupied Turkish territory between the old frontier and the line of the rivers Chorokh and Tortun and the mountain range of

Tchakhir Baba. A violent counterattack made by the Turks at Zinatcher was repulsed. In the course of an engagement in the valley of Oltichai 200 Cossacks charged on horseback to the trenches, where they dismounted. Leaving their well-trained horses to look after themselves, the Cossacks dashed into the Turks and put them to the sword. Two days later a Turkish official report from Constantinople via wireless to Berlin and London very briefly announced: "On the Caucasian front we occupied enemy positions in the district of Olti, on the Russian border of Transcaucasia."

The operations in the Dardanelles apparently had but little effect on Turkish activity in the Caucasus, for by June 19, 1915, they had replaced the Ninth Army Corps which had been captured by the Russians at Sarikamish, and had also restored and supplied with ammunition the Tenth and Eleventh Corps, which were seriously reduced in numbers by fighting and disease. The main Turkish concentration was taking place about this time against Olti, Melo, and Kiskin, outside of which line the First and Sixth Corps and the remainder of Halil Bey's army were drawn up. Here the Turks undertook some cautious offensive maneuvers, besides attempting to prevent the Russians from outflanking Erzerum. Some of the Kurdish leaders who were responsible for the Armenian massacres in the Van district voluntarily surrendered to the Russians and were deported to the interior with their dependents.

On June 20, 1915, in a battle near Olti, fifty-five miles west of Kars, 200 Russians were killed and prisoners and war materials were taken. By June 24, 1915, the Russians had occupied Gob, a town twenty-five miles north of Lake Van. A general movement of Russian troops toward Bitlis, where the armies of two Turkish commanders were concentrated, pointed to a favorable situation in the Caucasus from the Russian standpoint. Gob and Bitlis are connected by several comparatively good roads. But matters now began to quiet down somewhat—activities on both sides decreased. Russian sentiment had grown strong in North and Central Persia, a fact accentuated by the spirit displayed among the Moslem sects. Various isolated mountain tribes met the Russians with declarations of allegiance —obviously the safest policy to adopt with a powerful conqueror. Disease and famine stalked through the smoldering district of Van; only one doctor was available for 40,000 people —a large number of them in dire need of medical assistance.

In the first week of July, 1915, lively fighting was reported to have occurred north and south of Lake Van and south of Olti. A Turk force of 30,000 men, concentrated to the east of Bitlis, were being hard pressed by the Russians. Organized massacre of Armenians in Bitlis was regarded as an indication that the Turks intended to retreat from that point. They had also distributed 40,000 rifles among Kurds in the Mush Valley for use against Armenians.

Up to July 6, 1915, there had been only an artillery duel in the coast region, and a Russian motor boat sank a Turkish sailing vessel. South of the Kara Dagh range a Russian detachment encountered a regiment of Turkish infantry with artillery, machine guns, and two squadrons of cavalry. The Turks were again reported as coming off second best with considerable damage inflicted upon them. A Turkish offensive west of Ahlavat also failed.

After the Russians penetrated to Mush (eighty-three miles south of Erzerum), and Plian, Halil Bey, commander of the Turkish forces in the Caucasus, reorganized his army, bringing its strength up to 90,000, including six divisions of infantry, one of cavalry, and a large body of Kurds. General Eudenitch, the Russian commander, thus found himself confronted with the alternative of hastily attempting to concentrate his forces in the face of a strong Turkish army, or to retreat and thus expose a large Armenian population to Turk and Kurdish revenge. The main Russian army withdrew along the right bank of the Euphrates, the Turks occupying the left bank, July 22-25, 1915, being held in partial check by rear-guard actions.

On August 1, 1915, Halil Bey's forces came into contact with a considerable body of Russians at Palantchen, on the left bank of the Euphrates, twelve miles southwest of Kara Kilissa. The Russians had taken positions on a line extending from the northeast to the southwest from Darabi, six miles north of Kara Kilissa, to Djamschato, six miles southwest of the important Akhtunski Pass, covering the roads to Erivan, in Transcaucasia. In opposing this front the Turks exposed their communications, then 150 miles long, to attack from the direction of Sarikamish. The violent and picturesque fighting that developed during the first week of August will be described in the next volume.

The Turkish and Persian borders had meanwhile settled down to comparative quiet. Up to this stage the Russian commander had made no attempt to advance to Erzerum, though there were strong grounds for belief that the defenses of that fortress were by no means so strong as had been supposed or represented.

Russia was waiting her time in this theatre of war: her object was merely to hold the gate. She had just suffered severe reverses in Galicia and the Carpathians, and was now fighting desperately to avoid the great enveloping movement engineered by all the skill and weight of Von Hindenburg and Von Mackensen on her own territory of Poland and Russia itself.

PART XI—THE WAR IN AFRICA

CHAPTER LXXVII

THE CAMEROONS

THE war in Africa smoldered and flamed during the second period from February to August, 1915. The fight for the colonial possessions became a struggle for existence.

During the spring of 1915 the fighting in the Cameroons was generally favorable to the allied arms. In April the advance of the French and British troops forced the Germans to transfer their seat of Government from Buëa to Yaunde. In this month, Colonel Mayer's French column succeeded in pushing its way over the River Kele, while about the same time a British detachment seized a bridge across Ngwa.

On May 11, 1915, the station of Escha was taken. The Germans who occupied a strong position at Njoke were driven out, and the place was occupied by the British on May 29, 1915.

In the hinterland, along the Sanga River, the French columns had met with continued success in harrying and driving out the enemy. The Germans displayed great bravery, and offered stubborn resistance, but were forced to fall back on fortified Monso. Here they held out for some days, when they were forced to capitulate, and considerable stores of guns and ammunition fell to the victors.

The French troops continued their successful drive by taking Assobam and Besam on June 25, 1915, and then occupied the important post of Lomji, in the capture of which, the Belgian soldiers furnished invaluable assistance, proving themselves to be skillful and fearless fighters.

What especially contributed to make the Allies' successes easier in this section of the war area was the revolt of the natives against their German masters. The Germans during their retreat had burned villages and destroyed a vast amount of property which so enraged the natives that many deserted. Having a perfect knowledge of the country it was easy for them to escape capture. It was stated that many hung around the German flanks and took revenge on their former masters by hindering their retreat and by occasionally sniping the German officers.

The natives of the Cameroons were not generally trusted by the Germans, and were forbidden to fish in the streams of the country, lest they should furnish information to the enemy.

Countercharges of British cruelty were brought at this time by certain German missionaries of the Basle Mission, on the Sanga River. It was claimed that British troops promised to reward natives for delivering Germans into their hands, and for killing them. A number of Germans, it was stated, had been cut to pieces, while others had been tortured and delivered to the British. It was charged against the French military authorities that German prisoners had been deported to French Dahomey where they were forced to labor under black overseers. These charges were denied by the accused in each instance.

During April and May, 1915, there was sharp fighting on the Nigeria frontier. The large native town of Gurin, just inside British territory, was attacked by a German force from Garua in April. The contingent numbered sixteen Europeans, and about 350 natives. It was equipped with some large guns and Maxims. For the defense of the town there was only a small garrison of forty native troops commanded by Lieutenant Pawle. For seven hours the garrison held off the enemy, when he was forced to retire. During the struggle Lieutenant Pawle, the gallant commander of the garrison, was killed. The news of this engagement was carried by native soldiers who escaped from Gurin, to Colonel F. G. Cunliffe at Yola, who immediately set off with a detchment of the African Frontier Force, arriving on the scene of the siege the day following. After being joined by a body of French troops, he moved on to capture Garua where the British had met with disastrous defeat in August, 1914.

Since that time the four forts of the town had been greatly strengthened and every preparation was now made for a stout resistance. The British and French having intrenched themselves, the British guns began a vigorous bombardment of the forts. During the night sapping and mining went on steadily, enabling the British to move their trenches gradually nearer their objective.

The siege lasted from May 31 to June 10, 1915, when the forts surrendered. The allied troops entered Garua on June 11, taking over thirty-seven German, and 270 native prisoners, while great quantities of arms, ammunition and stores became their prizes. It was said that the garrisons of the forts might have held out much longer if they had not lost their nerve and become panic-stricken, which caused many desertions. It was a remarkable feature of this spirited struggle that the Allies did not lose a man.

Leaving Garua, the British and French troops now moved on Ngaundere, capital of the Adamawa District, which was taken with insignificant losses to the Allies on July 29, 1915. The retiring Germans were closely pursued to Tangere, which stands on a plateau nearly 4,000 feet high. This place was captured by the allied forces July 12, and attempts made by the Germans to regain it eleven days later were repulsed.

Early in August, 1915, the British captured Gaschaka and Koncha, when the heavy rains suspended for the time any further military operations. Meanwhile the French force had been working its way toward Yaunde, occupying the station of Dume on the way. The arrival of French troops at this town seems to have surprised and dismayed the Germans, who hastily abandoned several fortified places and destroyed their transport. They continued, however, to hold the hill above Dume for some time, but were driven out by a French detachment after a short struggle. From Dume a French column was dispatched against Abong-Mbong.

At the beginning of the fall of 1915, the Germans still held Yaunde, and a district in the center of the country, but the Cameroons could no longer be considered a German possession.

CHAPTER LXXVIII

BRITISH CONQUEST OF SOUTHWEST AFRICA

OUR attention is now drawn to Southwest Africa. In the first week of February, 1915, the Germans made a determined effort to break through the encircling armies that were closing in on them. Kakamas on the Orange, where a British garrison was stationed to protect Schuit Drift, was fiercely attacked on February 5 by about 600 Germans, well equipped with Maxims and machine guns. They were beaten off after a short engagement with a loss of nine men killed, twenty-two wounded, and fifteen taken prisoners. On the Union side the casualties were one killed, and two wounded.

On February 22, 1915, General Botha's army being ready, he moved out of Swakopmund, and on the following day occupied the stations of Nonidas and Goanikontes, meeting with only slight resistance. Nearly a month was now spent in preparing for the advance on the capital, Windhoek. Careful reconnoitering of the enemy's positions was made, and an advanced base was established.

On the night of March 19, 1915, two mounted brigades left the post at Husab to clear the railway line. General Botha accompanied the first brigade, which was commanded by Colonel Brits, their object being Riet, an important place south of the railway, where it was known that the enemy was strongly prepared. Riet was of utmost importance to the Union force for it commanded the highway to Windhoek. It was planned that while Colonel Brits's brigade attacked Riet the Bloemhof Commando was to execute a flank movement and seizing Schwarze Kopje to endeavor to cut off the enemy's retreat.

At daybreak on March 20, 1915, the brigade reached the German position. The right rested on the Swakop stream; the left on the foothills of Langer Heinrichberg, while the artillery was effectively placed so as to command the river and highway. Assisted by the guns of the Transvaal Horse Artillery a frontal attack was made, and the fighting became general. With varying fortunes it continued until the evening when the Germans were finally driven out and dispersed.

The second brigade commanded by Colonel Celliers had been directed to cut the railway line between Jakalswater and Sphinx. He was to attack the former place after blocking the way, in case any reenforcements should be sent by the enemy from Windhoek. Celliers succeeded in cutting the railway and seized a train containing supplies for the Germans, but his attack on Jakalswater was a failure, and the enemy made forty-three of his men prisoners.

General Botha was so confident of the ultimate success of his campaign, that he was not disposed to imperil his chances by any hasty operations, and so his progress toward Windhoek was at first necessarily slow. The nature of the country afforded the enemy many natural advantages and unfortunately the Union forces were not provided with aeroplanes, which would have proved invaluable in scouting.

Pforto, a station on the line where the Germans occupied a strong position, was surrounded by a column led by Colonel Alberts. The enemy had two large guns and a number of Maxims. A charge by the Union force and the effective work of their battery soon silenced the enemy's artillery. The Germans had lost twenty killed, of whom three were officers, when they surrendered unconditionally. There were 210 prisoners taken, four guns and a large quantity of ammunition.

General Botha was engaged in April and May, 1915, clearing the railway system of the enemy. To prevent any flank attacks it was necessary to hold the two main lines, which run from

Swakopmund north to Grootfontein, Tsumeb, and to Windhoek. This line being cleared for fifty miles, Colonel Skinner and the Kimberley Regiment were stationed at Trekopje, which became the Union railhead.

On April 26, 1915, about 700 Germans and a dozen guns vigorously assailed this encampment and for four hours the fight raged with varying consequences. The Germans under a withering fire from their batteries tried to surround the Union trenches to enfilade them, but were forced to retire, when they had got within 150 feet of their objective, leaving twenty-five killed and wounded behind them. The Union force lost eleven men, of whom three were officers, and forty wounded.

Meanwhile, the southern army was actively engaged. Sir Duncan Mackenzie's column had dispersed the Germans and taken some booty from one or two places near Luderitz Bay, and had seized many miles of railway. On February 22, 1915, his advance guard occupied Garub, a station seventy miles inland. Here a company of Union scouts pushed after the retiring Germans, and in a skirmish with mounted men protecting a troop train their leader was wounded. They were forced to retire, leaving one of their comrades a prisoner in the hands of the enemy. The British camp at Garub was also attacked by a hostile aeroplane which dropped hand grenades and shells, but there were no casualties.

Aus, an important station fifteen miles from Garub, was next occupied by Mackenzie. The place was evacuated without a struggle, but it showed that much work had been done to fortify it, and that the enemy had intended to resist. Owing to the rapid movements of the British force the Germans had abandoned everything, though several mines exploded when the town was occupied.

Turning now to the movements of General Smut's army in the south. Colonel Van der Venter, who commanded an important section of the army, crossed the Orange River and occupied a group of stations, including Nabas, Velloor, Ukamas, Jerusalem, and Heirachabis.

On the last day of March, 1915, Van der Venter's force was engaged in several skirmishes in which one man was killed and two wounded, while six of the enemy were killed and twenty-eight taken prisoners. At this price the stations of Platbeen and Geitsaud which yielded a great quantity of supplies and horses and live-stock were occupied.

On April 30, 1915, Van der Venter occupied Warmbad, the railway terminus, without opposition and pushing forward along the line his men entered Kabus, a station sixty-five miles to the north, two days later.

General Smut met Van der Venter at Kalkfontein on April 11, 1915, where plans were laid to drive the Germans from Karas Mountains where they occupied some strong positions. The enemy was attacked in three columns, advancing from different points. Finding themselves threatened on all sides, the Germans made no resistance and abandoned everything.

On April 17, 1915, Van der Venter entered Seeheim, the Germans fleeing in such hot haste that they could not stop to destroy the bridge over the Great Fish River. Colonel Berrange's force which had set out from Kimberley was now in touch with Van der Venter's column. At Hasnur near Rietfontein, Berrange took an intrenched position with slight losses and after frequent skirmishes and hard fighting joined Van der Venter's forces near Keetmanshoop, which surrendered to the combined forces April 20, 1915.

Sir Duncan Mackenzie's column left at Aus now struck out to the northeast with his mounted men and occupied the towns of Bethany and Berseba without meeting resistance and April 24, 1915, reached Aritetis on the railway, seventy miles north of Keetmanshoop, General Mackenzie could now act in conjunction with Van der Venter against the Germans retreating from Seeheim and Keetmanshoop. At Kabus, twenty miles north, in an indecisive engagement with the enemy, the Union forces lost twenty-two men taken prisoners, while the Germans numbering about 600, continued their retreat, their objective being Gibeon, where they hoped to entrain for the capital, Windhoek. General Mackenzie therefore sent a small party to destroy the railway to the north of Gibeon, while the Ninth Brigade was to engage the enemy. This body was defeated by the Germans with severe loss. They took some seventy prisoners and forced the Ninth Brigade to fall back on the main body.

On the morning of April 28, 1915, Mackenzie led his whole force against the Germans in a dashing attack that drove them from the field, and his cavalry continued to pursue them over twenty miles of country. The rocky and irregular character of the ground in this neighborhood made it difficult for cavalry operations, and the Germans made good their escape. The British lost three officers and twenty men killed; the wounded numbered fifty-five, of whom eight were officers. Among the killed was Major J. H. Watt of the Natal Light Horse. The British captured from the enemy seven officers, and about 200 men. They also released seventy of their own soldiers who had been made prisoners by the Germans on the previous day.

The booty that fell to the victors included field guns and Maxims, transport wagons, and large numbers of live stock. It was at Gibeon, where this battle was fought, that Sir George Farrar was killed in a railroad accident on May 18, 1915. His important services in the Commissariat Department during the invasion of the colony had contributed to making the successes of the Union forces possible. His career had been full of adventure. He was sentenced to death for the part he had taken in the Jamieson raid, and had fought against the Boers in 1899-02.

While General Mackenzie was successfully operating around Gibeon, General Botha's troops were active in the north; but nothing of importance occurred until May 1, 1915, when Kubas was hurriedly evacuated by the Germans and occupied by General Brits. Here, it was discovered that the Germans had made elaborate preparations for resistance, but—became panic-stricken by the sudden and unexpected arrival of Union forces. Miles of intrenchments surrounded the place, and a hundred contact mines were discovered and removed. From this point Colonel Brits continued his advance, and encountered the enemy at Otyimbigue, sixty-one miles from the capital of Windhoek.

After a spirited skirmish the place was taken, the Germans losing twenty-eight men as prisoners. Continuing their victorious advance the Union forces captured Karibib, an important railroad junction, and Johann Albrechtshöhe and Wilhelmstal were next occupied.

With General Botha threatening the capital from the west, and all the colony south of Gibeon in British hands, the greatest difficulties in the way of the invaders had been successfully overcome, and the end seemed to be near.

On May 10, 1915, General Botha was informed that Windhoek, the capital, was prepared to surrender. He set out at once for the town in a motor car accompanied by a small escort, and arranged with the Burgomaster of Windhoek the terms of capitulation.

On May 12, 1915, General Myburgh and a detachment of Union forces entered the town which contained at the time about 3,000 Europeans and some 12,000 natives.

Before the courthouse, in the presence of the town officials, and Union officers and men, a proclamation by General Botha in Dutch, English, and German was read, which placed the conquered districts under martial law, and which further expressed the hope that there would be no attempts to resist the Union forces as they must prove futile. The great wireless station at the capital, which kept the colony in touch with Berlin, was found to be uninjured, and with its capture the Germans lost their last wireless station outside of Europe. Thousands of cases of ammunition and parts of guns were among the prizes taken, while on the railway a number of locomotives and quantities of rolling stock were seized.

It now became the immediate business of General Botha's army to deal with those German straggling forces which remained still under arms in the north. In a few days following the occupation of the capital, Colonel Mentz found part of the enemy at Seeis, and without losing a man took 252 prisoners and a great quantity of booty. General Botha meanwhile occupied Omaruru, a station on the railway, and in the same week took possession of Kalkfield which was strongly intrenched, but which the Germans were compelled to abandon owing to Botha's adroit flanking movements. The Germans declining to make a stand, Botha's army swept victoriously onward.

In the last week in June, 1915, all the districts around Waterberg were cleared of the enemy. Leaving Okaputu in the evening of June 30, 1915, General Manie Botha with the Fifth Brigade got in touch with the Germans at dawn the next day near Osib, after a forced march of forty-two miles in sixteen hours. The Germans were driven off, and before nightfall Otavi was occupied. Here a good supply of water was found and as the country around is arid and like a desert, the loss of the town was a serious one to the enemy.

General Lukin with another brigade had set out from Omarasa at the same time as Manie Botha, and between them came General Botha and the Headquarters Staff.

The fight at Otavi was the last stand of importance made by the Germans. They had shown great bravery, but supplies were failing, they had been driven into the most inhospitable part of the colony, the natives were not always friendly, and during the first days of July, 1915, they made preparations to surrender.

The Union troops under General Myburgh, having left the railway, encountered a body of Germans sixteen miles south of Tsumeb and in the skirmish that followed lost one man and took eighty-six prisoners.

At Tsumeb, which Myburgh entered on July 8, 1915, some 600 more prisoners were taken, while he was able to release a number of Union comrades who had been left behind by the Germans in their hurried retreat. Colonel Brits had by this time reached the German port of Namutoni, where he took 150 prisoners, and released some Union captives, the last that remained in German hands.

Dr. Seitz, the Governor of German Southwest Africa, now opened communcations with General Botha concerning a surrender, and received the Union officer's terms in the form of an ultimatum. Botha stated that he and his troops stood ready to fight, if need be, another battle, but his terms were accepted before the time limit he had fixed expired.

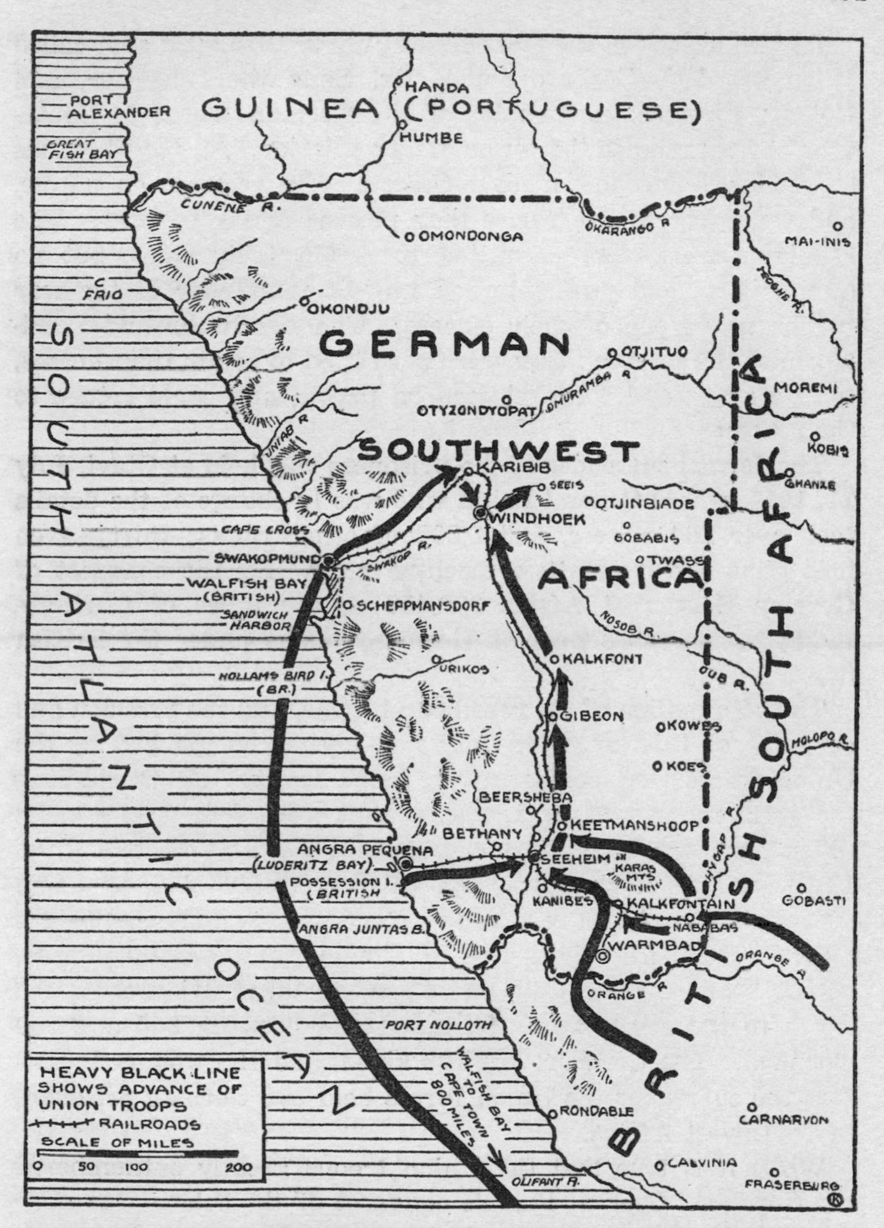

CONQUEST OF GERMAN SOUTHWEST AFRICA BY UNION TROOPS UNDER GENERAL BOTHA

At two o'clock in the morning of July 9, 1915, at a spot called Kilometre 500, General Botha, Dr. Seitz the Governor, and Colonel Francke, commander of the German troops in Southwest Africa, signed the terms of capitulation. All the Germans surrendered unconditionally. Officers were released on parole, and were free to live where they pleased in the country. The regular troops were permitted to retain their rifles, but no ammunition, and were interned for the remainder of the war in charge of one of their officers. The Landwehr and Landsturm of the reserve forces were permitted to retain their horses, but no arms, and were released on parole, and could return to their homes.

The formal surrender of the prisoners was held at Otavi, July 11, 1915, where General Lukin who was in charge of the details took over 204 officers, and 3,293 of other ranks; thirty-seven field guns and twenty-two machine guns. By the conquest of German Southwest Africa 322,450 square miles of territory, 113,670 more miles than all Germany, came under the British flag.

The suppression of the rebellion at home, and the invasion and conquest of this large territory had been accomplished by the Union forces with comparatively small loss of life considering the great number of engagements that were fought in a most difficult country for military operations. The best estimate gives 1,612 for both campaigns. The killed numbered 406, of whom ninety-six were killed in action by the Germans and ninety-eight by the rebels, fifty-eight died of wounds, and 153 by disease, accident, and other causes, and 606 were taken prisoners. The losses to the rebels were 190 killed and between 300 and 350 wounded. The Germans lost 103 killed, and 195 wounded. Before the surrender the Union forces held 890 German prisoners in Southwest Africa.

While it is true that the Union troops greatly outnumbered the Germans, General Botha's conquest of the colony was none the less a brilliant military achievement. The most dangerous foe that the Union soldiers encountered was not the Germans, but the deadly climate; the stretches of burning desert veld from eighty to a hundred miles wide, that had to be crossed in a heat that rose at times to 120° Fahrenheit in the shadow of the tents. All the supplies, the provisions for the men, and much of the water for their consumption had to be brought from Cape Town. The care taken in the commissariat department, and especially in the water supply, in a country where the enemy had polluted the wells, accounted for the general good health of the invading army. That 30,000 men should have been able to fight in such a difficult country for five months at a cost of less than 2,000 casualties was an experience rare in military annals, and reflects lasting credit on General Botha who planned the entire invasion.

The Germans, outmatched and outnumbered, avoided engagements whenever possible, but offered a stubborn resistance and fought with great bravery when there was no alternative. Once the Union forces were ready to advance, their rapid movements and forced marches took the Germans by surprise in the midst of their preparations, and baffled and bewildered them. Cut off entirely from help from the outside, and running short of ammunition which could not be replaced, their struggle could only result in one conclusion.

CHAPTER LXXIX

OTHER AFRICAN OPERATIONS

THE fighting along the African coast during this period was minor but picturesque. On February 26, 1915, the British military authorities announced that the coast of German East Africa would be blockaded on February 28, four days being allowed for the departure of neutral vessels. Some minor successes, chiefly naval, were obtained by the British during the month of March, when they occupied Shirati on Lake Victoria Nyanza and established there a base for armed steamers.

It was here on March 6, 1915, that the *Muanza*, the only

German armed steamer that remained on the lake, was destroyed by the British steamer *Winifred.*

In April, 1915, Major General Tighe, who had won distinction in the Indian Service, was appointed to command the British troops in German East Africa. During this month there was some desultory fighting along the edges of Kilmanjaro, and repeated but ineffectual attempts were made to cut the Uganda Railway line; otherwise there were no hostile movements worthy of note in this region.

On March 9, 1915, a German column, marching along the Maru River to invade the Karungu district on the eastern shore of Lake Victoria Nyanza, was defeated and scattered, after a short engagement, by a force of British troops under Colonel Hickson.

Along the region between the Uganda Railroad and the German frontier there were frequent skirmishes during May between British patrols and German troops, in which the losses were trifling on either side. The German forces had been operating for some time from the fortified port of Bukoba, and it was important to the future movements of the British that the place should be destroyed. On June 20 an expedition was dispatched by steamer from the British port at Kisumu, 240 miles away on the eastern shore; at the same time it was planned that British troops on the Kagora River were to cross the thirty miles that divided them from the German fortified port.

On June 25, 1915, Brigadier General J. A. Stewart, commanding detachments of the First Loyal North Lancashires, King's African Rifles, and the Twenty-fifth Royal Fusiliers reached Bukoba. The port was attacked by land and water. The British were in superior numbers, having only about 400 against them, but the Germans fought intrepidly, and their Arab allies showed great bravery. The British success was not easily won. The Germans lost most of their artillery and there were heavy casualties. The wireless station was ruined, boats in the harbor were sunk or captured, and the destruction wrought by the British on the port was complete.

The capture of Bukoka was important to the British, for as

a direct result the Uganda borders were kept clear of the enemy for the greater part of the summer of 1915.

The German town of Sphynxhaven on the eastern shore of Lake Nyassa was attacked on May 30, 1915, by a British naval force under Lieutenant Commander Dennistoun, supported by field artillery and a landing party of King's African Rifles. During the sharp, short engagement that followed the place was bombarded from the water, the enemy was driven out, and great quantities of rifles, ammunition, and military stores fell to the British.

The climatic conditions in the low-lying Nyassaland and Uganda borders in the summertime caused the British soldiers more suffering and deaths than their enemies. Insect pests like the tsetse fly swarm around Lake Victoria Nyanza, while different fevers of peculiarly malignant varieties lie in wait to attack the European. There is the terrible sleeping sickness that spares neither white nor black race. The great lake cannot be bathed in without danger for its abounds in crocodiles and hippopotami.

Guerrilla warfare was kept up during most of the summer of 1915 along the northeastern borders of Rhodesia and in Nyassaland. On June 28 the Germans were driven off when they attacked in two bands on the Saisa River, near Abercorn. A month later, having gathered 2,000 men, they besieged the place for six days, when British reenforcements arriving they were driven off. During these skirmishes and engagements the Belgian troops were of great service to the British in defending the frontier between Lake Mweru and Lake Tanganyika, and especially the western shore of the latter lake.

It was in this summer of 1915, during the early days of July, that the German cruiser, the *Königsberg,* met her end. Late in October of 1914 she was in shelter at a point some distance up the Rufiji River, where the water was so shallow that a ship of ordinary draft could not approach. When the British discovered the location of the cruiser they sank a collier across the mouth of the river to prevent the German boat from reaching the sea. The *Königsberg,* surrounded by forests and thick jungle growth, was exactly located by British aircraft. On July 4, 1914, Vice Admiral King Hall, commander in chief of the Cape station, entered the river with the monitors *Severn* and *Mersey* and opened fire.

The crew of the *Königsberg* had been active in fortifying their position during the time the cruiser had been sheltering in the river. They had established shore batteries with German thoroughness that commanded all the turnings of the river, and there were observation towers from which they could get the range of any vessel attacking. The British could not get a clear view of the enemy because of the dense jungle, but their aeroplanes were of great service in directing the action of the guns. There was never any doubt of what the ultimate fate of the *Königsberg* would be.

On July 4, 1915, the British bombarded the cruiser for six hours, when she was seen to be on fire. The attack for some reason was not renewed until July 11, 1915, when the cruiser was found to be completely destroyed, whether as the result of the British shells or because she was blown up by her own crew was not discovered at the time. The annals of naval warfare offer no more curious story than this of the German cruiser, which lay for so many months helpless in a jungle river, surrounded by steaming swamps, while far beyond lay the longed-for open sea.

PART XII—WAR IN ARABIA, MESOPOTAMIA AND EGYPT

CHAPTER LXXX

MESOPOTAMIA AND ARABIA

THE flames of war were sweeping across Mesopotamia and Arabia. In the last days of January, 1915, Lord Hardinge, Viceroy and Governor General of India, made a tour of the conquered territory around the Persian Gulf, and at Basra was received by the native community with an address of welcome, which expressed the hope of permanent British occupation.

Owing to the overflow of the Tigris and Euphrates in February and March, when the surrounding country is flooded, there was little fighting in those regions. But on March 3 the enemy appeared near Ahwaz, on the Karun River, where the British had a small garrison to protect the Anglo-Persian Oil Company's pipe line.

A contingent sent out from the town to discover the strength of the Turkish force, located them at Ghadir. The enemy was found to be about 12,000 strong, having been joined by a body of tribesmen from Arabia and Persia. As the British troops only numbered 1,000 men, there was imminent danger of them being cut off, and a hurried retreat was ordered. The Turks seemed determined that their enemy should not escape them, and used every effort to prevent a successful retreat. There was much hand-to-hand fighting before the British could struggle back to Ahwaz. As the Turks did not continue to attack it was to be supposed that they had lost heavily. The Anglo-Indian force had lost about 200. The colonel of the

Seventh Rajputs was wounded, and four of their white officers were killed.

On this day, March 3, 1915, a body of British cavalry reconnoitering toward Nakaila, about twenty-five miles northwest of Basra, was attacked while on their way back to camp by some 1,500 mounted Turks. The British pretending to retire, maneuvered to lure them on to a position where they had concealed infantry with machine guns and artillery. The Turks, quite unsuspecting a ruse came on, were met by a withering fire from the guns that sent them shattered and broken flying back to Nakaila. In this little fight the British had four officers killed and several severely wounded.

Reenforcements had been sent from India in anticipation of the end of the flood season, and Ahwaz and Kurna were greatly strengthened. Lieutenant General Sir J. E. Nixon, K. C. B., accompanied the new troops, and on his arrival took command of the entire force of between 30,000 and 40,000 men.

The Turks, who had also been largely reenforced with soldiers probably from Bagdad, on April 11 attacked the three British positions at Kurna-Ahwaz and Shaiba, the last a fort protecting Basra. Kurna was bombarded for two days, with small result. A bridge across the Tigris was partly destroyed, but they inflicted no casualties. Guns from the shore and those in H.M.S. *Odin* did effective work in scattering such of the enemy as appeared in boats. At Ahwaz large bodies of hostile cavalry could be seen against the sky line surrounding the British positions, but they did not attack.

The main object of the Turks was evidently to capture Basra, their attempts on Kurna and Ahwaz being merely feints to keep the British occupied while they struck a real blow at Shaiba. On April 12, 1915, an action began that lasted three days—one of the most notable fights in the history of this campaign. The attacking force was estimated at between 18,000 and 22,000 men. Perhaps 11,000 were regular infantry and cavalry from Bagdad, and 12,000 irregular levies of Kurds and Arabs. The Turkish infantry after some irregular artillery fire, commanded by German officers, advanced in the early morning of the 12th

MESOPOTAMIA—THE BRITISH OPERATIONS FROM THE PERSIAN GULF

toward the south-southwest, and west of the British lines. For three hours they were pressing forward, and then when the artillery fire fell off began to dig themselves in. An attack from the south was made in the afternoon, but was beaten off by the British before making much progress. The Turks were busy during the night of the 12th keeping up a spirited fire from rifles and machine guns, and by morning were found to have occupied some houses on a rising ground to the north of the British position. An Anglo-Indian force easily dislodged them from this place, and a counterattack made by the Turks from the west was repulsed with a loss to them of several hundred prisoners. The British also captured eighteen officers and two guns.

The British had repulsed all attacks, but the most difficult part of their task now lay before them, for the Turks were strongly intrenched near Basra some four miles from the British lines. On April 14, 1915, the Anglo-Indian force moved from camp toward Zobeir to the south, and driving off the Turks from their advanced position found themselves in front of their main lines. Some 15,000 Turkish soldiers and six big guns occupied well-concealed trenches in a tamarisk wood. The Anglo-Indian troops began their advance toward the enemy at 11.30 in the morning, and continued for five hours across a bare plain under a fierce sun and a pitiless heat. Not an enemy could be sighted, but a continuous fire, too accurate to be pleasant to the advancing host, came from the concealed trenches. At about 4.30 p. m. the 117th Mahrattas and Dorsets had led the way into the trenches, and, the whole line uniting in a great charge, the Turks were driven out at the point of the bayonet and dispersed. The Anglo-Indian troops however had purchased their victory dearly. There were some 700 casualties. Lieutenant Colonel H. L. Rosher of the Dorsets, Lieutenant Colonel T. A. Britten of the 110th Mahrattas, and Major J. C. M. Wheeler of the Seventh Lancers were among the seventeen British officers killed.

The routed Turks had fled toward Nakaila, and were vigorously pursued by the victors. They tried to escape by land and water. A dozen boat loads of fugitives were overhauled or sunk. The Turks lost about 2,500, of whom 700 were prisoners in

British hands. Great quantities of stores, ammunition and guns were also captured. The region around Basra was now cleared of Turkish soldiers for a distance of fifty miles.

On April 17 the Anglo-Indian cavalry occupied Nakaila. The rout of the Turks was complete, and it was said that in their retreat they were attacked by their former allies the Arabs, who turned on them as soon as the tide of battle went against them.

During the greater part of the month of May the British were occupied in clearing the territory of the Turks that remained. At Kurna and Ahwaz and their neighborhood the enemy had gathered in sufficient numbers to give some trouble. A British contingent was dispatched to drive them out of the Ahwaz locality, but the Kharked River was in flood, and severe sand storms hindered progress, so that before the Turkish camp could be reached the enemy had vacated Persian soil and fallen back to Amara.

General Gorringe, who commanded the British troops, now set about punishing those tribes which had been assisting the enemy. Some surrendered and gave up a number of rifles and arms. Others were disposed to show resistance, but the British easily defeated them, cleared out their strongholds, and destroyed some of their property.

On May 31, 1915, the Turks had become threatening in the vicinity of Kurna, and a British expedition consisting of soldiers and sailors set out at 1.30 a. m. to attack them. By wading and in boats the British surprised the enemy's position, two miles from the town, and soon silenced his guns by superior artillery work. The heights were won by midday, and the Turks took to flight, leaving three guns and about 250 prisoners behind them. They retreated to Amara as the force from Ahwaz had done. Their flight was so precipitate, that tents were left standing, as they took to mahalas and steamers on the river to escape. The British naval flotilla carrying General Townshend and Sir Percy Cox, Chief British Resident of the Gulf, was in pursuit of the fleeing Turks. Their gunboat *Marmaris* was sunk, and the transport *Masul* captured. Two lighters containing field guns, mines, and military stores were also taken, and about 300 prisoners.

Amara, the important business town on the Tigris about sixty miles from Kurna to which the Turks had fled, surrendered to the British June 3, 1915, its garrison of 1,000 becoming prisoners of war. In the town and vicinity 80 officers and some 2,000 men were also captured, and large quantities of ammunition, 13 guns, 12 steel barges, and 4 river steamers.

The whole of the country between Amara and the sea was now in British hands, and the Turkish forces in Mesopotamia had been partly destroyed and so demoralized that it was unlikely that they would soon take the offensive again.

In the last weeks of July, 1915, they again became troublesome. On July 24 the British, under General Gorringe, advanced to attack Nasiriyeh. The town was shelled by gunboats, and after a prolonged struggle the enemy retired, and the British occupied the place on the following day. They had captured during the fight 1,000 prisoners and 13 guns, while the dead Turks numbered about 500. The British casualties were between 300 and 400. During this engagement the fiercest foe the British had to contend against was the excessive heat, which registered as high as 113, and caused great suffering and some deaths.

Along the Euphrates, between Sukh-es-Sheyukh and Nasiriyeh, operations now began that lasted for twenty days. The country around here is peculiarly difficult for military movements, presenting a network of marshes and canals. The Turks occupied intrenched positions at the entrance of Kut-el-Hai Channel on the main line of communication between the Tigris and Bagdad. A British force was dispatched from Kurna to attack these positions. The expedition was supported by extemporized gunboats, and took the waterway of the Euphrates and Hamar Lake. Their progress was fiercely opposed by the Turks, who hovered about their flanks. The river had overflowed it banks, and inundated the neighboring country so that marching was difficult. It was necessary to drag boats over the land in some places along the advance. But the British troops were successful when reaching their objective. One regiment outflanked the enemy's gun position on the right bank, and during the engagement the Turks lost 7 officers and 83 regular troops and Arabs. The British casualties were 109. There were 25 killed.

CHAPTER LXXXI

SYRIA AND EGYPT

AFTER the declaration of war against Turkey, the allied war vessels were concentrated in the Levant and Red Sea to watch the coasts of southern Asia Minor, Syria, and Turkish Arabia. On the Syrian coast there was only one point where a naval force could effectively attack communications between Constantinople and the Turkish forces. This was the little town of Alexandretta, and the shore north to Payaz, a small village. The Turks, if they wished to reenforce their Syrian army must move their men, guns, and stores up a mountainous road over the Amanus from Baghche to Radju, or risk great losses by the coast route between Payaz and Alexandretta. The Turks took this chance, and were successful, for there was no allied warship in the Gulf of Alexandretta to oppose their progress. On December 17, 1914, H.M.S. *Doris,* a protected cruiser, appeared off Alexandretta and destroyed four bridges on the road and railway between that town and Payaz. The captain of the *Doris* sent an ultimatum to the Turkish commandant of Alexandretta demanding the surrender of the town, failing which he threatened bombardment of the place. To this the Turks paid no attention. A second ultimatum brought forth a telegraphic message from Djemal Pasha at Damascus, threatening to execute allied subjects interned in that city if any Ottoman noncombatants were killed at Alexandretta by the British guns. The captain of the *Doris* promptly replied that Djemal Pasha would be held responsible for the execution of allied subjects, if he dared to carry out what he proposed. Thanks to the influence brought to bear on the Porte by the American Embassy at Constantinople, the Ottoman military authorities in Syria became more reasonable, and finally agreed to blow up the two railway engines at Alexandretta themselves, much of the war material having been removed from the town while negotiations were pending.

During the first three months of 1915 there was only one fight of any importance on the coast of the Gulf of Alexandretta. On February 6 a landing party from H.M.S. *Philomel* was subjected to heavy fire from a concealed trench where eighty Turks were located. Six of the British and New Zealanders who formed the crew of the *Philomel* were wounded, three mortally. The cruiser promptly avenged their death by steaming in and opening a point-blank fire on the trenches with her 4.7-inch guns. More than fifty of the Turks were killed or badly wounded, the high-explosive shells shattering some to pieces. After this salutary lesson the Turks at Alexandretta did not seek any further encounters with the sailors of allied war vessels.

The British cruisers were late in arriving in the Gulf of Alexandretta, and had lost some opportunities to injure the enemy by their delay, but now they did valiant duty in preventing the Turks from sending any number of men or stores to Aleppo for the Caucasus, Mesopotamia, or the Egyptian border by the coast route, which would greatly have facilitated their movements. They were forced, owing to the vigilance of British warships, to send their troops and munitions over the Giaur Dagh by the pass called the Syrian Gates, between Cilicia and northern Syria, a rough, mountainous region, with bad roads, that made progress extremely difficult.

At the beginning of the allied operations against the Dardanelles, the observation of the Syrian coast was taken over entirely by the French fleet.

On April 19, 1915, the Turkish intrenchments at El Arish were bombarded by the French battleship *St. Louis*. The Turks had some fifteen or twenty field guns, and replied vigorously, but only one shell hit the battleship, which did no damage. The Turks suffered some losses. In the early part of May the big camp at Gaza, where numbers of Ottoman soldiers were gathered to be reviewed by Djemal Pasha, was shelled by the *St. Louis*, when some fifty Turks were killed by French shrapnel, and perhaps as many more wounded.

On April 29, 1915, the cruiser *D'Entrecasteaux* worked effectively on the Cilician coast, shelling the trenches at Taruss, while her hydroplane, dropping a bomb on the railway tracks, blew up trucks laden with high explosives and wrecked the railway station. On May 10 the Turks at El Arish were again shelled by the guns of the *Jeanne D'Arc*.

On Ascension Day, Alexandretta was the scene of some spirited work, in which the cruiser *D'Estrées* played the leading part. M. de la Passadière, her commander, demanded of the Kaimakam that the German flag should be hauled down that was flying over the German Consulate. The Turkish commander sent no reply, and it was pretended that he was ill or absent. M. de la Passadière having fixed a time limit when the flag must be hauled down, cleared his decks for action and trained the ship's guns on the consulate building. At the expiration of the time limit he opened fire, and the consulate was reduced to ruins. The only casualties were three Turkish soldiers, who, in spite of warning, had remained near the building.

The captain of the *D'Estrées* on May 14, 1915, destroyed a petrol depot which might be used to supply hostile submarines, and which contained over 1,000 cases. A few days earlier a much larger depot containing some 20,000 cases at Makri on the southern coast of Cilicia had been destroyed by the cruiser *Jeanne D'Arc*.

Budrum on the southwest coast of Asia Minor in the Gulf of Halicarnassus was bombarded for a serious act of Turkish treachery. The captain of the *Dupleix* had sent two boat crews to parley with the authorities, when they were fired upon by armed Turkish civilians and some soldiers. About twenty French soldiers were killed or captured as a result of this treacherous act, concerning which the Ottoman authorities published a communiqué in which they described the incident as the repulse of a landing force. The French losses were quickly

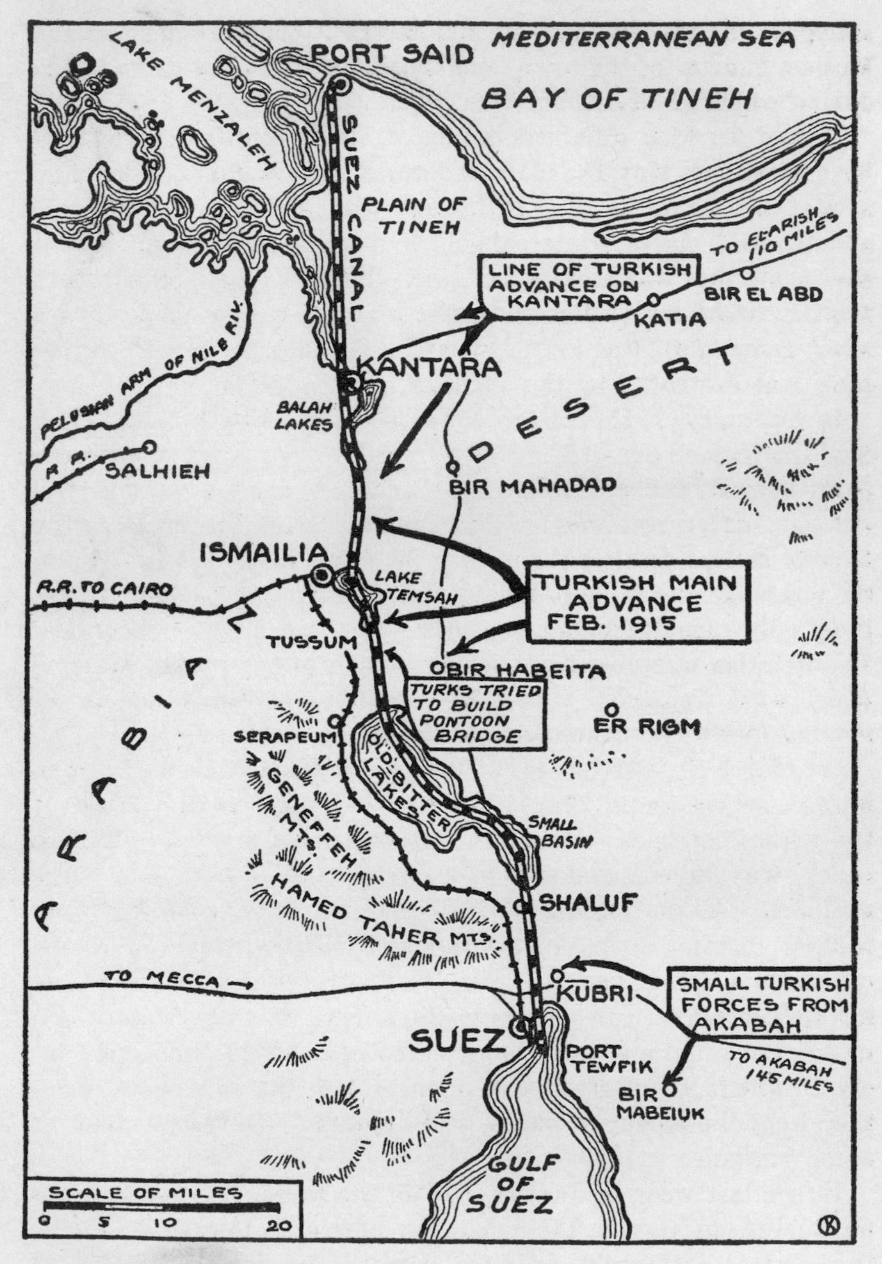

THE TURKISH ATTACK ON THE SUEZ CANAL

avenged, for the *Dupleix* at once began a bombardment of the Moslem quarter of the town, and continued firing for three hours during which great damage was done.

Armed Turkish inhabitants perpetrated a similar outrage on boat parties on May 18, 1915, at Banias, near Latakia; a tug and a boat belonging to the *D'Estrées* were fired on from roofs and landing places while chasing a merchantman belonging to the enemy that was seeking refuge in the port. As a punishment for the treachery of the civilians, who had posed as peaceable inhabitants until the French boats came into port, part of the town was destroyed by the shells of the *D'Estrées*.

In February, 1915, toward the close of the month, in the Red Sea, the French armored cruiser *Desaix* landed a reconnoitering party near Akaba, and found the Turks occupying a neighboring village. After receiving reenforcements from the cruiser, the French sailors drove out the fifty or sixty Turks hiding among the houses of the village, killing and wounding a dozen of them, their only casualty being one man, who was slightly wounded. The Red Sea was now patrolled by vessels of the Indian Marine, which were frequently successful in making captures, and in removing mines from the Gulf of Akaba.

On March 21, 1915, H.M.S. *Dufferin* at Mutweilah on coast of Midian, where an old Turkish fort is located, was the victim of the white-flag trick. Through this treacherous act one British sailor was killed, and an officer and nine other men were wounded. In the middle of May, H.M.S. *Northbrook* captured a dhow, having on board six German officers belonging to the merchant marine, and ten men who were trying to reach one of the Turkish Red Sea ports to the north. In these waters and in the Levant there were many incidents of this character, insignificant in themselves, but important in the aggregate, since they kept the enemy worried, and created a wholesome fear of allied vigilance.

In the last week of January, 1915, the three Turkish columns advancing on Egypt, the northern marching toward Kantara, the central and main advance headed for Ismailia, and the southern, whose objective was Suez, had been located, and were under surveillance of allied aeroplanes. By January 26 advanced guards of the central and southern columns were discovered near the canal. The central column was at Moia Harab, and some thousand men were also discovered at Wadi Um Muksheib. The southern column was found to be located at Bir Mabeiuk. On this same date British troops engaged the northern Turkish column a few miles east of El Kantara, losing in the skirmish five men and one officer. It was now evident to the British that the Turks were about to begin the main attack on the canal. Consequently the Auckland and Canterbury Battalions were dispatched to Ismailia; the Otago and Wellington Battalions were sent to El Kubri, and the New Zealand Infantry Brigade was sent up by rail from Cairo.

While this was transpiring on land, H.M.S. *Ocean, Swiftsure, Clio,* and *Minerva* joined the French warship *D'Entrecasteaux* and H.M.S. *Hardinge* and two torpedo boats already stationed in the canal. For three or four days following there were numerous skirmishes between enemy outposts and British patrols, the most effective work being wrought by allied aeroplanes and hydroplanes, which dropped bombs on the Turks as they swept over them and killed many camels and men. Lieutenant Patridge of the Indian Army Reserve of Officers and a French pilot lost their machine outside the British lines through the engine breaking down, and on returning to camp at night were shot and killed by a British picket.

On February 1, 1915, Djemel Pasha's main force occupied Katayib el Kheil, some low hills east of the southern end of Lake Timsah. The Turkish commander had every reason to feel satisfied with the progress he made in bringing his army across the desert in good condition, and with only the loss of a few deserters from among the irregulars. As many Tripolitan, Algerian, and Indian pilgrims had been forced to join the army by the persuasion of the leaders of the irregular troops, the Turkish force had increased in numbers.

Djemel Pasha's plan was to attack the canal with the main force, made up of the Twenty-fifth Division, and all, or part of the Twenty-third Division, which were to force their way between Serapeum and Tussum, while his right wing by a feint attack was to hold the British force at the Ismailia Ferry bridgehead. El Kantara was to be attacked by the northern column, while at the same time to prevent reenforcements from arriving, a demonstration was to be made at Ferdan. The southern column was directed to carry out the same tactics at Kubri, near Suez, which, as was subsequently shown, they did most ineffectually.

In the morning of February 2, 1915, an Indian reconnoitering force met the Turks about four miles east of the Ismailia Ferry. In the desultory action that followed, the British troops tried ineffectually to draw the Turks within range of their main position, and a violent sand storm arising in the afternoon, the engagement ended. The Turks retired and intrenched themselves about 2½ miles southeast of the Ferry post. On this same afternoon the Twenty-fifth Division of the Turkish army had arrived at a point within four or five miles of the canal. Their scouts were already established on the eastern bank, which is backed by trees, brushwood, and sand hills, affording excellent cover for infantry. A narrow sandy beach, not more than 9 feet wide extends along the foot of the eastern bank. The Turkish advance was made after night had set in, the Twenty-fifth Division, with pontoon companies and engineers of the Fourth and Fifth Army Corps, being first to reach the canal. They brought with them some twenty pontoons, and five or six rafts constructed out of kerosene cans fastened in wooden frames.

The first comers were followed by a part of the Seventy-fifth Regiment, old fighters from Tripoli and the Balkans; "Holy Warriors" as the Arabs called them. About 3 a. m. they had gained the openings along the canal bank, the most northerly of which being within a few hundred yards of the Tussum bridgehead. The remainder of the Seventy-fifth Regiment covered them from the left. Toward Serapeum, some distance south, the Seventy-fourth Regiment was stationed.

The night was dark and thickly clouded, and from the silence on the western bank of the canal the Turks must have believed it to be unoccupied. That they were entirely confident of success was shown in a letter afterward found on a dead Turkish officer and dated February 2. After describing the hard march across the desert, he concluded, "And to-morrow we shall be across the canal on our way to Cairo!"

The Turks crowded on the narrow strip of beach or in the gaps in the banks, and suffered heavily from the fire of this mountain battery. A number of their boats which left the shore were [illegible]. The Sixty-second Punjabis left their cover under a with[illegible] and pluckily charged down the bank to repel the T[illegible] tempts to make a landing. Toward Tussum, farthe[illegible] field battery belonging to the East Lancashire Div[illegible] ported by New Zealanders of the Canterbury Battali[illegible] a rattling fire, to which the Turks immediately replied with machine guns and rifles. The small torpedo boat *O-*[illegible] with its crew of thirteen now took part in the fray by dashing up the canal and landing a few men at a point south of Tussum.

At the first gray light of dawn the action became general, and fresh forces entered the conflict. The Turks on the eastern bank who had occupied the day line of the Tussum post now advanced, protected by artillery, against the bridgehead, while the Serapeum post was assailed by another body of troops. On the canal and Lake Timsah the allied warships opened fire, and continued it for some time. From the slopes of Katayib el Kheil three batteries of Turkish field guns replied, doing considerable damage to every visible target. But they had not taken careful observations of the British positions, and the carefully masked Territorial battery between Tussum and Serapeum was not discovered. This battery, aided by the New Zealanders, almost silenced the Turkish fire from the eastern bank, and enabled them to attend to the reserves of the enemy now seen advancing on the desert to the east. Four of the Territorial gunners were wounded by the Turkish batteries. A pontoon which the Turks had pushed across the canal in the dark was sunk, but until daybreak those who had engineered this work managed to keep afloat, and continued sniping with some damage to British artillery horses until they were rounded up and taken prisoners by some Indian cavalry.